Isaiah 1–39

Westminster Bible Companion

Series Editors

Patrick D. Miller
David L. Bartlett

Isaiah 1–39

WALTER BRUEGGEMANN

Westminster John Knox Press
Louisville, Kentucky

Book design by Publisher's WorkGroup
Cover design by Drew Stevens

First edition
Published by Westminster John Knox Press
Louisville, Kentucky

This book is printed on acid-free paper that meets the American National Standards Institute Z39.48 standard. ⊗

PRINTED IN THE UNITED STATES OF AMERICA

98 99 00 01 02 03 04 05 06 07—10 9 8 7 6 5 4 3 2 1

Library of Congress Cataloging-in-Publication Data

Brueggemann, Walter.
    Isaiah / Walter Brueggemann. — 1st ed.
        p.   cm. — (Westminster Bible companion)
    Includes bibliographical references.
    Contents: v. 1. 1–39 — v. 2. 40–66.
    ISBN 0-664-25524-8 (v. 1 : alk. paper). — ISBN 0-664-25791-7 (v. 2 : alk. paper)
    1. Bible. O.T. Isaiah—Commentaries.   I. Title.   II. Series.
BS1515.2.B669 1998
224'.1077—DC21   98-16400

Contents

Series Foreword

This series of study guides to the Bible is offered to the church and more specifically to the laity. In daily devotions, in church school classes, and in listening to the preached word, individual Christians turn to the Bible for a sustaining word, a challenging word, and a sense of direction. The word that scripture brings may be highly personal as one deals with the demands and surprises, the joys and sorrows, of daily life. It also may have broader dimensions as people wrestle with moral and theological issues that involve us all. In every congregation and denomination, controversies arise that send ministry and laity alike back to the Word of God to find direction for dealing with difficult matters that confront us.

A significant number of lay women and men in the church also find themselves called to the service of teaching. Most of the time they will be teaching the Bible. In many churches, the primary sustained attention to the Bible and the discovery of its riches for our lives have come from the ongoing teaching of the Bible by persons who have not engaged in formal theological education. They have been willing, and often eager, to study the Bible in order to help others drink from its living water.

This volume is part of a series of books, the Westminster Bible Companion, intended to help the laity of the church read the Bible more clearly and intelligently. Whether such reading is for personal direction or for the teaching of others, the reader cannot avoid the difficulties of trying to understand these words from long ago. The scriptures are clear and clearly available to everyone as they call us to faith in the God who is revealed in Jesus Christ and as they offer to every human being the word of salvation. No companion volumes are necessary in order to hear such words truly. Yet every reader of scripture who pauses to ponder and think further about any text has questions that are not immediately answerable simply by reading the text of scripture. Such questions may be about historical and geographical details or about words that are obscure or so loaded with meaning that one cannot tell at a glance what is at stake. They may be about the fundamental meaning of a passage or about what connection a particular text might have to our contemporary world. Or a teacher preparing for a church school class may simply want to know: What should I say about this biblical passage when I have to teach it next Sunday? It is our hope that these volumes, written by teachers and pastors with long experience studying and teaching the Bible in the church, will help members of the church who want and need to study the Bible with their questions.

The New Revised Standard Version of the Bible is the basis for the interpretive comments that each author provides. The NRSV text is presented at the beginning of the discussion so that the reader may have at hand in a single volume both the scripture passage and the exposition of its meaning. In some instances, where inclusion of the entire passage is not necessary for understanding either the text or the interpreter's discussion, the presentation of the NRSV text may be abbreviated. Usually, the whole of the biblical text is given.

We hope this series will serve the community of faith, opening the Word of God to all the people, so that they may be sustained and guided by it.

Introduction

The book of Isaiah is like a mighty oratorio whereby Israel sings its story of faith. Like any oratorio, this one includes interaction among many voices, some of which are in dissent. Like any oratorio, this work requires a rendering; and because each interpretive rendering (including this one) takes on a peculiar character, no one rendering may claim to be the "correct" one. Like any oratorio, moreover, this one conveys its primary themes with great authority, so that they persist through the vagaries of many imaginative interpretations. In this oratorio, a primary theme is the predominant and constant character of Yahweh, who looms over the telling in holy sovereignty and in the faithful gentleness of a comforting nursemaid. All said, the book of Isaiah is a remarkable artistic achievement wherein the artistry is a match for the awesome, inscrutable Character whose tale it tells.

In broad sweep, the story told in the book of Isaiah is the long account of Israel's life in the midst of a demanding sequence of imperial powers. The book of Isaiah has in its purview an international geopolitical horizon. The book traverses the chronology of the Assyrian Empire from the incursions of Tiglath-pileser III (745–727 B.C.E. [Before Common Era—formerly known as B.C.]) to the miraculous deliverance of Jerusalem from Sennacherib in 701; the Babylonian Empire under the domination of Nebuchadrezzar; and the radically altered policies of the Persian Empire under Cyrus that resulted in a benign support of emerging Judaism. The interaction between Judah and the several imperial powers is a key element in the staging of the story.

The book of Isaiah, however, is not simply a telling of the political story of Judah, nor of the sequence of superpowers. It is not in the end an act of political theory or of history. What makes this rendering of Judah's life distinctive is that the story is told with unfailing attentiveness to Yahweh, who is reckoned to be the primal player in the life of Judah and in the life of the world around Judah. The book of Isaiah, with wondrous artistry,

1

manages to hold together the realities of lived public history in that ancient world and the inscrutable reality of Yahweh, who is said here to impinge decisively in that history. Thus the book of Isaiah is neither "history"
in any modern sense of the term nor "theology" in any conventional way.

The convergence of history and theology here results in a quite distinctive genre of documentation for which the best term we have is
prophecy. Prophecy in this context may be understood as a *redescription* of
the public processes of history through which the purposes of Yahweh are
given in human utterance. As a consequence, any human decision—
whether by Judean kings or by imperial overlords or by authorized
priests—is reckoned to be penultimate, for what is ultimate is the resolve
of Yahweh and the capacity of Yahweh to do something utterly new in such
processes that appear to be settled and autonomous. Yahweh, as given us
in the Isaiah tradition, is endlessly surprising, disjunctive, and elusive, so
that the book of Isaiah does not yield a smooth presentation of sovereignty,
but proceeds by disjunctive fits and starts, some unbearably harsh and
some astonishingly healing. The hearer of the book of Isaiah must endlessly marvel at a text that dares to make this Disjunctive One available
through artistic imagination, with the "nuts and bolts" of Judean history
following meekly in the wake of that Holy Resolve.

The horizon of long-term *international history* and the *cruciality of Yahweh* for the telling of that history are even more focused, however, for in
the end the book of Isaiah is an oratorio about *the suffering and destiny of
Jerusalem*. The city is regarded as the center of Yahweh's peculiar attentiveness, as the seat of the world's best hopes for well-being, and as the site
of the most profound disobedience and recalcitrance. Jerusalem is taken in
this tradition as an epitome of Yahweh's creation, which owes its life to
Yahweh and which seeks with great resourcefulness to have a life other
than the one Yahweh would give.

It is Jerusalem that is *under judgment* and that draws the negating attention of Yahweh (3:1, 8). It is Jerusalem that is *addressed in exile*, in recognition of its need and in assurance commensurate with its need (40:2; 44:28).
It is Jerusalem that is imagined *healed, restored, ransomed, forgiven* (65:18–19).
It is Jerusalem, the meeting place of divine will and historical reality, that is
the recipient of Yahweh's judgment and Yahweh's renewing comfort and
mercy. All of this is described at the outset, where the whole course of Jerusalem and the entire sequence of the book are laid out (1:21–27).

We late Western, Christian readers of course are not in Jerusalem. We
read only at a distance. But we continue to pray for the peace of Jerusalem,
for as peace comes there, we shall all be made whole.

MODELS OF INTERPRETATION

The book of Isaiah has been assessed through a variety of approaches, of which we may identify three quite distinct models:

1. *A pre-critical, or traditional, understanding*, still found in some quite conservative scholarship, keeps the entire book of Isaiah connected to the prophet Isaiah of the eighth century B.C.E. Much of the first part of the book refers beyond question to such a historical character. But with equal clarity it is certain that much of the later part of the book refers to circumstances and events long after the lifetime of the prophet. This reality poses no problem for what is essentially the traditional approach, for with the genre of "prophecy," it is entirely credible to judge that the eighth-century prophetic figure, by special grace as a prophet, was able to anticipate all that comes subsequently in the book. There is nothing intrinsically impossible about such an approach. It is nonetheless important to note that with the rise of modern theories of knowledge and specifically given "historical criticism," such an approach has been commonly rejected in the interpretive world represented by this series and by the church traditions related to it.

2. *A critical understanding* of the book of Isaiah is reflective of the intellectual world of the West in the eighteenth and nineteenth centuries that focused on historical issues. Scripture interpretation in such a posture sought to situate every book of the Bible and every major part of every book of the Bible in an appropriate historical context. As concerns the book of Isaiah, long and sophisticated historical study produced a long-standing scholarly consensus that is still found in most informed books on Isaiah.

According to that critical consensus, chapters 1—39 are linked to Isaiah of the eighth century B.C.E. in the context of the Assyrian Empire between 742 and 701. Chapters 40—55 are commonly dated to 540, just at the moment when the rising Persian Empire displaced the brutal and hated domination of Babylon. And chapters 56—66 are dated later, perhaps 520, when Jews who had returned from exile went about the critical and difficult task of reshaping the community of faith after its long, exilic jeopardy.

The judgments made in this approach concerning the divisions of the book of Isaiah, now referred to by the shorthand references First Isaiah, Second Isaiah, and Third Isaiah, largely continue to dominate scholarship. The gain of such an approach is the insistence that the theological claims of the text are evoked by and addressed to particular, sometimes recoverable, historical situations. Unfortunately, the assigning of parts of the book of Isaiah to particular historical contexts has led to an inadvertent judgment that the "Three Isaiahs" only exist back-to-back as an editorial convenience, but without integral connection to each other.

3. Although a critical understanding of the book continues to be nearly unanimous among interpreters, by the end of the twentieth century, with some critical distance from the assumptions about knowledge that seemed to be givens, it is not surprising that scholarly attention and energy have more recently moved away from common critical judgments in a canonical direction. *The canonical study of the book of Isaiah* continues to recognize that the book is a literary complexity. Representative of the newer approaches are the essays in *New Visions of Isaiah*, edited by Roy F. Melugin and Marvin A. Sweeney. A canonical approach is not a return to a traditional approach. The newer perspective seeks to understand the final form of the complex text as an integral statement offered by the shapers of the book for theological reasons.

This approach by scholars is relatively recent, and a great deal more work is yet to be done in this regard. To illustrate this perspective that seeks to relate elements of the book that critical judgment has separated, I cite two cases.

First, many scholars have pointed to the theme of "former things and new things," as in 43:18–19:

> Do not remember the former things,
>   or consider the things of old.
> I am about to do a new thing;
>   now it springs forth, do you not perceive it?

When attention is paid to this theme, it may be noticed in 9:1 ("former time . . . latter time"), in what is likely an early text, and in 65:16–17 ("former troubles . . . former things"), surely a late text. That is, the theme is evident in every major part of the book. It is argued in a canonical perspective that "former things" refers to the harsh judgments of Yahweh culminating in the destruction of Jerusalem and the Exile, and "latter things" are the promises of Yahweh for the restoration after the Exile. When these historical matters are related to the literature of the book of Isaiah, they correlate as "former things" in the judgment texts of chapters 1—39 and the "latter things" as the promises of chapters 40—66. Matters are much more complex than this, but the themes provide a guiding principle for interpreters that gives primary attention not to apparent historical contexts but to the shape of the canonical literature.

A second gain of the canonical approach is in a study of the call narrative of 6:1–10 (11–12). Whereas earlier scholarship has treated this text as the report of an intense personal experience of the prophet, canonical perspective takes the text as a literary-canonical marker whereby Yahweh's harsh verdict against Jerusalem is commended:

> 'Keep listening, but do not comprehend;
> keep looking, but do not understand.'
> Make the mind of this people dull,
> and stop their ears,
> and shut their eyes,
> so that they may not look with their eyes,
> and listen with their ears,
> and comprehend with their minds,
> and turn and be healed.

The intention that Israel should not "turn and be healed" is a governing motif of chapters 1—39. Such a perspective invites the thought that 40:1–11, also a report of a "heavenly consultation," announces the gospel of forgiveness (vv. 2–9) that governs chapters 40—66. Thus 6:1–10 (11–12) and 40:1–11 are taken as parallel declarations whereby the large themes of judgment and promise that permeate the book of Isaiah are rooted in visions of heavenly decision making. The assumption, moreover, is that whatever personal, psychological experience may lie behind these two texts, they now function primarily as literary points of reference in the larger canonical book.

The canonical approach, which is only at the beginning of its interpretive work, draws upon historical-critical gains but moves beyond them toward theological interpretation. This latter perspective is the one in which I have tried to work in this study.

DIRECTIONS OF INTERPRETATION

The book of Isaiah is such a rich, dense, and complex work that it is open for interpretation in various directions:

1. The book of Isaiah has been a fertile interpretive field for Christian theology. Positively, one may say that the book of Isaiah is enormously generative and suggestive, and therefore it is open for being drawn into a variety of interpretive molds, among them that of Christian faith. But it must always be recognized that much Christian reading has flatly

preempted the text and forced upon the text readings that are far removed from its seemingly clear intent. Readers of Isaiah who are situated in the Christian church would do well to read representative Christian interpreters. For example, John Calvin's impressive commentary moves, characteristically, directly into christological interpretation whereby references to Israel are routinely taken to refer to the church. We likely need to relearn both how to make such an interpretive move and to notice the preemptive quality of such a maneuver.

Consideration should be given to the remarkable book of John F. A. Sawyer, *The Fifth Gospel: Isaiah in the History of Christianity*, which explores Christian usage of the book of Isaiah through the history of reading. Sawyer traverses the entire theological-liturgical tradition of the church and pays attention to such focal themes as "Virgin Birth," "Suffering Servant," and "Messiah." The title of the book reflects the claim of early teachers in the church who concluded that along with the four Gospels of the New Testament, Isaiah is a "gospel" that fully contains the crucial claims of Christian faith.

2. It is a matter of considerable importance, in my judgment, that Christians should not preempt the book of Isaiah. It is legitimate to see how the book of Isaiah fed, nurtured, and evoked Christian imagination with reference to Jesus. But that is very different from any claim that the book of Isaiah predicts or specifically anticipates Jesus. Such a preemption, as has often occurred in the reading of the church, constitutes not only a failure to respect Jewish readers, but is a distortion of the book itself. It is strongly preferable, I suggest, that Jews and Christians together recognize that the book of Isaiah is enormously and generatively open in more than one direction. No interpretive tradition is able to monopolize and close interpretation. This is a difficult and important question to which respectful attention must be paid.

3. Beyond the particular Christian claims the church might make, it is important to recognize that the book of Isaiah provides a large rereading of historical reality that is strikingly pertinent to the current condition of Western culture. On that pertinence, I commend especially Daniel Berrigan's *Isaiah: Spirit of Courage, Gift of Tears*. Berrigan's rereading is uncommonly poignant and makes immediate contact with our human crisis.

The "map" of Israel's life in the book of Isaiah is broadly preexilic/exilic/postexilic. Although those labels refer to actual historical crises in the ancient world, it is possible to see that this sequence around *displacement* and *restoration* is peculiarly pertinent in our particular time and place. The displacement (and subsequent exile) is a credible way to characterize Western culture, given the collapse of traditional certitudes and the demise of a covenantal social infrastructure (see Walter Brueggemann, *Cadences of Home: Preaching Among Exiles*). Western culture now faces a displacement that may indeed be expressed as an exile (see Frederick Buechner, *The Longing for Home: Recollections and Reflections*). And like the book of Isaiah, serious people are now disputatiously engaged in a struggle for the shape of the future, the outcome of whose struggles we are not able to see. One cannot, in reading Isaiah, disregard the concrete particularity of the text and simply *read past* that concreteness. But one can *read through* the concrete particularity into our own time and place, for it turns out that our time and place is much like that time and place. Believing people (Jews and Christians), moreover, dare to imagine that the same Holy One who acted in that time and place in disruptive and embracing ways still continues to disrupt and embrace even now. Thus the relevance of the text is evident. It cannot be arrived at too easily, but it is an insistent relevance that cannot be put off for too long either.

4. In the end, the book of Isaiah has continuing power among us, not because of historical critical judgments or because of canonical discernments, but because of the theological *stuff* of the text, given as image, theme, and phrase. This text tradition that insists upon the centrality of *the Holy One* is a *gospel* (40:9; 41:27; 52:7; 61:1). It is news about what God has decided, decreed, and is doing that makes a decisive difference in the world. It is a summons to *faith* (7:9; 30:15) that insists that Yahweh be relied upon in every circumstance of life. The *gospel* to be received in *faith* is an offer of *comfort* (40:1; 49:13; 51:3; 52:98; 61:2; 66:13) in the midst of every crisis. Such claims are endlessly problematic in a time and place such as ours, where the credibility of such gospel claims is difficult. I hazard that such claims are no more problematic now than they were when first asserted. But such a problematic does not deter the voice of the text and its claims. When circumstance is taken too seriously, either in self-confidence or in despair, the text keeps ringing in our doubting ears:

> For my thoughts are not your thoughts,
>   nor are your ways my ways, says the LORD.
> For as the heavens are higher than the earth,
>   so are my ways higher than your ways
>   and my thoughts than your thoughts.
>   (55:8–9)

1. "Holy, Holy, Holy Is the Lord of Hosts"
Isaiah 1—12

It is conventional to regard the initial twelve chapters of the book of Isaiah (along with chapters 28—31) as the primary work of the eighth-century prophet Isaiah. Certainly, the editorial notice of 1:1 situates the material in the eighth century. Moreover, the specific confrontation with King Ahaz (7:1–25) and the frequent references to Assyria (7:17, 20; 8:4, 7–8; 10:5–15; 11:16) anchor this material and its speaker, Isaiah, in the latter half of the eighth century. There is no doubt of the historicity of the events reflected therein, nor of the prophet Isaiah, nor of the utterances assigned to him. It is evident that the person of Isaiah occupied defining space in the theological memory, hope, and imagination of Israel.

However, primary attention is now given by scholars not to the initial utterances of the prophet but to the final form of the text as we have it. That is, editorial work by many hands over a long period of time has shaped and reshaped prophetic utterance in order to create a theological message that has been durable and canonical in Judaism. Although that theology is surely *seeded* by the eighth-century prophet, there is no doubt that the completed theological claim of the book of Isaiah runs well beyond the initial utterance of the eighth century. We may, moreover, see this canonical achievement on exhibit even in chapters 1—12, which are commonly thought to be the primary work of eighth-century Isaiah.

The work of eighth-century Isaiah, with particular reference to King Ahaz and the crisis of the Syro-Ephraimite war (Judah's war with Syria and Israel) is to summon Judah to radical trust in Yahweh, the God of Israel. But because the king and those around him did not share that trust in Yahweh, they succumbed to Assyrian power. The prophet took submission to Assyrian power to be a wholesale rejection of Yahweh, which inevitably brought Yahweh's wrath upon the city of Jerusalem. This deeply negative verdict upon eighth-century Jerusalem is funded and reinforced by what must have been a shared prophetic conviction (shared at least by his contemporary, Amos) that disregard of Yahweh's will in public life leads to subsequent trouble in public life. It is this ethical linkage that constitutes the core of prophetic discernment.

Because Isaiah trusts in Yahweh's fidelity, however, this prophetic tradition has difficulty accepting that Yahweh in wrath will finally terminate the beloved city and its people. So there continues to sound, amidst the harsh judgment, the assertion of Yahweh's resolve to do newness that is grounded not in Israel's merit or repentance but in Yahweh's own determination. And beyond the rootage of the prophet in the David-Zion traditions of graciousness, there is no doubt that later editorial work in the Isaiah tradition had on its horizon not only the *destruction* of Jerusalem in the sixth century but the modest *recovery* of the city at the end of the sixth and into the fifth century. Those historical realities thus provide substance for the theological conviction of Yahweh's *judgment* and Yahweh's renewing *mercy*. Thus, both *rootage in traditions* of prophetic rigor and David-Zion hope and the *lived experience of displacement and homecoming* together produced in the Isaiah tradition a two-stage presentation of Yahweh-with-Jerusalem: two stages of judgment and renewal. In later Isaiah, this becomes a prominent theme concerning "the former things" and "a new thing" (43:18–19). What is remarkable is that this scheme for the final form of the text, which is especially influential in the later tradition of Isaiah, is already decisive for the shaping of chapters 1—12, which are most clearly linked to Isaiah in the eighth century.

As a consequence of this editorial conviction rooted in both *theological tradition* and *lived experience*, we are able to see that this two-stage pattern is decisive for chapters 1—12. Thus, after the orientating statement of 1:1, the book of Isaiah presents a long introductory "speech of judgment" (1:2–31) that is followed by the powerful promise of 2:1–4. In parallel fashion, the extended "speech of judgment" in 2:5–4:1 culminates with the promise of 4:2–6 concerning the returning remnant. Things are more complicated in the middle portion of 5:1–9:7, but we notice even here that the culminating verdict of "distress and darkness, the gloom of anguish" (8:22) constitutes "the former time" (9:1), which is followed by "the latter time" (9:1), articulated in the exuberant promise of 9:2–7. And in the judgment speech of 9:8–10:4 we are reassured by the hope of a remnant in 10:5–27a, when Assyria is to be overcome "in a very little while." (The pattern in 5:1–10:27a is not as clear as elsewhere.) The final statement of judgment in 10:27b–34 is answered by the series of promissory assertions in 11:1–16 and most especially by the visionary oracle of 11:1–9.

Thus we are able to see that the primary tone of these chapters, largely from the eighth century, is *judgment*. But that harsh judgment is decisively punctuated and reshaped by the *promises* of 2:1–4; 4:2–6; 9:2–7; and 11:1–9, together with other less formidable affirmations in 10:5–27a and 11:10–16. In the final form of the text, there is no doubt that the promise prevails. The tradition of Isaiah, already in chapters 1—12, refuses to give finality to the harsh judgment that is so palpable and that cannot be denied. In the end, it is not the pain of the historical process but the wonder of Yahweh's resolve that will carry the day. For that reason, this daring and massive statement culminates in the unreserved, celebrative, exuberant doxology of chapter 12.

It is difficult to know how much of the material of hope comes from the prophet of the eighth century and how much is later editorial work. It seems clear that the prophet himself is grounded in traditions that permit hope in the face of dire circumstance. However that matter may be decided, the finished literary product that became canon is—as it always is in the production of biblical literature—a combination of *deeply rooted, tenacious tradition*, which already has its mind made up, and *poignantly faced, honestly embraced lived experience*. These two together—tradition and experience—produce what becomes the normative claim of faith in the book of Isaiah. What is said is honestly impinged upon by lived reality, but there is more at work here than what the world notices about reality.

The book of Isaiah, then, including chapters 1—12, is *theology*. That is, it has a determined perspective on reality with Yahweh at its center. The two-stage presentation of Yahweh's life with Jerusalem, the "former times" and the "latter times," is as important a resource for Christians as it is for Jews. That two-stage perception, so profoundly formative for the book of Isaiah, was readily taken up by Christians in the acknowledgment of the crucifixion and resurrection of Jesus. It is for that reason that the promises offered by the Isaiah tradition are so readily reread with reference to Jesus. In doing so, it is important for Christians to keep in mind that we are second readers and that our reading is always a rereading.

AN OVERTURE
OF THE MAIN THEMES
1:1–2:4

This opening presentation provides an overture to the entire book of Isaiah. As we will see, the book of Isaiah reflects upon, interprets, and shapes Israel's imagination over a long sweep of the history of Jerusalem—from royal *prosperity* through exilic *displacement* to modest *rehabilitation*. The present first chapter has all of this sweep in purview and enunciates the themes that will be predominant in all that is to follow. The book of Isaiah is fully aware of the historical and geopolitical vagaries that beset Jerusalem. It insists, however, upon redescribing those ups and downs with primary reference to the character and resolve of Yahweh, the God of Israel, whom it regards as the primary agent in the destiny of Jerusalem.

Locating the Book (1:1)

1:1 **The vision of Isaiah son of Amoz, which he saw concerning Judah and Jerusalem in the days of Uzziah, Jotham, Ahaz, and Hezekiah, kings of Judah.**

Like many of the prophetic books of the Old Testament, the book of Isaiah begins with an editorial comment that situates the book to follow. In good journalistic fashion, we are quickly given four pieces of "who, when, what" data. First, the "source" is Isaiah, son of Amoz. We know nothing about this historical personage except what can be deduced from the book itself. Moreover, if "Isaiah" is understood as a historical figure (as seems beyond dispute), then this verse pertains only to portions of the book found in chapters 1—39, for it is clear that subsequent chapters are situated well after the eighth-century figure.

Second, the subject of what follows is "Judah and Jerusalem." We will be able to see that each part of the long sweep of the book is indeed preoccupied with Jerusalem and Judah, "in life and in death"; that is, *in monarchic Israel* and *in exile,* and then in the new life finally given to Jerusalem *after the Exile.*

Third, the time line offered concerns four kings. Of these, Jotham is relatively unimportant and does not figure in the book of Isaiah (cf. 2 Kings 15:32–38). His father, Uzziah (= Azariah), was a notably strong king whose long reign was prosperous (2 Kings 15:1–7), though he seems only to provide the entry point for the ministry of Isaiah (cf. Isa. 6:1). Thus, of the four kings named, only two figure significantly in the book that follows. Ahaz is commonly regarded as a weak ruler and, from a Yahwistic perspective, vacillating and eventually unfaithful (734–715; cf. 2 Kings 16:1–20). His son Hezekiah is commonly assessed as a strong, independent, and reliable king, a sharp contrast to his father (715–697?; cf. 2 Kings 18:1–20:21). Hezekiah receives extended, favorable treatment in the biblical recounting of Israel's history. The two kings together provide a backdrop for the prophet, who is situated in royal history but not defined by it. These two kings, in fact, pertain to only a brief slice of the apparent chronology of the book of Isaiah (735–690) and perhaps are regarded editorially, in the larger sweep of the book, as symbols for *weak Yahwism* and *strong Yahwism*, postures of faith and power with which prophetic faith must contend in every context in every generation.

From a historical perspective, Ahaz and Hezekiah are reference points in the monarchic period, that is, in the eighth century. Ahaz models a weak king who jeopardizes the realm, and Hezekiah models a strong king who enhances the realm. Although the book of Isaiah undertakes specific monarchic history, however, it characteristically looks past monarchic history with one eye in order to keep in mind the larger sweep of the history of Jerusalem that extends through the end of monarchy (up to 587), through the Exile (587–537), and into the postexilic period (perhaps as far as 520).

It is for that reason necessary (and demanding) to read Isaiah with a bifocal vision, focused both on near history and on far history, both viewed from a deeply committed Yahwistic perspective. Read in the long perspective of the book of Isaiah, Ahaz is a metaphor for the refusal of Jerusalem to trust Yahweh, whereby Israel comes to failure and exile; conversely, Hezekiah is a metaphor for the trust that Israel may have in Yahweh, which makes possible an enduring communal existence into and beyond exile. Thus the data of verse 1 offer both historical particularity and a more generalizing model, and the reader must always attend to both, even as the text itself seems characteristically to attend to both at the same time.

Fourth, we are told that what follows in the book of Isaiah is a "vision." The book of Isaiah presents itself as testimony to the presence and purpose of Yahweh. We are put on notice of a peculiar presentation of history that has Yahweh's holiness at its center. We may anticipate, for that reason, that what follows will not accommodate itself to any conventional notion of historical reality or political possibility.

Chapters 1—4 together prepare us for an extraordinary redescription of historical experience viewed in terms of Jerusalem's God-given, God-governed destiny. Although we have an interest in the human voice that testifies, this first verse invites us to look beyond "Isaiah" to the true Subject of the vision and the real Author of Jerusalem's destiny, who is Yahweh.

An Initial Negative Judgment (1:2–3)

1:2 **Hear, O heavens, and listen, O earth;**
        for the LORD has spoken:
      I reared children and brought them up,
        but they have rebelled against me.
      3 **The ox knows its owner,**

and the donkey its master's crib;
but Israel does not know,
my people do not understand.

These two verses provide a basic theme by which to enter the book. They consist in a summons to heaven and earth (v. 2a), an affirmation of Yahweh's generous attentiveness (v. 2b), and an indictment of unresponsive, recalcitrant Israel (v. 3). The force of the two verses is to assert that the situation between Yahweh and "my people," as the book begins, is one of disruption, alienation, and contradiction. The book of Isaiah is evoked by an assertion on Yahweh's part that Israel, in its willful stupidity, has disrupted what might have been an amiable, reliable, sustaining relationship.

The call to heaven and earth is a rhetorical assertion of indignation on Yahweh's part. Yahweh summons cosmic witnesses to observe the mess that has become of the relationship with "my people." Because Yahwism is monotheistic, Yahweh cannot summon other gods to observe, and so instead summons the most formidable of creatures, heaven and earth. Israel's failure in its response to Yahweh is a matter of cosmic concern, now made evident to the whole known world.

In the abrasion now made cosmically public, Yahweh is not at fault. Indeed, Yahweh has been a caring, attentive parent who brought Israel to adulthood. The two verbs "reared" and "brought up" suggest nurture that brought a child—small, weak, and vulnerable—to strong viability (cf. Hos. 11:1–3). The verbs serve to acquit Yahweh of any wrongdoing in the relationship.

By contrast, Israel is completely responsible for the disruption. Israel "rebelled." The term is one of an active resistance. Israel has intentionally refused a relationship with Yahweh that is proper and indispensable to its very character. In verse 3, the poetry employs a telling image to further expose Israel. Yahweh's relationship to Israel is like that of an owner of an ox or a donkey. The animal is completely dependent, and the owner is completely reliable. The animal unreservedly trusts the owner, trusts even though such animals are not excessively bright or discerning. It is first nature (not second nature) for a donkey or an ox to know instinctively that to survive depends upon trust of the master. Israel, by contrast, refuses this most elemental relationship of trust upon which everything depends, and has indeed sloughed off the very relationship that would make its life viable. Israel is dumb, to its own hurt. Unlike a knowing donkey, Israel will starve to death by rejecting its master. What a way to begin a book of the Bible!

Primary Themes of Guilt, Punishment, and Rejection (1:4–17)

1:4 Ah, sinful nation,
> people laden with iniquity,
> offspring who do evil,
> children who deal corruptly,
> who have forsaken the LORD,
> who have despised the Holy One of Israel,
> who are utterly estranged!

5 Why do you seek further beatings?
> Why do you continue to rebel?
> The whole head is sick,
> and the whole heart faint.
6 From the sole of the foot even to the head,
> there is no soundness in it,
> but bruises and sores
> and bleeding wounds;
> they have not been drained, or bound up,
> or softened with oil.

7 Your country lies desolate,
> your cities are burned with fire;
> in your very presence
> aliens devour your land;
> it is desolate, as overthrown by foreigners.
8 And daughter Zion is left
> like a booth in a vineyard,
> like a shelter in a cucumber field,
> like a besieged city.
9 If the LORD of hosts
> had not left us a few survivors,
> we would have been like Sodom,
> and become like Gomorrah.

10 Hear the word of the LORD,
> you rulers of Sodom!
> Listen to the teaching of our God,
> you people of Gomorrah!
11 What to me is the multitude of your sacrifices?
> says the LORD;
> I have had enough of burnt offerings of rams
> and the fat of fed beasts;

I do not delight in the blood of bulls,
  or of lambs, or of goats.

¹² When you come to appear before me,
    who asked this from your hand?
    Trample my courts no more;
¹³ bringing offerings is futile;
    incense is an abomination to me.
  New moon and sabbath and calling of convocation—
    I cannot endure solemn assemblies with iniquity.
¹⁴ Your new moons and your appointed festivals
    my soul hates;
  they have become a burden to me,
    I am weary of bearing them.
¹⁵ When you stretch out your hands,
    I will hide my eyes from you;
  even though you make many prayers,
    I will not listen;
    your hands are full of blood.
¹⁶ Wash yourselves; make yourselves clean;
    remove the evil of your doings
    from before my eyes;
  cease to do evil,
    ¹⁷ learn to do good;
  seek justice,
    rescue the oppressed,
  defend the orphan,
    plead for the widow.

The theme of rebellion, announced in verses 2–3, is now explicated in great detail. This extended poem, a characteristic "lawsuit" speech whereby Yahweh indicts and then sentences Israel, consists of four elements: a general indictment (v. 4), a lament about Israel's true and pitiful situation (vv. 5–9), a refusal to heed Israel in time of need (vv. 10–15), and a summons to reformation (vv. 16–17).

Verse 4 follows the general indictment of verses 2b–3 with a massive, comprehensive catalogue of the full Old Testament inventory of vocabulary for sin. The people is said to be "sinful," "with iniquity." These two terms, together with "rebel" in verse 2, form the primary triad for sin in the Old Testament. They are followed in the third and fourth lines of the verse with two other general terms, "do evil" and "deal corruptly," after which come two very strong, active verbs, "forsake" and "despise." For the purposes of our study, it is not necessary to differentiate among these several terms. What counts is the cumulative force of the whole of the vocabulary. In as many ways as is possible, the poem asserts that Israel is fully turned against Yahweh, against the relationship that promises life. The last line of verse 4 is a difficult phrase. In its place it seems to make a climactic claim that Israel has become completely alien (other) to Yahweh, the very God with whom it had an intimate relationship. All of that relationship has been forfeited, so that Israel is now alone—made so by its own stubbornness.

In this verse, we may notice two other matters. One is the first mention (of many to follow in the book) of Yahweh as "the Holy One of Israel." The phrase is a poignant one. It acknowledges at the same time that (a) Yahweh is indeed linked intimately to Israel, but (b) Yahweh is holy, that is, awesome, unapproachable, and not to be presumed upon. The phrase is a kind of contradiction, witnessing to the dangerous freedom of Yahweh and to the disastrous future Israel generates for itself by its Yahweh-mocking conduct. Finally, the verse is introduced by an exclamatory "ah." The translation "ah" is much too weak. The older translation "woe" more nearly voices the ominous tone of what follows. Israel is put on notice, at the very outset, that its life with Yahweh has become acutely problematic. As a result, its life in the world is deeply at risk. The poet prepares us to watch while this beloved creature of Yahweh engages in self-destruction.

In verses 5–8, the consequences of the actions of verse 4 are now explicated. The poet first appeals to a metaphor of deep wound and sickness. The body politic of Judah is profoundly weak and ailing, from head to foot. There is no "soundness" (health, wholeness), for its body has become all bruises, sores, and wounds. These wounds, moreover, are unattended. Judah may not have noticed, but Judah is in a very bad way, near to death.

In verse 7, the metaphor of verses 5–6 is unpacked. The poetry concerns the land of Judah and its cities. The land is occupied, presumably (as we will see) by the Assyrians. Like every occupying army, the Assyrians do their share of burning, looting, and devouring. (The term for "foreigners" here is the same as "estranged" in verse 4.) Things have gone terribly wrong. The land is disrupted by war and alien presence, when what is intended was a peaceable land shared only by Israel and Yahweh. The military occupation is not only physically dangerous; it is abhorrent to those who imagined a peaceable vision. Indeed, "daughter Zion" (v. 8), or Jerusalem, stands alone and exposed with all the land leveled around it. The city stands exposed on the landscape, like a garden booth in a patch of vines, dangerously obvious and therefore vulnerable. Scholars believe that this verse may allude to the Assyrian invasion under Sennacherib when the land was massively devastated. Thus the occupying Assyrian army is deftly identified as a consequence of Israel's rebellion against Yahweh. At the same time, in the larger scope of the book, the text looks beyond Assyria to the ultimate devastation of the Babylonians. Both devastations and all devastators are present to the imagination of the poet.

In verse 9 the poet makes a remarkable move. Judah faces "the Lord of hosts," a phrase perhaps better translated here as "the God of the troops." The Holy One of Israel is, in Yahweh's own person, a dangerous military power. The warring God has left "a few survivors," else Jerusalem would be as devastated as Sodom and Gomorrah. The poet alludes to the old Genesis story of cities left without a survivor, totally destroyed by Yahweh (Gen. 19:24–25). It is the survival of "the few" (who presumably have gone into exile) that distinguishes Jerusalem, city of Yahweh, from Sodom and Gomorrah, cities rejected by Yahweh. The cities are alike in every regard, certainly alike in their alienation from Yahweh and in their just dessert of Yahweh's anger. By the end of verse 9, the massive exposé of Judah has reached its extremity. The poet has made the case that Jerusalem now has Yahweh as its uncompromising adversary.

The poet goes one step further in verses 10–15. In verse 9, the poem offers an important contrast of Jerusalem with the cities of Genesis. Now, in verse 10, the imagery of verse 9 is taken up again. Only now, in poetic imagination the rulers and people of Jerusalem are identified and addressed as Sodom and Gomorrah instead of being contrasted with them. The beloved Holy City has been renamed by the most abhorrent name imaginable, the most despicable, deplorable name available (cf. Jer. 23:14; Ezek. 16:46–49; Hos. 11:8; Amos 4:11). It is now this completely abhorred community that is summoned to listen one more time.

At the center of Jerusalem, of course, stands the temple. The temple is the place of much priestly activity, and the purpose of such activity is to remain connected to Yahweh. The priestly activity is a "means of grace," making communion possible. But of course no "means of grace" could possibly relate this belated Sodom to Yahweh. Yahweh proceeds to enumerate the priestly offerings of communion, and in naming them, rejects them: sacrifice, burnt offerings, fatlings, blood of bulls, lambs, and goats! All were heretofore accepted, legitimated offerings; all are now flatly rejected. Yahweh does not need them (cf. Psalm 50:8–13). Yahweh does not want them. Yahweh will not accept them. The same goes for all the periodic liturgies of festival and sabbath. Yahweh rejects them because Israel's gestures of worship are no longer vehicles for a serious relationship. The offerings are dishonest. Yahweh will no longer participate in the charade of receiving gifts from people who are not sincere. Indeed, Yahweh "hates" the charade and is exhausted by so much dishonest religion. Note well, what is rejected are Jerusalem's best gestures toward Yahweh. The core action toward Yahweh is prohibited: The relationship is over and finished!

There was a time in liberal Protestantism when the rejection of cultic worship by the prophet was interpreted to mean that God did not approve of high, liturgical, sacramental churches, so that in principle God opposed priestly activity. Such a reading must surely be resisted, because it was only an act of self-congratulations by low-church, Protestant communities. If, however, we read on to verse 15, low-church practice fares no better in this indictment, because God also will not hear prayers from this distorted community. It is not a particular, priestly practice that is rejected by Yahweh. It is rather every effort at communion that is rooted in pretense, dishonesty, and disobedience.

It is difficult to imagine a more massive rejection of God's people on God's part than this. In truth, the poem asserts, Yahweh is finished with this people and with its activities in the Jerusalem temple. God will not look. God will not listen. God will not attend. God will not respond. Judah is now on its own—without God. And Judah on its own, so the poet asserts, cannot manage any better than can a donkey without a master. The end of verse 15 sounds like a point of final termination.

For that reason, we are not quite prepared for verses 16–17, which suggest that there is yet a route back to Yahweh. We will see this inclination often in the book of Isaiah. This particular prophetic tradition is as honest and as harsh as the traditions of Jeremiah and Ezekiel. But it is much more reluctant than are they to anticipate the complete nullification of Israel. The book of Isaiah endlessly seeks, against the terrible consequences Judah deserved, to keep a hope alive for this people of God.

The hope offered here is a series of nine imperatives suggesting that Israel can be restored to Yahweh, but only with profound, intentional changes. The actions required are not the ones dismissed in verses 10–15, but are more elemental. It is as though the poet says, for Yahweh, "Don't talk of love, show me!" The actions urged, if Judah is to have a chance, are of two kinds. First, in the center of the urging (v. 16b) are three general statements about evil and good. That seems too obvious, except that Israel had lost its way even on such elemental categories (5:20). Restored relationship with Yahweh requires good in the place of evil. Israel must engage in ritual purification because it has been defiled and made unacceptable to the holy God (v. 16). The "washing" here to be done is the same as that which David offers in Psalm 51:2, only here it is Israel who must wash, that is, the whole people. We will see in 6:5 that the prophet is not indifferent to ritual cleansing. Life with Yahweh must be undefiled, and the community must use the available means to become ritually acceptable.

Second, the last four lines in verse 17 concern social relationships of justice to the oppressed, the orphan, and the widow. This triad refers to those in the community who are weak, vulnerable, without an advocate, and so subject to political exclusion and economic exploitation. Isaiah, as is true of the Mosaic-prophetic tradition generally, always has an eye out for socioeconomic-political issues. An appeal to the authority of the Bible, in all its literalness, is phony if these issues are not front and center. Notice that the offer of restitution of this devastated community concerns every dimension of Judah's life: right worship (*holiness*) and right neighbor practice (*justice*). Indeed, Judah is lost unless there is a total and radical reorientation of its entire life. Its only hope is to cease to be seedy, disreputable Sodom, because Sodom has no more future with Yahweh in Isaiah than it did in the book of Genesis. Thus the "not knowing" of verse 3 is at unbearable cost. The poet confronts the community of Israel with the central life-or-death Yahwistic question: Existence is on the terms of Yahweh or there is no existence. There is no third alternative!

An Ominous Bed for Renewal (1:18–20)

1:18 **Come now, let us argue it out,**
     says the LORD:
   though your sins are like scarlet,
     they shall be like snow;
   though they are red like crimson,
     they shall become like wool.
19 **If you are willing and obedient,**
     you shall eat the good of the land;
20 **but if you refuse and rebel,**
     you shall be devoured by the sword;
   for the mouth of the LORD has spoken.

In the present arrangement of chapter 1, verses 2–3 have expressed the governing problematic of the poetry—Israel's self-destructive stupidity. Then in an extended and daring scenario, verses 4–17 have explored the implications of the assertion of verses 2–3, that is, the termination of Israel. Now in verse 18, that long scenario is ended, and the poetry returns in great sobriety to the judicial case put before the witnesses in verse 2. It is as though God now says to Judah, "Let's get serious." This summons is in the language of adjudication. Judah must make some choices and has very little room for maneuverability. A real change is possible. The bloody color of sin can turn to the innocence of snow. What has been the crimson mark of disobedience can become innocence again. This is remarkable and unexpected good news. The God who is prepared to terminate a relationship offers a way back to that relationship, but it will not be easy!

Israel has now only two choices, and each choice carries a clear and unavoidable consequence. They are choices that hover over and haunt the entire book of Isaiah in every season of its long story. In verses 19–20, the poetry offers an unambiguous choice that reiterates the options of the tradition of Deuteronomy 30:15–20. Israel can now, yet again, *choose life* or *choose death*. Israel can choose obedience, which means to acknowledge that life is given by and referred back to this other One, the Holy One in Israel. Israel can choose to refuse that relationship and continue to rebel in its self-indulgent autonomy. That is a genuine and urgent choice.

But choices are not in a vacuum. Every choice entails a future. The choice of obedience is a choice of fruitful, blessed, productive land. That is, the working of creation in life-giving ways depends upon Israel's obedience to torah. The choice of rebellion is to be "devoured." The word used in verse 20 is the same as that used in verse 7; the devouring is by the Assyrian army (perhaps an image for the belated coming of the Babylonian army). The consequences of choice take place in lived reality—productive land or occupying army. But the consequences, either way, are at the behest of Yahweh: "The Lord has spoken." Notice, the "vision" of Judah's choosable future is not commonsense or conventional politics. This overwhelming poetry has at its center the conviction that lived, public life pivots around the covenantal requirement of the Holy One. To order public life in disrespect and disregard of the Holy One is to be exposed in a flattened cucumber patch, with nowhere to hide—and to be leveled like Sodom! The news for Jerusalem is not good, but there is a chance!

The Whole Drama of Life-Death-New Life in a Nutshell (1:21–27)

1:21 **How the faithful city**
    has become a whore!
        She that was full of justice,
    righteousness lodged in her—
        but now murderers!
    22 **Your silver has become dross,**
        your wine is mixed with water.

23 **Your princes are rebels**
  and companions of thieves.
Everyone loves a bribe
  and runs after gifts.
They do not defend the orphan,
  and the widow's cause does not come before them.

24 **Therefore says the Sovereign, the LORD of hosts, the Mighty One of Israel:**
  Ah, I will pour out my wrath on my enemies,
    and avenge myself on my foes!
25 **I will turn my hand against you;**
  I will smelt away your dross as with lye
    and remove all your alloy.
26 **And I will restore your judges as at the first,**
  and your counselors as at the beginning.
Afterward you shall be called the city of righteousness,
  the faithful city.

27 **Zion shall be redeemed by justice,**
  and those in her who repent, by righteousness.

The poetry now turns to a reflective response upon the devastating verdict just announced upon wounded, near-to-death Jerusalem. In the center of this unit, the elements of a prophetic lawsuit against Judah are voiced: indictment (vv. 21c–23) and sentence (vv. 24–26b). What surprises, however, is that the lawsuit utterance is framed in verse 21ab by a positive retrospect and in verse 26cd by a positive anticipation beyond the judgment.

The city is remembered as it once was (v. 21). The verse begins with an ejaculatory "how," expressing astonishment and grief at the drastic change. The initial word is the same as that used at the beginning of Lamentations 1:1, which grieves the devastation of the same city. The city is remembered as having been faithful in some time past, filled with justice and righteousness, and fully permeated with covenantal practices that enhance the entire community. But now the city is likened to a whore—fickle, self-indulgent, unprincipled. The shabby present is even more pitiful when contrasted with the memory. Now everything precious has been devalued by distortion and abuse: silver cheapened, wine watered down, princes now in anarchy and lawlessness. Everything has gone to the dogs! Everyone is on the make. Everyone seeks self-advancement, and no one cares anymore for the public good. When there is such self-serving and self-seeking, moreover, the needy of society predictably disappear from the screen of public awareness. Widows and orphans are the litmus test of justice and righteousness (cf. 1:17). On this test, Jerusalem fails completely and decisively. The large theological issues of life with Yahweh boil down to the concreteness of policy toward widows and orphans.

Then follows a massive prophetic "therefore" (v. 24). The preposition announces the sure consequence of such a failure. The consequence is the savage work of the sovereign God. Jerusalem is not autonomous, is not free to pursue its own indulgent agenda. Yahweh has a peculiar purpose for Jerusalem and will act in severe ways against the city that fails in that purpose. The poetry of punishment picks up on the silver/dross imagery of verse 22. The process will now be reversed. What had been cheapened by an impure mix of metals will now be purged. The purging of course entails fire, burning away the impurity. Thus, without saying so the poet anticipates for Jerusalem "the fire next time" that is yet to come. Jerusalem is under threat, as the entire book of Isaiah knows. That threat will destroy the monarchy and cause a reversion to the judges and counselors, the anarchic situation of the days of the book of Judges. Jerusalem is not permitted to enjoy the sure structures of order and government if those orders renege on their proper function of obedience to Yahweh. We have in these verses, in a nutshell, the primary claims of the early Isaiah tradition. The city has failed Yahweh's torah purpose of neighborliness. It will for that reason suffer devastation.

In the end we are surprised by verse 26cd: Afterward! The end is not yet. The devastation is not the last word. After all of that, after defeat, after exile, the city will again become its true self, a practitioner of righteousness and faithfulness, the very terms of verse 21. Likely the poetry has in view here the later utterances of chapters 56, 58, 60—62, which pertain to Jerusalem's hoped-for recovery after exile. There is hope, but it is deeply postsuffering hope. Yahweh's wrath is deep and serious and will be outlasted only by Yahweh's resolve to bring Jerusalem to its true and proper function as a place of justice. The poet looks historical threat full in the face but holds out for the holy purpose of Jerusalem, which runs through the threat of history and even beyond that threat.

A Response of Modest Hope and Large Devastation (1:28–31)

1:28 **But rebels and sinners shall be destroyed together,**
      and those who forsake the LORD shall be consumed.
  29 **For you shall be ashamed of the oaks**
        in which you delighted;
      and you shall blush for the gardens
        that you have chosen.

³⁰ **For you shall be like an oak**
   whose leaf withers,
   and like a garden without water.
³¹ **The strong shall become like tinder,**
   and their work like a spark;
they and their work shall burn together,
   with no one to quench them.

These verses form a reprise on the main themes of this chapter. Verse 27 follows closely the accents of verse 26cd, which in turn echo verse 21ab. Jerusalem will indeed come to justice and righteousness, that is, the care of widows and orphans. That much is promised. The following "but" of verse 28, however, looms large and severely qualifies the promise of verse 27. Indeed, verses 28–31 comment on those, surely many, perhaps most, who will not share in the good "afterward." Because of the harshness of verses 28–31, it is clear that the promise of verse 27 is partial and conditional. It pertains only to those who repent in justice and righteousness. The rest, surely the majority, are those already considered in verses 2–3 who resist Yahweh. For these there is no hope. They will be consumed (cf. vv. 7, 20), eaten alive in one gulp. In verses 22–23, the poetry has traced the negative transformation of everything of value. Now, in verse 29, the "oaks" and "gardens"— embodiments and symbols of growth, power, and self-generated vitality—will shrivel, dry up, and fail. The presumed strength and virility of the powerful will evaporate in the drought. The image of drought in verse 30 is followed in verse 31 by the image of fire. Both fire and drought will terminate, but fire is more abrupt, more violent, more total. There is a hope in verse 27, but it is lean and conditional. Only the repentees dare look beyond the devastation. For most, those who surely refuse to repent, there looms only violent and painful nullification. This long chapter begins the "vision." It is a vision of a beloved city deeply under threat, under threat from the very Holy One who caused it to prosper in times past.

Hope in Latter Days (2:1–4)

2:1 **The word that Isaiah son of Amoz saw concerning Judah and Jerusalem.**

   ² **In days to come**
      the mountain of the LORD's house
   shall be established as the highest of the mountains,
      and shall be raised above the hills;
   all the nations shall stream to it.
   ³ **Many peoples shall come and say,**

> "Come, let us go up to the mountain of the LORD,
>   to the house of the God of Jacob;
> that he may teach us his ways
>   and that we may walk in his paths."
> For out of Zion shall go forth instruction,
>   and the word of the LORD from Jerusalem.
> ⁴ He shall judge between the nations,
>   and shall arbitrate for many peoples;
> they shall beat their swords into plowshares,
>   and their spears into pruning hooks;
> nation shall not lift up sword against nation,
>   neither shall they learn war any more.

These verses constitute a separate poetic unit. This is clear both because of the new introductory formula of verse 1 and because the same poem, with slight variations, is used in Micah 4:2–4. It must have been a familiar and popular poem, existing on its own. Clearly, its placement here, just after the harshness of chapter 1, is a later editorial maneuver. Perhaps it should be treated independently, but it is not unimportant that this poetic unit follows the first chapter. Its placement reflects a characteristic tendency of the final form of the text of Isaiah. For all of its harshness, the tradition of Isaiah characteristically moves to hope. In largest scope, after the judgment of chapters 1—39, the Isaiah tradition considers new possibilities for Jerusalem in chapters 40—66. Here, on a much smaller scale, the Jerusalem tradition looks beyond "the coming fire" (1:31) to "the latter days."

These verses are "the word" that the prophet "saw." That is, they continue to partake, in a distinctive way, of the "vision" identified in 1:1. The poet looks beyond the sure and coming devastation to Yahweh's larger, long-term intention. The anticipatory aspects of the Isaiah tradition are not unlike Martin Luther King Jr.'s "I have a dream" speech. This tradition has an anticipation for the future rooted in the deeper resolve of Yahweh, a future not yet seeded in historical circumstance. The poet imagines a smaller, burnt, purified Jerusalem with a wholly new future.

In time to come—we do not know when—in Yahweh's good and sure time, Jerusalem will loom large and tall as a reference point for the nations. That will be when the city has become a place commodious for widows and orphans, when the city is marked, as it surely will be, by faithfulness, justice, and righteousness. In that time Jerusalem will be like a magnet, drawing all the nations of the world toward its peculiar authority. Norman Gottwald suggests that the image of the poem is something like an effective United Nations, where the nations can come in concert, drawn by a shared offer of well-being, where war will be unnecessary and no longer an available practice of the nations (*All the Kingdoms of the Earth*, 199–203).

The nations will want to come to Jerusalem because in Jerusalem Yahweh is fully present as the source of all life for the world. In Jerusalem, moreover, is the torah of Yahweh (here rendered as "instruction") that will make available to the nations Israel's Yahweh-given secret for peace. That is, the torah is the clue for peace in the world. Yahweh will become the arbiter, the world court, so that matters will be decided equitably, without recourse to violence, force, or war. The nations, presumably, will accept the verdicts of Yahweh, because Yahweh is so obviously effective, wise, and just. The acceptance of such a governance will permit serious and complete disarmament.

The nations will not need to defend against each other, because Yahweh will establish a *pax Jerusalem* through which all will be safe and prosperous, indeed, "all will be well." Earlier the poet had observed negatively: silver to dross; wine to water; princes to thieves (1:22–23). Now the transformation is positive: swords to plowshares; spears to pruning hooks (2:4). There will be a cessation of political and economic oppression and threat. Moreover, there will be an end to hateful, divisive ideology. The nations will learn peace—and will practice it!

It is astonishing that after the deep threat of chapter 1 the "vision" moves beyond the threat without denying it. In the end, after the threat is implemented—as surely it will be—Jerusalem so radically criticized is still the seat of the world's best possibility. Jerusalem is the dramatic center of the new governance whereby Yahweh's will will "be done on earth as it is in heaven."

YET AGAIN, MASSIVE JUDGMENT AND RESILIENT HOPE
2:5–4:6

This extended passage is evidently composed of a series of smaller units, now arranged to comprise a larger whole. Isaiah 2:5 would seem to be an introductory appeal for the entire unit, though that is uncertain. In the main, we may distinguish between the long section of 2:6–4:1, a series of prophetic indictments and sentences, and the promissory oracle of restoration after the devastation in 4:2–6. Thus the completed unit reiterates the primary themes and movement of 1:2–2:4 and, like that unit, completes an *oracle of judgment* with a *promise of restoration*. The tradition of Isaiah is completely convinced that Jerusalem is to be severely punished; it is equally convinced that punishment will not be the final settlement of the city, even if the restoration is modest and after the fact of devastation.

A Summons to Renewed Obedience (2:5)

2:5 **O house of Jacob,**
come, let us walk
in the light of the LORD!

This brief verse seems to stand alone as a liturgical summons to trust in Yahweh. I have placed it with verses 6–22, regarding it as a summons for which the remainder of the chapter is a basis, giving a reason for heeding the summons to trust. It is alternatively possible to treat the verse as a climax to the promissory vision of verses 1–4, inviting Judah to embrace the vision of a torah-based peace. Either way, the verse is a bid for loyalty to Yahweh, either to receive the goodness promised in verses 1–4 or, as I think more likely, as an invitation to shun the threat so powerfully voiced in the verses that follow.

The address, "house of Jacob," treats the community as children of the great promises in the Genesis narratives, and is offered as a call to worship. But entry into this worship entails an embrace of the commandments. The verb "walk" bespeaks torah obedience. It is worth noting that the reference to Yahweh, the subject of obedience, is not simply Yahweh, but "light of the Lord (= Yahweh)." The phrasing could possibly allude to Yahweh's light in creation, which overpowers the chaos of darkness. Or it could refer to temple presence, or alternatively to relief from oppression, as in 9:2. Any of these readings suggests an appeal to the visual world of presence in the temple, the world of presence in which the tradition of Isaiah is situated. The alternative to "the light of the Lord" is defeat and death (cf. Isa. 60:1–3).

A Vision of Yahweh-Sent Violence (2:6–22)

2:6 **For you have forsaken the ways of your people,**
O house of Jacob.
Indeed they are full of diviners from the east
and of soothsayers like the Philistines,
and they clasp hands with foreigners.
⁷ **Their land is filled with silver and gold,**
and there is no end to their treasures;

their land is filled with horses,
>and there is no end to their chariots.
⁸ Their land is filled with idols;
>they bow down to the work of their hands,
>to what their own fingers have made.
⁹ And so people are humbled,
>and everyone is brought low—
>do not forgive them!
¹⁰ Enter into the rock,
>and hide in the dust
from the terror of the LORD,
>and from the glory of his majesty.
¹¹ The haughty eyes of people shall be brought low,
>and the pride of everyone shall be humbled;
and the LORD alone will be exalted
>in that day.
¹² For the LORD of hosts has a day
>against all that is proud and lofty,
>against all that is lifted up and high;
¹³ against all the cedars of Lebanon,
>lofty and lifted up;
>and against all the oaks of Bashan;
¹⁴ against all the high mountains,
>and against all the lofty hills;
¹⁵ against every high tower,
>and against every fortified wall;
¹⁶ against all the ships of Tarshish,
>and against all the beautiful craft.
¹⁷ The haughtiness of people shall be humbled,
>and the pride of everyone shall be brought low;
>and the LORD alone will be exalted on that day.
¹⁸ The idols shall utterly pass away.
¹⁹ Enter the caves of the rocks
>and the holes of the ground,
from the terror of the LORD,
>and from the glory of his majesty,
>when he rises to terrify the earth.
²⁰ On that day people will throw away
>to the moles and to the bats
their idols of silver and their idols of gold,
>which they made for themselves to worship,
²¹ to enter the caverns of the rocks
>and the clefts in the crags,

from the terror of the LORD,
  and from the glory of his majesty,
  when he rises to terrify the earth.
22 Turn away from mortals,
  who have only breath in their nostrils,
  for of what account are they?

This extended poetic unity, in its main structure, concerns rather conventional prophetic emphases on indictment and sentence. The poem accents Judah's deep jeopardy in the face of Yahweh's judiciary activity. Yahweh holds Israel to high covenantal expectations, and when those are disregarded, punishment comes. What may interest us, however, is not the familiarity of the primary themes but the daring and venturesome rhetorical patterns employed, which are quite remarkable. The covenantal, judicial verdict is given immediately in verse 6: Yahweh has forsaken Yahweh's special people. God has given up on Israel, because Israel has been hopelessly unresponsive to Yahweh's covenantal requirements. The prophet could make no more dreadful announcement, for Israel's security and well-being in the world depend upon linkage to Yahweh.

The poem then begins to provide the grounds upon which Yahweh made this decision of rejection. The indictment of Israel is dominated by the repeated use of forms of the term "full," used four times. In verse 6, the community is *filled* with non-Israelites of two sorts. Diviners and soothsayers are agents of alien religious practices that are not covenantal and not oriented to obedience, but are a way of manipulation and control that seeks to manage without God (cf. Deut. 18:9–13). These religious seductions are matched by "traders." "Clasping of hands with foreigners" means to enter into economic agreements that erode the distinctive self-identity of Israel. The prophetic tradition, long before Karl Marx, understood that distorting religion and distorting economics provide mutual reinforcement and together seriously impinge upon the character and identity of the community. Thus the summons to "walk in the light of the Lord" (v. 5) is a call away from religious and economic accommodation that inevitably slackens and weakens Israel's Yahwistic character. Jerusalem is endangered precisely because Judah has forgotten or neglected the particularity of its historical destiny and the concrete disciplines that sustain that destiny.

From this general accommodation, certain things inevitably follow: (a) The land is *full* of silver and gold. That is, the community has become an intentional, aggressive money economy, enormously affluent and on the make, which evokes a crisis in Israel of "God and mammon" (cf. Matt. 6:24). (b) The land is *full* of horses and chariots, that is, weapon systems.

This arsenal, which has been amassed by the central royal government, was not needed until Judah became an accommodationist money economy in pursuit of affluence and tried to live "like all the nations." As the community gains more wealth, it must perforce find means of protection, which of course contributes to the vicious, endless cycle of security and anxiety. (c) Along with money and weapons comes a land *full* of idols, projections of self-achievement, self-security, and self-congratulations. The triad of money-weapons-idols forms a convergence that is at the core of Karl Marx's critique of an alienating society. This threefold "fullness" has decisively shifted the identity of the community, which now neither depends upon Yahweh (being self-sufficient) nor obeys Yahweh (being autonomous). No wonder Yahweh has rejected! Thus we are able to see that the poem provides an acute social analysis of the self-destructiveness of a post-Yahwistic society. This analysis, which pertains to an ancient society, is a workable model for our continuing social analysis of our own time and place, an analysis that is at the heart of prophetic faith.

Verse 9 draws a conclusion from this analysis of "fullness": "And so . . . " Consequently everyone is brought low, humbled, jeopardized, at risk. In prophetic logic, this is the inevitable outcome of self-indulgence. But of course the conclusion is ironic. The claim that raising one's self in such a way brings one low points on to the cadences of the crucifixion: "He humbles those who are exalted." The actual effect of such *fullness* is an inescapable *emptiness*, life emptied of well-being, security, and joy. This is "gaining the whole world and losing one's soul." The poem observes that what Judah most craves is what it surely cannot have on these terms. The last line of verse 9 is odd. The prophet has addressed God in verse 6, and now, in what appears to be a throwaway afterthought, the prophet again speaks to God, adding personal urgency to the weight of the evidence. On formal grounds, this people cannot be forgiven and restored to relationship with Yahweh. Beyond that, it is clear that the prophet himself wants for Judah no such restoration. The prophet aligns himself with the indignation of God in concluding that reconciliation is not possible and should not be possible. The line reinforces the sense of hopelessness for Judah that the poem intends to assert.

In the extended section of verses 11–18, the poet meditates on the theme of "humbling." "Haughty eyes" bespeak self-confident avarice. Everything seen and everything imaginable is sought on one's own terms—no hesitation, no apology, no reluctance, only shameless self-assertion. This is rank consumerism! But to no avail. The verbs of devastation in verse 9 are reiterated—in reverse order—"brought low, humbled." It is Yahweh, only

Yahweh, who now will be lifted up in exaltation. Yahweh is not user friendly. Rather, Yahweh is elevated while all others are lowered. Judah had come to think that Yahweh was one piece of its landscape, so that all of it would be enhanced together, Yahweh and Judah. Not so! Yahweh is not part of Judah's landscape, but stands free, alone, detached, over-against.

In verses 12–17 we arrive at the rhetorical center of the poem. Yahweh has scarcely been mentioned in this poem; but now Yahweh appears with full title, "Lord of Hosts"—that is, Yahweh in awesome, ferocious power; Yahweh in battle dress ready for a moment of self-assertion, combat, and triumph. Those who thought they were Yahweh's allies and beneficiaries turn out to be adversaries. Everything turns on "the day." "The day" is a frequent reference in the prophets to the moment of Yahweh's intense mobilization to reassert Yahweh's own governance (cf. Amos 5:18; Zech. 1:10, 14). In this dramatic moment Yahweh is over-against all rivals and all would-be allies. Thus, in verses 12–16 we have a tenfold use of the preposition "against." The ten objects are all figures for arrogance, pride, self-sufficiency, autonomy. The first two objects in verse 12 are general references to self-enhancement. In verse 13 two metaphors are used, "cedars of Lebanon, oaks of Bashan," bespeaking impressive visible strength as signs of pride and sufficiency. In verse 14 the reference is to natural phenomena and in verse 15 to the accoutrements of royal power and prestige. In verse 16, "ships" and "beautiful craft" concern ambitious material equipment designed to enhance trade and therefore affluence. These several objects of Yahweh's opposition should not be studied as discreet references, but heard in their cumulative rhetorical effect. Yahweh has declared hostility against all efforts at autonomy and self-sufficiency. The ten objects look back to the "fullnesses" of verses 7–8, for they are the same. Judah has made sustained efforts at securing and enhancing its life apart from Yahweh, and Yahweh will have none of it. Thus the summons of verse 5 is that Judah should cease and desist from its self-sufficiency. This rhetorical torrent concludes in verse 17 with a reiteration of verse 11, which now functions as something of a poetic refrain.

In verse 8, the idols are attacked as emblems of self-sufficiency. In verse 18, the theme is taken up again. The term "idols" is used here to belittle and dismiss efforts at self-enhancement. It won't work! Effort to base life on one's own achievements is futile. A donkey cannot do without a caring owner! Verse 19 reiterates the warning and plea of verse 10. And that is followed in verses 20–21 with the image of Judah in profound panic with its hopeless, futile idols. In verses 11 and 19 Israel is urged to flee to the caves for safety, because Yahweh is going to hit the urban enterprise. The imagery is of frantic urban elites—the ones who trade, engage in commerce, manage the defense industry, and enjoy surplus wealth—heading for the hills, perhaps the caves by the Dead Sea. This is civil-defense evacuation! Their self-confidence and self-composure are completely shaken. And so they enter the caves to hide out from the threat of Yahweh. They enter caves filled with bat dung and mole dung. But besides being merely unpleasant, bats and moles are impure animals. Contact with them defiles and makes one religiously unacceptable. The poet offers a hideous contrast between affluent self-affirmation and the exposure and humiliation of hiding out with subterranean creatures who disqualify urban elites from life with Yahweh.

One can imagine, moreover, that, as they flee, the Jerusalemites will debate what of their precious treasures to take with them, as fugitives are wont to do. Perhaps they will take their most precious properties, their images of silver and gold. The picture—not a pretty one—is one of profound incongruity. The fugitives arrive at the caves with their signs of wealth and well-being. But of course the caves are inhospitable. Judah is now in deep dung! And there, their idols have no value but are only a burden. In fear and desperation, they scuttle their gods, giving them over to the other cave dwellers in order to travel light, perhaps to save their skins but nothing else. So they end, completely empty-handed, all of their resources to no avail, all of their fullness from verses 6–8 now spent. In verse 21, the summons of verses 10 and 19 is sounded yet one more time.

Understand, all of this utterance is only a poetic act of imagination. Its force is not intended to be rational. The poet is not making an argument about policy, nor is this a prediction of what is to come. It is rather a rhetorical assault on a numbed community of elites; it sends a "wake-up call," inviting them into a scenario of life that had seemed, until its utterance, impossible for those so well defended. The poem comes to Judah like something of a nightmare, intruding into a well-defended Judah, exposing Jerusalem as not at all well defended, now without resources and helpless. The dismantling of the well-regarded and well-regarding city happens because Yahweh is the key character in this scenario, the very character excluded from the enlightened world of aggressive, affluent autonomy. Yahweh, it is clear, will not be squeezed out of Jerusalem so long as there are poets to keep life more open than *full gold* and *full horses* and *full idols* ever intend.

Finally we arrive at verse 22, which makes yet a final appeal. The verse stands outside the intense rhetoric of the preceding and seems to function as a counterpoint to the appeal of verse 5. It speaks a powerful imperative: "Turn away." Except for the strategic imperatives of "enter" (vv. 10, 19), this is the first substantive imperative. Now the poet bids Judah come to its senses and leave off its self-destructive craving for autonomy. Leave off trust in "mortals." The Hebrew is bald: '*adam* = humankind. The same term has been used in verses 9, 11, 17, and 20, there rendered "people." Leave off human self-securing. Leave off all the efforts at money, weapons, and idols, which generate phony assurances that have no force when Yahweh is mobilized. The problem with "humans" is that they have no breath in their nostrils; that is, they are fragile, mortal, dependent, finite. They are not generative of breath as is Yahweh with Yahweh's "spirit," but are only needy recipients of the life Yahweh grants. How futile, how silly to trust human guarantees that cannot endure!

The poet addresses a community that has been deeply seduced into a false way of life. The trouble is rooted in the common, ordinary propensity to self-sufficiency that requires large doses of self-deception. Perhaps every community in turn falls for it. But surely not Judah, which had an alternative with Yahweh and should have known better. But now, the poet focuses on this community, which in its profound stupidity (cf. 1:3) rejects its sure source of life. We are now able to see how the invitation of verse 5 stands as a countertheme to the haunting exposé of verse 22. Trust in human capacity is failed and futile. Jerusalem has available this extraordinary alternative of life with Yahweh, summoned in obedience, guaranteed by presence. The bad choice, life without Yahweh, is an empty-handed choice, driven underground for life, midst the defiling dung, with moles and bats. The options are stark. The poet, however, is not yet finished.

Loss—When Yahweh "Takes Away" (3:1–12)

3:1 **For now the Sovereign, the LORD of hosts,**
    is taking away from Jerusalem and from Judah
  support and staff—
    all support of bread,
  and all support of water—
2**warrior and soldier,**
    judge and prophet,
    diviner and elder,
3**captain of fifty**
    and dignitary,
  counselor and skillful magician
    and expert enchanter.
4**And I will make boys their princes,**
    and babes shall rule over them.

⁵ The people will be oppressed,
   everyone by another
   and everyone by a neighbor;
the youth will be insolent to the elder,
   and the base to the honorable.

⁶ Someone will even seize a relative,
   a member of the clan, saying,
"You have a cloak;
   you shall be our leader,
and this heap of ruins
shall be under your rule."
⁷ But the other will cry out on that day, saying,
"I will not be a healer;
   in my house there is neither bread nor cloak;
you shall not make me
   leader of the people."
⁸ For Jerusalem has stumbled
   and Judah has fallen,
because their speech and their deeds are against the LORD,
   defying his glorious presence.

⁹ The look on their faces bears witness against them;
   they proclaim their sin like Sodom,
they do not hide it.
Woe to them!
   For they have brought evil on themselves.
¹⁰ Tell the innocent how fortunate they are,
   for they shall eat the fruit of their labors.
¹¹ Woe to the guilty! How unfortunate they are,
   for what their hands have done shall be done to them.
¹² My people—children are their oppressors,
   and women rule over them.
O my people, your leaders mislead you,
   and confuse the course of your paths.

In these verses, the poet seeks yet again, as in 2:9–21, to help his listeners imagine a scene of utter loss, confusion, and vulnerability. The words are not a description of what is, but of what may be and will be, because Yahweh will terminate the fraudulent, self-indulgent society of Judah. In these verses, everything follows from the thesis sentence of verse 1. In that verse, three matters are underscored. First, we have the only mention of Yahweh in the entire unit that follows (except the reference in verse 8, which is derivative).

Yahweh is here given an ominous title, "Sovereign, the Lord of hosts"—severe, solemn, strong, dangerous. Second, the verb of Yahweh's action is "take away," remove, cause to be without. We are not told how this happens. The poet has no curiosity about the process. Third, Yahweh will enact this negative verb against Judah and Jerusalem. The city and its environs are full—as we have seen—of money, weapons, and gods (vv. 7–8). All of that is about to be emptied by the awesome irresistible force of Yahweh.

The remainder of this unit, through verse 12, is a characterization of life in Jerusalem when Yahweh has taken everything away. The summary of loss is given in verse 1a, where the term "support" is used three times: "support and staff (masculine and feminine), support of bread, support of water." Jerusalem will shortly lack the basic supplies of bread and water for life. The line may anticipate famine and drought, or perhaps the "devouring" of resources by an occupying army (cf. 1:7). We are not given any specifics. We are only invited to imagine a land now completely destitute, without elemental resources.

The list of verses 2–3 is odd, both because it is a pure list of social roles, without verbs, and because we are given no clue about how this inventory relates to verse 1. The list includes all the roles of leadership in the community—religious, political, and military. The odd slippage between verse 1 and verse 2 allows that all of these leading citizens will lack bread and water. Or alternatively, perhaps these are the "support and staff," the stuff of social life that will now be missing. Either way, the destitution envisioned means that the social infrastructure of Judah is now completely in jeopardy. And because all of these roles have lost their force and their authority, the civil order of the community is deeply at risk.

The risk is articulated in three ways: (1) Unqualified, immature people—young boys and babes—will be cast in leadership roles; that is, in place of judges, elders, captains, and dignitaries (v. 4). (2) The conventional lines of respect and deference upon which society depends will disintegrate. Society will become a jungle of rapacious exploitation in which generational and class distinctions that give status and stability will be overturned (v. 5). Everyone will prey upon everyone, the sort of world experienced as unbearable by Job (Job 30), when one's social location is nullified. (3) There will be a complete vacuum of leadership (vv. 6–7). Circumstance will become so unbearable, social prospects so dismal, that none will be willing to take leadership responsibility. In these quick verses, the poet sketches out a completely failed, hopeless community—all because the Sovereign has "taken away."

Verse 8 draws a provisional conclusion. All of this is in prospect for

Jerusalem, because city and regime have organized their life against Yahweh, defying Yahweh's preeminence. Note well, the defiance and resistance to Yahweh are not direct and explicit. Presumably there was still lots of "religion" (cf. 1:10–15). Rather, the defiance concerns self-indulgent autonomy in matters economic, military, and political, at the high cost of the viability of the community. The poet imagines a sociopolitical world that is saturated with the severity of Yahweh.

The unit ends in verses 9–12 with a retrospect on the inversion of society just described. The poet observed the despair and desperation in this Sodom-like environment. Jerusalem is recipient of a woe (v. 9), a grieving acknowledgment of a complete breakdown. There are some who are innocent (righteous), who still get along. The poet, however, has no interest in them. It is the guilty who are the subject of the woe (v. 11). They now are victimized by the results of their own choices and policies. The news for them is not good. The sorry situation of verse 12 recalls verse 4. The void of responsible leadership has devolved authority upon women and children who are unable to do good, but who exploit, mislead, and confuse. Everything that made life livable in a patriarchal framework has now been forfeited. Notice how close to social reality the poet remains. This is not some large, floating theological verdict. This is a verdict "on the ground," in the midst of the daily demands of living together, eating, drinking, and surviving. Judah is paralyzed when Yahweh "takes away."

Yet More Loss—More "Taking Away" (3:13–4:1)

3:13 The LORD rises to argue his case;
    he stands to judge the peoples.
  14 The LORD enters into judgment
    with the elders and princes of his people;
  It is you who have devoured the vineyard;
    the spoil of the poor is in your houses.
  15 What do you mean by crushing my people,
    by grinding the face of the poor? says the Lord GOD of hosts.

  16 The LORD said:
  Because the daughters of Zion are haughty
    and walk with outstretched necks,
    glancing wantonly with their eyes,
  mincing along as they go,
    tinkling with their feet;
  17 the Lord will afflict with scabs

the heads of the daughters of Zion,
and the LORD will lay bare their secret parts.

¹⁸ In that day the Lord will take away the finery of the anklets, the headbands, and the crescents; ¹⁹ the pendants, the bracelets, and the scarfs; ²⁰ the head-dresses, the armlets, the sashes, the perfume boxes, and the amulets; ²¹ the signet rings and nose rings; ²² the festal robes, the mantles, the cloaks, and the handbags; ²³ the garments of gauze, the linen garments, the turbans, and the veils.

²⁴ Instead of perfume there will be a stench;
    and instead of a sash, a rope;
and instead of well-set hair, baldness;
    and instead of a rich robe, a binding of sackcloth;
    instead of beauty, shame.
²⁵ Your men shall fall by the sword
    and your warriors in battle.
²⁶ And her gates shall lament and mourn;
    ravaged, she shall sit upon the ground.
4:1 Seven women shall take hold of one man in that day, saying,
    "We will eat our own bread and wear our own clothes;
    just let us be called by your name;
        take away our disgrace."

This theme of social loss and dislocation is continued through four small poetic units, all of which address the same issues of loss and deprivation. In *verses 13–15*, the poet uses the formal language of the courtroom, not unlike 1:18. Yahweh as judge and prosecutor brings a case against Judah. The case does not name all of the inhabitants of Judah as defendants. Rather, the accusation is filed against "elders and princes," those in roles of leadership, influence, and power. It is worth noting that the "princes and elders" named here are the same as those listed in verses 2–3, though there rendered in English as "elders and captains." The poet is discerning enough to see that the distortion of social relationships is not in the first instance a work of all citizens, but characteristically the work of "opinion makers" who are on the make at the expense of their fellow citizens. The charge is direct: "You," not everyone, but "You" (v. 14). "You" have confiscated vineyards and houses. The seizure perhaps has not been violent, but rather accomplished through the inexorable workings of economic processes governed by rules that deliberately favor some at the expense of others.

In language that is clearly parallel to that of Amos (Amos 4:1), the poet observes social differentiations that have contributed to the crisis. In verse 15, the first line concerns "my people"; the second line has, in parallel, "the poor." In this particular case, it is "the poor" who are said to be "my people." This is a strong example of God's preferential option for the poor, for the God of Hosts is peculiarly allied with the poor as their legal advocate against the leadership class. Thus the poet is able to hold together most skillfully the *large jeopardy* of the community with a quite *concrete social analysis.*

This acute social analysis continues to operate in the second poetic unit, *verses 16–17,* where the indictment is against "the daughters of Zion." This phrasing, of itself, has no very clear reference. In context, however, the addressees would seem to be the elite women of the urban establishment, in an exposé not unlike Amos's "cows of Bashan" (Amos 4:1). That is, the prophets appear to see women as the engine of consumerism, driving the wanton exploitation and destruction of the poor. Now it may be that this prophetic propensity is sharply sexist and inordinately abusive of women. It is clear, however, that in verses 2–3 and 14, a vigorous critique, in a different way, is addressed against male leadership. In any case, in these verses the poem seems to address the conspicuous consumption and wanton exhibitionism of the wealthy. The poet offers us an image of something like an "Easter parade"—perhaps a "Passover parade"—some quite public occasion when the most self-indulgent in Jerusalem show off themselves and their extravagance. In reading this I am reminded of Edward Elgar's "Enigma Variations," in which the music mimics the steps of different persons entering the room with their various distinctive paces and postures. So here, the poet in great detail mocks the strutting, self-announcing arrogance of those who parade themselves and their finery; he comments on necks extended, eyes cutting at an angle, feet walking in tiny steps—all gestures calculated to call attention to those who are attired in finery of the most exotic sort. All this transpires while widows and orphans are denied life (1:17)!

The poet sketches out shameless luxury in order to drop verse 17 with its abrupt, devastating reversal. The heads of these women must have endured long hours being caressed in a beauty parlor—and now they are a mass of scabs and sores! The finery of dresses must have been artistically designed— and now the women endure mocked exposure of brutalizing slavery! We are told nothing about how this abrupt reversal happens, for it can happen this quickly only in abrupt rhetoric. We are told only "Yahweh will afflict."

Of course, it is the abruptness that is the point of the rhetoric. These Jerusalemites who spend their profligate days in clubs and at fashion shows assumed, without any serious reflection, that their extravagance would endure to perpetuity. And now, "Yahweh will afflict!" This reversal in Jerusalem anticipates the like reversal for Lady Babylon in the later testimony of Isaiah (47:1–3). There as well, the reversal is abrupt, inexplicable, and unexpected. There as well, it is a rhetorical maneuver that has only Yahweh as the agent of change and the warrant for change. The God of the book of Isaiah, according to the poet, moves quickly and devastatingly, precisely in places that thought themselves to be immune. The poet will use nothing of explanatory comment. The coming displacement is only rudely and tersely announced. The hearers are left to pause in alarmed reflection and dismay. How scandalously unthinkable that the finely clothed are now to be naked in their secret parts! The honored and glorified are now to have exposed genitals, candidates for gross and limitless abuse. The poet is not "nice." Nor is the God of the poet nice. The speech works to assault even the numbed resistance of those who knew "It can't happen here."

The poet goes further with the same theme in the third poetic unit, *verses 18–23*. This unit is only an inventory of items that supplement what has just been stated. Again three things interest us. First, it is Yahweh who will act. Yahweh here receives no extra title or modifier. By this time Yahweh is known in the poem in all of the ferocious potential of Yahweh's character. Second, the verb "take away" is reiterated from verse 1. This God is not yet finished subtracting from the city too secure and too full. And third, the reversal will be "in that day," the time already cited in 2:12. The poet knows that Jerusalem's time in Yahweh's hand is freighted with an ominous schedule. At the behest of Yahweh, the turn of times is about to break. When it breaks, moreover, everything taken for granted will be broken open. No one in Jerusalem, no one in the power structure, no one in the public horizon of extravagance can do anything to stop the day Yahweh has set.

Now the poet becomes specific. It is as though the poet has probed the clothes closets and dressers of the most fashionable women in the city. Or it is as though he has spent time in the most exclusive shops in downtown Jerusalem, watching the most popular purchases. He lists them all, twenty-one items. The vocabulary is exotic. The poet is able to make distinctions in the massive extravagance. He names the articles one by one, and with each one makes the exposé of self-indulgence more biting. The list is monotonous. It is intended to be. There is no rhetorical development, no inflection, no verb, no emphasis. The list, which intends to be cumulative in its repetition, advertises the self-indulgence that will bring ruin to the infrastructure of the city. In this section of the indictment, it is as though the poet can think of nothing to say or needs to say nothing more. The list itself, if it is noticed and heeded item by item, carries its own massive indictment.

The shoppers and owners of all this stuff no doubt did not set out to be greedy. It happens a little at a time. Of course, today's luxuries become tomorrow's necessities, because "everyone" has a nose ring! The purchase and possession seem so incidental, so taken-for-granted, so far removed from deep issues of social infrastructure. Nonetheless the poetry haunts all those who can hear and notice. The investments that have seemed so innocent and natural and commonplace are now redescribed and resituated by *the agent* (Yahweh), *the verb* ("take away"), and *the time* ("that day"). What was treasure becomes threat.

Now the poet breaks into the fourth poetic utterance, *3:24–4:1*. But for all the length of verse 24, there is not yet a verb. There is an exchange being wrought, in the status of Jerusalem, inscrutably, inexplicably. It just happens, all in and of itself, without agent, without intention, without Yahweh. Five times, relentlessly, the word "instead" is repeated. In each case, the change is a negation, a loss, a deprivation, a humiliation. We have seen that this long chapter, which offers a nightmare future to self-indulgent Jerusalem, is governed by the verb "take away" (vv. 1, 12). Now we are led to see what is left when all of the splendor and comfort and well-being are subtracted and "taken away":

> instead of perfume . . . stench;
> instead of sash . . . rope;
> instead of well-set hair . . . baldness;
> instead of rich robe . . . sackcloth;
> instead of beauty . . .

The last item lacks a counterpart in the Hebrew, perhaps lost, perhaps missing for dramatic effect . . . unthinkable, unutterable! The first cluster of terms—perfume, sash, well-set hair, a rich robe, beauty—betokens affluent Jerusalem, women and perhaps men who spend time and energy in grooming, appearance, and comfort, with much leisure. And then follows the stark contrast—stench, rope, baldness, sackcloth. Tersely the poet images a world of horrors—grief, sadness, humiliation, filth, slavery, acute discomfort, suffering. One can experience, in poetic imagination, the harsh rope against a pampered skin; the crude, hurried shaving of hair so long cared for, now cut short for utilitarian purposes.

If verse 24 is a vision of the fate awaiting the women of Jerusalem who "glance wantonly" and "mince" (v. 16), then verse 25 more quickly provides a parallel fate for the courageous husband-soldiers who in two short lines are completely routed. Their lives were invested in protection of the luxury of verses 16–23. Now their deaths permit the deprivation of verse 24. So for the women (v. 24), so for the men (v. 25), and finally, so for the city (v. 26).

Jerusalem, the proud city, whose gates are lifted up in pride, power, and joy at the coming of the "King of glory" (Psalm 24:7–10), now droops in grief at the absence, the failure, and the resulting barbarism. The first line of verse 26 stays with the visual image of city gates. The second line moves to an alternative metaphor, now a city raided and cleaned out, robbed of everything. The NRSV rendering of "ravage" moves the verb in a violent direction, exposed, vulnerable, violated. The city is as vulnerable as the women, as exposed as the men; and all will suffer together—physical loss, emotional displacement, profound humiliation. Everyone—everything "taken away."

The poet traces, in hyperbolic terms, the destruction of the city (4:1). Men and women will be killed. But men more so! Always in war, more men die. The outcome is a great disproportion of women who are still alive. Women in that ancient world, however, were endlessly exposed and under threat, needing, as a patriarchal society required, male provision and protection. We have already seen the death of leadership on a public scale. "Boys and babes" will fill the vacuum (v. 4). "Children and women" will be leaders (v. 12). And now in 4:1, what was a public crisis in verses 4 and 12 becomes as well a domestic, family crisis (cf. 3:6). The ratio of women to men, anticipates the poet, is seven to one. There are not enough men to go around. They have all died! In a patriarchal society, the women will be frantic. They each need a man to provide food and clothing and protection and stability.

But there are not enough men to generate so much food and clothing. In their desperation, the women will themselves supply their own food and clothing. The expectation made of the few surviving men is lessened. The men need not even "do," but only "be." The women—utterly displaced, exposed, vulnerable, without social location or assurance—want only a name. In our more-or-less emancipated society, the sense of humiliation at being man-less is not easy to appropriate. The premise of the poetry, nonetheless, requires that we allow the women this sense of themselves. In addition to physical risk, to be man-less is to be shame-filled. So desperate are the women that they will accept any man because everything is "taken away."

At the end of this dreadful scenario, with the physical, societal, and personal, we are in the midst of the sure ruins left by the war. Given eighth-century Isaiah, the reference could be to Assyrian devastation. Given the entire book of Isaiah, the devastation is more likely the work of Babylon. But given Yahweh as the subject of the twice-used verb "take away," the scenario pertains not just to a historical crisis, but to the sure destiny of beloved Jerusalem whenever it imagines itself autonomously self-sufficient, when it indulges itself so much without notice for the disintegration of the societal fabric. The inventory of ornamentations among the affluent in verses 18–23 is only a few verses removed from diminishment of the poor of verses 14–15. The two are related to each other. And adjacent to "the poor" in verses 14–15 are the "widows and orphans" of 1:17, 23. The poet connects what self-sufficiency and extravagance always seek to de-link. We are left at the end of 4:1 with the camera slowly, so slowly panning what might have been, and what is "instead" all "taken away."

Life Reserved, Safe but Modest (4:2–6)

4:2 **On that day the branch of the LORD shall be beautiful and glorious, and the fruit of the land shall be the pride and glory of the survivors of Israel. ³ Whoever is left in Zion and remains in Jerusalem will be called holy, everyone who has been recorded for life in Jerusalem, ⁴ once the Lord has washed away the filth of the daughters of Zion and cleansed the bloodstains of Jerusalem from its midst by a spirit of judgment and by a spirit of burning. ⁵ Then the LORD will create over the whole site of Mount Zion and over its places of assembly a cloud by day and smoke and the shining of a flaming fire by night. Indeed over all the glory there will be a canopy. ⁶ It will serve as a pavilion, a shade by day from the heat, and a refuge and a shelter from the storm and rain.**

This prose oracle, like the poem of 2:1–4 before it, is surely an independent rhetorical unit. It is introduced by the promissory formula "on that day," which regularly begins a new unit, and which indicates an imaginative reach into the future, beyond all present circumstance. Though it is independent, we take notice of its remarkable placement here. It is difficult to imagine what ought to have come next in the prophetic utterance after the devastating scenario of 4:1. What would one say next after such a scenario of violent loss?

Nonetheless, by this juxtaposition, we are able to see yet again the characteristic rhetorical strategy of the book of Isaiah. The portions of the book that seem to be early (i.e., from the eighth century) are preoccupied with the devastation of the city. That devastation is never soft-pedaled or toned down. From the outset, however, the book of Isaiah in its edited, completed form already sees ahead in these early chapters to the crisis and possibility of Judaism beyond the devastation of the Exile. There will indeed be restoration in Jerusalem! The book of Isaiah knows that, not only because this book is saturated with later witnesses who lived in the midst of the belated restoration after the disaster, but because this tradition, at its core, is completely certain of Yahweh's resilient resolve to do good for the beloved city.

Circumstances of restoration permit reportage as anticipation. Beyond circumstance, however, we are dealing with prophetic certainty that appeals to the One who presides over the coming of new circumstance. That is, this hope does not depend only upon "sight," but also upon "faith" in the God who presides over the death and over the new life of the city.

The future of Jerusalem here anticipated "on that day" is one in which the splendor, loveliness, and productivity of the land, so recently devastated, will be fully restored (v. 2). It is as though all the powers of creation are again mobilized for fruitfulness and well-being. This offer of hope is more fully articulated in the fuller poetic statement of 62:1–12, wherein Yahweh is fully present to Zion so that Zion may be secure and prosper.

The glorious promise given here, however, is voiced with a sobering qualification. The ones who will receive and benefit from this reassertion of blessing are not the whole community, but only "a few survivors" (1:9). Thus, even the hope of the book of Isaiah, resilient as it is, is not so innocent as to imagine that all who were lost shall be restored. No, not all. The oracle concerns the "survivors" (= fugitives), the ones "left," the ones who "remain." The coming beneficiaries constitute only a portion of the community, perhaps only a small portion, but a portion now regarded as holy. These are the ones "recorded for life." The others are referred to here only by their absence. The ones now lost are not survivors, not called holy, only written down for death (cf. Ezekiel 9—10).

The promise of the oracle, so extravagant at the outset of verse 2, is in fact a quite restricted offer for a quite precise constituency. It is likely that the oracle envisions something like a separatist (postexilic) community of those who practice the disciplines of holiness, who maintain the kind of disciplined orderliness that makes possible the presence of God and consequently the proper fruitfulness of creation. Thus the promise of blessed earth in verse 2 and the mention of the holy ones in verse 3 evoke, at the same time, the exilic reference to blessed earth in Genesis 1 and the holy community in the book of Leviticus.

Just beneath the surface of this assurance to those "called holy" is a flint-shaped attack on all the "others." It is because of them that there had to be a "spirit of judgment and burning," that is, a forceful purgation of all that characterized Jerusalem, that made it unclean and therefore unsuitable for Yahweh's presence. The mention of "filth" here refers to the impure blood discharge of women, and "bloodstains" refers to menstrual emission. Thus the defilements here refer to rigorous priestly restrictions, though the assertion may now have a more general, metaphorical scope than the original. In any case, the destruction of the city is a response to defilement that must be judged and purged. It is scarcely news that in the prophetic traditions the judgment of exile is punishment for disregard of Yahweh's command. What interests us here is the clear distinction between the unclean and the holy (cf. Ezek. 22:26), so that the judgment is caused by some, and it is others who receive new life after the violent and summary purgation. These categories seem to reflect a late, postexilic community in which disputes (such as those in Malachi, Ezra, and Nehemiah) about the quality of cultic life and obedience became urgent and overriding. This reference perhaps suggests when this promise was voiced and the shape of the promise that has sociopolitical concreteness to it.

In verse 5, the oracle moves past the judgment (apparently 587 B.C.E. and the Exile to Babylon) and looks to a rehabilitation of the temple and a restored, reassuring presence of Yahweh. This verse has quickly overcome the devastation of the Exile. It begins with a verb "create," which portrays Yahweh doing an utterly new thing, but a new thing reminiscent of the old tabernacle of Moses (cf. Exodus 35—40). It is again "cloud by day and fire by night," signs of Yahweh's sure protective presence in the community as it was in the wilderness with Moses (cf. Exod. 40:34–38). In that ancient provision, the cloud and fire hovered over the glory, the visible presence of Yahweh. Now the signs of presence are "over all the glory."

The oracle employs a series of vehicles to convey the protective assurance of presence. The "canopy," a covering also used for the symbolic shielding of the bride (Joel 2:16) or bridegroom (Psalm 19:6), is like a vast tent covering. It performs the function of pavilion, shade, refuge, and shelter. The language is not unlike that of Psalm 121:5–8, in which Yahweh's own self is a protective covering day and night against the sun and moon and any other danger. The dialect of assurance here concerns the accoutrements of the remembered temple. They are used, characteristically, to bespeak safety and protection guaranteed by God's presence. That canopy, however, is only for the purified community, after "the spirit of burning." Thus the tradition of Isaiah is restorative. It offers, however, only a certain kind of restoration, only for the most serious and devoted of Yahweh's people. The others have perished in their self-preoccupation, completely off the screen of Yahweh's protective generosity.

We may pause to consider the odd juxtaposition of 2:6–4:1 and 4:2–6. The assortment of themes of indictment and judgment that bespeak profound loss is massive, total, and unrelenting. It concerns the whole city and especially the privileged. In the face of such a judgment, the oracle of promise in 4:2–6 strikes one as a quite muted resolution. To be sure, it is enough of a resolution for those "called holy," for they are fully assured and fully protected by Yahweh's presence.

Such a muteness is modest, however, in the face of the great devastation here envisioned. It is clear that the completed, edited juxtaposition of the two passages sheds no tears for those most jeopardized by their self-indulgent fullness. Life moves on, and certainly the book of Isaiah moves on. In this later embrace of holy disciplines, Judaism was able to jettison those who brought death to its city. The judgment is harsh, and the recovery is a gingerly compensation. There is nothing easy or accommodating in the newness, as was already anticipated, perhaps, in the resolve to "smelt away your dross" and "remove all your alloy" (1:25). The fire does burn and consume (1:31), and there is no retrieval. By the time we reach 4:2–6, the editors of the book of Isaiah have already carried us into postexilic debates about purity and holiness and the shape of the community of survivors (cf. Isa. 56:3–8). There is a hope, but it is a hope now sober and rigorous.

When we reach the end of chapter 4, we have completed the extended introduction to the book of Isaiah. By regarding 2:1–4 as a countertheme and conclusion to 1:3–31, and observing 4:2–6 as a countertheme and conclusion to 2:6–4:1, we are able to see that the introduction to the book of Isaiah is arranged in two extended units, each of which entails an abrupt reversal from judgment to hope. In 1:3–2:4, an assertion of severe judgment (1:3–31) is followed by a wondrous vision of a peace-generating city (2:1–4). Comparably, in 2:5–4:6 the judgment of 2:6–4:1 is followed by the promise of 4:2–6. In both cases of the positive anticipations of 2:2–4 ("in days to come") and 4:2–6 ("on that day"), we are not prepared for the reversal and affirmation. Thus, in the midst of each extended unit, between 1:31 and 2:12 and between 4:1 and 4:2, the literature makes a major break and moves abruptly from judgment to hope.

The reversal, break, and affirmation foreshadow the larger shape of the book of Isaiah, with the structural break between chapter 39 and chapter 40. This literary arrangement, moreover, alludes to and perhaps evokes in Israel's imagination the "historical" experience of reversal, break, and affirmation that come between the destruction of 587 and the end of exile and anticipated homecoming of 540. These literary articulations provide an "explanation" for such a decisive reversal. Short of explanation, however, it is unmistakably the claim of the Isaiah tradition that this break and reversal that constitute the pivot of Israel's life (as construed in the tradition of Isaiah) is rooted in and authorized by the resolve of Yahweh to do good for and in and through Jerusalem. Behind that resolve, the tradition neither expects us nor permits us to go.

ANGER NOT YET TURNED
5:1–10:4

This extended middle section of chapters 1—12 is complex and intricately woven together. At the outset, the parable of 5:1–7 sets the tone of failure, rejection, and judgment. There follows in 5:8–25 a series of woes culminating in 5:25 with the verdict "His anger has not turned away." It is readily noted that the material of 5:8–25 with its woes and the verdict of 5:25 has a counterpart in 9:8–10:4. This later section reiterates the verdict of 5:25 as a refrain in 9:12, 17, 21, and 10:4, and adds an additional woe in 10:1, which brings the total number of woes to seven. Now it may be that 5:8–25 (with the introductory parable of 5:1–7 and an addendum in 5:26–30) together with 9:8–10:4 at one time constituted a single literary unit. If that is so, it is an utterance of uninterrupted negativity.

Into the midst of this extended unit has been inserted a large block of material that scholars regard as a personal memoir or testimony, because it features first-person utterance and alleged first-person experience of the prophet (6:1–9:7). Indeed, it is this material (along with chapters 36—39) that tells us everything that we think we know of the prophet. This first-person material—which portrays a tough, theologically rooted prophet—includes ⌐a call narrative (6:1–13),⌐ an encounter with King Ahaz (7:1–8:15),⌐and instruction to "disciples" that bespeaks both judgment (8:16–22) and newness (9:1–7).⌐ The "memoir," now framed by 5:1–30 and 9:8–10:4, reflects the same two-stage faith reflected elsewhere. It denies nothing but finishes with great affirmation: "The zeal of the LORD of hosts will do this" (9:7). The "this" may refer to the oracle of restoration in 9:2–7. In context, however, the "this" of Yahweh's zeal includes both the *judgment* of "former time" and the *assurance* of "latter time." All of Zion's life and destiny, so the prophet attests, is within the scope of Yahweh's zeal.

A HARSH VISION OF TERMINATION
5:1–30

Although apparently a distinct literary piece, there is no doubt that chapter 5 continues and reiterates the theme of judgment against Jerusalem that we have found massively voiced in 1:3–31 and 3:1–4:1. This long chapter consists of a love poem (vv. 1–7), a series of "woe sayings" (vv. 8–23), and an assertion of judgment through a foreign invasion (vv. 24–30).

A Love-Song Become Judgment (5:1–7)

5:1 Let me sing for my beloved
          my love-song concerning his vineyard:
     My beloved had a vineyard
          on a very fertile hill.
  2 He dug it and cleared it of stones,
          and planted it with choice vines;
     he built a watchtower in the midst of it,
          and hewed out a wine vat in it;
     he expected it to yield grapes,
          but it yielded wild grapes.

  3 And now, inhabitants of Jerusalem
          and people of Judah,
     judge between me
          and my vineyard.
  4 What more was there to do for my vineyard
          that I have not done in it?
     When I expected it to yield grapes,
          why did it yield wild grapes?

  5 And now I will tell you
          what I will do to my vineyard.
     I will remove its hedge,
          and it shall be devoured;
     I will break down its wall,
          and it shall be trampled down.
  6 I will make it a waste;
          it shall not be pruned or hoed,
          and it shall be overgrown with briers and thorns;
     I will also command the clouds
          that they rain no rain upon it.

  7 For the vineyard of the LORD of hosts
          is the house of Israel,
     and the people of Judah
          are his pleasant planting;
     he expected justice,
          but saw bloodshed;
     righteousness,
          but heard a cry!

These verses quickly articulate a long history between Yahweh and Yahweh's beloved that begins in affection and tenderness (the wondrous mem-

ory of Yahweh's initial saving intervention in the life of Israel; vv. 1–2) but ends in harshness and trouble (the punishment of exile; vv. 5–6). The move from wondrous beginning in affection to harsh destruction is made because of the failure of Israel to "produce" (the recalcitrance of the monarchial period during which Israel refused to be obedient to the torah expectations of Yahweh; vv. 3–4). The poem quickly and in large sweep reviews the entire life of historical Israel in relation to its theological identity.

At the outset we are not told who the speaker is nor what the relationship is between the parties of the love song. Only later, in verse 7, do we learn that Yahweh is the speaker-singer who sings of beloved Israel. The "love song" in fact is sustained only through verses 1–2. Although we expect Yahweh to be the speaker in this poem, in fact someone else, presumably the prophetic poet, sings on behalf of "my beloved" (= Yahweh) concerning "his vineyard" (= Israel). The assignment of roles in the poetry is not very clear, but the intention of the prophetic utterance is unmistakable. The landowner (Yahweh as owner of all the land; cf. Exod. 19:5; Lev. 25:23; Psalm 24:1) is deeply devoted to the vineyard and showers upon it rich attentiveness and much hard work, doing all the things necessary to maximize the productivity (i.e., the well-being) of the vineyard. That attentiveness of God for God's people and land is voiced in the verbs "dug, cleared, planted, built, hewed out." The verbs bespeak complete and demanding devotion.

We are surprised, however, that the last verb is "expect." That is, the lavish care given to the vineyard is not disinterested. The vineyard owner expects something in return for all the effort. Of course the owner expected fruit, good produce. That is the purpose of a vineyard. Almost tersely we learn in verse 2 that the vineyard owner is disappointed, for all that resulted from the lavish care are pitiful, unwanted wild grapes.

Verses 3–4 constitute a reflective interlude in the poem, which now becomes disputatious and ceases to be a love song. That is, the failure of adequate response causes the poetry to change genres and tone of expression. Something is deeply amiss between vineyard owner and vineyard. The governing verb "expect" is reiterated (v. 4), again to end in disappointment. The initial zeal and energetic devotion of the owner have cooled completely. The ardor is spent; the vineyard has failed; the relationship is in deep jeopardy, for the owner has given up on the vineyard.

After the interlude, the owner speaks again (vv. 5–6). Now we hear a new series of verbs, negative verbs, that undo the constructive effect of the verbs in verses 1–2. Now the verbs are "remove, break down, make waste, command (drought)." Moreover, these verbs, which concern the withdrawal of care and protection, permit a second series of verbs in the passive, "be devoured, be trampled, not be pruned or hoed, be overgrown." The vineyard so enhanced by the attention of the vinekeeper is now exposed and vulnerable, and it is to be damaged irreparably. Everything for the vineyard depends upon the owner, who is now completely alienated and uncaring. It has taken only six verses to move from positive imagery to unqualified devastation, all because of the failure of the vineyard to meet the expectations of the owner. The outcome of the poem is to present a picture of a garden now completely abandoned; that is, Judah carried into exile, abandoned, left to its own inadequate resources.

Verse 7 functions to decode the love song-become-dispute-become-judgment. The subject of the poem is Israel-Judah, accountable to "the Lord of hosts," that is, the God who is ferocious in power. The shift from positive to negative verbs turns on the third use of the term "expect" (v. 7). The vineyard = Israel is to produce. When it does not produce, it can no longer count on Yahweh's attentive protection. The poetry assumes all of the rigorous demand of the old Mosaic covenant, perhaps in the form of a Deuteronomic theology of blessing and curse. But the decoding goes further. The "expectation" of good grapes is in fact "justice and righteousness." The two terms together concern Yahweh's command to Israel, that Israel should be a community that practices generative, positive social relationships without abuse or exploitation. That command and expectation of Yahweh, however, are profoundly disappointed by the course of Israel's life. Israel has not produced justice but bloodshed. The term "bloodshed" (offered as a play on words in Hebrew: *mišpāḥ* = "bloodshed" instead of *mišpāṭ* = "justice") means "outpouring," thus the outpouring of lifeblood through exploitative social practice; that is, the kinds of economic transactions that abuse, injure, and slowly bleed the poor to death. The "bloodshed" that concerns the poet is not thuggery and murder, but the more subtle, slower, but equally decisive killing through economic policy against the vulnerable and resourceless.

The wordplay, *mišpāṭ-mišpāḥ*, is seconded by a second wordplay. Yahweh expects righteousness (*ṣĕdaqâ*), that is, equitable, generative social relations; but instead Israel produced "outcry" (*ṣĕ'āqâ*), that is, the feeble social protests of those who are victimized by rapacious social policy. In this remarkable wordplay, the poet has moved from horticulture (grapes) to social relations, always the primal agenda of the prophetic tradition. Even in the wide, demanding sphere of social relations, however, the prophet is not content to speak generally of in-justice and un-righteousness (as in Jer. 22:13), but takes up terms that are brutally concrete in asserting that Israel has completely reneged on the most elementary social relations between the powerful and the powerless that Yahweh "expects" from this beloved people. It is no wonder that the vineyard is abandoned to destruction. That is, in the view of the book of Isaiah, Judah is given over to the dangers of exile and annihilation. Thus in a quite fresh idiom, the prophetic tradition, yet one more time, promises that the failure of Judah will bring its consequent historical destruction.

This text and its imagery are taken up in imaginative ways in New Testament teaching. The "love song" becomes the base line for the parable of Jesus in Matthew 21:33–41, which now receives a decisive christological turn. Indeed, now the accent is not on the vineyard as such, but on the *owner's son* who is heir, an heir now murdered by the tenants. In the more familiar imagery of John 15, the relationship of vine and branches is taken up. Although the imagery is tilted in very different directions, in one regard the use is closely paralleled. The branches are to "bear fruit." That is what is "expected," as in the love song. And where that expectation is not met, trouble comes upon the community around Jesus, as it did in Isaiah's Jerusalem. Here the fruit is "love," but such love is not far removed from Israel's notion of "justice and righteousness." In both cases, an intensely generous gift of relationship carries with it rigorous and insistent expectations about which there is no compromise or negotiation. The landowner is acquitted. The failure is that of the vineyard, which now suffers the consequences of its own lack of productivity. The vineyard has failed to enact its true character. And now, says the tradition of Isaiah, patience has run out. The time of the vineyard is ended. It will become, as we say in the South, only a patch of kudzu vine.

A Grief Anticipated (5:8–25)

5:8 **Ah, you who join house to house,**
> **who add field to field,**
> **until there is room for no one but you,**
> **and you are left to live alone**
> **in the midst of the land!**
> 9 **The LORD of hosts has sworn in my hearing:**
> **Surely many houses shall be desolate,**
> **large and beautiful houses, without inhabitant.**
> 10 **For ten acres of vineyard shall yield but one bath,**
> **and a homer of seed shall yield a mere ephah.**

> 11 **Ah, you who rise early in the morning**
> **in pursuit of strong drink,**

who linger in the evening
   to be inflamed by wine,
¹² whose feasts consist of lyre and harp,
   tambourine and flute and wine,
but who do not regard the deeds of the LORD,
   or see the work of his hands!
¹³ Therefore my people go into exile without knowledge;
their nobles are dying of hunger,
   and their multitude is parched with thirst.

¹⁴ Therefore Sheol has enlarged its appetite
   and opened its mouth beyond measure;
the nobility of Jerusalem and her multitude go down,
   her throng and all who exult in her.
¹⁵ People are bowed down, everyone is brought low,
   and the eyes of the haughty are humbled.
¹⁶ But the LORD of hosts is exalted by justice,
   and the Holy God shows himself holy by righteousness.
¹⁷ Then the lambs shall graze as in their pasture,
   fatlings and kids shall feed among the ruins.

¹⁸ Ah, you who drag iniquity along with cords of falsehood,
   who drag sin along as with cart ropes,
¹⁹ who say, "Let him make haste,
   let him speed his work
   that we may see it;
let the plan of the Holy One of Israel hasten to fulfillment,
   that we may know it!"
²⁰ Ah, you who call evil good
   and good evil,
who put darkness for light
   and light for darkness,
who put bitter for sweet
   and sweet for bitter!
²¹ Ah, you who are wise in your own eyes,
   and shrewd in your own sight!
²² Ah, you who are heroes in drinking wine
   and valiant at mixing drink,
²³ who acquit the guilty for a bribe,
   and deprive the innocent of their rights!

²⁴ Therefore, as the tongue of fire devours the stubble,
   and as dry grass sinks down in the flame,
so their root will become rotten,
   and their blossom go up like dust;

for they have rejected the instruction of the LORD of hosts,
   and have despised the word of the Holy One of Israel.

25 Therefore the anger of the LORD was kindled against his people,
   and he stretched out his hand against them and struck them;
   the mountains quaked,
and their corpses were like refuse
   in the streets.
For all this his anger has not turned away,
   and his hand is stretched out still.

The judgment against Jerusalem is pronounced in parabolic, lyrical form
in verses 1–7. That judgment is implemented in the historical process long
after the prophet Isaiah in the eighth century, for the destruction of the
city does not come until the incursion of the Babylonians in the sixth century (587). The book of Isaiah, however, can use materials concerning the
Assyrian threat against the city in the eighth century (a threat that did not
succeed) for the longer, later vision that concerns the Babylonian disaster.

The announcement of judgment is offered in verses 8–25 in a genre very
different from that of verses 1–7. It is much more didactic than is the poetry of verses 1–7. This material consists of six woes (vv. 8, 11, 18, 20, 21,
22), followed by two prophetic sentences (vv. 24, 25). The woes are introduced by a term that bespeaks the grief of death, rendered in NRSV as
"Ah." The form of utterance expresses anticipated mourning for those
who are sure to die for their unacceptable behavior. The mood is not condemnation but sadness. In the woe sayings, there is not even any deathly
intervention from God. It is as though the behavior condemned itself and
carries the verdict of death.

The first woe (vv. 8–10) is an anticipated lament for those who will come
to grief for an inequitable economic practice in which those who are prosperous, aggressive, and greedy eventually confiscate and possess the houses
and fields of their more vulnerable neighbors. The combination of "houses-
fields" likely alludes to the warning against coveting in the tenth commandment (Deut. 5:21). In prophetic usage this warning does not pertain
to particular acts of greed but to a general economic policy and frame of
reference whereby big landowners buy up and crowd out small farmers in
what we might now term agribusiness. This economic procedure, which
destroys the neighborly fabric of the community, apparently was wide-
spread in eighth-century Judah and was regarded by the prophets as a grave
violation of Yahwism. They insisted that Yahweh had a stake in maintain-
ing small-scale farming and in resisting large concentrations of land and

wealth. A rereading of John Steinbeck's *The Grapes of Wrath* is illuminating concerning this social reality and social protest.

The severe and solemn response of Yahweh to this betrayal of Yahwistic neighborliness is twofold (vv. 9–10). It is anticipated that many "large and beautiful houses," emblems of rapacious economic policy, will be desolate, no doubt left so by ruthless invading armies (cf. Amos 3:15). It is further anticipated that the devastation that leaves houses desolate will also leave the land damaged so that it will not produce. That is, war with all its violence assesses a heavy cost against the capacity of the land to produce. "Bath" and "ephah" are weights used to measure grain production. It will take large acreage to produce small crops. Thus the threat of Yahweh matches the affront: The big, avaricious landowners intended to become rich and prosperous at the expense of their neighbors, but their own actions and policies would leave them diminished with poor crops. Prophetic faith makes remarkable ethical linkages, suggesting that exploitation of neighbors would result in diminished productivity of the land. Who would have thought it—except Israel's prophets!

The second woe is the most extensive of the series and the most ominously implemented (vv. 11–17). The action condemned is strong drink. It is likely that the real concern is not alcohol but rather self-indulgence and self-absorption. (See Amos 6:4–6 for a parallel condemnation of a like practice.) The accumulation and concentration of land, produce, and wealth considered in the first woe invites inordinate self-regard and self-indulgence. Such foolishly gotten and foolishly used wealth tends to desensitize. In this case, the woe warns those who become insensitive to the workings of Yahweh in their very midst. And because this woe stands between mention of "justice" in verses 7 and 16, we may surmise that as the self-indulgent disregard Yahweh, so they likewise disregard their neighbor. They see and care only for themselves.

Although such actions and policies do not seem exceptional to those who engage in them, they meet with an abrupt prophetic "therefore," which asserts consequences not expected among the desensitized perpetrators (v. 13). There will be exile, that is, deportation and displacement! The most securely situated will be disrupted and displaced. The exile will drive the nobles to hunger and the multitudes to thirst. All classes of society will meet disaster when the elemental infrastructure of society fails. For a second time the consequence is a direct inversion of the affront. In verse 8, the affront is *many houses* and the consequence is *devastated homes* (v. 9); in verse 11, the affront is self-indulgent *feast* and the consequence is *hunger and thirst* (v. 13). In this daring Yahwistic rhetoric, the linkage between affront and consequence is the adversarial intention of Yahweh. The prophets are not social scientists who linger over "cause and effect" explanations. In the world of Yahweh's governance, such destructive acts and policies cannot be undertaken without accountability. There are ethical requirements writ large and indelibly into the processes of society, and they must be honored.

The harsh anticipation of verse 13 is reiterated and intensified in verses 14–15. With another "therefore," the poet imagines a huge, gaping black hole in reality, the black hole of death. Jerusalem—its nobles and its multitudes—will be swallowed up, devoured, and wiped out of the historical process. The list of the condemned is given twice, the second time in reverse order: "*nobility* . . . multitude . . . throng; people . . . everyone . . . *haughty.*" The first and last elements in the enumeration are the privileged who are the special target of this threat. The rhetoric of verse 15 is reminiscent of 2:9–17. The "troubles" come upon Jerusalem because the city imagines itself autonomous from Yahweh.

The sequence of offenses (vv. 11–12) and consequences (vv. 13, 14–15) constitute a rather conventional rhetorical unit. But verses 16–17 move in different imagery that complements the extremities of exile and Sheol. Yahweh is enhanced by the concrete human practice of justice and righteousness (see also v. 7). That is the only way to "magnify" God. The conclusion of verse 17 offers a seemingly idyllic picture of a pastureland well ordered with sufficient provision for well-being. The metaphor of pasture is often used to bespeak a well-ordered society. But here it is "among the ruins," suggesting that what is well ordered is in fact a sheep pasture in downtown Jerusalem. What had been a busy, prosperous urban area with all the prerequisite public buildings and banks now is a peaceable pasture where there is no disturbing urban activity (cf. Mic. 3:12). The picture is not unlike many urban centers now given up to failure. Of course, Jerusalem—like every such urban center—thought "it couldn't happen here!"

Verses 18–23, in much more terse fashion, offer four woes identifying the causes for the coming grief in Jerusalem. What poses as *grief* in the woe saying, however, is in fact *judgment* for Jerusalem's distorted behavior. In the first of these woes, the poetry contrasts the actual conduct of Jerusalem (v. 18) with its obtuse theological verbalization (v. 19), exposing the hypocrisy and self-deception in the contradiction between deed and word. The actions condemned are generic, with the terms "iniquity, falsehood, sin"—nothing specific (v. 18). The prophet uses the image of a bundle of sins all tied up and carried, as a peasant might carry produce: Jerusalem has a full load of sin!

The speech of Judah is filled with eagerness and expectancy, wanting to know what Yahweh's intention is (v. 19). It is as though Judah is so shameless that it is unaware that it will receive only judgment from Yahweh. It assumes that what "the Holy One of Israel" gives will be welcome and positive. This mocking attribution utters Isaiah's most solemn title for Yahweh, "the Holy One of Israel," now coupled with the terms "haste, speed," which in 8:2–3 are part of a proper name signaling Yahweh's ominous, harsh coming intervention. But here these "innocent" ones are so unknowing that they do not know they are asking for Yahweh's harshness. Thus the woe is for a community so preoccupied with itself that it is completely unaware of the exposed and dangerous situation it has created for itself vis-à-vis Yahweh. This unawareness that evokes an ill-advised welcome of Yahweh is not unlike the expression of contradiction in Amos 5:18–20 (also a woe) and Jeremiah 7:9–10. It is as though Jerusalem is theologically narcoticized.

The brief woe of verse 20 states a series of three distortions, suggesting that Jerusalem has completely lost its powers of discernment and discrimination, presumably because it is so self-indulgent that it can no longer see reality beyond its own short-term benefit. The point is perhaps the use of euphemism in public discourse that disguises what is in fact reality, as in the current talk of our society wherein "downsizing" means unemployment, "opportunity" means the unrestrained, unregulated power of the strong, and "law and order" means a vengeful defense of the status quo. The distortion may be a lack of any reference point, resulting in confusion, or it may be deliberate deception done to obscure what is going on, like the much later "detoxifying" of language through euphemism in the Nazi death camps (Robert J. Lifton, *The Nazi Doctors: Medical Killing and the Psychology of Genocide*, 202). The woe certifies that manipulation and deception that cover over exploitative brutality will come to a harsh and sorry end.

The third woe in this set of four briefly warns against autonomy, wherein one's wisdom and various kinds of technical knowhow are exercised without any larger reference point, that is, without reference to the covenantal requirements of Yahweh (v. 21). Such moral autonomy is sure to evoke social disaster, even though the "wise and shrewd" always imagine themselves to be immune from threat.

Finally, in verses 22–23 the poetry returns to the self-indulgence of drinking (cf. v. 11). As in the previous reference, the issue is not alcohol, but the consequences of such self-indulgence. The issue is the distortion of public order, the collapse of an equitable judicial system whereby for a price courts will rule for those who exploit others; conversely, the innocent—

here the vulnerable, weak, exposed innocent—have no chance for the favor of the court. The poet understands that the disappearance of a reliable judiciary assures the complete collapse of a viable human community.

The effect of these six woes is cumulative. The poetry presents a society that has lost its center, its reference, its focus, its purpose, and its chance for well-being. Thus the woes are followed by two abrupt, heavy, harsh prophetic "therefores" (vv. 24, 25), voicing Yahweh's negative resolve. In the first "therefore" (v. 24), the indictment is that Israel has rejected Yahweh's torah, or law, as the norm and guide for social order. This rejection is tantamount to rejecting Yahweh, for in Israel, Yahweh is never available apart from torah. The consequence of such a rejection is given in a series of metaphors—fire, rot, dust—all of which bespeak failure and nullification. In this utterance the sorry end to come is still vague and poetic.

The second "therefore" (v. 25) becomes explicit. Now Yahweh will actively intervene with anger and with outstretched hand, that is, with direct, forcible engagement. Indeed, the negative force of Yahweh is so strong as to evoke images of death.

The Land Now Desolate (5:26–30)

5:26 **He will raise a signal for a nation far away,**
   and whistle for a people at the ends of the earth;
   Here they come, swiftly, speedily!
   [27] **None of them is weary, none stumbles,**
   none slumbers or sleeps,
   not a loincloth is loose,
   not a sandal-thong broken;
   [28] **their arrows are sharp,**
   all their bows bent,
   their horses' hoofs seem like flint,
   and their wheels like the whirlwind.
   [29] **Their roaring is like a lion,**
   like young lions they roar;
   they growl and seize their prey,
   they carry it off, and no one can rescue.
   [30] **They will roar over it on that day,**
   like the roaring of the sea.
   And if one look to the land—
   only darkness and distress;
   and the light grows dark with clouds.

These verses extend the threat of verse 25 to ensure that the point is not missed. The threat becomes more specific than heretofore about the large geopolitical vista of the book. The threat is not "supernatural." Rather, it is political, military, concretely savage. All of Yahweh that appears in these verses is the opening, "He will raise" (v. 26). That is all; the rest is "a nation far away." The threat is invasion by a massive foreign army. That much anybody can see in the course of the public process. It takes a Yahwistic believer, however, to imagine that what is seen as geopolitical reality is at the behest of Yahweh.

The intention of the poetry is to make the threat awesome and deeply unsettling by portraying the unnamed invader as massively and impressively as possible. It is "a nation far away" that comes "swiftly and speedily," not what Jerusalem had asked when it asked for Yahweh's "plan" to come with speed and haste (v. 19). This coming nation is indeed Yahweh's "plan," a plan to undo the Holy City. The enemy is powerful, strong, well-equipped, irresistible, determined. The "nation from afar" is like a relentless lion that will "carry off" (= exile), leaving only ruin and devastation. (See Amos 3:12 on the residue of "two legs, or a piece of an ear.")

What becomes of the land, now desolate, from which all have been deported? The land is darkness and distress, all darkness and cloud, utterly failed, hopeless, resourceless, lifeless, abandoned. The listener is invited to a vision of an ominous, eerie city, so unlike the current picture of self-indulgence, deception, and uncaring insensitivity. "The nation from afar," instrument of Yahweh, is unnamed. In the context of eighth-century Isaiah, that nation is surely Assyria, the first large geo-military threat to Jerusalem (cf. 10:5; 36–37). In the larger view of the book of Isaiah, the threat is Babylon, who eventually destroyed the city as Assyria could never do. The unnamed instrument of Yahweh is Assyria—or Babylon—or whoever needs to be identified in a particular moment of threat. The historical references provide the theological model. Finally, as scripture the poetry asserts that within the historical process, even God's beloved people are not safe, not protected, when their life departs from Yahweh's intention.

These verses draw the inescapable, heavy, threatening conclusion of the several assertions of 1:2–31; 2:6–4:1; 5:1–7; 8–26; This sustained rhetoric of threat has been interrupted only by the restorative visions of 2:1–4; 4:2–6. More that is positive will come later in the book of Isaiah. Thus far, however, we are still being led by the rhetoric toward the coming loss, the jarring recognition that Yahweh's awesome way in the world is harshly demanding. The prophet makes daring linkages between self-indulgent economic policy and practice and the coming devastation. These linkages make sense only in a world of Yahweh's intentionality. They are linkages about which the people in this text are always relearning, always being re-instructed, always reobserving in the arena of our own life in the world. We finish with this long announcement of governing themes diminished, bereft, in darkness and distress, hardly daring to hope. That is, in my judgment, exactly where this poetry intends to leave us.

A VISION, A CALL, A NULLIFICATION
6:1–13

This unit of text consisting in the commissioning of the prophet may be divided into two parts: the *commissioning* (vv. 1–8), and the *message* entrusted to the prophet as the message bearer of the heavenly government of Yahweh (vv. 9–13).

A Vision that Recruits (6:1–8)

6:1 **In the year that King Uzziah died, I saw the Lord sitting on a throne, high and lofty; and the hem of his robe filled the temple. ² Seraphs were in attendance above him; each had six wings: with two they covered their faces, and with two they covered their feet, and with two they flew. ³ And one called to another and said:**
  "Holy, holy, holy is the LORD of hosts;
  the whole earth is full of his glory."
⁴ The pivots on the thresholds shook at the voices of those who called, and the house filled with smoke. ⁵ And I said: "Woe is me! I am lost, for I am a man of unclean lips, and I live among a people of unclean lips; yet my eyes have seen the King, the LORD of hosts!"
  ⁶ Then one of the seraphs flew to me, holding a live coal that had been taken from the altar with a pair of tongs. ⁷ The seraph touched my mouth with it and said: "Now that this has touched your lips, your guilt has departed and your sin is blotted out." ⁸ Then I heard the voice of the Lord saying, "Whom shall I send, and who will go for us?" And I said, "Here am I; send me!"

The vision report purports to be an immediate and direct experience of God's holiness on the part of the person of Isaiah. A great deal of scholarly attention has been given to the possibility that the narrative reports on a direct, personal, emotional experience of God, or alternatively, an experience that is cultic in nature, for the symbolism of the Jerusalem temple is paramount in the account.

Whatever may have been the personal dimension of the reported experience (in which the text seems to have no special interest), it is generally recognized that the call narrative is a highly stylized, intentionally structured literary unit. On the one hand, the text is commonly taken as a *classic outline of right worship*, which is sequenced as (a) praise (vv. 1–4); (b) confession (v. 5); (c) forgiveness (vv. 6–7); and (d) commissioning to a prophetic vocation (v. 8). On the other hand, if one reckons with the highly stylized character of the text, one may consider that the chapter concerns not its impact upon the *person* of the prophet who is here authorized, but its impact upon the *prophetic book*. That is, the narrative account seeks to claim that the prophetic book—understood as utterance from a divinely called and appointed prophet—can claim continuing "prophetic authority" from on high, long after the prophetic personality has departed the historical scene. In a canonical approach to the book of Isaiah, this unit makes a claim that its utterance is indeed divinely authorized, for the authorization pertains not only to the immediate utterance of verses 9–13, but also to the entire text of Isaiah in which this specific account is embedded. Thus we may look past the authorization of the prophet (which is indeed evident) to the authorization of the book that continues to speak authoritatively to the faithful for the coming generations of the community that heeds the text. The prophetic word and the prophetic book that continue to haunt us are derived from and witness to the intention of God's own purposes for the world.

The account reports an activity in the throne room of heaven where the holy God sits, high and elevated in splendor, surrounded by awesome and impressive attendants to the divine presence. The account assumes a polytheism that peoples the heavens with many gods, angels, and servants of the high God (cf. 1 Kings 22:19–23 and the reference to God's "ministers" in Psalm 103:20–21). The scene is royal; this is "The King." The mention of King Uzziah, who died in 742 (cf. 1:1), serves perhaps simply to date the reported experience or perhaps to contrast the transitoriness of human kings with the abiding quality of the divine king.

In the vision, Yahweh massively occupies and dominates the heavenly throne room to which "Isaiah" (person, book?) is wondrously given access. This earthly intruder into the heavenly scene observes the seraphim, the heavenly winged servants of Yahweh in rapt attentiveness, utterly devoted to Yahweh, fluttering around the Holy One, honoring him and covering him in order to guard and enhance Yahweh's holiness. The primary activity that fills the throne room with glad surrender is the seemingly unending doxology of the divine choir. It sings of the holiness, the splendor, the glory, the unutterable majesty of the ruler of heaven whose awesome governance extends over all the earth. (This vision of doxology is echoed in the scenario of heaven in Rev. 4:8 where the same threefold "holy" is sounded again to the same overwhelming God.) This moment of praise (which the prophet observes) is indeed an event behind which it is not possible to go for explanation. We are here at the core of holiness from which is decreed all that happens everywhere in creation. The song of the heavenly choir begins in holiness and ends in glory, both terms acknowledging the odd, overwhelming otherness of God. The attempt to verbalize the effect of God's holiness evidences that God's presence is incalculable, before which everything must yield. The characterization may be *cultic*, that is, in ritual routinization, but the rhetoric is that of a disruptive sudden and direct appearance of God.

The overwhelming sense of God's holiness (vv. 1–4) evokes a massive contrast in verse 5. The prophet-observer, in the presence of Yahweh's holiness, has a fresh sense of himself, his inadequacy, his lack of qualification to be in the holy presence. As the words have clustered to name Yahweh's majesty, so the terms converge to bespeak inadequacy—"woe, lost, unclean!" The terms indicate that the prophet-observer is in dire straits, now put profoundly at risk. He is "reduced to nothing" (Calvin). There is no coziness here, for God's presence is a source of deep jeopardy. Indeed, in his lack of competence, these inadequate eyes have seen "the King," "the Lord of hosts!" Both of these terms articulate majestic sovereignty, likely reflecting the liturgic cadences of the Solomonic temple (cf. Psalm 24:7–10). The vision of God evokes the undoing of the human participant. Already in 1:4, the prophet had condemned the community. Now he stands within that community, condemned along with all the others.

In verses 6–7, however, we learn that the God whose royal person undoes and dismantles is also the God who has procedures and means for reclamation of the one undone. The seraph, one of the awesome functionaries of Yahweh's royal court, effectively ministers to the overwhelmed and disqualified human speaker. The application of live coals to the person of the human speaker is a dangerous, painful, perhaps cultic enterprise (cf. Jer. 1:9). The effect is a complete purgation and rehabilitation, expressed in parallel terms, "guilt departed, sin blotted out." In this act, which overrides human circumstance, the human participant is now qualified with all disability overcome. The rehabilitation permits the human agent a legitimate place in the very presence of God.

However, the legitimate admission is not, as verse 8 immediately makes clear, for enjoyment of the divine presence. The throne room of God is the policy room of world government. There is business to conduct. There is creation to manage. There are messages to be sent. The government of Yahweh (notice the plural "we," not unlike the plural for "government" in British English) needs a carrier. There is a discussion about whom to dispatch, not unlike 1 Kings 22:20. Immediately, apparently without reflection upon the cost, the recently rehabilitated human agent is promptly recruited into the work of God's government: "Send me." He could not, we may imagine, resist the chance. He got all he bargained for and more!

This well-known narrative moves quickly from *the vision of splendor* to *the awareness of inadequacy* to *readiness for dispatch.* Because the movement is so clear and the drama is so profound, as I have indicated, the text has often been taken to be either biography—that is, the commissioning of a prophet—or a model for worship. Without gainsaying either of these two perspectives, more recent scholarship, in addition, suggests that this visionary report has a literary function in the shape of the book of Isaiah. That is, what is here enacted is not personal message, but canonical-literary authorization. Thus the narrative legitimates some extended portion of the book of Isaiah, the portion that announces judgment on Judah and Jerusalem. (See the counterpart positive authorization of the book of Isaiah in 40:1–11.)

A Message of Nullification (6:9–13)

6:9 And he said, "Go and say to this people:
    'Keep listening, but do not comprehend;
       keep looking, but do not understand.'
10 Make the mind of this people dull
       and stop their ears,
       and shut their eyes,
   so that they may not look with their eyes,
       and listen with their ears,
   and comprehend with their minds,
       and turn and be healed."
11 Then I said, "How long, O Lord?" And he said:
   "Until cities lie waste
       without inhabitant,
   and houses without people,
       and the land is utterly desolate;
12 until the LORD sends everyone far away,
       and vast is the emptiness in the midst of the land.
13 Even if a tenth part remain in it,

it will be burned again,
like a terebinth or an oak
  whose stump remains standing
  when it is felled."
The holy seed is its stump.

The "message" of verses 9–13 constitutes a focal point and epitome for "the message" of the book of Isaiah. This perspective moves in the direction of literary authorization and away from the biographical or liturgical.

And what a message it is! The prophetic message is that "this people," presumably Judah and Jerusalem, should "not comprehend," "not understand," "not look," "not listen," "not comprehend." It is the decree of Yahweh's government that Israel should have all of its senses dulled and numbed beyond notice. All of its organs of perception—heart, eyes, ears—must fail. And the reason: If they *notice*, they will *turn*. And if they *turn*, they will be *healed*. But the intent of the government of God is negative: Not to notice and so not to turn; not to turn and so not to be healed! The intention of the decree of Yahweh is that Judah and Jerusalem should be narcoticized so that they will not be healed. God wills an unhealed people!

This is not what we might expect, but of course prophetic assertion is most often not what is expected. This is indeed a countermessage, countering official religious assumptions that God always wills good.

The shock of the message is enough to evoke a questioning protest from the prophet: "How long?" (v. 11). The question is a characteristic utterance of complaint in Israel (cf. Psalm 13:1–2). The question does not want an answer about length of suffering, but it suggests that God is unfair or inattentive, and that the speaker (prophet, Judah, Jerusalem) deserves something better from God.

The answer from God, given immediately, without hesitation or qualification, is *until!*

    until the failure of cities, houses, land;
    until the land has a profound massive abandonment;
    until only 10 percent remain,
      and then a fire,
      and then only a stump.

That is, until . . . termination! The message resulting from this vision of God's majesty is an Israelite future of nullification, a ceasing to be in the world. The burden of the oracle is that God has given up on this beloved people and will no more protect them, but will actively intervene to undo them.

The nullification is qualified only with the enigmatic statement at the end of verse 13 (not unlike the modest hope of 4:3). The three words that comprise this last statement are not clear, something about holy seed from stump, something about the impossible possibility of new life from deep failure, something that the book of Isaiah, as we have seen in 2:1–4 and 4:2–6, relentlessly asserts, never able to leave the terrible message finally at nullification and termination.

It is possible to take this defining oracle simply as judgment, harsh and unqualified. If, however, we take this oracular announcement in the context of the entire book of Isaiah, we already know that the long-term vision of the book concerns the deep loss of Jerusalem *and its fragile restoration.* The first part of the book concerns the devastating loss of the holy establishment, the most trusted place (Jerusalem and its temple), the very place where God's vision of presence is given. The last line of verse 13 looks quickly beyond the loss, but with only an enigmatic trace of assurance. The focal disclosure dominating "Isaiah" in the eighth century is nullification, an anticipation two centuries in fruition, but as sure as a decree from the heavenly throne.

It is stunning that this harsh, pivotal statement from Isaiah looms large in the use of the Old Testament in the New. In all four Gospels, verses 9–10 are quoted with reference to Jesus. It is evident that prophetic faith in ancient Israel was not heeded or accepted by kings or people, and this led to the wholesale rejection of Israel as God's people. Similarly, it is evident that the demanding message and person of Jesus were widely rejected; the early church had to ponder long that rejection. In the Synoptic tradition (Matt. 13:14–15; Mark 4:12; Luke 8:10), our verses are quoted as judgment upon those who do not properly understand and receive Jesus. In John 12:37–43, the same verses are quoted to comment negatively on those who suffer from spiritual blindness and do not properly discern Jesus—who he is and what he requires. And in Acts 28:26–27, it is the reality of Jewish resistance to Jesus that opens the way for Paul's Gentile mission. The imagination of the early church is saturated with the realism of the oracle of Isaiah. The early church is able to see that the *rejection of Jesus* is parallel to the *rejection of the prophetic word.* In both cases, the texts are haunted by the awareness that the resistance is in some odd way initiated by God's own negation.

The oracle that results from this large vision of God is harsh—harsh in its nullifying of Jerusalem and harsh in its second usage concerning Jesus.

It is harsh to recognize that the rule of God is rejected by God's own people. It is enigmatic to see that the rejection is not only willful hard-heartedness, but is decreed by God, decreed because God wanted(?) the defeat of Jerusalem; wanted(?) the resistance of unbelievers to Jesus.

It is clear in this hard saying, even if much else is not clear here, that the purposes of God are at work in the midst of severe human obduracy. There are no easy healings. There are no ready turnings. The healings are not readily available, and the turnings are too demanding. There is no easy gospel, no cheap grace, no good word that gives assurances to those who drop by hoping for a quick and comfortable deal. And that leaves, in these cases, only obtuseness and its terrible consequences.

Those dulled and numbed are headed toward termination. These words sound ominous in a society like ours, deeply narcoticized not only by chemical dependence, but by a host of numbing dependencies: poverty and wealth in the extreme, brutality, militarism, self-indulgence—the same list of which the ancient poets spoke so relentlessly. *Not noticing* leads to *termination*. Not noticing may not evoke a supernatural swoop of nullification directly from heaven. It may come more like a thief in the night, too quiet to be noticed until it is too late.

To be sure, there is comfort at the end of the oracle. But it is only late, a seeming afterthought. It is a small, thin comfort of a holy seed from the stump. But first the stump! The stump of failure and termination rooted in numbness and hard-heartedness. The book of Isaiah knows the stump of 587 B.C.E. when all was lost. The Gospel writers know the Friday stump of crucifixion. It will not surprise us that our verses of narcotization leave us deeply stumped. The prophetic drama does not permit a rush to post-exile, even as the gospel does not permit a rush past Friday to arrive too early and too easily at Sunday.

AN UNCOMPROMISING
EITHER/OR FOR JERUSALEM
7:1–25

This long chapter is one of the most complex and elusive in the entire book of Isaiah. We may consider it in three parts: (1) a narrative of confrontation between the prophet and the king, Ahaz, in the midst of an acute political-military crisis (vv. 1–9); (2) continued confrontation around the much-noticed "prophetic sign" (vv. 10–17); and (3) a collection of four enigmatic prophetic anticipations for Jerusalem (vv. 18–25). The entire chapter makes clear that prophetic faith is inescapably situated midst the vagaries of the historical-political process, and it is in such a context that the concrete risks of faith must be run.

The Demands of Faith (7:1–9)

7:1 **In the days of Ahaz son of Jotham son of Uzziah, king of Judah, King Rezin of Aram and King Pekah son of Remaliah of Israel went up to attack Jerusalem, but could not mount an attack against it.** 2 **When the house of David heard that Aram had allied itself with Ephraim, the heart of Ahaz and the heart of his people shook as the trees of the forest shake before the wind.**
3 **Then the LORD said to Isaiah, Go out to meet Ahaz, you and your son Shear-jashub, at the end of the conduit of the upper pool on the highway to the Fuller's Field,** 4 **and say to him, Take heed, be quiet, do not fear, and do not let your heart be faint because of these two smoldering stumps of fire-brands, because of the fierce anger of Rezin and Aram and the son of Remaliah.** 5 **Because Aram—with Ephraim and the son of Remaliah—has plotted evil against you, saying,** 6 **Let us go up against Judah and cut off Jerusalem and conquer it for ourselves and make the son of Tabeel king in it;** 7 **therefore thus says the Lord GOD:**

    It shall not stand,
      and it shall not come to pass.
    8 **For the head of Aram is Damascus,**
      and the head of Damascus is Rezin.
(Within sixty-five years Ephraim will be shattered, no longer a people.)
    9 **The head of Ephraim is Samaria,**
      and the head of Samaria is the son of Remaliah.
    If you do not stand firm in faith,
      you shall not stand at all.

The occasion for the meeting of prophet and king is the threat of attack upon Jerusalem by its two small northern neighbors, Israel and Syria (Aram) (cf. 2 Kings 16:5–9). (In passing, it may be noticed that the contemporary geopolitics of the region are unchanged. The government in Jerusalem continues to be threatened by its small northern neighbors, Lebanon and Syria.) King Ahaz is inspecting the city waterworks, likely in anticipation of a siege on the city. It is clear that the king is not only worried about security, but in fact is deeply frightened and intimidated by this northern threat. Indeed, he is so frightened that he is about to make a major policy decision to appeal for help to Assyria, the great and awesome empire to the north of Israel and Syria. (Assyria was situated in the territory of present-day Iraq.) Thus the king is about to appeal to a greater threat (Assyria) against a lesser threat (Israel, Syria), a decision that reflects short-term panic and long-term foolishness. But because his heart shook "as the trees of the forest shake before the wind," such panic and foolishness become the ground for policy formation (v. 21; cf. Lev. 26:36).

It is to be noted that in verse 2, the king is referred to not merely by his name, but formally as "The House of David." This appellation suggests that our narrative is concerned not only with this specific military crisis, but also with the long-term reality of the Davidic dynasty, with all of the theological freight that is carried by that dynasty. As long ago as 2 Samuel 7:11–16, the House of David received an unconditional, long-term assurance of support from Yahweh, that is, a theological support for a sociopolitical institution. The House of David may rest secure in Yahweh's steadfast loyalty. That is the core truth of the regime and its core ideological claim, indeed its *raison d'être*. Only now, in panic and foolishness, the House of David considers alternative means of security that in effect deny the cruciality of Yahwistic fidelity, that is, alternative to reliance upon Yahweh. Thus a concrete policy decision is understood to be a far-reaching theological departure whereby the state forfeits its Yahwistic ground for existence.

Into that situation of threat, panic, and foolishness comes the prophet, dispatched by Yahweh. He meets Ahaz, who functions in the book of Isaiah as a representative embodiment of fickleness and unfaith. The prophet is accompanied at this meeting by his son, "*Sheár yashub.*" The name of the boy is reckoned by interpreters to be a powerful assertion. The translation of the name, "a remnant shall return," introduces a special notion of Isaiah, namely, "a remnant." In context the term is ominous. It alludes to the conviction of the Isaiah tradition that Jerusalem will be destroyed and its inhabitants will be deported into exile, which is tantamount to death. And from the death of exile only a small portion of the population will eventually be returned to Jerusalem in order to resume life. Thus the name of the boy might be more fully "[Only] a remnant shall return [from exile]." The reference is essentially bad news, because in the long-term perspective of the book, *the exile is certain*, and from exile *only a small portion will survive* as identifiable Jews.

To be sure, in a later context, the "remnant" might be taken as assurance, when it is understood as "[*at least*] a remnant will return [*to the homeland*]." But it can be heard as assurance only in the actual context of exile, an actual context not yet even on the horizon of the king. So the presence of the little boy along with the prophet and the king adds to the gravity of the exchange. The name of the boy puts the king on notice. The king is well advised to consider a greater threat than these small neighbors.

The centerpiece of the exchange between prophet (the voice of Yahweh's sovereign rule) and the king (the panicked carrier of Davidic possibility) is the prophetic oracle that radically redescribes the context of the city (vv. 7–9). The prophet is instructed by Yahweh to address the king with a characteristic salvation oracle that offers assurance (v. 4). The assurance is given in four invitational imperatives urging the king to move out of his panic. The ground of this assurance is that the threatening powers are "smoldering stumps." (Calvin says "tails.") That is, the prophet employs derisive rhetoric about "a burnt out case" in order to mock the threat.

The prophet invites the king to courage, based on a reassessment of political reality. The continuing assertion of the prophet is that these two posturing kings—Rezin and "the son of Remaliah" (he refuses to utter the name of the illegitimate claimant of power, Pekah)—will not last and do not in fact constitute a serious threat. Therefore Ahaz would be foolish indeed to shape policy in response to them. The prophet engages in political analysis of the international scene. He offers a scenario that is quite at odds with that of the king, for the king's perception is completely skewed by fear. The judgment made here about Judah's true military situation is perhaps "disclosed" by Yahweh, for this is "Thus saith the Lord." Whatever such a phrase might mean, it seems clear that the prophet (and the prophetic tradition generally) is capable of acute social analysis, international as well as domestic. The world looks very different when the observer is not consumed by fear.

The political analysis offered by the prophet to the king, moreover, is drawn to a rhetorical climax in verse 9b, wherein the prophet issues one of his most pivotal utterances. We may notice two rhetorical features of this utterance. First, the last two lines of verse 9 begin with "if." The prophet lays upon the policy making of the dynasty a condition. Indeed, it is a Yahwistic condition. The future depends upon the king's trusting and acting in certain ways that preclude policy formation out of Yahweh-denying panic and foolishness. This conditionality is astonishing, for the entire Davidic theology since 2 Samuel 7 is without condition, as though the dynasty enjoyed a blank check of Yahwistic assurance. No, maintenance of the Jerusalem regime is based on an elemental theological requirement.

Second, the oracle contains the double use of the term "have faith" ('āman), that is, "rely, trust." This usage of the term is important because this same term is at the heart of Davidic theology upon which the Jerusalem regime heavily relies:

Your house and your kingdom shall be *made sure* (*ne'ĕmān*) forever before me.
(2 Sam. 7:16a)

My *faithfulness* (*'ămûnâ*) and steadfast love shall be with him; . . .
but I will not remove from him my steadfast love,
  or be false to my *faithfulness* (*'ămûnâ*).
(Ps. 89:24a, 33)

King Ahaz is invited, in the midst of this pressing concrete crisis, to re-consider and reembrace the profound assurance of Yahweh given long ago to his family and his regime. And now the king is required by the prophet, by appeal to the very ideology upon which the king relies, to get his mind off the immediate threat and off the pseudo-help of Assyria (which is no help at all), and to focus upon the single true source of assurance and well-being. Yahweh's fidelity is rooted in the decree of heaven but impinges directly and poignantly upon worldly decisions.

It is commonly agreed that this utterance of the prophet is a (the?) piv-otal text upon the meaning of *faith* in the work of Isaiah and, indeed, in the entire Old Testament. Faith ("stand firm in faith") is not a matter of in-tellectual content or cognitive belief. It is rather a matter of quite practi-cal reliance upon the assurance of God in a context of risk where one's own resources are not adequate. It means to entrust one's security and future to the attentiveness of Yahweh—to count God's attentiveness as adequate and sure, thereby making panic, anxiety, or foolishness unnecessary and inappropriate. It is to know one's self safe in risk because of an Attending Other whose resources are mobilized and whose commitments are unfail-ing. It is to place one's self into the reliable care of another.

The affirmation of verse 9b is the completion of the summoning im-peratives of verse 4. These imperatives—take heed, be quiet, do not fear, and do not let your heart be faint—are commonly understood as the sort of rhetoric used in ancient Israel when Israel is engaged in military con-flict or is being mustered for battle that is filled with great threat (cf. Deut. 20:3). The importance of this parallel to a situation of war is that the invi-tation *not to fear* but *to faith* is not a bourgeois notion of safety when "all is well," as though it were an invitation to complacency. It is, rather, pre-cisely for times of conflict, threat, and danger, when circumstance dictates fear rather than trust. The prophetic summons to faith is an urging that the king engage in an attitude and a practice of confidence that flies in the face of an unambiguous circumstance of danger. Faith is a refusal to give in to the threats of undoing posed by these small northern neighbors, and to proceed in confidence in the face of such self-evident danger. Notice, moreover, that Ahaz is not called to a spiritual enterprise but to a concrete, public action as king that proceeds on the conviction that Yahweh stands at the center of the crisis and will prevail. The crisis revolves around this Yahweh upon whom the dynasty in Jerusalem is founded, but about whom Rezin and "the son of Remaliah" know nothing.

The importance of this assertion of trust can hardly be overstated. It is most unfortunate that, in the long history of the church, "faith" has been almost everywhere transubstantiated into "belief," which transposes the concrete practicality of trust into a cognitive enterprise. How ludicrous that in the long, oppressive history of orthodoxy—which guards cognitive formulations—that those who enforce *right belief* seem most often to be themselves unable or unwilling to engage in *deep trust*. It is this deep trust in the midst of risk, so deep that it redefines the situation, that is reiterated in the lyrical words of Paul, that great voice of faith. Notice how Paul employs a military metaphor not unlike that of Isaiah: "No, in all these things we are more than conquerors through him who loved us. For I am convinced . . . " (Rom. 8:37–38). Paul's key insight on faith (cf. Gal. 2:16), moreover, is echoed in Martin Luther, who understood Isaiah precisely. Luther casts his great hymn of faith in military metaphor:

> A mighty fortress is our God,
> A bulwark never failing.

The negative counterpart sounds like it is addressed directly to Ahaz:

> Did we in our own strength confide,
> Our striving would be losing.

Luther continues the military imagery as he turns his poetry in a christological direction:

> Christ Jesus, it is he;
> Lord Sabaoth his Name,
> From age to age the same,
> And he must win the battle.

The assurances of Paul and Luther, which have dominated the mind of much of the church, stay close to Isaiah. Ahaz is called to live in an alternative world governed by this faithful God and by none other. Habitation in this alternative world, moreover, has immediate and concrete implications for the practice of life. The dynasty is being summoned back to its radical roots.

A Sign of Assurance (7:10–17)

7:10 **Again the LORD spoke to Ahaz, saying,** [11] **Ask a sign of the LORD your God; let it be deep as Sheol or high as heaven.** [12] **But Ahaz said, I will not ask, and I will not put the LORD to the test.** [13] **Then Isaiah said: "Hear then, O house of David! Is it too little for you to weary mortals, that you weary my God also?** [14] **Therefore the Lord himself will give you a sign. Look, the young woman is with child and shall bear a son, and shall name him Immanuel.** [15] **He shall eat curds and honey by the time he knows how to refuse the evil and choose the good.** [16] **For before the child knows how to refuse the evil and choose the good, the land before whose two kings you are in dread will be deserted.** [17] **The LORD will bring on you and on your people and on your ancestral house such days as have not come since the day that Ephraim departed from Judah—the king of Assyria."**

The confrontation of prophet and king continues. It is a continuation of "faith versus fear" and the two worlds that result from faith or from fear. We are not given the reaction of the king to the prophetic summons of verse 9b. What follows in verses 10ff. suggests that King Ahaz refused the call of Isaiah to radical faith. Thus, in verse 10 an apparent refusal escalates the encounter. Now it is "the Lord" (not Isaiah) who takes the next step. God says, "Ask a sign." That is, defiantly, "Do you want me to prove it to you?" "Do you want me to give evidence?" (v. 11). The king piously refuses the offer (v. 12). The prophet (now prophet, not God) reprimands the king for refusing to engage the offer, and now he proceeds with a sign that the king had not requested and did not want. The sign is "a visible gesture" whereby the theological claim of God is made concrete and therefore inescapable. (Notice the like function of "signs" in the Exodus narrative [Exod. 4:8–17, 28–30; 10:1–2] and in the Fourth Gospel [4:48; 20:30].)

The sign in this utterance has become one of the pivots of theological interpretation (vv. 14–17). We may comment on four issues related to the sign. First, *a young woman* will bear a child. The woman seems incidental for the sign, for it is the child and not the woman that claims attention. Nonetheless, "the young woman" has been an important issue in interpretation, largely because of the way in which she turns up in the New Testament as "the virgin Mary." Concerning "the young woman," scholars have used great energy attempting to identify her, variously proposing that she is the wife of the prophet, the wife of the king, an incidental woman without special identity, or even a mythical being. There is no compelling or decisive evidence in any of these directions. Her identity is not important.

Her status has been of as much interest to interpreters as her identity. The phrase "young woman" (*'almâ*) means a woman of marriageable age,

but it completely begs the question of virginity. It is undoubtedly clear that
a status of virginity is not of any interest or importance for the sign of Isaiah. Indeed, most of the ancient translations of the term have left that question open. But the Septuagint and, derivatively, the Vulgate, which have
dominated Christian reading of the text, have rendered "virgin." It is this
reading that has become decisive for New Testament usage (cf. Matt.
1:123; Luke 1:17), and that has then led to a rich tradition of church theology on "The Virgin Mary," articulated as it is, even in the creed (see
Sawyer, *The Fifth Gospel*, 65–82). Two matters are clear: (1) The Isaiah passage per se has no interest in the virginal status of the woman. It is not interested because the focus is not on the birth but on the child. (2) The
church's subsequent development of the interpretation of the virgin, rich
tradition as it is, cannot be said to be "wrong," but it can be said to go in a
quite fresh direction, surely other than the Isaiah text itself.

Second, the crucial element in the sign concerns the child whose name
is "Immanuel," that is, *God is with us*. We have seen a particular child's
name in 7:3, there a quite ominous name. Here this child's freighted name
is positive and reassuring, for it asserts the entire affirmation of Davidic
theology rooted in the ancient oracle of 2 Samuel 7. The child is to be a
visible, physical, concrete reassertion of the core conviction of royal Israel that God is present in and with and for Israel as defender, guardian,
and protector, so that Israel need not be afraid. Indeed, Ahaz in this context need not be afraid and, therefore, need not turn to the savage resource of Assyria. It is this confidence about which Israel sang in the
temple:

> God is our refuge and strength,
>   a very present help in trouble.
> Therefore we will not fear, though the earth should change,
>   though the mountains shake in the heart of the sea; . . .
> God is in the midst of the city; it shall not be moved;
>   God will help it when the morning dawns . . . .
> The LORD of hosts is with us;
>   The God of Jacob is our refuge.
>   (Psalm 46:1–2, 5, 7)

(This psalm is conventionally linked to the time of Isaiah, and it is the
source of Luther's great hymn, *A Mighty Fortress*.) Thus the child is a visible summons to faith, the faith to which Ahaz has been summoned in
verses 4 and 9, and that he has, in his fearfulness, completely abandoned.

Third, the function of the child is to *monitor the time* of the current threat of the northern neighbors, a time that will be short indeed (v. 16). It is conventionally reckoned that a child knows the difference between "good and evil," right and wrong, by two years of age. Thus by two years of age, that is, two years from the moment of utterance by the prophet, the two kings—Rezin and "the son of Remaliah"—will be terminated. That is, the threat noted in verses 7–9a, which preoccupies the king, is a short-term danger and should not be taken as seriously as does the king. It is the lack of trust in Yahweh and his consequent fearfulness that causes the king to misassess his true circumstance and tempts him with the pseudo-help of Assyria. His is *not* a world without Yahwistic reliability. It should be noted, in the move from the reassuring name in verse 14 to the reassuring time in verse 16, that verse 15 is odd. It is most likely that "curds and honey" refer to a time of abundance, prosperity, and well-being. If so, then the lines suggest that this child, by two years, will face no threat of war but will live in peace and prosperity. There will be a return to glad normalcy, because "God is with us."

Thus *the woman, the named child,* and *the time* all converge to offer the king assurances that may override his panic and his dangerous misreading of military-political reality. Isaiah issues an offer of well-being that the king cannot accept. King Ahaz comes to represent, in the tradition of Isaiah, not simply a weak, vacillating king, but *Judah in its unfaith,* Judah in its disregard of Yahweh, and so Judah that chooses for itself the troubles of forsaking Yahweh. It is likely that Ahaz's resistance to faith—and the sign of faith—leads to verse 17, our fourth consideration. Ahaz refuses "God with us." Ahaz proceeds to live and conduct policy minus Yahweh, that is, minus the assurance and guarantees of Yahweh. From a Yahwistic-prophetic perspective, of course, such a decision is a disaster.

In the context of this wondrous sign and assurance, we are not prepared for the harshness of verse 17. The verse makes sense only on the basis of the refusal of Ahaz. There is now going to come trouble in Judah not known since the split of the kingdom in 922, big trouble. The rhetoric of trouble, even on the lips of this eloquent poet, fails. The real danger—which Ahaz does not yet perceive—defies rhetoric. And so the announcement breaks off in midsentence, and the poet blurts out, "the King of Assyria"! That is the big trouble to come. Geopolitically, Assyria is the great threat of the north, which makes northern Israel and Syria look completely unimportant. Specifically, this king is Sennacherib, the ruthless monarch who assaulted Jerusalem (cf. 36:1; 37:17–37). The naming of Assyria, the great, brutal superpower, abruptly undoes all the assurance of verses 4, 9b, 14–16. The book of Isaiah plunges the hopeless king—with hopeless people—into the

cauldron of Assyrian rapaciousness and brutality. It could have been otherwise! But the king could not trust. And so comes devastation at the behest
of Yahweh, the very God who offered to be "with us," but is now "against
us," concretely, devastatingly in the form of Assyria. The awesomeness of
the tradition of Isaiah is that it asserts the issue of faith/fear as a great public policy issue. Faith matters to life and death, to war and peace, to prosperity and destruction, to concrete decisions in the real world. This
tradition dares to assert that the future of Jerusalem—seat of David, seat of
Yahweh—depends upon adjudicating the offer of faith and the temptation
of fear. As belated readers, we may ponder how the fear/faith issue is yet at
work in other cities and other nation states. Decisions for life and death,
war and peace, prosperity and devastation, now as then, are made without
even a recognition that faith is not a churchy thing, but it is a basis for radical alternatives in socioeconomic, political, military policy. As the prophet
said, "No faith . . . no future!" (v. 9b).

Unwelcome Futures (7:18–25)

7:18 **On that day the LORD will whistle for the fly that is at the sources of
the streams of Egypt, and for the bee that is in the land of Assyria.** [19] **And they
will all come and settle in the steep ravines, and in the clefts of the rocks,
and on all the thornbushes, and on all the pastures.**

[20] **On that day the Lord will shave with a razor hired beyond the River—
with the king of Assyria—the head and the hair of the feet, and it will take
off the beard as well.**

[21] **On that day one will keep alive a young cow and two sheep,** [22] **and will
eat curds because of the abundance of milk that they give; for everyone that
is left in the land shall eat curds and honey.**

[23] **On that day every place where there used to be a thousand vines, worth
a thousand shekels of silver, will become briers and thorns.** [24] **With bow and
arrows one will go there, for all the land will be briers and thorns;** [25] **and as
for all the hills that used to be hoed with a hoe, you will not go there for fear
of briers and thorns; but they will become a place where cattle are let loose
and where sheep tread.**

There have now been collected as an addendum to the prophet-king encounter four anticipations of the future of Judah, all introduced by "on that
day," a day not yet known but already decreed by Yahweh (vv. 18–19, 20,
21–22, 23–25). The concrete decisions the king makes—in fear and not in
faith—have drastic, far-reaching consequences. Either way—in fear or in
faith—the king sets the future in motion. These oracles, ostensibly a con-

tinuation of verse 17, articulate the ominous future Ahaz has chosen for his city and his people. These oracles are all Yahweh-driven, though only the first two (vv. 18–19, 20) explicitly name Yahweh; the other two (vv. 21–22, 23–25) voice the outcomes understood as deriving from the will of Yahweh. They are not, however, simply decrees from *the government of Yahweh*. They are, at the same time, characteristically, situated in *the real world of geopolitics*. Isaiah will not permit Judah to withdraw into a religious cocoon, because Yahweh is ruler in the real world of power.

The first oracle appeals to vivid imagery to imagine the invasion of Egypt and Assyria upon the land of Judah (vv. 18–19). To be sure, the Isaiah tradition is primarily preoccupied with Assyria. The inclusion of Egypt as the alternative superpower is perhaps hyperbole, in order to exhibit Judah as completely exposed and vulnerable to international threats. Judah is under assault and helpless. The oracle seems to explicate the abrupt "the king of Assyria" in verse 17.

The second oracle again bespeaks devastation at the hand of Assyria (v. 20). The "razor" here refers to the standard brutal military practice of shaving captives in order to humiliate them and reduce them visibly to servility (cf. 2 Sam. 10:4–5; Isa. 3:17). The process includes the shaving of head and beard; the "hair of the feet," moreover, is a euphemism for the shaving of genital hair, all the more to contribute to humiliation. Judah will be made completely servile to Assyria! The anticipation is reflective of the reported public submission of Ahaz to Assyria: "I am your servant and your son" (2 Kings 16:7). The single source of freedom of action in the world is Yahweh. That source rejected, Ahaz and his people must live in an Assyrian world, on Assyrian terms, which are terms of subjugation, servility, and humiliation.

The third oracle echoes verse 15 and seems not so negative as its counterparts (vv. 21–22). Indeed, it may be a positive anticipation of a new beginning of well-being. If so, it is an odd and unexpected statement here. But perhaps even if it is positive, one is struck by the modesty of the vision, modest after devastation. Thus it may be that here the devastation is past, and one begins again, lowly, in new life. This anticipation is perhaps congruent with the "remnant shall return" of 7:3. The bad news is *only* a remnant. The good news is *a remnant*. The bad news is only one cow and two sheep. The good news is an abundance of milk for "everyone that is left"!

The fourth oracle completes the picture of devastation that Ahaz has brought upon his people (vv. 23–25). This brief unit is dominated by the threefold use of "briers and thorns." Now, there are still a thousand vines, rich, prosperous agriculture. Then, in an awful time sure to come, the rich vines will be displaced by briers and thorns. All agricultural abundance will cease. The land so fertile and blessed will revert to desolation and abandonment. The routines that make for life will be terminated. There will be hunting there, but no cultivation, only an open grazing land (cf. Mic. 3:12). Israel is abandoned, left to the elements. Life is no longer viable.

The chapter moves from the crisis of invasion and siege by Israel and Syria (v. 5) to the final devastation by Assyria (vv. 18–25). Between these ominous options of Israel-Syria at the beginning and Assyria at the end, there has been a third alternative. The alternative of *faith in Yahweh* offered by the prophet has given Judah a chance for well-being. It was a chance made viable by a child named *God with us*. But Ahaz, emblem of fickle Israel, could not choose it. There was "a road less traveled," but he could not take it. And so death. The book of Isaiah moves its inexorable way to nullification.

Two readings have dominated this text. One can make a *historical reading* of Ahaz in the eighth century B.C.E., where the issues are clear enough. Or one can make a *christological reading* and draw this text toward the story of Jesus and his virginal mother. Both of these readings have long-established legitimacy. My urging, however, is that we keep focus upon *the offer of faith*. The enduring community of this text—synagogue and church—still lives in a world of ominous circumstance and is ever again invited to accept at face value the threat of circumstance. But faith is to resist circumstance and to continue "a more excellent way," a way with no guarantees beyond promises and the One who makes those promises. When and where church and synagogue embrace such assurances and act publicly upon them, the governments of the world could not long resist or refuse. Evidently, in the wake of Ahaz, we have been choosing—in panic and foolishness—the way of the bee and the fly, the razor, and the brier long enough. The non-negotiable verdict of the prophet still lingers: No faith . . . no future! The news is that the people of this text—in panic and foolishness—all too often choose against their own future, the one Yahweh would give.

PUBLIC JUDGMENTS, HIDDEN HOPES
8:1–22

This chapter is even more obscure and problematic than the preceding one. The geopolitical context is the same as that in chapter 7, namely, a threat by Israel and Syria against Judah, and a temptation to appeal to Assyria for aid against Israel and Syria (see chapter 7 for a fuller comment). This chapter is most difficult to interpret for two reasons. Many of the phrases and images in the text are obscure and beyond recognition. More than that, some of the governing metaphors are seemingly ambiguous, so that one cannot be certain when the intention is judgment and when it is hope. Whatever can be said in this chapter is of necessity provisional.

Perhaps the greatest learning from this difficult chapter is how tentative our reading and interpretation of the Bible must be. If one did not notice this, one could be overly impressed by those who seem to know completely and without question what the Bible says, what it means, and how it applies. Closer examination of such absolutism discloses that such certainty applies only to a few selected portions of the Bible, and then often by overriding and disregarding the elusiveness that is intrinsic to the text. That elusiveness stems in part from the fact that we are dealing with very old texts in phrasing and imagery that are remote from us, plus a long process of not very adequate textual transmission. In addition to that, however, the elusiveness concerns the very elusiveness of God, so that voices like Isaiah, authoritative as they are, are not always clear on what must be said. Their saying is couched in rhetoric that is open. In any case, we see enough of elusiveness to be cautious and reluctant toward interpretations that are too loud, too certain, and too unforgiving of alternatives.

The large issue of the chapter concerns *faith in Yahweh*. As a countertheme we may notice several places at which the prophet stands apart from his community, so that we see hints of an emerging alternative community. We may divide the chapter into five elements that in part seem to be floating literary/rhetorical fragments that form no sustained or coherent argument.

Fear and Faith . . . Again (8:1–8)

8:1 Then the LORD said to me, Take a large tablet and write on it in common characters, "Belonging to Maher-shalal-hash-baz, 2 and have it attested for me by reliable witnesses, the priest Uriah and Zechariah son of Jeberechiah. 3 And I went to the prophetess, and she conceived and bore a son. Then the LORD said to me, Name him Maher-shalal-hash-baz; 4 for before the child knows how to call "My father" or "My mother," the wealth of Damascus and the spoil of Samaria will be carried away by the king of Assyria.

5 The LORD spoke to me again: 6 Because this people has refused the waters of Shiloah that flow gently, and melt in fear before Rezin and the son of Remaliah; 7 therefore, the Lord is bringing up against it the mighty flood waters of the River, the king of Assyria and all his glory; it will rise above all its

channels and overflow all its banks; 8 it will sweep on into Judah as a flood, and, pouring over, it will reach up to the neck; and its outspread wings will fill the breadth of your land, O Immanuel.

These verses may be divided into two parts, between which King Ahaz apparently made his decision for Assyria, a policy decision the prophet regards as a disastrous rejection of Yahweh. Verses 1–4 continue the argument of 7:1–17, in which the king is urged not to fear excessively the momentary threat of Syria and Israel. We are here introduced to the name of yet a third child, "Spoil speeds, prey hastens." This child and the name are applied precisely to the political crisis facing Judah. The name is taken to assert that the wealth of Damascus (capital of Syria = "spoil") and the spoil of Samaria (capital of Israel = "prey") will all be promptly carried away to Assryia. That is, these nations will be overcome by Assyria, and therefore Ahaz need not fear them. Moreover, the threat of these two small kingdoms will evaporate in nine months, that is, by the time this baby can say "mamma" and "daddy." (Notice that the time here is less than the two years given as an assurance in 7:16.) Thus the assurance given yet again by a child is parallel to that of 7:14, 16.

After verse 4 and before verse 5 everything has been decided. Ahaz has capitulated to the pressure of Assyria (cf. 2 Kings 16:7–8). Now in verses 5–8, the fateful decision is underscored and condemned, and is shown to be a foolish and devastating one. Judah (and the king) had a choice (cf. Deut. 30:15–20). One choice—now rejected—was to choose "the waters of Shiloah" (v. 5). This enigmatic phrase apparently refers to an internal water supply in Jerusalem (the river Gihon?), which made Judah safe from siege (cf. 1 Kings 1:33, 38; Psalm 46:4). The reference seems to cohere with Yahweh's promise to keep Jerusalem safe, a promise made precisely to the dynasty of David.

Ahaz, however, is too fearful. The choice alternative to the peaceable stream of sustenance is a raging river, ostensibly the Euphrates but in substance the massive, brutalizing power of Assyria. Verses 7–8 explicate the metaphor of raging waters to the fullest in order to bespeak the coming rule that will be savage and chaotic. The imagery refers to the surging of chaos that will flood all of Judah and wash away all of its certitudes. Judah has made the wrong choice by being excessively reliant upon military power to the neglect of its own peculiar assurance from Yahweh. The last phrase of verse 8—"Immanuel"—seems to be a mocking reminder of what might have been. It asserts that Judah is the people with whom Yahweh is reliably present. Ahaz, now having disregarded that fundamental assertion, has concluded that Yahweh is *not* with Judah. And where Yahweh is not!?, other choices may be exercised, even if they lead to death.

An Interlude of Assurance (8:9–10)

8:9 **Band together, you peoples, and be dismayed;**
   listen, all you far countries;
 gird yo urselves and be dismayed;
   gird yourselves and be dismayed!
 [10] **Take counsel together, but it shall be brought to naught;**
   speak a word, but it will not stand,
   for God is with us.

These poetic verses form an interlude in this devastating message. Until now, the address of Yahweh has been variously the prophet Isaiah, the king, or the people Judah. But now the address is "you peoples" (plural), presumably Assyria and the other states that prey upon Judah. The imagery is reminiscent of Psalm 2, which portrays the nations making a concerted assault on Yahweh's rule, attacking Jerusalem and the Davidic king who resides there. As in Psalm 2, all of the enemies of Yahweh gang up on the city, except here the poetry is dominated by "be dismayed!" Three times the nations are invited to "be dismayed," because their assault upon Yahweh and upon Jerusalem is futile. And why? Because of *Immanuel!* It is striking that whereas "Immanuel," the theological slogan that mobilizes all of Davidic theology, is used ironically as rebuke in verse 8, it is here used seriously and affirmatively. In verses 7–8 we are given a picture of a *wholesale defeat* of Jerusalem. In verses 9–10, in stark contrast, we are given *massive assurance* of the well-being of Jerusalem. Perhaps the two themes are sequential: first the devastation; then the assurance. Or perhaps they simply reflect the intrinsic ambivalence of the theological tradition, perhaps— now a greater perhaps—reflective of Yahweh's own ambivalence toward this utterly beloved, utterly recalcitrant people. The remarkable reality is that the tradition of the text does not permit either sentiment to defeat the other. Both judgment and assurance are there. Both are real. Both must be heeded. Yahweh is serious, and the historical process is open.

Yahweh as Judah's Only Real Problem (8:11–15)

8:11 **For the LORD spoke thus to me while his hand was strong upon me, and warned me not to walk in the way of this people, saying:** [12] **Do not call conspiracy all that this people calls conspiracy, and do not fear what it fears, or**

be in dread. ¹³ But the LORD of hosts, him you shall regard as holy; let him
be your fear, and let him be your dread. ¹⁴ He will become a sanctuary, a
stone one strikes against; for both houses of Israel he will become a rock one
stumbles over—a trap and a snare for the inhabitants of Jerusalem. ¹⁵ And
many among them shall stumble; they shall fall and be broken; they shall be
snared and taken.

The text takes an intimate, confessional turn in these verses. Now the
prophet declares what he himself has heard from Yahweh. God has compelled him to distinguish himself from "this people." Isaiah now offers himself as a counterforce, operating at odds from the people. The people,
especially the king, are preoccupied with the Israel-Syria "conspiracy." But
they have it all wrong. Here the text reiterates the verbs of 7:4: "Do not
fear" what they fear. "Do not be in dread" of what they dread. It is not Israel and Syria that must be feared, for their days are numbered. For the
prophet, it is Yahweh who requires all attention, no one else. "Lord of
hosts"—the title bespeaks great military power—is the one to fear, the one
before whom to be in dread; that is, Yahweh is the real "conspirator" against
Judah. Yahweh is the one who is causing trouble for Judah, and the king
misconstrues everything because the king does not acknowledge Yahweh
to be so crucial. In verses 14–15, it is evident that the prophet takes up the
old reassuring theology of Zion, the one sung about in the Psalms, and
turns it against Zion. Yahweh, the rock of security, is now the rock for stumbling. Yahweh, the one who protects from snare and trap, has now become
snare and trap. And because Yahweh is a powerful adversary, big trouble
comes to Judah. The words pile up: stumble, fall, broken, snared, taken!
The book of Isaiah sees clearly the deathly slope of Judah at the hands of
Assyria, then at the hands of Babylon, all the time at the hands of Yahweh.

Yahweh as Jerusalem's
Only Real Possibility (8:16–22)

8:16 Bind up the testimony, seal the teaching among my disciples. ¹⁷ I will
wait for the LORD, who is hiding his face from the house of Jacob, and I will
hope in him. ¹⁸ See, I and the children whom the LORD has given me are signs
and portents in Israel from the LORD of hosts, who dwells on Mount Zion.
¹⁹ Now if people say to you, "Consult the ghosts and the familiar spirits that
chirp and mutter; should not a people consult their gods, the dead on behalf
of the living, ²⁰ for teaching and for instruction?" Surely, those who speak
like this will have no dawn! ²¹ They will pass through the land, greatly dis-
tressed and hungry; when they are hungry, they will be enraged and will

curse their king and their gods. They will turn their faces upward, [22] or they will look to the earth, but will see only distress and darkness, the gloom of anguish; and they will be thrust into thick darkness.

In verse 11, Isaiah has been "seized" to see differently. And now, in verse 16, he acts to give evidence of his alternative view. He not only has discerned reality differently, Yahwistically, but he also makes provision to assure that his alternative vision of reality will endure and continue to be available and authoritative. Verse 16 is of special interest because it suggests that the prophet had a circle of colleagues (followers?) who shared his vision. Among them, moreover, he left affidavits of his alternative view of reality. Scholars speculate that this might be the seed of the book of Isaiah, or perhaps at least 6:1–9:7, which oddly contains first-person statements. The testimony of the prophet, which is to endure into the future, is left as an enduring evidence that Judah need not practice its self-destructive panic. There is "a more excellent way," a way loaded with risks, a way of faith. Isaiah's enduring warning is not unlike the categories of Barbara W. Tuchman in *The March of Folly*, who understands "folly" to be public policy operating even in the face of compelling, wise opposition. The record of Isaiah testifies to the compelling evidence that exhibits current royal policy as foolishness.

In these verses, the prophetic stance on Judah's life is contrasted to that of "official Jerusalem." There is a strong urging from the populace to enlist other, that is, non-Yahweh religious authorities, in order to consult other religious techniques. To no avail, says the prophet! Those who do that will end in despair and desperation, for there is no such help. Those who go down the road of self-help—religious or any other technology—will end in distress, darkness, gloom, anguish, thick darkness, the darkness of inscrutable absence, of failure, of silence. The phrases are heaped up to make the negative point.

There is, however, an alternative that the prophet champions: "I will wait for the LORD, . . . I will hope" (v. 17). To be sure, Yahweh is hiding his face. And where Yahweh's face is hidden, deathly trouble is sure to come. But the hiddenness of Yahweh is not forever! The hiddenness is for now in all its severity, but there will be an "afterward" (cf. 1:26). Isaiah—and so he urges his followers—will not submit to this frantically chosen gloom but will live in determined and unflinching anticipation that Yahweh will yet enact another, alternative, new thing.

Indeed, it is definitional to the book of Isaiah that judgment is regularly juxtaposed to hope. The prophet never for an instant doubted a devastation to come from Yahweh because of massive unfaith. But the prophet knew with equal certainty that newness from Yahweh would follow. The capacity of the prophet to say both things, to insist fully upon both without either eliminating or silencing the other, is the measure both of his theological conviction and of his rhetorical eloquence.

The text pertains, on the face of it, to the crisis of Ahaz with Israel, Syria, and Assyria. The history lesson warrants our attention because we notice in this history traces of our own time and place and of our God in that time and place. Theological interpretation, however, does not linger in history lessons. "The testimony" is "bound up" (cf. v. 16) and kept available even until now, even until our own reading, until our own time and place. When we read in our time and place, we do not read in escapist fashion back to the circumstance of Ahaz. We read, if we read seriously at all, of testimony preserved for us.

We read about this Yahweh, who is fear and dread in our own world of alarm and dismay. We ourselves read as a nation state now warmly embraced by a powerful military ideology. We United States citizens are not, to be sure, the suppliants of a great superpower as Ahaz was of Assyria, for we *are* the superpower recruiting and seducing suppliant states for our grand designs of a "new world order." We ourselves are now members of churches so secularized that Isaiah's rhetoric sounds obscurantist, if we hear it at all. And then we are given pause over the simplicity of the claims enduringly made here. What if it is true that the story of the world has at its center this Force of power and purpose who is our only Problem and our only Possibility? One cannot move readily from the savage abruptness of Isaiah to the smoothnesses of modernity or to the vagaries of theology given with too much scholastic certitude. One must decide to host the abruptness and then to wonder, What if Yahweh is the only "conspiracy," and all else is paranoia?

There is no overwhelming evidence for this alternative construal of reality, only three children named "A Remnant Shall Return," "Immanuel," "Spoil Speeds, Prey Hastens." These odd, seemingly quixotic names stand against the insistence of Assyrian superpower and endless religious consultation. What gives us pause is that we hear the sounds of "the mighty flood waters," and we have less reason to be certain. We wonder and are perplexed, even like those ancient Israelites—only now in our time and place, in our circumstance and our rationality. The "testimony sealed up" for now requires us, in any case, to wonder. Moreover, it authorizes our being haunted in ways that refuse explanation by any of the interpretive "civil engineers" who explain away the flood waters.

A GREAT DAVIDIC NEWNESS
9:1–7

9:1 But there will be no gloom for those who were in anguish. In the former
time he brought into contempt the land of Zebulun and the land of Naph-
tali, but in the latter time he will make glorious the way of the sea, the land
beyond the Jordan, Galilee of the nations.
> ² The people who walked in darkness
>   have seen a great light;
>   those who lived in a land of deep darkness—
>   on them light has shined.
> ³ You have multiplied the nation,
>   you have increased its joy;
>   they rejoice before you
>   as with joy at the harvest,
>   as people exult when dividing plunder.
> ⁴ For the yoke of their burden,
>   and the bar across their shoulders,
>   the rod of their oppressor,
>   you have broken as on the day of Midian.
> ⁵ For all the boots of the tramping warriors
>   and all the garments rolled in blood
>   shall be burned as fuel for the fire.
> ⁶ For a child has been born for us,
>   a son given to us;
>   authority rests upon his shoulders;
>   and he is named
>   Wonderful Counselor, Mighty God,
>   Everlasting Father, Prince of Peace.
> ⁷ His authority shall grow continually,
>   and there shall be endless peace
>   for the throne of David and his kingdom.
>   He will establish and uphold it
>   with justice and with righteousness
>   from this time onward and forevermore.
>   The zeal of the LORD of hosts will do this.

This familiar and beloved oracle offers to Judah, driven as it is to distress,
darkness, gloom, and anguish, yet another chance in the world. The poetic oracle beginning in 9:2 is introduced by what seems to be a prose tran-
sition in 9:1. In the Hebrew text this verse 1 is the final verse of chapter 8,
so that it looks back to the ominous judgment of 8:22 as well as forward to
the promised well-being of the oracle.

Verse 1 is organized around the contrast between "former time" and "latter time." In the context of chapters 6—8, the "former time" is apparently the time of failure and oppression under the rule of Ahaz. The "latter time" apparently is the time after Ahaz when new royal leadership (Hezekiah) makes new "peace and prosperity" possible. Thus the oracle articulates a radical and decisive break in the fortunes of Judah, when all that is "dark" will be overcome by "a great light," namely, a new David.

When this contrast of "former/latter" is read in the larger context of the book of Isaiah (as in 43:18–19), then the "former time" is apparently the entire preexilic and exilic experience of abuse and suffering, and the "latter time" is the time of homecoming and restoration in the land. Because this oracle has been taken over by the church and read christologically, this same contrast can be understood as "B.C.E." (B.C.) and "C.E." (A.D.), so that it is the coming of Christ that marks the decisive turn toward well-being.

It is evident that this eloquent poetry admits of a multilayered reading. In the first instance, nonetheless, the oracle apparently concerned the joyous announcement of the birth of a new Davidic king who would have the authority, resolve, and capacity to reverse the fortunes of Judah. Because Ahaz, in this part of the book of Isaiah, is the embodiment of failed leadership, his son Hezekiah is reckoned to be the celebrated subject of this oracle. And indeed Hezekiah became, as we will see (cf. Isaiah 36—39), a vigorous agent for the recovery of Judah, even in the face of Assyrian power. But because the poetry is lyrical and was no doubt liturgical in its setting and has since been resituated in the canonical book of Isaiah, we need not insist too closely on the Hezekiah connection. Rather, what we have is a glorious, celebrative affirmation that Yahweh, through a human Davidic king, will create a wondrous new possibility for Judah that is unqualified and unconditional. The theological point is Yahweh's capacity and resolve for a newness that is completely fresh and without extrapolation from anything that has gone before.

The poem may be marked by three moments. First, verses 2–3 announce the spectacular newness that will be visible in the sociopolitical horizon of Judah. The "darkness" refers to a situation of despair and oppression at the hand of Assyria (cf. 8:11; 9:1). And now light! "Light" is regularly linked to the coming of Yahweh's "glory," that is, to the visible evidence of Yahweh's splendor, majesty, and sovereignty. This is the coming of Yahweh vigorously into the life of Judah where there had been only absence.

That "darkness into light," moreover, evokes unrestrained celebration and rejoicing (v. 3). The poet, in an attempt to voice the depth and power of joy, cites two parallel situations of joy, the most extreme, exuberant cases thinkable. One is *the joy of harvest*, when the crops are secure from the threats of weather and abundance is guaranteed for another season. Such an occasion of harvest regularly evokes much drinking, after the fear and anxiety that the crop would be lost (cf. Psalm 126:6). The second parallel is *the division of conquered booty*, when an enemy has been defeated. The joy is in part the celebration of goods long coveted and now finally available, and in part simply the exultation of conquest and triumph. It is like harvest and like conquest when "the light" comes.

Second, the transformation to be wrought is a vigorous military one (vv. 4–5). The "yoke" and "rod" bespeak oppression, perhaps in the form of heavy imposed imperial taxes by the Assyrians. The turnabout here anticipated is like "the day of Midian," when Gideon won a great and completely unexpected victory over the oppressive Midianites (see Judg. 6:2–6). Overcoming Assyrian oppression is as inexplicable as was the defeat of Midian, but in the same miraculous way, it is here assured. The expected and welcome defeat is not a spiritual or religious or "nice" one. It is brutal military activity whereby the equipment of the enemy soldiers, all bloodied in the much killing, is burned as an act not only of elimination of weapons, but also of gloating and consequent humiliation of the enemy (cf. Psalm 46:8–9). Through a historical agent, Yahweh will terminate the hated empire in a violent, forcible way.

Only in the third and final section of the poem is the royal agent mentioned (vv. 6–7). Until now no agent is named; the newness is the work of Yahweh. But now it is a child, a son, an heir to the throne! The birth of an heir to the throne of David, expected to be more effective than his predecessor, is of course cause for great celebration—partly authentic joy, partly managed royal propaganda. The well-known series of royal names for "the new king" is likely ritualized hyperbole. It asserts that the new king will meet every expectation of the populace and will perform well every responsibility of the royal office. Thus the king will be wise, shrewd, and discerning ("*wonderful counselor*"), able to do incredibly shrewd things, surely a contrast to the foolish policies of his predecessor. The second title, "*mighty god*," should not be understood in a belatedly substantive, trinitarian category nor as a claim of divinity. Rather, the language means that the new king will be filled with all the powers (especially military) that are required. The phrase "*everlasting father*" is not easy, but likely relates to the generative, guaranteeing powers of the king, a massive antidote to anxiety when things seem to be out of control. Nothing will be out of control in the new administration. "*Prince of peace*" characterizes the new ruler as one who will preside over, maintain, and perhaps impose an order on reality that is in stark contrast to the chaos of the regime of Ahaz. These royal titles are conventional in such displays of dynastic authority and are often thought to be derived from antecedent Egyptian liturgies. Be that as it may, the titles are now laden with Israel's covenantal lore, and for Christians they have been preempted by the claims of Jesus. The force of the titles is cumulative. All of them together assure a new, well-ordered, properly functioning, reliable, life-giving public domain. There is nothing privatistic or personalistic about this vision. It concerns a new deployment of positive public power and embodies "the kingdom of God."

The follow-up of the titles anticipates an awesome regime, with three important marks (v. 7). First, there will be no limit. The scope of "peace and prosperity" will be enormous. There are no doubt traces of latent imperialism here, a dream of "Greater Israel" (cf. Gen. 15:18–21). Second, the seductions of imperialism are checked by the qualities of "justice and righteousness." These two terms, rooted in the covenantal-prophetic tradition, bespeak a social order and arrangement of public power that are equitable and humane, with institutional safeguards and passionate communal commitments that preclude acquisitive avarice and exploitation of the little ones by the big ones. The same word pair, justice and righteousness, is reflected in the liturgical-ideological program of the regime in Psalm 72:1; and in an assertion requiring shameless inventiveness, the tradition dares to claim, in the mouth of the queen of Sheba, that Solomon has ruled in justice and righteousness (1 Kings 10:9). Moreover, the same word pair in Isaiah 5:7, as part of a wordplay, makes clear that it is precisely "justice and righteousness" that is the intention of Yahweh for Israel. Indeed, the prophetic tradition dares to claim that it is justice and righteousness, that is, properly deployed social power, and not arms, that will make the nation secure. Thus the new king will govern in a way that gives sustained well-being to the realm. Third, this new rule will endure "now and forever," as only a regime of justice and righteousness could.

The final phrase of the oracle is unexpected and powerful (v. 7b). This new regime, which gives an entirely new possibility for life in Judah, is because of Yahweh's jealousy. The term rendered "zeal" appeals to Yahweh's passionate, emotionally driven commitment that is twofold. On the one hand, Yahweh is zealous for Judah and Jerusalem, and will see that the city prospers. On the other hand, Yahweh has zeal to maintain Yahweh's own reputation and credibility. Those two passions converge, and Yahweh will act forcibly in behalf of Judah and in behalf of self-regard. That is, the new social possibility for Judah is rooted in Yahweh's most elemental intensity.

The phrase of verse 7b, however, as it offers and assures, also warns. It retains for Yahweh the credit for the newness and refuses to cede too much credit to the coming king or to the dynasty. The king is a key player in the newness, for the newness is indeed social, political, and military. It is not, however, the "zeal of the king" that will do this. The resolve and passion is deeper than that of the king. The determination for social newness is rooted in "The Lord of Hosts." The phrase alludes to Yahweh's limitless military capacity. It also recalls the vision of Isaiah 6:5: "Yet my eyes have seen the King, the LORD of Hosts!" The newness of Judah is indeed a massive decree made by the government of heaven. The new David will enact on earth a chance for justice, righteousness, and peace—the key marks of viability, the very marks forfeited in the foolishness and panic of Ahaz.

The powerful, visionary poetry of this oracle permits more than one reading. It takes on a life of its own, claiming freedom from the Ahaz/Hezekiah matrix of the eighth century. Such a freeing from the Ahaz context has already happened in the book of Isaiah, wherein the notion of "former/latter" moves in larger scope to exile and homecoming. And in the usage of Matthew, the interpretive freedom taken with this passage is immense (Matt. 4:13–17). According to Matthew, Jesus relocates so that "what had been spoken through the prophet Isaiah might be fulfilled." This claim of course does not mean that the poet in Isaiah 9:1–7 had Jesus in mind or "predicted" Jesus. It means rather that the text, powerful and generative as it is, surges beyond its "original setting" to illuminate and redescribe new situations. The text is "reheard" in the Matthew community as a disclosure of Jesus' ministry. In this rehearing, the text speaks of the great reversal now to be caused by Jesus. He is now the "great light" that will transform. We notice, moreover, that the action of Jesus, as given us in Matthew, takes place amidst the ominous arrest of John the Baptist, that is, in the face of oppressive, imperial power. And we note that Jesus, out of that Isaiah text, preaches "the kingdom of heaven," that is, proclaims a counterreality that challenges even the rule of Herod.

The text permits many such rehearings, because God is always recruiting human agents to enact the Great Reversal about which Yahweh had persistent "zeal." For Christians, the decisive rehearing of the text pertains to Jesus, who is the great light in the darkness. But even that rehearing with reference to Jesus is not exclusive. Alongside that we may entertain many rehearings in which new human agents enact the light that shines in the darkness. The transformative zeal of Yahweh for new *peace and prosperity* marked by *justice and righteousness* is undiminished and undeterred. For that reason, new contexts for joy, evoked by Yahweh's unconditional, unqualified newness well up in places where the darkness seemed to perpetuity. It is not, for the darkness has not overcome the light.

ANGER STILL "STRETCHED OUT"
9:8–10:4

9:8   The Lord sent a word against Jacob,
       and it fell on Israel;
    9 and all the people knew it—
       Ephraim and the inhabitants of Samaria—
       but in pride and arrogance of heart they said:
   10 "The bricks have fallen,
       but we will build with dressed stones;
     the sycamores have been cut down,
       but we will put cedars in their place."
   11 So the LORD raised adversaries against them,
       and stirred up their enemies,
   12 the Arameans on the east and the Philistines on the west,
       and they devoured Israel with open mouth.
     For all this his anger has not turned away;
       his hand is stretched out still.

   13 The people did not turn to him who struck them,
       or seek the LORD of hosts.
   14 So the LORD cut off from Israel head and tail,
       palm branch and reed in one day—
   15 elders and dignitaries are the head,
       and prophets who teach lies are the tail;
   16 for those who led this people led them astray,
       and those who were led by them were left in confusion.
   17 That is why the Lord did not have pity on their young people,
       or compassion on their orphans and widows;
     for everyone was godless and an evildoer,
       and every mouth spoke folly.
     For all this his anger has not turned away,
       his hand is stretched out still.

   18 For wickedness burned like a fire,
       consuming briers and thorns;
     it kindled the thickets of the forest,
       and they swirled upward in a column of smoke.
   19 Through the wrath of the LORD of hosts
       the land was burned,
     and the people became like fuel for the fire;
       no one spared another.
   20 They gorged on the right, but still were hungry,
       and they devoured on the left, but were not satisfied;

they devoured the flesh of their own kindred;
21 **Manasseh devoured Ephraim, and Ephraim Manasseh,**
     and together they were against Judah.
For all this his anger has not turned away;
     his hand is stretched out still.

10:1 **Ah, you who make iniquitous decrees,**
      who write oppressive statutes,
  2 **to turn aside the needy from justice**
      and to rob the poor of my people of their right,
    that widows may be your spoil,
      and that you may make the orphans your prey!
  3 **What will you do on the day of punishment,**
      in the calamity that will come from far away?
    To whom will you flee for help, and where will you leave your wealth,
  4 **so as not to crouch among the prisoners**
      or fall among the slain?
    For all this his anger has not turned away;
      his hand is stretched out still.

Back-to-back with the wondrous anticipation of verses 1–7, we are hit heavily with a long speech of judgment against "Israel/Jacob." It is likely that poetry concerning "Jacob/Israel" originally concerned the Northern Kingdom, Israel. In the final form of the text, the same poetry is reappropriated for the Southern Kingdom of Judah. Thus the usages are not always consistent. The juxtaposition of hope and judgment is characteristic of the tradition of Isaiah. Indeed, it is this juxtaposition that constitutes the primary mystery of Israel's faith and the primary rhetorical achievement of the Isaiah tradition.

The most prominent feature of this extended poetry is the fourfold refrain that we have already encountered in 5:25: "For all this his anger has not turned away,/his hand is stretched out still" (9:12, 17, 21; 10:4). We can begin our discussion with the refrain and then work backward to the declarations that result in the refrain. The poem is tightly disciplined around these reiterated refrains.

The cause of Judah's coming trouble, the "all this" of the refrain, concerns its refusal to attune its life to Yahweh's intention. The God who governs the life processes of Israel, according to Isaiah, is awesome, ferocious, and uncompromising. "All this" evokes on Yahweh's part enduring anger, because Yahweh will not tolerate the mockery of Yahweh's sovereignty. The means of sovereign anger is "his hand is stretched out still." The phrase is of special interest because it is the phrase used positively for the Exodus (6:6).

Israel is rescued from Egyptian slavery because of Yahweh's "outstretched arm." What is astonishing is that the same "outstretched arm" that saved is now extended in hostility against Israel, Yahweh's current adversary (cf. Jer. 21:5). The same determined energy that saved Israel at the outset of its life is now determined energy to punish, if not to destroy.

It is self-evident that this is an odd way of speaking and an odd way of understanding the public processes of power. It is nonetheless a way that is standard in the Old Testament. Israel has rhetoric whereby it voices observed reality as a mode of Yahweh's governance. Others might see the danger of the Arameans and Philistines differently, but not Israel, because for Israel everything is referred to the agency of Yahweh. In freedom and determination Yahweh responds harshly to Israel's unresponsiveness. And so the crisis of the eighth century is understood as a covenantal-theological-Yahwistic crisis that cannot be overcome or relieved, except by dealing with the demands of Yahweh.

Israel, even until late, could have avoided this turn of affairs. Israel could have "turned," that is, repented (v. 13; cf. 6:10). Israel could seek Yahweh, that is, direct its attention wholly to the presence and purpose of Yahweh (Amos 5:4, 6). But, says the prophetic tradition, Israel not only offended Yahweh, but when warned, refused to change and continued in its recalcitrance (cf. 2 Kings 17:13–18).

It is likely that the tradition of Isaiah, in its use of this refrain, appeals to conventional, stylized forms of speech, suggesting that each "blow from Yahweh" is designed to elicit repentance. And if it does not, then comes another blow. Thus, in Leviticus 26 we have a reiteration of this process:

> And if in spite of this you will not obey me, I will continue to punish you sevenfold for your sins. . . . If you continue hostile to me, and will not obey me, I will continue to plague you sevenfold for your sins. . . . If in spite of these punishments you have not turned back to me, but continue hostile to me, then I too will continue hostile to you: I myself will strike you sevenfold for your sins (Lev. 26:18, 21, 23–24).

Many scholars, moreover, believe that our text reflects and is parallel to Amos 4:6–11, wherein a series of smitings is said to be motivation for turning. Amos concludes each one with the formula: "Yet you did not return to me" (vv. 6, 8, 9, 10, 11). Where Israel does not return, Yahweh remains angry. Where Yahweh remains angry, trouble comes, and Israel continues in jeopardy.

The long recital of judgment (marked by the reiterated refrain) touches upon familiar themes: Israel and its leadership have been arrogant and ir-responsible, so that Yahweh must punish. Thus "pride and arrogance" are named in verse 9, obtuseness and a refusal to recognize trouble in verse 10, a refusal to "turn" or "seek" in verse 13, all are "godless and evildoers" in verse 17, and because of greediness they devour each other in internecine conflict (vv. 20–21a). The irresponsible conduct of Judah sets it in pro-found opposition to Yahweh.

As a consequence that is inescapable, according to Israel's prophetic cal-culus, judgment must surely come. This punishment comes in the form of threatening foreign armies that are at the behest of Yahweh (v. 12a). The punishment, instigated by Yahweh and executed by foreigners, has caused a brutal diminishment of the people, especially the leadership (vv. 14–18), so that Israel must now live in a context where there is no pity, compas-sion, or mercy (v. 17a). In an alternative image, "wickedness" has broken out like a consuming fire, so that the whole land is burned and none is spared (vv. 18–19). This vexing characterization appeals to a variety of metaphors that are rich and elusive. Among them, one more time, is "briers and thorns" (v. 18; cf. 7:23–25). And yet for all their variation, we may judge that all these several images speak primarily of war and inva-sion. There is explicit reference to the Arameans and Philistines as threat-ening adversaries (v. 12). It is most likely, moreover, that "cutting off head and tail" relates to the brutality of war (v. 14), and that the absence of com-passion, which thereby exposes the vulnerable (v. 17), is a consequence of military action, as is the wholesale burning. Without being reductionist, the punishment is enemy intrusion before which Israel is helpless.

As is often the case, one may notice the daring linkage uttered by the prophet:

> Cause: Refusal to live as Yahweh commands.
> Result: Brutality at the hands of foreign enemies.

The prophet insists that the public process is a moral fabric. There are deep costs for the violation of the purposes of Yahweh, costs that are as-sessed not "supernaturally" but through the ongoing affairs of nations. Thus the prophet manages to keep together, as Israel's prophets regularly do, the uncompromising theological *claim of Yahweh* and the seeming *va-garies of life* through which that theological intentionality is enacted.

Although 10:1–4 belongs to the sequence of 9:8–21 because of the re-frain in verse 4, we may also notice its very different rhetorical character. It is linked to 9:8–21 by the refrain. Verses 1–3, however, have more in common with the "woe series" of 5:8–23. As we have seen in those sayings, here as well the term "woe" ("ah") introduces a warning that those who act *foolishly* will come to a sorry end. It is characteristic of woe sayings that the bad consequences come intrinsically with the foolishness, that is, without any intervening, punishing agent.

The "foolishness" chosen here concerns the practice of social exploitation by the manipulation of the legal process. The prophet understands—long before Karl Marx—that "law making" is the privilege of the powerful, most often done to their own advantage. The writing of law turns out to be "the writing of oppression" whereby exploitation of the vulnerable—widows and orphans—is completely legal. However, here the distorting process of such law making is brought under the aegis of "woe." Such a process ensures trouble, vexation, and eventually death.

In verse 3, as we have seen in 5:9, 13–17, 24–25, the "pure woe saying" is reinforced by prophetic threat, thus introducing an agent of punishment. There will be "a day of punishment." Such actions as those here condemned do not go unnoticed or unrequited! There is coming a *Shoah*, a devastating storm, and there will be no safe place, no place to hide, no refuge. The imagery is reminiscent of 2:20–21, wherein even the wealthy and powerful are forced to run and hide, without their wealth. When the judgment comes, as it surely will, the wealth secured by legal but unacceptable means will be abandoned. The poet anticipates a drastic social reversal wherein the wealthy, powerful, and manipulative will be recast as desperate fugitives, now placed in enormous jeopardy.

It is important, in my judgment, that the prophets be understood as poets. They are seeking, with enormous inventiveness, to enable their listening contemporaries to construe their lives Yahwistically. They insist (and so they utter) that Yahweh is an active and defining focus for life, without which focus public life in Israel is sure to be misconstrued, falsely understood, and faithlessly lived. It is easy in our secularized time and place to find such a Yahweh-reference more than a little naive, and surely life can be well imagined and well understood without reference to Yahweh. But it must have been equally easy to do so in that ancient context. It is easy (easier!) to perceive reality in terms of practical politics than it is to situate a decisive Yahweh at its center. According to this prophetic tradition, however, such a construal of reality is deeply misjudged and will never bring security, well-being, or joy. Yahweh is the inescapable Character at the center of things. Yahweh is, insists the poet, currently deeply offended and mobilized to wound. All this from Yahweh can be avoided, but the requirement for such avoidance is taken by Judah to be too heavy, for it entails the complete reorientation of public life. For that reason the hand of Yahweh remains vigorously and hostilely stretched out. Such poetry is an odd rendering of reality. But Bible believers do indeed operate with such an odd sense of reality as the only version of reality that makes sense of the world at hand.

FAITH REQUIRED IN THE MIDST OF GLOBAL THREAT 10:5–34

The tradition of Isaiah articulates faith on a large scale, resisting any safe, private, or conventional categories. We have already seen that the Isaiah tradition thus far has had Assyria in purview as the defining reality of geopolitics (5:26; 7:17; 8:4, 7). Now in yet another complicated and unclear chapter, the hearer of this text is plunged into the large, demanding world of geopolitics, face-to-face with the threats and temptations of a superpower. The text consists of a variety of fragmentary pieces that were likely accumulated over a long period of time; some of the "superpower" texts likely are addressed to superpowers later on the horizon of Israel, for whom Assyria is now a metaphor. We may divide the chapter into four parts, even though any such division must override and ignore some of the complexities of the rhetoric.

A Tool Become Too Arrogant (10:5–19)

10:5 **Ah, Assyria, the rod of my anger—**
>   **the club in their hands is my fury!**
>   6 **Against a godless nation I send him,**
>>   **and against the people of my wrath I command him,**
>   **to take spoil and seize plunder,**
>>   **and to tread them down like the mire of the streets.**
>   7 **But this is not what he intends,**
>>   **nor does he have this in mind;**
>   **but it is in his heart to destroy,**
>>   **and to cut off nations not a few.**
>   8 **For he says:**
>   **"Are not my commanders all kings?**
>   9 **Is not Calno like Carchemish?**
>>   **Is not Hamath like Arpad?**
>>   **Is not Samaria like Damascus?**
>   10 **As my hand has reached to the kingdoms of the idols**

whose images were greater than those of Jerusalem and Samaria,
¹¹ shall I not do to Jerusalem and her idols
    what I have done to Samaria and her images?"

¹² When the Lord has finished all his work on Mount Zion and on Jerusalem, he will punish the arrogant boasting of the king of Assyria and his haughty pride. ¹³ For he says:
    "By the strength of my hand I have done it,
        and by my wisdom, for I have understanding;
    I have removed the boundaries of peoples,
        and have plundered their treasures;
    like a bull I have brought down those who sat on thrones.
¹⁴ My hand has found, like a nest,
    the wealth of the peoples;
and as one gathers eggs that have been forsaken,
    so I have gathered all the earth;
and there was none that moved a wing,
    or opened its mouth, or chirped."

¹⁵ Shall the ax vaunt itself over the one who wields it,
    or the saw magnify itself against the one who handles it?
As if a rod should raise the one who lifts it up,
    or as if a staff should lift the one who is not wood!
¹⁶ Therefore the Sovereign, the LORD of hosts,
    will send wasting sickness among his stout warriors,
and under his glory a burning will be kindled,
    like the burning of fire.
¹⁷ The light of Israel will become a fire,
    and his Holy One a flame;
and it will burn and devour
    his thorns and briers in one day.
¹⁸ The glory of his forest and his fruitful land
    the LORD will destroy, both soul and body,
    and it will be as when an invalid wastes away.
¹⁹ The remnant of the trees of his forest will be so few
    that a child can write them down.

The large vista of prophetic faith has viewed even Assyria as a tool in Yahweh's hand whereby fickle Judah might be punished. The tool (rod, staff, axe) is only to enact Yahweh's harsh intention for Judah. But Assyria has taken on a life of its own in disregard of Yahweh's intention. This long poetic unit features three "voices." In verses 5–7, Yahweh speaks, characterizing Assyria's true situation. Yahweh has dispatched Assyria in anger against Judah, but Assyria has gone beyond Yahweh's mandate and has acted arrogantly and with craven ruthlessness. The chosen instrument has gotten too big for its imperial britches and has acted autonomously. This poetic unit begins with "ah" (woe; not unlike 5:8–23, 10:4), only now the ominous verdict is not against Judah but against Assyria.

The manifestation of arrogance is exhibited when the prophet places a boasting speech in Assyria's mouth (vv. 8–11). Thus Assyria is the second voice. It may be that this speech of arrogance reflects actual Assyrian propaganda recorded in royal annals. But it is also the case that the prophets like to place self-indicting utterances in the mouth of their opponents. The Assyrian boast concerns the unrestrained power of conquest that treats Jerusalem like every other nation, without any allowance made for the Yahwistic distinction of Judah.

In verse 12 the prophet, the third voice, announces the coming intention of Yahweh to punish the arrogant empire of Assyria. This rhetoric, Yahweh-driven as it is, simply takes for granted that Assyria, like every nation and every center of power, is subject to Yahweh's governance. That is a claim about which Assyria knows nothing and in which Judah in its anxiety does not trust. But of course prophetic utterance does not defer either to external Assyria or to internal cowardice, but proceeds, undeterred, to map out in utterance the alternative world of Yahwism.

Assyria's arrogant self-assertion continues in verses 13–14. The Assyrian empire indicts itself by admitting that it has violated international order by removing national boundary markers. This territorial rapaciousness, which inevitably causes deep political disorder and much suffering, is acutely caught in the metaphor of verse 14. Assyria seizes what belongs to others like a nest-robber taking eggs. Assyria is indeed like a fox in a chicken-coop!

At the end of this unit, Yahweh, who stated the problematic in verses 5–6, now returns to issue a verdict on the empire (vv. 15–19). The rhetorical question of verse 15, referring back to verse 5, requires a negative: "No," the axe is not to lord it over the woodsman. "No," the saw is not to dominate the forester. "No," Assyria is not to be autonomous in relation to Yahweh, the governor of all nations. Inescapably there follows a prophetic "therefore" (v. 16). There will be failure even among Assyria's "stout warriors." The Assyrians may have had great military successes. They cannot, however, succeed where Yahweh turns against the empire. Indeed, Yahweh will not only *cause* a fire, but will *be* a fire that devours the "thorns and briers" of Assyria. Notice how the notion of "thorns and briers," heretofore a threat against Judah (5:6; 7:23–24; 9:18), has now become a threat against Assyria. This poetry reuses the notion of "remnant" we have already seen, only now it is the remnant of the arrogant empire.

The anticipated devastation is massive. Prophetic faith, with enormous rhetorical nerve, imagines Yahweh to be fully capable of routing and decimating the empire. Scholars have noticed the extremity of the language of fire and the absence of any concrete reference to Assyria, leading to the suggestion that this is a later addition to the text, an addition that moves in an apocalyptic direction, thus escalating the imagery of "Yahweh versus" every arrogant opponent.

The Turning of the Remnant (10:20–23)

10:20 On that day the remnant of Israel and the survivors of the house of Jacob will no more lean on the one who struck them, but will lean on the LORD, the Holy One of Israel, in truth. 21 A remnant will return, the remnant of Jacob, to the mighty God. 22 For though your people Israel were like the sand of the sea, only a remnant of them will return. Destruction is decreed, overflowing with righteousness. 23 For the Lord GOD of hosts will make a full end, as decreed, in all the earth.

The long rhetorical assault upon Assyria has as its counterpart good news for Judah. The elimination of Assyria (or any subsequent endangering superpower) entails liberation and well-being for Judah. The positive possibility suggested here and in verses 24–27a reflects a characteristic propensity of the Isaiah tradition to follow harsh judgment against Judah and Jerusalem (as in 9:8–10:4) with subsequent assurance. Here the assurance is for "the survivors." We have seen in 7:3 that the notion of a "returning remnant" is a harsh warning of destruction. Here that ominous anticipation is turned to a positive affirmation, albeit modestly positive and not overly exuberant.

The promise is that in time to come "the survivors" of Israel will not rely upon "this smiter," that is, upon Assyria. One of the great self-deceptions among those who distrust Yahweh is the strong temptation to trust the very agency that will destroy. Indeed, in our own time it takes little imagination to see how we have entrusted our security precisely to a technological-military enterprise that is only a pseudo-security that will not and cannot save.

The promise here is carried by three powerful terms: (1) The first, "*lean*," reminds one of the old gospel song about "leaning on Jesus, leaning on the everlasting arm." Our text places that pietistic sentiment in the real world of policy decisions. "Leaning" is not simply a pietistic slogan but has demanding implications for political-military policy. (2) Verse 20 culminates with "*in truth*." The term is the same root term as used in 7:9. The term identifies that upon which Israel genuinely relies. As we have seen in 7:9, the term alludes to the entire fabric of Davidic-messianic faith. To *lean in trust* requires complete reorientation of policy. (3) That complete reorientation is signaled by *"return"* in verse 21. This return is not primarily a geographical homecoming from exile, but it is a willing, unreserved reengagement with the sovereignty of Yahweh. The promise of the prophet is that the remnant will become a genuinely responsive people of Yahweh, not tempted or seduced by alternative securities or alternative loyalties.

After the use of these three words concerning anticipated fidelity, verses 22–23 appear to be an ominous qualification. It is as though the tradition is worried lest Judah (in exile) should be too much reassured. Thus verses 22–23 seem to take back what in verses 20–21 has just been given. It will be "only a remnant" in the midst of surging destructiveness that will lead to a "full end." The future of Judah is a long shot in a world where Yahweh has unleashed vigorous, large-scale destruction. There is nothing easy, obvious, or assured about this future "leaning."

A Future Become Like Past . . .
in a Little While (10:24–27a)

10:24 **Therefore thus says the Lord GOD of hosts: O my people, who live in Zion, do not be afraid of the Assyrians when they beat you with a rod and lift up their staff against you as the Egyptians did.** 25 **For in a very little while my indignation will come to an end, and my anger will be directed to their destruction.** 26 **The LORD of hosts will wield a whip against them, as when he struck Midian at the rock of Oreb; his staff will be over the sea, and he will lift it as he did in Egypt.** 27 **On that day his burden will be removed from your shoulder, and his yoke will be destroyed from your neck.**

These verses appear to be a still later addition to verses 20–23. Now speaks "The Lord of Hosts," the one seen by Isaiah in his defining vision (6:5), the one who commands immense military power beyond challenge. The utterance of the awesome One is a salvation oracle that intends to counter the fear of Judah that may lead to foolishness or to despair (cf. 7:4; 8:12). The utterance of Yahweh to counter the visible threat of Assyria! Word against circumstance! The odds seem long. But of course it is always *word* that the faithful trust *in circumstances* inviting deep despair and resignation. The word asserts that the circumstance of brutalizing Assyrian power is not to perpetuity.

It will end! When? Soon. How soon? "In a very little while" (v. 25). The phrase is not a prediction of a time schedule. It is an assuring invitation to hope, trust, and buoyancy. It will be "a very little while" before Assyrian power fades. But it will fade! It will end as soon as Yahweh's "indignation and anger" against Judah are spent. The perpetuation of Assyrian power is not dependent upon Assyrian policies or resources; it is dependent only upon Yahweh's inclination.

When Yahweh's inclination toward Judah is changed and consequently Yahweh's use of Assyria is done, everything will change. Whereas Assyria had been a "rod" of punishment, now there will be a "scourge" against Assyria. Yahweh will turn against the empire. Then will come a rescue of Judah, the same kind of rescue that Gideon miraculously wrought against the Midianites (cf. Judg. 7:22–25; cf. Isa. 9:4), the same kind of rescue that worked by the miraculous rod of Moses against Egypt (Exod. 14:16–31). As with Midian and with Egypt, the reversal of fortunes is completely inexplicable. Israel has no ground for hope against such formidable enemies. But it happens!

Now the prophetic tradition performs a remarkable rhetorical linkage, one compelling only for those with thick memories. The circumstance of Israel in relation to any of the late superpowers is very grave. Hope is rooted not in reference to the monarchy, but in Israel's most elemental, primitive, unreflective narrative recall. Assyria may have more modern technology and may have "advanced" to new stages of military cruelty, but in fact nothing important has changed in Yahwistic calculus. Yahweh's saving power surges where it will, and Judah lives by that power. And none of Judah's enemies, early or late, can resist the play of Yahweh's inscrutable power in the world. Those who remember know about Egypt and about Midian, about Moses and about Gideon, and do not doubt that what has been can be again, by the mercy and power of Yahweh.

A Reprise of Warning (10:27b–34)

10:27b **He has gone up from Rimmon,**
    28 **he has come to Aiath;**
    he has passed through Migron,
        at Michmash he stores his baggage;
    29 **they have crossed over the pass,**
        at Geba they lodge for the night;
    Ramah trembles,
        Gibeah of Saul has fled.
    30 **Cry aloud, O daughter Gallim!**
        Listen, O Laishah!
        Answer her, O Anathoth!

³¹ **Madmenah is in flight,**
　　the inhabitants of Gebim flee for safety.
³² **This very day he will halt at Nob,**
　　he will shake his fist
　　at the mount of daughter Zion,
　　the hill of Jerusalem.

³³ **Look, the Sovereign, the LORD of hosts,**
　　will lop the boughs with terrifying power;
　　the tallest trees will be cut down,
　　and the lofty will be brought low.
³⁴ **He will hack down the thickets of the forest with an ax,**
　　and Lebanon with its majestic trees will fall.

By verses 26–27 we have arrived at an assurance that permits unqualified buoyancy. As a result, we are not prepared for these final verses of the chapter. They narrate a military assault against Jerusalem. Scholars think that the geographical detail and precision of verses 27a–34, which name places of march and places of bivouac, may be a recall of an actual assault on the city, perhaps by the Assyrian armies. It is worth tracing the names and reconstructing the route of invasion on a good map. What interests us, however, is the fact of the invasion whereby "he will shake his fist" at Zion (v. 32). The promise of deliverance in verse 25 is "in a very little while." Before that, however, there is the little while of historical reality with all its brutality. Jerusalem is always exposed "for a little while." The realism is never compromised. And even in a Christian retelling of the messiah who will "after three days rise again," there is always "great suffering" (Mark 8:31). There is nothing easy about biblical assurances, for Yahweh's people live in the real world, subject to its profoundly unsettled character.

The last two verses of the poem echo 2:12–17. There is a terrible "againstness" in the intention of Yahweh. These verses perhaps serve two functions. First, they sound the realism that, in the face of Assyria, Jerusalem was indeed brought very low, very low even in spite of the great promises to David. But second, these verses likely create a context for the Davidic oracle of 11:1–9. There will be a shoot from the stump. But first, it is the axe that produces the stump. Judah always lives at the extremities of danger and gift. The rhetoric of verses 33–34 voices such an extremity, poised now for the counterextremity that is about to follow.

This long poetic unit is demanding, both because the historical references are elusive and because the rhetoric continually surprises with its disjunctions. It is important, in any case, not to be lost in the detail. What counts finally is Yahweh's claimed authority, even over the superpower to the great benefit of Judah. Readers in the United States might grasp the full weight of the text if we hear the text more poignantly in our role as part of the Assyrian superpower that we are, rather than the little, vexed remnant community. Of course, Jews and Christians in the United States are some of both. We are invited to the agility of more than one reading, for we are addressed in our brutal practice of domination *and* in our needful exile.

BEGINNING YET AGAIN
11:1–16

The conclusion of chapter 10 leaves the listener gasping (vv. 33–34). The axe chops, and the lofty are brought low. The subject of 10:27b–34 is Jerusalem. The poet once more anticipates the devastation of the Holy City. I begin our consideration of chapter 11 against the backdrop of 10:33–34, because such a backdrop of fallenness is characteristic of Isaiah. Things will come to a sorry state of judgment. But then follows chapter 11, with its inexplicable announcement that Yahweh will work a newness out beyond the dismal state of 10:33–34! The tradition of Isaiah never ceases to be astonished at the newness and never fails to summon God's people to hope and expectation in the face of discouraging circumstance.

A Shoot of Newness (11:1–9)

11:1 **A shoot shall come out from the stump of Jesse,**
       and a branch shall grow out of his roots.
  2 **The spirit of the LORD shall rest on him,**
     the spirit of wisdom and understanding,
     the spirit of counsel and might,
     the spirit of knowledge and the fear of the LORD.
  3 **His delight shall be in the fear of the LORD.**

   He shall not judge by what his eyes see,
     or decide by what his ears hear;
  4 **but with righteousness he shall judge the poor,**
     and decide with equity for the meek of the earth;
   he shall strike the earth with the rod of his mouth,
     and with the breath of his lips he shall kill the wicked.
  5 **Righteousness shall be the belt around his waist,**
     and faithfulness the belt around his loins.

6 **The wolf shall live with the lamb,**
    the leopard shall lie down with the kid,
  the calf and the lion and the fatling together,
    and a little child shall lead them.
7 **The cow and the bear shall graze,**
    their young shall lie down together;
    and the lion shall eat straw like the ox.
8 **The nursing child shall play over the hole of the asp,**
    and the weaned child shall put its hand on the adder's den.
9 **They will not hurt or destroy on all my holy mountain;**
  for the earth will be full of the knowledge of the LORD
    as the waters cover the sea.

This familiar and eloquent passage of promise begins with a stump, a terminated plant from which nothing can grow. (See 6:13 for "stump" used
with a different Hebrew word.) The context is a deep failure of the Davidic dynasty, the one that had carried the hopes of Judah. The deep failure assumed here could be in a crisis of Ahaz or Hezekiah, or it could
possibly refer to the exile of the sixth century. We are not told. Either way,
Judah's Davidic hopes are spent.

And now, in the face of that spent hope, the poet asserts a new generativity with a sprout, unnamed and unidentified, but a faint sign of life,
growth, and possibility. The promissory oracle thus articulates the coming of a new royal figure in time to come who will positively enact all that
is best in royal power, all that the Davidic kings heretofore had failed to
accomplish. The explanation offered for this inexplicable coming reality is
"the spirit of the Lord" (v. 2). We are here not to think in later trinitarian
categories of the church, but rather with appeal back to the coming of Yahweh's generative, irresistible, authorizing "wind" upon David as it was
given and then withdrawn from Saul (see 1 Sam. 11:6; 16:13, 14, 16). The
"spirit of Yahweh" is a force that enlivens, gives power, energy, and
courage, so that its bearer is recognized as one designated, who has the capacity to do what the world believes is impossible. There is no doubt that
the Davidic house claimed to be the habitat of Yahweh's transcendent
power. More practically, we are able even in our own time to identify in
public life those whom "the force" attends. The "spirit" is a self-starter
who generates new historical possibility where none was available. And
when "the force of Yahweh" surges upon this "sprout" wrought from "the
stump," Judah will have in its midst an agent of new possibility who counters all its despair.

The primal gift given to the new king by the spirit is a capacity for wise

discernment, in order to enact the very realities betokened by the royal titles of 9:6. There will be the "wonderful counselor," "prince of peace," the
one who by judiciousness will create a fully functioning social apparatus.
The coming one is marked by "the fear of the Lord," that is, the kind of
piety that makes one's life fully congruent and resonant with the intention
of Yahweh. Clearly, the coming king is in deep contrast to all those Davidic figures of the past who failed in all of these regards.

The primary function of the coming king is *judicial* (vv. 3b–5). It is the
work of the king as judge to sort out conflicting interests and claims, to settle social disputes, to make it possible for every subject to be assured of
security and well-being. Indeed, Solomon had already prayed, so it is reported, for "an understanding mind to govern your people, able to discern
between good and evil" (1 Kings 3:9). And David before him had been cun-
ningly commended as "like the angel of God, discerning good and evil" (2
Sam. 14:17). The tradition of Isaiah, moreover, had itself seen that the failure to discriminate and identify good and evil will lead to rapaciousness
(5:20) and eventually death (10:1–3).

The king is to practice righteousness and equity that are not based on
surface appearances or on what is said, because a discerning ruler is not to
be influenced by gestures of the wealthy or swayed by the manipulations
of the powerful. The poetry here taps into a deep and primal conviction,
known throughout the ancient Near East generally and in Israel, that the
royal government is *The Equalizer*, to intervene in behalf of the poor and
the vulnerable (widows and orphans) who are unable to supply their own
social leverage. Similarly, the crucial programmatic royal statement of
Psalm 72:1–2, 4 holds this responsibility for the monarch:

> Give the king your justice, O God,
>   and your righteousness to a king's son.
> May he judge your people with righteousness,
>   and your poor with justice. . . .
> May he defend the cause of the poor of the people,
>   give deliverance to the needy,
>   and crush the oppressor.

King Josiah, moreover, is celebrated for such an exercise of kingship (Jer.
22:15–16), and the Jeremiah tradition offers this mandate for the coming
king:

> Act with justice and righteousness, and deliver from the hand of the op-
> pressor anyone who has been robbed. And do no wrong or violence to the

alien, the orphan, and the widow, or shed innocent blood in this place. . . .
The days are surely coming, says the LORD, when I will raise up for David
a righteous Branch, and he shall reign as king and deal wisely, and shall execute justice and righteousness in the land (Jer. 22:3; 23:5).

Conversely, the Ezekiel tradition faults the monarchy precisely for its failure in this regard, a failure that leads to exile (Ezek. 34:2–6).

It is impossible to overstate the cruciality of this vision of justice for the
coming ideal king, the importance of which is evident in a society like ours,
wherein governmental power is largely in the hands of the wealthy and
powerful and is operated almost exclusively to their own advantage and
benefit. Such an arrangement of public power is a complete contradiction
of the biblical vision of government.

The public responsibility of the king for justice and righteousness exercised in fidelity requires that the royal government should have at its disposal leverage for sanctions, penalties, and punishments for those who
violate the vision. The positive power to create social good requires the capacity for curbing "the wicked." Thus the king has the capacity to "smite"
and to "slay" the wicked, who are here seen to be those who prey upon, exploit, and abuse the meek, vulnerable, and poor.

This "theory of government," articulated in lyrical fashion, is pivotal for
discerning Israel's prophetic notion of what is possible. First, it reminds us
that for all of royal Israel's accommodationism and opportunism, it still kept
alive a sense of its distinctiveness as a community committed to justice in
public affairs, justice for the weak and vulnerable. Second, insofar as this text,
with its clear messianic flavor, can be drawn upon as an illumination of Jesus,
it is a reminder that Jesus cannot be reduced to privatistic salvation or to
sacramental operations, but that Jesus was received, celebrated, and eventually crucified precisely for his embodiment and practice of this vision of social possibility. Third, any derivative theory or practice of public power that
claims to be "biblical" must attend to issues of economic justice for the vulnerable. This "theory of government" is not primarily concerned to create
free space for "the working of the market" in the hands of the powerful or
for the policing of personal morality, but for the maintenance of economic
viability for all members of society. It is clear that this "spirit" is in the business of making systemic reparations for the poor and the marginalized. Indeed, the clothing of the coming king, that is, his visible political platform,
has slogans written all over it: righteousness, justice (v. 5).

At verse 6, the poet makes a vast leap into a new field of imagery, now
anticipating a transformed creation, with a deep revision of animal-human

relationships (vv. 6–8). The imagery of "lion-lamb" is familiar to us, but we have yet to grasp its importance for human policy and conduct. The poet imagines a coming time, under good governance, when all relationships of hostility and threat, in the animal world as in the human environment, shall be overcome. There will be conciliation and peaceableness among these species that have been at war with each other since the beginning of time. This lyrical statement is one of the most remarkable assertions in the Bible that there will be "all things new" in creation when God fully authorizes the right human agents.

The phrasing is so overwhelming that a commentator (at least this one) is at a loss to know how to interpret adequately its majestic scenario. Let me suggest the following:

(1) It is important that this vision of new creation in verses 6–8 is linked to verses 1–5, even though it is not evident how they are related. I suggest that the new scenario for "nature" is made possible by the reordering of human relationships in verses 1–5. *The distortion of human relationships* is at the root of all *distortions in creation.* So in the narrative of Genesis 3, surely a backdrop for this lyrical vision, it is a *human* violation of God's order that produces the enemies of *nature.* In our own time, put more practically, human avarice and greed, implemented with limitless and shameless technology, now drive the animal kingdom to bizarre forms of devouring and destruction. Peaceableness in the created order requires, first, the enactment in the human community of a conciliation that is fundamentally economic. We have yet to relearn what the Bible knew—that adversarial human transactions foul the nest for all creatures.

(2) My mention of Genesis 3 suggests that the Davidic king is imaginatively linked to the "First Earthling" (Adam) in Genesis 1—3. Surely the coming king is not to be understood simply as a functionary of the Jerusalem establishment. In an appeal to larger biblical imagery, the Davidic king to come is a cosmic player. Thus David is in some sense the "Adam" of Genesis 1, given dominion over the earth and all its creatures; of Genesis 2, summoned to "till and keep" the earth; of Genesis 3 as the agent of primal disorder. It is the Davidic king in Psalm 8:6–8, of whom it is affirmed:

> You have given them dominion over the works of your hands;
>   you have put all things under their feet,
> all sheep and oxen,
>   and also the beasts of the field,
> the birds of the air, and the fish of the sea,
>   whatever passes along the paths of the seas.

By extrapolation, the rulers of the nations (and of the transnational corporations who are the real rulers) are cast in the role of the ones with dominion and responsibility, who with their great military chutzpah and their almost limitless technological capacity are summoned to have dominion. Their proper work is to "till and keep" the earth, to turn it from life to death, and to make it possible for the earth to function fruitfully. Human power matters to the health of the earth.

(3) Given all that we know about the animal kingdom—all that we know of aggression from Konrad Lorenz, Annie Dillard, and all the rest—it is clear that aggression and domination belong to the animal world, and it was ever thus. Therefore this poetic scenario is unreal. However, this poem is about the impossible possibility of the new creation! The coming king will not only do what the world takes to be possible, but will also do what the world has long since declared to be impossible. If there is a coming time when "death will be no more" (Rev. 21:4), then it is entertainable that devouring competition and the old practice of the big ones eating the little ones is not the wave of the future. Everything depends upon a ruler whose slogan is "righteousness," a ruler whose rule will permit children to play at the snake's hole. And that does not even mention the huge deposits of nuclear waste that turn up in the neighborhoods of the poor. The rightly governed world will indeed be detoxified, no more a threat to the poor, the meek, the children, the lamb, the kid. The new world will indeed be safe for the vulnerable.

As the poem moves to a larger sphere in verses 6–8 after the political dimension in verses 1–5, so in verse 9 the rhetoric moves to a yet larger scope, now the whole of creation. "My holy mountain," that is, Zion, will be a place of harmony and peaceableness where "the prince of peace" will rule. But the well-being of Jerusalem is only emblematic. The real gain is that the earth—the whole earth, all of creation—will be full of the knowledge of Yahweh, the same knowledge given by the spirit in verse 2. John Calvin comments: "If this fullness of knowledge takes possession of our minds, it will free us from all malice" (*Isaiah* I, 387).

The poem is about deep, radical, limitless transformation in which we—like lion, wolf, and leopard—will have no hunger for injury, no need to devour, no yearning for brutal control, no passion for domination. This radical renovation is anticipated by Paul in Romans 8:19–23. Moreover, one of Paul's disciples dares to voice the human dimension of this renovation:

> But now you must get rid of all such things—anger, wrath, malice, slander, and abusive language from your mouth. Do not lie to one another, seeing that you have stripped off the old self with its practices and have clothed

yourselves with the new self, which is being renewed in knowledge accord-
ing to the image of its creator. In that renewal there is no longer Greek and
Jew, circumcised and uncircumcised, barbarian, Scythian, slave and free; but
Christ is all and in all (Col. 3:8–11).

The transformation is vastly public and intimately personal. It is a gift and
then a vocation. It is of course not possible—except that the sprout comes
from the stump by the spirit!

The Shoot Now International (11:10–11)

11:10 **On that day the root of Jesse shall stand as a signal to the peoples; the
nations shall inquire of him, and his dwelling shall be glorious.**
   ¹¹ **On that day the Lord will extend his hand yet a second time to recover
the remnant that is left of his people, from Assyria, from Egypt, from Pathros,
from Ethiopia, from Elam, from Shinar, from Hamath, and from the coastlands of the sea.**

These two verses are likely an addition to the lyrical poem of verses 1–9,
which reaches its unmistakable climax in verse 9. The new element in verse
10 is that the newness is for *the peoples, the nations* (plural). Such a scope for
the new rule might be implied in verses 6–9, but it is not articulated. The
tradition of Isaiah, after the fashion of 2:1–4, imagines Jerusalem as the initiating point of newness for the entire international community. Only
here, in contrast to 2:1–4, it is not Zion and Torah, but it is "the root of
Jesse" that will be the guiding flag and summoning symbol (i.e., the way of
well-being) for all nations. Thus in this one verse the vision goes public
beyond Jewishness.

The openness to an international scope is continued in verse 11, but
with a different accent. Whereas verse 10 seems to extend the presence of
Yahweh to *the nations*, verse 11 is concerned with *the Jews who are scattered
everywhere in exile.* "A second time" refers to Yahweh's gathering activity
after "a first time," which was a scattering enterprise. The scattered exiles
are assured of a homecoming, so that the "remnant" now concerns a large
company of Jews now given a powerful, positive assurance.

It is evident that this entire unit of verses 1–10 concerns a king at the edge
of the horizon of the eighth century. The prophetic tradition stayed close to
its own time, place, and circumstance. The poem is not a prediction of Jesus,
nor even an anticipation of one so remote. Nonetheless, the church has long
found this text illuminating of Jesus, for in the imagination of the church it
is Jesus who embodies and enacts what is promised here. Such a rereading of

the text is legitimate and proper, for these great texts evoke and permit many rereadings. That is not the same, however, as treating it as a "prediction," but it is a responsible way of interpretation that establishes linkage between Jewish expectation and the powerful, compelling reality of Jesus. We have seen that the text moves from public history (vv. 1–5) to creation (vv. 6–9) in its anticipation. It is worth noting that in the pondering of the church, there is a similar tendency to move, in characterizing Jesus, from public history (the Synoptic gospel) to a cosmic Christ (the Johannine testimony). In the pattern of the Pauline trajectory of New Testament faith (which has largely dominated the imagination of Protestantism), there is a move from the "the human predicament" (Romans, Galatians) to cosmic reordering (Ephesians, Colossians). Thus the sequence of topics in this text is not without our own late, Christian appropriation.

The Great Ingathering (11:12–16)

11:12 **He will raise a signal for the nations,**
> **and will assemble the outcasts of Israel,**
> **and gather the dispersed of Judah**
>> **from the four corners of the earth.**
> [13] **The jealousy of Ephraim shall depart,**
>> **the hostility of Judah shall be cut off;**
> **Ephraim shall not be jealous of Judah,**
>> **and Judah shall not be hostile towards Ephraim.**
> [14] **But they shall swoop down on the backs of the Philistines in the west,**
>> **together they shall plunder the people of the east.**
> **They shall put forth their hand against Edom and Moab,**
>> **and the Ammonites shall obey them.**
> [15] **And the LORD will utterly destroy**
>> **the tongue of the sea of Egypt;**
> **and will wave his hand over the River**
>> **with his scorching wind;**
> **and will split it into seven channels,**
>> **and make a way to cross on foot;**
> [16] **so there shall be a highway from Assyria**
>> **for the remnant that is left of his people,**
> **as there was for Israel**
>> **when they came up from the land of Egypt.**

I have suggested that "the shoot from the stump" may perhaps refer to hope for the monarchy after its termination in the Exile. That is a possible but not necessary reading of verse 1. There is no doubt, in any case, that verses 12–16 contain a promise made precisely to exiles, for the book of Isaiah, in its belated formation, is preoccupied with the future of the exiles.

The subject of verse 12, "he," is the shoot of Jesse. It is this coming, anticipated king whose last work is the ingathering of the exiles from across the world. The wording of verse 12 picks up the reference of verse 10 to "signal." I imagine this to be like the umbrella that European tour guides hold high for members of the tour group to see and to follow. "He" will provide a means of assembling and gathering all the exiles in a great homecoming. The ultimate hope of Isaianic Judaism is a joyous homecoming of homeless, displaced, despairing Jews who, by the vagaries of history and by imperial policies of deportation, have been scattered to the winds.

Upon return home, the now ensconced exiles may quarrel (v. 13). Indeed, the verse likely reflects the bitter quarrels of Judeans and Samaritans (Ephraim) in the postexilic period concerning who should exercise domination in the community of Jews. But, it is promised, such quarreling will stop. The "prince of peace," who can stop the hostility of wolves and kids and lions and lambs, can surely stop the internecine wars of Israel (cf. 9:20–21). It is appalling, but characteristic, that family feuds in religious communities are the most brutal and uncaring. But it will not be so, because the one propelled by God's spirit will blanket the earth with God's assurances and so with well-being.

Verse 14 makes clear that it is *internal* reconciliation in the community that counts, that is, reconciliation of north and south, Judah and Samaria. For in this verse, the returned exiles are permitted some violent triumphalism over non-Jewish neighbors with whom there are old scores to settle. Clearly, "the prince of peace," who means to gather all nations and all peoples, is not yet finished (v. 10). Amidst the large hopes of Judaism, there are yet notes of realism about old feuds unended and old hates unrequited. This verse is perhaps an acknowledgment that human fratricide is a more intransigent reality than even that of lion and lamb in the animal world. The promise made here is not romantic!

As quickly as possible, so it seems to me, the poet moves past that unhappy note of realism to a final great articulation of harmony (vv. 15–16). Now it is Yahweh (and not the son of Jesse) who will do the liberating work. Yahweh will make passage out of Egypt possible (v. 15). Yahweh will make passage from Assyria possible (v. 16). Surprisingly, the verse concerning safe passage home alludes to the Exodus. This will be a great liberation, and all of God's people will come home. The book of Isaiah will have more to say of this expectation. What is clear is that the newness of

God is here so massive and so concrete that all the circumstances of despair are overcome.

We are invited to ponder a poetic scenario that is designed to foster hope precisely in a world that appears to be completely shut down.

1. This text cannot be drawn too close to Jesus. Yet in Christian imagination it is clear that it is Jesus who came to the lost house of Israel, who ministered to the lost, and who portrayed the shepherd seeking the lost sheep (Luke 15:3–76), surely a story that in some way refers to the scattered of Israel.

2. Beyond the particular Jewish reference to lost exiles, a theme that invites the state of Israel to be seen as a great "ingathering," and beyond the specific New Testament rhetoric about Jesus, it is crucial to recognize that ours is a world with a huge company of exiles, of homeless and displaced persons. These exiles are not simply accidents or "the less fortunate." They are the sure and inescapable outcomes of military and economic policies of the superpowers (and of lesser imitating powers) who aim at a monopoly of wealth and power. We live in a world that is vigorously and relentlessly exile producing. In the face of that shameless reality of public life, there stands (only?) this poem and the assurance "a remnant shall return." The tradition of Isaiah is sure of God's intention to *gather*. To be sure, the horizon concerns the scattered Jews, but the "signal" is raised for all peoples and all nations. It is asserted that the powers of the empire cannot retain as bondaged property the exiles that the "shoot" wants free.

3. This text is indeed a recipe for the impossible. Like every poet, this one has the freedom (and obligation?) to say what cannot be explained. Thus:

- It is impossible to imagine a government genuinely committed to justice for the poor and righteousness for the meek.
- It is impossible that there will be a reconciliation of the animal world.
- It is impossible that "they will not hurt or destroy."
- It is impossible that there will be a homecoming of the wounded and despairing.

All of this is impossible, because the status quo is too recalcitrant and the managers of the status quo too much enjoy advantage commensurate with leverage. It is all impossible—and so we are resigned to the possible, which entails endless injustice, relentless hostility, pervasive displacement, all adding up to despair. We are resigned to the possible as the *world* defines the possible, except for this text and others like it. Those who make a difference, who refuse the closing down of creation in brutality, cling to the poem. That is how the poem has become canon—by people clinging to it. We still cling to it; moreover, we cling to it when we hear it, almost without thinking, daring to answer, "The Word of the Lord . . . thanks be to God."

4. The text that moves from the familiar in verses 1–5 to the exotic in verses 6–9 culminates in the unfamiliarity of homecoming in verses 12–16. The text, I have insisted, cannot be drawn too close to Jesus. It is nonetheless worth noticing that the cadences of homecoming echo in Christian liturgy. And so, mindful of our exile-producing world, the church engages in countercultural subversion when it hears the promise: "Then people will come from east and west, from north and south, and will eat in the kingdom of God. Indeed, some are last who will be first, and some are first who will be last" (Luke 13:29–30). The Eucharist, to be sure, is provisional. It is, at a minimum, a way to continue to host the impossible promise entrusted to the inexplicable "shoot."

PRAISE AND THANKS BEYOND WRATH
12:1–6

12:1 **You will say in that day:**
 I will give thanks to you, O LORD,
  for though you were angry with me,
 your anger turned away,
  and you comforted me.

 [2] **Surely God is my salvation;**
  I will trust, and will not be afraid,
 for the LORD God is my strength and my might;
  he has become my salvation.

 [3] **With joy you will draw water from the wells of salvation.** [4] **And you**
  will say in that day:
 Give thanks to the LORD,
  call on his name;
 make known his deeds among the nations;
  proclaim that his name is exalted.

 [5] **Sing praises to the LORD, for he has done gloriously;**
  let this be known in all the earth.
 [6] **Shout aloud and sing for joy, O royal Zion,**
  for great in your midst is the Holy One of Israel.

The first editorial unit of the book of Isaiah comes to a conclusion with this hymnic affirmation. Although this hymnic unit echoes some accents of chapters 1—11, it is essentially a hymn of the sort found in the book of Psalms. Most likely the editors of the book of Isaiah have taken already extant materials and placed them here in order to give positive closure to this large unit of text.

The doxology may be divided into two parts, marked by the double introduction of verses 1, 4, "in that day." The first hymnic unit is verses 1–3, governed by the phrase "in that day." This doxology is introduced by an instruction to someone (singular), perhaps Israel, perhaps a "messenger," to be ready to praise "in that day" (v. 1). This latter formula is characteristic in prophetic rhetoric for a promise from God that is sure but not yet in hand. The doxology is an act of confident hope that things in time to come (we know not when) will be happily resolved. The conclusion of chapters 1—12 is an act of buoyant and determined hope that refuses to give in to debilitating present circumstance.

The doxology is to be one of thanks, of glad acknowledgment of Yahweh's goodness and generosity. In verse 1 we see reflected Isaiah's characteristic two-stage faith, of judgment and hope, of "former time" and "latter time" (cf. 9:1). The former time is a time of wrath, when Yahweh treats Jerusalem harshly. This time of wrath makes sense both to the theological tradition of Israel (because of torah violation) and historically (because of the abuse wrought on the city in the historical-political process). The doxology, however, does not linger over the wrath that is undeniable. The doxology moves past the suffering, in anticipation to be sure, to postwrath time when Yahweh's anger is assuaged, guilt is paid for, and Yahweh is ready to "comfort" Israel (cf. 40:1–2). We should notice that the use of "comfort" here anticipates the more familiar use of the term in 40:1, and that in Isaiah it characteristically refers to homecoming from exile. Thus, in the final form of the book of Isaiah, already in chapter 12 we are invited to look past eighth-century trouble to sixth-century deliverance from exile.

It is commonly recognized that verse 2 echoes in quite literal form Exodus 15:2, which celebrates the Egyptian deliverance. The deliverance here anticipated is, like the Exodus, a second exodus, a theme to become prominent in later Isaiah (see more immediately the allusion of 11:16). The God who was angry is now acknowledged to be Israel's great friend, advocate, ally, support, and only hope. It is this Yahweh who can and will, in great authority and power, completely transpose historical conditions. Although the verse is clearly stylized, we may also notice familiar accents of Isaiah. The second line of the verse nicely contrasts *trust* and *fear*,

precisely the contrast that the prophet put before the king in 7:4–9; 8:12.
The doxology, representative of Israel's most durable faith and in stylized
form, sounds the accents that have informed the prophet.

The conclusion of verse 3 bespeaks unqualified joy at the well-being Yahweh will give in time to come. "Drawing water" may have been an actual ritual, a sacramental act dramatizing the new gifts of Yahweh (Wildberger).
Calvin regards it as a figure of speech, "a very beautiful metaphor":

> [E]verything necessary for supporting life flows to us from the undeserved
> goodness of God. And since we are empty and destitute of everything good,
> he appropriately compares the mercy of God to a *fountain*, which satisfies
> those who are thirsty and dry, refreshes those who are parched with heat,
> and revives those who are worn out with fatigue (*Isaiah* I, 401).

The second part of the chapter begins with a formula parallel to that of
verse 1, only now the addressee is plural—presumably restored Israel gathered in exuberant worship. The summons to praise, characteristically, is in
a series of imperatives. Israel has now received unexpected and unmerited
goodness from Yahweh, and so is under obligation to give public voice to
the miracle of homecomings and restoration. Thus Israel restored is called
to give thanks, call upon the name, make known, praise, shout, sing for joy.
Israel cannot now restrain itself, for the unexpected, undeserved, inexplicable has happened. It is the sort of thing about which one cannot keep
quiet. The *news* must be shared!

What has happened are Yahweh's "deeds" (v. 4), what he has "done gloriously" (v. 5). It is conventional in Israel's doxology that the deeds mentioned lack specificity, so that any particular use of the hymn can permit
particular content to be included or inferred. Because this hymnic material
is rooted in an old and deep doxological tradition, reference here is probably made to all the saving transformations in the life of Israel, going back
to the Exodus. But because the hymn now is situated where it is, the deeds
likely refer to the Isaianic preoccupation with the rescue of Jerusalem and
the return of the exiles. That particular reference point, so important to the
tradition of Isaiah, in the doxological practice of Israel is only one characteristic example of Israel's ongoing construal of lived reality as a series of
inexplicable, gracious transformations wrought by Yahweh.

In its doxology, Israel's exuberance knows no restraint or limitation.
Thus the witness of praise is to be "among the nations," "in all the earth"
(vv. 4–5). The tradition of Isaiah is open to a horizon larger than Israel,
able to envision a time of recovery for Jerusalem not only as a cherished

Jewish habitat, but also as a rallying point for all nations who join in praise of Yahweh (cf. 2:1–4). Holy presence in Zion is an enormous assurance to the remnant of Judah, but it is equally an invitation to those beyond the remnant of Judah.

Chapters 1—12 have *uttered Jerusalem* to its sorry judgment and have *imagined Israel* in the nadir of its existence, due to its recalcitrance. None of this is here denied. But if these chapters constitute an intentional unit, then it is important that Israel's final word is praise and thanks. That is because Yahweh's final act is *not wrath but comfort*. Yahweh does indeed do harsh work. In the end, however, Yahweh will do otherwise. Yahweh will give an abundant life. Of this Israel must sing. To this, all the others are invited as well.

2. Yahweh's Rule in World Perspective
Isaiah 13—23

Although chapters 1—12, the primary texts related to the historical figure of the prophet Isaiah, have been concerned with the destiny of Judah and Jerusalem, it is evident that the larger horizon of this prophetic tradition is international in scope. This is especially evident in the recurring attention already given to Assyria, the defining superpower of Isaiah's eighth century. The prophetic tradition knew well that the future of Judah and Jerusalem could not be understood apart from larger geopolitical realities. It also asserted, moreover, that both the future of Judah and Jerusalem as well as the future of the other nation-states with which Judah is variously ally, co-conspirator, trading partner, and adversary are commonly under the decisive rule of Yahweh.

This latter theme of Yahweh's governance of the international process is the central theme of chapters 13—23. It is asserted therein that Yahweh is the sovereign governor of every nation-state. For the most part, this sovereign purpose portends punishment, suffering, and nullification for the several nation-states that are characteristically seen as opposed to the rule of Yahweh. The nature of that opposition is not often spelled out but comes under the general rubric of autonomy, self-sufficiency, and hubris. This collection of oracles variously considers Babylon as the leading superpower on the horizon of the book of Isaiah (13:1–14:23), Assyria as the older and representative superpower (14:24–27), Philistia (14:28–32), Moab (15:1–16:14), Damascus (17:1–3), Ethiopia (18:1–7), Egypt (19:1–25), Babylon yet again (21:1–10), Dumah (21:11–12), "the desert places" (21:13–15), Kedar (21:16–17), and Tyre (23:1–18). Characteristically, the oracles announce judgment against these nation-states, often vigorously portraying an assault and consequent suffering, and summoning the people to wailing, lament, and grief for the suffering consequent upon Yahweh's judgment. The primary theme of these chapters is the nonnegotiable, demanding, insistent rule of Yahweh before which every power must submit.

Often implied and occasionally asserted is the claim that Yahweh has a "plan" that overrides the intentions and policies of these several nation-states (e.g., 23:8–9). Yahweh's "plan" is not a large, fixed blueprint of world history. Rather, it is an *ad hoc* intention as a particular utterance, designed to resist and counter the "plan" of autonomy by the nation-states. Thus the rhetoric of "plan" is a device to speak of a *countergovernance* of the world that the would-be autonomous states do not acknowledge but cannot resist.

There is no doubt that these oracles arise in particular sociopolitical-military contexts. It is evident that such contexts were important in shaping the oracles, but the recovery of such contexts is often notoriously problematic, enigmatic, and obscure. (For one excellent discussion of these issues, see Norman K. Gottwald, *All the Kingdoms of the Earth: Israelite Prophecy and International Relations in the Ancient Near East.*) Without doubting such contextualization, it is equally evident that the literary-theological intent of the oracles no longer pertains to these original contexts, for such a historical context as an interpretive horizon would promptly render the oracles irrelevant to the reader. It is evident that in the canonical shaping of the book of Isaiah, these oracles now function *in the book of Isaiah* in order to advance the general theme of Yahweh's sovereignty. Because our interpretive interest is in the canonical intention of the oracles, I have paid little attention to original historical contexts, about which scholars are in any case most often unsure and in disagreement.

The dominant theological theme of these oracles, to which the following discussion gives primary attention, is the nullification of autonomous states at the behest of Yahweh's sovereignty. Within that general theme, we may notice two related and subordinate themes. First, there is no doubt that the sovereign nullification of these nation-states has as a practical and inescapable by-product the emancipation and well-being of Judah. Indeed, it may be that Yahweh's concern for Judah is a driving force for Yahweh's action against the other states. Thus the fall of Babylon permits the prospering of "Jacob" in its own land (14:1–2). The soon-to-be reestablished Davidic monarchy assures the reemergence of steadfast love, faithfulness, and justice in time to come (16:1–5). The beautiful people of Ethiopia will bring gifts to Zion (18:7–8). Israel will be a partner in a new geopolitical arrangement for peaceableness (19:24–25). The recovery of Tyre will bring extravagant gifts to the people of Yahweh (23:18).

Having said that, it is remarkable that even in this general assault upon foreign nations, Israel is also threatened with judgment. Israel will be brought low like Damascus for its disregard of Yahweh (17:4–14). Judah and Jerusalem will be exposed and vulnerable for "looking" in the wrong place for protection (22:1–14). In these oracles, exceptional as they are, Israel/Judah is treated alongside other nations, without privilege, and is in the same way threatened for the same unresponsiveness to Yahweh.

Second, there is no doubt that these oracles are to some extent open-ended. That is, they keep receiving ongoing interpretation in the form of additions and supplements. Characteristically, these extended interpretations move in an apocalyptic direction. I would note two of the most remarkable cases of this. In 19:1–15, Egypt is given rather predictable condemnation. But then, in a series of brief prose additions, this text anticipates the restoration of Egypt, both as a recipient of Yahweh's Exodus attentiveness (19:19–22) and as a full member of Yahweh's reconstituted beloved people (19:24–25). In 23:1–14, Tyre is roundly condemned and headed for disaster. In verses 17–18, however, the recovery of Tyre's remarkable economy is anticipated, which now includes a completely new, willing orientation to Yahweh.

What strikes me about these oracles is their remarkable variety and density and interpretive potential. It is correct to group the oracles under a general rubric of "Oracles Against the Nations," as commentators regularly and legitimately do. Having done that, however, in hearing the text we must not be excessively dominated by the general theme but must pay close attention to the detail, in which there is rich and unpredictable variation. Much of this variation and supplementation can of course be explained through historical-critical work. Beyond that, however, the interpreter notes *how seriously historical reality is taken* and *how freely and enigmatically Yahweh's governance is uttered and enacted.*

Finally, as a complete and inexplicable surprise in this section is the narrative of 22:15–25. The narrative purports to be a "local" account of an administrative crisis and the resolution of a personnel problem. As my commentary makes clear, however, the narrative is now shaped canonically to assert the pivotal themes of Judah's coming *disgrace* (v. 18) and in sequence Judah's assured, coming *throne of honor* (v. 23). Even in such an apparently mundane account as this, the book of Isaiah remains focused on the two-stage vision of *inescapable punishment* and *buoyant assurance.*

A DAY OF HARSH SOVEREIGNTY
13:1–22

This long series of "Oracles against the Nations" asserts Yahweh's coming sovereignty over many nations, states who were geopolitical threats to

Judah. It is no doubt crucial that among these threats the first to be singled out is Babylon, the dominant superpower in the sixth century and surely the pivotal feature in the geopolitical landscape of the book of Isaiah. John Calvin comments:

> When various changes are taking place, some think that God sports with the affairs of men, and others, that everything is directed by the blind violence of fortune. . . . [V]ery few are aware that these things are appointed and regulated by the purpose of God. There is nothing of which it is more difficult to convince men than that the providence of God governs the world . . . [that] all might understand that those calamities did not take place but by the secret and wonderful purpose of God. (*Isaiah* I, 406–407)

A Claim of Credibility (13:1)

13:1 **The oracle concerning Babylon that Isaiah son of Amoz saw.**

The extended utterance of chapter 13 is introduced in a way that purports to identify its author. This superscription, parallel to those of 1:1 and 2:1, credits the oracle to the eighth-century prophet. Scholars, however, are divided on whether this oracle is in fact from the eighth century, for it may reflect a later venue. If it is from the eighth century, then Babylon here may be, as Calvin suggests, a figure for Assyria. At a minimum, the final form of the text intends to give canonical linkage to the prophet and therefore legitimacy to the utterance. Second, it is an "oracle seen." (The same mix of "seen" and "spoken" is evident in Amos 1:1.) The visual aspect may suggest that the prophetic is here tilted toward the apocalyptic, a later propensity toward *visions* of disaster. The accent on the visionary, characteristically a later propensity, would seem to question a dating to the eighth century, so that the data given here are ambiguous. The verse clearly intends to situate the oracle in the orbit of the "prophet of record."

Mobilization for the Onslaught (13:2–5)

13:2 **On a bare hill raise a signal,**
    cry aloud to them;
  wave the hand for them to enter
    the gates of the nobles.
  3 **I myself have commanded my consecrated ones,**
    have summoned my warriors, my proudly exulting ones,
    to execute my anger.

⁴ Listen, a tumult on the mountains
     as of a great multitude!
  Listen, an uproar of kingdoms,
     of nations gathering together!
  The LORD of hosts is mustering
     an army for battle.
⁵ They come from a distant land,
     from the end of the heavens,
  the LORD and the weapons of his indignation,
     to destroy the whole earth.

In vivid imagery, the poem offers a picture of a great invasive army march-
ing against established power. These verses provide a scene wherein
armies are mobilized, a great throng of warriors is mustered, and the
march begins. One can imagine a noisy, boisterous, buoyant band of warriors now getting the march under way. In verses 2–3, we do not know who
speaks. It is only "I myself" who is the commander. It is this commander
who issues an order: "raise a signal." That is, give the signal so that the
armies are prepared to move. The command is a quite personal one; he orders "my consecrated ones," "my warriors," "my exulting ones," to act out
"my anger." The military force is immense and irresistible, and it is now
to move against "the gates of the nobles," that is, against powerful, established power. This is not a declaration of war; that has already been done.
We are now witnessing the initial move of the actual assault.

   What strikes one, for all the vivid imagery, is how little we are told. We
do not know who commands. We do not know who constitutes the army.
We are ignorant of the enemy or the provocation. All this is left unsaid because the poem aims at our emotions. We are invited to sense that a proud,
stable world is now placed in acute jeopardy.

   In verses 4–5, the noise of many troops is continued. Listen! You can
hear them. The words translate into neighing horses, cursing soldiers, and
clattering armor. The troops are massive. And now—it can be held off no
longer—we learn the name of the commander. It is "Yahweh of Hosts,"
the lord of the troops, the same terrifying God the prophet has already encountered in 6:5. The God of this poetry operates under military imagery!

   The armies of Yahweh, massive and formidable, are recruited from
everywhere. All nations muster at his behest. This operation is as big as the
Normandy landing! The imagery is cosmic: "end of the heavens." And the
goal is a match—to destroy "the whole earth." The phrases are nicely com-
plementary: "of the heavens" = sources of the troops; "destroy the whole

earth" = object of Yahweh's fury. We know nothing yet of the cause of conflict. What we do know is that the "nobles" assaulted are surely vulnerable and unable to resist this coming army of Yahweh, which has unlimited resources and manpower. We watch and wait while "Yahweh of troops" asserts control over earth as in heaven.

The Day Producing Agony and Anguish (13:6–8)

13:6 Wail, for the day of the LORD is near;
    it will come like destruction from the Almighty!
  7 Therefore all hands will be feeble,
    and every human heart will melt,
    8 and they will be dismayed.
Pangs and agony will seize them;
    they will be in anguish like a woman in labor.
They will look aghast at one another;
    their faces will be aflame.

The theme of Yahweh's coming onslaught of established power is continued. Only now the imperative is escalated from "listen" (v. 4) to "wail," that is, howl in anguish. The poem appeals to the ominous "day of the Lord" (cf. Isa. 9:4 on "the day of Midian"), presumably a military occasion when the irresistible force of Yahweh's resolve takes the form of destructive, threatening invasion (cf. Amos 5:18; Zeph. 1:14–16). The established powers are not stable or strong enough to be safe from the onslaught of Yahweh. The political-historical process is not managed well enough to be protected from Yahweh's ultimate sovereignty. The coming of Yahweh is identified by appeal to an old name for Yahweh bespeaking awesome, primordial power, "Almighty" (*shaddai*; v. 6).

The poet, however, does not focus upon Yahweh's coming, as in verses 3–5, but upon the consequences for those under assault. These are "the nobles" (v. 2). Characteristically, the poet enacts a great inversion whereby stable, viable public power is reduced to feebleness, fearfulness, dismay, agony, and anguish. The poet sketches out a scenario of frantic hopelessness, powerlessness, and vulnerability, for which "a woman in labor" is taken as a metaphor of needful distress. Nothing is said about how this invasion is implemented. The poet acknowledges no proximate agents; it is directly and consummately Yahweh who will end all that is settled.

"I Will Put an End" (13:9–16)

13:9 See, the day of the LORD comes,
     cruel, with wrath and fierce anger,
   to make the earth a desolation,
     and to destroy its sinners from it.
 10 For the stars of the heavens and their constellations
     will not give their light;
   the sun will be dark at its rising,
     and the moon will not shed its light.
 11 I will punish the world for its evil,
     and the wicked for their inequity;
   I will put an end to the pride of the arrogant,
     and lay low the insolence of tyrants.
 12 I will make mortals more rare than fine gold,
     and humans than the gold of Ophir.
 13 Therefore I will make the heavens tremble,
     and the earth will be shaken out of its place,
   at the wrath of the LORD of hosts
     in the day of his fierce anger.
 14 Like a hunted gazelle,
     or like sheep with no one to gather them,
   all will turn to their own people,
     and all will flee to their own lands.
 15 Whoever is found will be thrust through,
     and whoever is caught will fall by the sword.
 16 Their infants will be dashed to pieces
     before their eyes;
   their houses will be plundered,
     and their wives ravished.

This long section of poetry, portraying Yahweh's invasion and consequent distress, begins with a second reference to "the day of the Lord" (v. 9). It is Yahweh with military ferociousness who now will dominate the landscape, even though the nobles had imagined that their life had been secured against Yahweh's insistent rule. The poet must engage in "limit expressions"—that is, exaggerated, picturesque imagery—in order to communicate "limit experiences" of public life being dismantled by Yahweh's holiness.

We have seen in verse 5 the cosmic dimension of this poem as Yahweh's forces come "from the end of the heavens." Now, in an effort to state the threat in the most severe way imaginable, the poet brings the cosmic dimension of "the day" to sharper focus (v. 10). As Israel could anciently imagine the sun and moon poised in Israel's interest (Josh. 5:20), so now stars, sun, and moon—all creatures of Yahweh—refuse to function in order to permit the darkness of death that Yahweh wills in the earth. The political-military crisis is given cosmic scope because the one who sends the armies is the creator of the heavens and the governor of the earth.

It is Yahweh alone who speaks and acts as a first-person agent (vv. 11–13). The poetry is saturated with "I, I, I"; Yahweh has declared war on evil, the wicked, the pride of the arrogant, the insolence of tyrants. All of this is a raw challenge to Yahweh's rule, and it will not be tolerated. We are already on notice that Yahweh is angry (v. 3). And now the anger is given full play. The God who musters (*pqd*; v. 4) is the God who punishes (*pqd*; v. 11)—the same verb. The term bespeaks Yahweh's forceful, decisive entry into a situation with devastating consequences.

The anger of verse 3 produces the "therefore" of verse 13. Yahweh is offered as an agent of unrestrained, unbridled resolve. Yahweh is offended and will stop at nothing to punish and to destroy those who refuse to submit. There is nothing here of love, of reason, of corrective, redemptive punishment. What the poet gives on behalf of Yahweh is raw, boundless rage. In order to voice the rage, moreover, the poet must push beyond conventional political analysis to speech that surges beyond history to cosmos. The poet envisions the entire creation—heaven and earth—now under assault, now destabilized, now threatened in its very being, because the "Lord of Hosts" is angry (v. 13).

The decisive verbs in verse 13 are "tremble" and "shake." These are no routine terms. They are words used in Israel's most extreme rhetoric to articulate the shattering of the stable foundations of reality. The scholarly term for such rhetoric is *apocalyptic*, and here the Isaiah tradition moves in a distinctively apocalyptic direction. We must, however, not permit such an interpretive category to slot the terms, as though to explain and domesticate them and fit a scheme. Rather than fit them into an explanatory category, we do better to pay attention to the emotive intention of the poetry, to see the safest, most formidable establishment in the world now assaulted and helpless, because Yahweh will not let such an enterprise endure. The threat from Yahweh is *raw rage*, linked with *righteous indignation*. The trigger is evil and wickedness, rendered only in the most generic terms. Yahweh will not tolerate a mocking, even by the most formidable alternative power on the map!

The poet portrays the devastation as massive. Human persons will be scarcer than gold (v. 12)—there will be so few left. They will be vulnerable like gazelle and sheep are vulnerable to wild animals—exposed, helpless, mute—running for their lives but to no avail (v. 14). The ones caught will be ruthlessly treated, stabbed, bloodied by the sword. If verse 15 pertains to the soldiers, that is, to the men, then all of their dependents are named in verse 16: babes, wives, houses. This is not conquest in the interest of confiscation. This is simply destructive rage voiced in shameless verbs: dashed, plundered, ravished. The poet is on a roll of the most extreme rhetoric available. Such rhetoric is required to assert how it is when Yahweh is fully mobilized in Yahweh's awe-filled, awful sovereignty. Yahweh's commitment against pride and insolence is not a reasonable, calculated matter. It is Yahweh's "gut reaction," Yahweh's deepest interest completely beyond calculation. One might observe that Yahweh's negative energy is paralleled to that of the insolent and the proud, as though Yahweh beats his enemies at their own game by their own weapons. Such a critique, however, is outside the scope of the poet. Nothing will deter the poet from the extremity of public reality rooted in the extremity of Yahweh.

Finally, the Specificity of Babylon (13:17–22a)

In verses 2–16, one is struck by the lack of specificity. The added superscription of verse 1 links the oracle to Babylon. In the poem itself, however, the threat is generic. It is an outraged, outrageous presentation of Yahweh's massive, brutal rule. But the poem completely lacks concrete reference. Indeed, the references are open and generic enough that they can be applied and reapplied to any "enemy of Yahweh," and we may imagine by extrapolation, any brutalizer of God's people. The focus is only secondarily upon the enemy, for the poem primarily concerns Yahweh's complete power and authority.

13:17   **See, I am stirring up the Medes against them,**
        who have no regard for silver
        and do not delight in gold.
   18 **Their bows will slaughter the young men;**
        they will have no mercy on the fruit of the womb;
        their eyes will not pity children.
   19 **And Babylon, the glory of kingdoms,**
        the splendor and pride of the Chaldeans,
     will be like Sodom and Gomorrah
        when God overthrew them.
   20 **It will never be inhabited**
        or lived in for all generations;

Arabs will not pitch their tents there,
   shepherds will not make their flocks lie down there.
²¹ But wild animals will lie down there,
   and its houses will be full of howling creatures;
there ostriches will live,
   and there goat-demons will dance.
²²ᵃ Hyenas will cry in its towers,
   and jackals in the pleasant palaces;

Only in verses 17–19 do we finally get any specificity with reference to the Medes and the Babylonians-Chaldeans. It is as though these verses now seize upon generic rhetoric and bring it down to an actual crisis. In assessing this specificity, three options are available: (1) The poem from the outset has concerned Babylonia, which would bring the poem into line with the later parts of the book of Isaiah when Babylon was a looming and decisive threat for Judah in the sixth century. (2) The poem originally concerned Assyria, the nemesis of Judah in Isaiah's eighth century, and has been reassigned to serve the later part of the book of Isaiah, so that an older text is redeployed. (3) Babylon is not to be taken too literally but functions as a figure for any and every geopolitical power that runs against the intention of Yahweh. Whatever may have been the historical locus and interest of the poem in its primary utterance, there is no doubt that the poem in its canonical place can function in this latter way, as a model concerning every challenge to the power of Yahweh. Thus again we attend to the historical realism of the book of Isaiah but then accept a rereading as a legitimate reading of a canonical text.

The focus of the poem as it now stands—reading from verse 19 and informed by verse 1—is the harsh, abrupt, irresistible inversion of mighty Babylon (cf. Isa. 47:1–4). Babylon was indeed a "wonder of the world," advanced in every way—artistically, culturally, scientifically. Now that great city-empire is reduced to a state like Sodom and Gomorrah, primary emblems of complete devastation. The Isaiah tradition has already applied this devastating figure to Judah (1:9–10). But here it is used for arrogant Babylon, now to be completely devastated and left helpless, without resource or possibility.

The agents of this devastation are "the Medes" (v. 17). This is the first time in the poem that a proximate historical agent is named. "The Medes" are a sixth-century state that arose to threaten the domination of Babylon. Not much is known about them, and in the context of the Isaiah tradition we may take "Medes" to be a reference to the better known, more easily identified Persians, with their leader Cyrus. Indeed, in Isaiah 41:25

and 45:1, 13 Cyrus is said to be "stirred up" (using the same verb) as are the Medes here. Thus the poem identifies the historical force that will terminate Babylonian power. Even though it is the Medes (or Persians, or Cyrus), that historical agent is "stirred up" by Yahweh, who sets in motion the historical operation that terminates Babylon. Babylon will now receive its just due. As Babylon showed "no mercy" (v. 18; cf. Isa. 47:6; Jer. 50:42), so it will receive no mercy. History is the march of harshness against the harsh, and there will be no resistance. Yahweh is the one who is the impetus for the rise and fall of the great powers. And now Babylon is in free fall.

The poet will not stop until the new Sodom-Gomorrah status of Babylon is explicated. The city once proud and arrogant now will be a permanent ruin, so devastated and leveled that it will never recover. In these final verses, the poet engages in a torrent of rhetoric commensurate with that of verses 14–16. Not even Bedouin shepherds will go near the ruined city. At best, the ruined city, with its half-leveled temples and craters of palaces, will be a haven for wild animals and scavengers who are dangerous, ominous, and forbidding. The place where life was focused now becomes a habitat for deathliness. These *antihuman creatures* who inhabit the ruins— never tamed, never useful, never safe—will occupy and recharacterize the place. The poet is at pains to portray an occupation of the ruins that completely redescribes the place. The poet is not content with ominous creatures being there: They will "lie down"—the same word used for "comfort" in Psalm 23:2. The place will be full of these threatening creatures, lots of them. The goat-demons will "dance" where once elegant princesses danced. The jackals will enjoy "pleasant palaces," as though they leisurely stroll the terraces and enjoy state dinners. The reversal could not be more total, or more mocking, or more repulsive.

Deathliness Close at Hand (13:22b)

13:22b **its time is close at hand,**
        and its days will not be prolonged.

The entire scenario of verses 17–22a is initiated and governed by one verb, "I am stirring up." All the rest is derived from this verb. The entire historical process of reversal unfolds on its own. It needs only this authorizing trigger. Then sounds a final affirmation: Soon! The inversion is about to happen. In the seventh century it was soon for Assyria, though Assyria did not know it. In the sixth century it was soon for Babylon, though Babylon did not notice. It is always soon for the tyrants and exploiters, but it seems to belong to tyranny and exploitation not to notice until it is too late.

The ones who notice—because of these poets—are the ones needful, the ones who stay close to the rhetoric of Yahweh, the ones capable of hosting in their utterance another agent, the ones who trust in the very Yahweh who is never on the screen of the tyrants. Thus the poem, with Yahweh at its center, is thrown into the benumbed face of the tyrant. The poet engages in raw rage, in elegant exaggeration, in ironic celebration of the inversion. The poetry is characteristically irrelevant to "the nobles." The victims of pride and insolence, however, cling passionately to this rhetoric, because they have no other resource. The poetry is adequate for such folk. It need only last a little while, because the poetry in all its threat need persist only until "Soon!"

INVERSION, COMPASSION, HOMECOMING
14:1–2

> 14:1 **But the LORD will have compassion on Jacob and will again choose Israel, and will set them in their own land; and aliens will join them and attach themselves to the house of Jacob. 2 And the nations will take them and bring them to their place, and the house of Israel will possess the nations as male and female slaves in the LORD's land; they will take captive those who were their captors, and rule over those who oppressed them.**

The harsh dismantling of "Babylon" in chapter 13 has important spin-offs for the Jewish community that was contained within Babylonian domination. None of that spin-off, however, was voiced in chapter 13, even if it is clearly implied. In these verses, what may be inferred from chapter 13 is now made explicit.

Babylon had shown "no mercy" toward Israel (cf. 47:6), but was relentlessly brutal, as it was toward all of its conquered colonies. But now Yahweh will have mercy, occupying the space left by the nullification of Babylon. Israel had long ago been chosen by Yahweh (cf. Deut. 7:7–11), but the Exile had been experienced as an "unchoosing," a rejection by Yahweh. Now Israel is chosen again, again designated by Yahweh as a special, beloved community. As Babylon knows a great reversal from pride to nullification, so commensurately, Israel knows a great reversal from suffering to compassion and chosenness.

This new status as Yahweh's beloved, restored people, however, is not

simply a religious reassurance. The new status has important and direct sociopolitical aspects. Not only will Judah now go back home in joy and in
well-being. En route home, Israel will be accompanied by aliens, that is,
non-Jews, who will be linked to the Jewish community. The statement at
the end of verse 1 lacks specificity. We are not told what this "escort"
means.

We are astonished to have the matter explained in verse 2. The "aliens"
will have their "place" in Jewish society as slaves when Israel "possesses the
nations." Israel in exile still has the cadences of "possession" deep in its
imagination from the ancient memories. From Abraham to Joshua, Israel
is a landless community that dreams of land with all the privileges and securities and advantages that go with it. Among those privileges is the capacity to create a permanent underclass of non-Jews who are to do menial
tasks for the ease of Israel. There is here no acknowledgment that such a
radical reversal that subjugates others is problematic.

The text imagines a complete social reversal. Not only will the bondaged
Jews be freed; they will in turn bondage the aliens. The great reversal is
more fully voiced in Jeremiah 30:16:

> Therefore all who devour you shall be devoured,
>   and all your foes, everyone of them, shall go into captivity;
> those who plunder you shall be plundered,
>   and all who prey on you I will make a prey.

This people who had suffered now will enjoy new well-being at the expense of others.

The vision of enslaving others suggests that Israel was not saturated
with Exodus memory, or at least it did not extend the notion of Exodus
emancipation to others. The lack of sensitivity in the text concerning this
matter does not need "explaining" by us. But we do wonder about such a
vision. Perhaps the vision of enslaving others reflects the resolve of the
poet to state the reversal with complete consistency. Or perhaps there is
reflected here the first wave of exuberance in which the recently bondaged
can think of no one but themselves. Or perhaps this is a measure of the ideological contamination of faith whereby the triumph of Yahweh readily
slides into the triumph of God's people. In any case, we can see that biblical rhetoric operates in the world of real people. And when real people—
even real believing people—come to daily reality, their visions of faith take
peculiar, and sometimes shameless, concrete form. Emancipation from exile does not mean that the struggle for faith is ended. It only transposes

that struggle into a new arena of fresh possibilities, fresh temptations, and fresh compromises. Good news can move quickly to new modes of exploitative behavior, all under the aegis of God's gifts.

WELCOME TO DEATH!
14:3–23

This quite distinct poem continues the accent of 13:1–22 concerning the utter defeat of Babylon by Yahweh, which in turn points to a positive reversal of the fortunes of Israel (14:1–2). Although the general theme is congruent with chapter 13, the poetic imagery here is even more extreme. It appeals to ancient mythological rhetoric concerning primordial struggles, looks toward the future in apocalyptic ways, and uses daring figures of a rich, peopled, conflicted, lively cosmos. The phrasing of the poetry intends not simply to state a verdict on the tyrant, but to make that verdict emotively available to the listening community of staggered, hope-filled Jews.

Leisure for Taunting (14:3–4a)

14:3 **When the LORD has given you rest from your pain and turmoil and the hard service with which you were made to serve,** 4a **you will take up this taunt against the king of Babylon:**

The promise of 14:1–2 and indeed the very structure of the book of Isaiah anticipates a time when Judah will be relieved of all of the abusive pressures of exile, a relief made possible by Yahweh's "Day" when the exploitative overlord will lose control. The rhetoric of this anticipation in these verses concerns "hard labor" reminiscent of the Exodus narrative (cf. Exod. 5:4–21) as well as a slight reference to the Flood narrative (cf. Gen. 5:29). Thus we have the verb "give rest" (*nûaḥ*), from which comes the name *Noah*. By appeal to these traditions, the text holds out a promise for a coming time of well-being when Judah is free from all imperial pressure. One of its important opportunities, in such freedom, is to engage in a mocking song against the tyrant. Such a mocking song may be simply an emotional catharsis of pent-up feeling and an act of vengeance, but it is also an active, vocal way of claiming God-given freedom. In any case, the verses prepare us and introduce the anti-Babylonian poem to follow.

Finally Sabbath Rest (14:4b–7a)

14:4b **How the oppressor has ceased!**
      How his insolence has ceased!
  5 **The LORD has broken the staff of the wicked,**
      the scepter of rulers,
  6 **that struck down the peoples in wrath**
      with unceasing blows,
    that ruled the nations in anger
      with unrelenting persecution.
  7a **The whole earth is at rest and quiet;**

These beginning verses take the form of a lament, as though the poem is an act of grief over the death of an empire, or more personally over the death of a particular tyrant. But of course the rhetoric is a trick (not unlike the rhetorical trick of 5:1–7). What purports to be a statement of grief is in fact an utterance of celebrative gloating. At long last, Yahweh has broken the power of the oppressor, the one who acted in arrogance and wickedness, who assumed complete autonomy and freedom to engage in exploitative brutality. In a world governed by Yahweh, nobody is free to practice exploitative brutality, but the tyrant always learns that too late.

The double use of the word "cease" in verse 4b is *shabbat* (= sabbath). There is now a complete "cessation" of tyrannical power, a cessation like Israel stopping work on the sabbath. The Babylonian way of power in the world is now completely nullified and eliminated. The "sabbath" of such abuse is caused by the Lord of the sabbath, who is powerful, relentless, and determined to prevail. This Yahweh is angry at the unspeakable violation of Yahweh's own purpose; and so "with blows," that is, assault that will not stop, the empire is terminated. Yahweh meets violence with overwhelming force. And the result is that "the whole earth" has a rest. The poem understands imperial rule to have been global. In 13:5, it is "the whole earth" that is to be destroyed. But now "the whole earth" has been returned to Yahweh's good rule; thus it enjoys "rest and quiet," that is, ordered peaceableness. The first term, "rest," echoes verse 3; the second term, "quiet," is used often in the book of Judges to characterize the land when Yahweh has defeated the oppressor and has given Israel "breathing space." The poet readily presents Yahweh as the one capable of reordering public power on the largest thinkable scale, all to the advantage of "the land" and the people.

Welcome to Powerlessness! (14:7b–11)

14:7b   **they break forth into singing.**
    8 **The cypresses exult over you,**
        the cedars of Lebanon, saying,
    "Since you were laid low,
        no one comes to cut us down."
    9 **Sheol beneath is stirred up to meet you when you come;**
        it rouses the shades to greet you,
        all who were leaders of the earth;
        it raises from their thrones
        all who were kings of the nations.
    10 **All of them will speak**
        and say to you:
    "You too have become as weak as we!
        You have become like us!"
    11 **Your pomp is brought down to Sheol,**
        and the sound of your harps;
    maggots are the bed beneath you,
        and worms are your covering.

These verses report two responses to the defeat of the oppressor. First, the created order, embodied in cypress and cedar trees, is elated that the oppressor is nullified, because the rapacious exploitation of the earth is ended. With the new governance, no one will cut down the forest; the trees are relieved at their new lease on life. Invariably, oppressors who enslave people are also destructive of the ecological system. Arrogance toward human persons is reinforced by carelessness about the environment. The new rule of Yahweh is an assurance to all creatures. And so they sing (Psalm 96:11–12):

> Let the heavens be glad, and let the earth rejoice;
>   let the sea roar, and all that fills it;
>   let the field exult, and everything in it.
> Then shall all the tress of the forest sing for joy.

As Israel is free, so the trees are safe!

It is, however, the second response to the fall of the oppressor that is more interesting. The poet imagines a scene in Sheol, the dark netherworld where discarded people are housed who no longer have power for life. "Sheol" is not a place of punishment, but it is where the dead are kept in their

impotence. As the deposed oppressor arrives in Sheol, now completely removed from authority and utterly impotent—a suitable resident for Sheol—
all the others who used to be active authorities and great powers in the earth
(now become impotent) present themselves as a welcoming committee for
the new arrival into Sheol. They gather round the new arrival and recognize
him as one of their own, formerly powerful, now completely powerless.

In high irony, the poet has them welcome the new member of the powerless to their company: "You are like us"—powerless, no longer a force to
be reckoned with. It takes one to know one! The welcome on the part of
the Sheol residents who speak is wistfulness, for what once was for all of
them and is no more. For the poet, the speeches from Sheol constitute
high irony. The speech "rubs it in," so that this now feeble has-been should
be recognized for what he is, completely broken and irrelevant, warrant-
ing no attention at all.

The verdict of verse 11 articulates a complete reversal from *what was* to
what is. The new resident had been only recently surrounded by great pomp
and luxurious harps bespeaking leisure and self-indulgence (cf. Amos 6:5)—
but now there is the failed existence of Sheol. There had been a time of a
posh bed upon which to rest (cf. Dan. 4:4–5; Amos 6:4), but now there is
only a bed of maggots, that is, filth, abuse, and discomfort. There had been
a delicate covering for royal privilege, but now worms. How the mighty
have fallen! How the good life has been forfeited! Such a life cannot be preserved if one is in opposition to the strong rule of Yahweh. Everything treasured by the oppressor is now lost; his fate is mean, messy, and humiliating.

Notice that such poetry is profoundly subversive of every self-
congratulatory status quo. Whereas the rhetorical dismantling in all its
harshness may have been aimed at Babylon, in canonical form the onslaught
means to school the imagination of the community of faith. It intends to
provide a world in which abusive power is seen to be flimsy and precarious,
and sure to pass. So Judah relishes the poetry in its endless counterpower
and continues to cling to this horizon of Yahweh's governance, especially
in the face of oppressors who always seem strong to perpetuity. They are
not to perpetuity! They are fated to Sheol. The reception committee of impotence is already gathering to greet the next oppressor. And so Jews maintain by such poetry the capacity to wait, to resist, and not to give in.

You Are Brought Low (14:12–20a)

Now comes a long poetic section that ponders and celebrates the astonishing reversal that occurs in the historical process. The reversal happens in the

historical process, and one can, of course, identify "historical" reasons and agents for the fall of an abusive superpower. In the horizon of the biblical text, however, the reversal is not sociopolitical; it is rhetorical. The poem is something of a "performative utterance" whereby each time the poem is recited, the oppressed community of the faithful can witness again to the fall and can again celebrate and claim its new God-given freedom. Or in the hearing of the poem, the presently oppressed can engage in anticipation of a reversal, even if it has not yet begun in visible, sociopolitical terms.

Verse 12 with exotic rhetoric provides the themes for what follows and summarizes the demise.

14:12 **How you are fallen from heaven,**
     O Day Star, son of Dawn!
How you are cut down to the ground,
     you who laid the nations low!

It begins with "How" (like v. 4b), a term for a lament. It is as though one is invited to grief. Moreover, there is cause for grief. The oppressor had primordial ambitions to climb to heaven and to assume a place among the gods, to join the galaxy of the omnipotent (cf. Gen. 11:1–9). All of that is now lost and defeated. The phrase "Day Star, son of Dawn" surely appeals to older elemental myths about primordial ambition and pride. But even if we do not refer to the old myths, closer at hand we may consider the imagery of the movie *Star Wars* and the imaginative tale of cosmic, intergalactic conflict between the powers of good and evil. Here is the quintessential evil one, the cosmic brutalizer of the innocent who wants to usurp the throne room of the good. But alas! Such ambition cannot be realized. Such pretense cannot be sustained, for the destiny of such inappropriate cosmic ambition is "fallen, cut down, laid low"—utterly failed. One can grieve, imagining the illusion that produced such self-deception and disappointment. But in a mini-instant, the grief, only a staged ploy, turns to exuberance. In the world of the poet, the rule of good has withstood the threat! The world is safe, and we are delivered!

The false ambition of the oppressor is voiced in the arrogance of verses 13–14.

14:13 **You said in your heart,**
     "I will ascend to heaven;
I will raise my throne
     above the stars of God;
I will sit on the mount of assembly
     on the heights of Zaphon;

¹⁴ **I will ascend to the tops of the clouds,**
   I will make myself like the Most High."

Characteristically, the poets of Israel delight in placing extravagant self-indicting speeches on the lips of adversaries: "You said in your heart"; that is, "You imagined" (cf. Ps. 10:4, 6, 11; 14:1; Isa. 37:24–25; 47:8, 10). Such self-promoting imagination is dominated by a shameless "I":

> I will raise,
> I will sit,
> I will ascend,
> I will make.

All these assertions have to do with self-exaltation and self-elevation, all engineered by the "I." Of course, the oppressor (perhaps) does not say such things out loud, but only by acts of policy. The "I" of arrogance asserts autonomy, drives out Yahweh, and denies submission to Yahweh. That is what oppressive power in public policy is about.

It will not, the poem insists, work! (vv. 15–17).

14:15 **But you are brought down to Sheol,**
     to the depths of the Pit.
  ¹⁶ **Those who see you will stare at you,**
     and ponder over you:
   "Is this the man who made the earth tremble,
     who shook kingdoms,
  ¹⁷ **who made the world like a desert**
     and overthrew its cities,
     who would not let his prisoners go home?"

It cannot work because such arrogant agents are not in fact autonomous, are not free for exploitative policy, and cannot in the end occupy the throne room of heaven, for Yahweh is already there and takes up all the space. The arrogant speech of elevation (vv. 13–14) is countered by a disjunctive "But you." Now the "you" of the oppressor is drawn into the world of Yahweh's magisterial utterance and is therefore no longer autonomous. Indeed, the oppressor no longer acts but is acted upon, recipient of a future that Yahweh has decided.

The would-be "Day Star" is brought low (a deliberate contrast to the verbs of vv. 13–14), so low as to end in Sheol, place of utter powerlessness. The lowering is abrupt, complete, and dazzling, so dazzling that tourists come to ponder and be amazed at the reversal. They look upon the failed shell of power and wonder that this is the way of one who so recently dominated the earth, caused nations to tremble, reduced the earth in the devastation of imperial "progress," captured cities, and held prisoners. This is the one who seemed so massively in control that he could, without pause, do whatever abusive thing he chose to anybody. This is the one who did that—and now! The Bible believes in such inscrutable turns in public power. It witnesses some such turns, and it waits for others. It does not doubt, because there is a power far more reliable than this momentary terrorizer of the earth.

If "the Day Star" is failed in life, the failure continues to be evident in death (vv. 18–20a).

14:18 **All the kings of the nations lie in glory,**
each in his own tomb;
19 **but you are cast out, away from your grave,**
like loathsome carrion,
clothed with the dead, those pierced by the sword,
who go down to the stones of the Pit,
like a corpse trampled underfoot.
20a **You will not be joined with them in burial,**
because you have destroyed your land,
you have killed your people.

This poet cannot terminate the mocking and gloating until the argument is pressed to its furthest extreme. One might imagine it is enough to see the tormentor removed from power. But no, the tormentor is pressed even to the grave, so that the humiliating point is not missed.

It is conventional that kings are honored in death, given full ceremonial burials celebrated in awe and majesty—honor guard and all. That much is routine (v. 18). "But you" (v. 19)—by contrast—"you" are unlike all of these, dishonored in death as defeated in life. Tyrants imagine being honored; sometimes, however, the raging crowd will overcome protocol. So the Hapsburg bodies lie in a disordered warehouse in Vienna, and no one cares. Mussolini is savaged in death by a crowd that exposed his body in mockery. And Lenin's tomb is at the edge of dismantling. Abuse will not produce permanent honor, because the grip of fear will fail. The people will notice the pain and will surge against the royal self-presentation.

The same ignoble end for failed power is offered by Jeremiah (22:18–19) to the miserable king, Jehoiachim:

> They shall not lament for him, saying,
> "Alas, my brother!" or "Alas, sister!"

They shall not lament for him, saying,
  "Alas, lord!" or "Alas, his majesty!"
With the burial of a donkey he shall be buried—
  dragged off and thrown out beyond the gates of Jerusalem.

And before Jehoiachim, the despised queen Jezebel, so powerful and feared in life, is left for the dogs and survives only in the bony parts for which the dogs had no taste (2 Kings 9:34–35). The Bible knows that brutal power cannot last and regularly ends in humiliation. Here the poet envisions a dishonored royal corpse—no longer protected by a royal guard but now exposed to the deep rages of injustice and therefore trampled (v. 19), not buried (v. 20). It is not buried because people and land have been violated by rapacious autonomy. Some may celebrate "the glory that was Greece and the grandeur that was Rome." But not these Jews who knew that glory based on threat and grandeur rooted in exploitation will not endure. We readers in the opulent West, moreover, need not study ancient examples too long, but may ponder, through the pain, our own extravagance linked to abuse, surely productive of a waiting, enraged resentment. What goes up by self-will does indeed come down and down and down.

So Also the Heirs (14:20b–21)

14:20b **May the descendants of evildoers**
     nevermore be named!
  ²¹ **Prepare slaughter for his sons**
     because of the guilt of their father.
  Let them never rise to possess the earth
     or cover the face of the world with cities.

The poem, however, is not yet finished when the tyrant is incarcerated in the permanent land of the impotent. The poet looks past this former tyrant to the future. Such tyrannical clusters—dynasties, families, clans, organizations—have an amazing capacity for survival and reemergence. Always there is somewhere a hidden heir to the brutality who waits for a revival of power. Always there is a possible resurgence of barbarism. And so the poet is not content to carry the brutalizer to weakness. The heirs must be considered; the descendants of exploiters are prone to exploitation. For every Nebuchadrezzar, there is a neo-Nebuchadrezzar. Thus it is important that those now consigned to weakness should include all possible future carriers. The heirs must be obliterated. The sons must be executed. The name must be nullified (cf. Ps. 109:13). Steps must be taken to assure that the deathly possibility remains dead—to the third and fourth generations and forever. The permanent exclusion of the dynasty of abuse is the only sure way to guarantee that it will not happen again.

No Babylonian Remnant (14:22–23)

> 14:22 **I will rise up against them, says the LORD of hosts, and will cut off from Babylon name and remnant, offspring and posterity, says the LORD.** [23] **And I will make it a possession of the hedgehog, and pools of water, and I will sweep it with the broom of destruction, says the LORD of hosts.**

Israel's long taunt song is now certified by a final utterance in the mouth of Yahweh. The words are insistent. Here speaks "The Lord of hosts" (v. 22). The last phrase of verse 22 is "says the Lord." Yet one more time in verse 23, it is "The Lord of hosts." The one who causes the end of abuse now guarantees that it is indeed an end. It is Yahweh, not any human agent, who finally acts to eliminate oppression for the world of Judaism. The book of Isaiah has anticipated the remnant of Jews, a small company of survivors who outlast the vagaries of exile. Babylon, by contrast, will have no remnant, no little band of survivors, none. And because there are no survivors, the land of Babylon, heretofore so splendid, is now emptied and available for lesser creatures who do not exploit and who are no threat. (As in 13:21–22, we imagine a new occupancy of wild creatures—ostriches, goat-demons, hyenas, and jackals.) Here the new power is perhaps hedgehogs. A hedgehog is hardly royal splendor, but it will last longer than tyrants. The land is emptied, clear, abandoned. Such a scenario is an ominous threat to established power. To the listening exiles, however, it is good news. The poet has eliminated the tyrant. One can imagine this poem tasted like manna on the lips of the abused, who only dared a bit to hope for an alternative.

THE LORD OF HOSTS HAS PLANNED
14:24–27

> 14:24 **The LORD of hosts has sworn:**
>   **As I have designed,**
>   **so shall it be;**
>   **and as I have planned,**
>   **so shall it come to pass:**
>   [25] **I will break the Assyrian in my land,**

> and on my mountains trample him under foot;
> his yoke shall be removed from them,
>   and his burden from their shoulders.
> 26 This is the plan that is planned
>   concerning the whole earth;
> and this is the hand that is stretched out
>   over all the nations.
> 27 For the LORD of hosts has planned,
>   and who will annul it?
> His hand is stretched out,
>   and who will turn it back?

This oracle constitutes yet another oracle against a nation, this time Assyria. Although it seems to follow nicely in the sequence beginning with Babylon (13:1–14:23) and continuing with the Philistines (14:28–32), in fact this oracle is distinctive in two ways. First, it concerns Assyria, the great superpower from the time of eighth-century Isaiah (cf. 7:17; 8:4). As such it stands in close relation to Isaiah 1—12, unlike almost every other oracle in this section. Second, however, the Assyrian connection is limited to verse 25. The remainder of the oracle is large and generic in its assertion of Yahweh's sovereignty, generic enough that it may be regarded as a belated overture that summarizes the primary themes of the entire corpus of "Oracles Against the Nations."

As a generic introduction, we notice the awesome title "Lord of hosts" at beginning and end, a framing device for the entire oracle (vv. 24, 27). The indicative assertion of Yahweh's "plan" in verse 24 and the defiant rhetorical questions of verse 27 grandly assert Yahweh's governance of the entire geopolitical process. Yahweh has decided what will happen, and no counterplan, even that of a superpower, has a chance. Thus the main theme of the "Oracles Against the Nations" is *Yahweh's sovereignty over the international process,* so that even nation-states that imagine themselves to be autonomous finally will find themselves ordered and ruled by Yahweh's magisterial purposes.

Specifically, we are told in verse 25, it is Yahweh's plan that the imperial domination by Assyria will be terminated. The word pair "yoke, burden" echoes the phrasing of 9:4; 10:27 that apparently anticipates the overthrow of Assyria. If this oracle is indeed from the eighth century, then the text takes a long anticipatory look into the middle of the seventh century when Assyria began its slide into oblivion. Verse 26 follows the specificity of verse 25 by the largest claim imaginable concerning "the whole earth" (cf. 13:5). But of course Assyrian domination is so vast that the over-throw of Assyria does indeed concern the whole earth.

The specific claim of the oracle pertains to the eighth–seventh-century geopolitical crisis. If we "read beyond" the eighth century, as the final form of the text is wont to do, then this astonishing oracle asserts the intentional and certain governance precisely of political powers that imagine their own autonomy. It takes no great interpretive imagination to extrapolate how this might be read now by citizens of the United States, surely a su-perpower imagining its own autonomy. Now as then, the defiant rhetori-cal questions of verse 27 require an answer of "No one." No one can annul the plan of Yahweh or turn back the hand, then or now. It is perhaps not incidental that Yahweh's powerful resolve is articulated in the Exodus phrase "outstretched hand." The poem anticipates a large-scale emanci-pation from tyranny. The poet is unambiguously sure, in the face of every evidence to the contrary.

DO NOT REJOICE BUT WAIL
14:28–32

14:28 **In the year that King Ahaz died this oracle came:**
²⁹ **Do not rejoice, all you Philistines,**
 that the rod that struck you is broken,
 for from the root of the snake will come forth an adder,
  and its fruit will be a flying fiery serpent.
³⁰ **The firstborn of the poor will graze,**
 and the needy lie down in safety;
 but I will make your root die of famine,
 and your remnant I will kill.
³¹ **Wail, O gate; cry, O city;**
 melt in fear, O Philistia, all of you!
 For smoke comes out of the north,
 and there is no straggler in its ranks.

³² **What will one answer the messengers of the nation?**
 "The LORD has founded Zion,
 and the needy among his people
 will find refuge in her."

The superscription, echoing the formula of 6:1, places this oracle in the time of Ahaz, that is, during the lifetime of eighth-century Isaiah. It purports to address the Philistines, who continued to be a vexing partner and disturbance to Judah. The reference to Philistines may refer to the coastal cities never securely grafted into Judah. However that may be, the oracle continues to accent the large theme of Yahweh's governance over the nations, even though Yahweh is not explicitly mentioned until the promise of verse 32.

As it stands, the oracle contains a theme and a countertheme. The theme is that "you Philistines" are in for bigger trouble in the future than in the recent past. The Philistines are about to rejoice, apparently because a tyrannical oppressor ("rod") has been killed. If this oracle is placed in the eighth century, this death may refer to the death of one of the feared Assyrian rulers. The death of such a tyrant might indeed evoke celebration. Except, says the oracle, worse is yet to come. After the snake comes an adder, and after an adder a fiery serpent. The gravest threat is still in the future, a threat that dwarfs all past threats (v. 29). That threat is variously identified as famine or as "killing," perhaps either the result of military invasion (v. 30b).

In any case, the proper response to the crisis is not rejoicing (as is the temptation), but wailing (cf. 13:6). Wailing would constitute an accurate recognition of Philistia's true state, now in acute jeopardy (v. 31). The cause for legitimate "howling" in loss and grief is an ominous threat from the north, perhaps an invading army. That army is effective and tightly disciplined (no stragglers), and leaves a trail of smoke and destruction in its wake. Philistia is on notice of something like General Sherman's "scorched earth policy." Those who rejoice with such a threat at the threshold live in "lala land," out of touch with reality.

The countertheme, which the tradition of Isaiah can scarcely ever resist, is that as Philistia is routed, so Judah will be safe. In verse 30, an idyllic picture of "the poor" and "the needy" is offered in which they eat and lie down in complete security. The imagery echoes the more familiar Psalm 23:1–3. The theme is reiterated in verse 32, only more explicitly. It is Yahweh (now mentioned for the first time) who has founded and guaranteed Zion as a safe refuge for "the needy." It is enough that the oracle sounds afresh the certitudes of Zion theology that must have loomed large amidst the Assyrian threat and long after the Exile. It is, moreover, astonishing that verses 30 and 32 single out *the poor, the needy,* and *the afflicted.* This rhetoric may refer especially to the most desperate in the community. Or it may refer to the entire community of the pious, who in emerging Judaism are "the poor." Either way, their assured protection by Yahweh contrasts with the wretched future of the Philistines.

The oracle assumes a coming international upheaval more severe than anything in the past. In our belated reading, we are drawn to imagine that we (e.g., Christians) are protected and assured. Given our sociopolitical situation in the United States, however, we may take pause before the warning. For well-off U.S. Christians, we might be tempted to "rejoice" at the "virtues of capitalism" and all the expanding affluence of our society. The way I read this oracle, however, such rejoicing may be ill-founded and premature, perhaps based on a most seductive illusion that fails to notice the deeper jeopardy of a society not able to sustain its own poor.

The sequence of "do not rejoice . . . wail" anticipates Jesus' harsh notice to those who misconstrue (Luke 6:21, 25):

> "Blessed are you who *weep* now,
>   for you will *laugh*. . . ."
> "Woe to you who are *laughing* now,
>   for you will *mourn and weep*."

There is indeed "a time to weep, and a time to laugh" (Eccles. 3:4). The oracle is aimed at those who have not a clue about their time or their situation in a world governed by an adder-dispatching God.

HE WILL NOT PREVAIL
15:1–16:14

It is scarcely noteworthy that Babylon receives a position of primacy in an extended treatment in these oracles (13:1–14:23). Babylon after all dominated the international horizon in Israel's most generative period and, in the end, emerged as the focal subject of the Isaiah tradition. By contrast, Moab was not a major power and, so far as we know, never threatened Judah in an overwhelming way. It is for that reason that the oracle against Moab is remarkable for its passion and its extent (15:1–16:14).

We do not know why this is so. We do know that Moab interacted with Judah over a long period of time. That shared history is marked by proximity, for they shared a common border that was variously crossed as power waxed and waned. Because they had many common concerns and common enemies (cf. Gen. 19:30–38), their history was one of intimacy (dramatized in the Genesis narrative about the origin of Moab). That shared history was, finally, one of vexation. Although neither Judah nor Moab could finally threaten the other, each could harass and inconvenience the other, for they regularly interfered in the business of the other.

This oracle is exceedingly difficult in its geographical references and in the shape of its rhetorical intention. Indeed, commentators are able only to guess at its meaning and draw conclusions only of a general kind. This long oracle is a collection of smaller units that we may divide into four elements: (1) a lament over ruined Moab (15:1–9); (2) an exchange of request and response (16:1–5); (3) a second lament (16:6–11); and (4) a verdict of negation (16:12–14).

Even More! (15:1–9)

This oracle sounds a lament over the people and territory of Moab. It is possible, as in chapters 13—14 concerning Babylon, that what seems to be a lament over loss can actually function as a gloating, but that does not seem to be the case here. What impresses, rather, is the slow pace and comprehensive scope of the song of grief, which seems to be genuine, even though we do not know who speaks of "my heart." It is perhaps an articulation of grief that is so elemental that it cuts under national, ethnic boundaries and voices a common human response to the devastation of war. There is no qualification or softening of grief; the poet seems to send no hidden message.

The territory of Moab is devastated in a night raid (v. 1).

15:1 **An oracle concerning Moab.**

> **Because Ar is laid waste in a night,**
> **Moab is undone;**
> **because Kir is laid waste in a night,**
> **Moab is undone.**

Perhaps the timing suggests a sneak attack, lacking the honor of conventional warfare. The same two terms are reiterated: "laid waste" (*šdd*) bespeaks common brutality; "undone"—that is, reduced to complete dysfunction (6:5)—is by happenstance the same term used by the prophet in his vision of God's holiness. Moab is dismantled as a functioning state.

The appropriate response to such massive, brutal loss is ritual grief that is done in communal liturgical fashion (vv. 2–4).

15:2 **Dibon has gone up to the temple,**
> **to the high places to weep;**
> **over Nebo and over Medeba**
> **Noab wails.**
> **On every head is baldness,**
> **every beard is shorn;**

³ in the streets they bind on sackcloth;
    on the housetops and in the squares
    everyone wails and melts in tears.
⁴ Heshbon and Elealeh cry out,
    their voices are heard as far as Jahaz;
    therefore the loins of Moab quiver;
    his soul trembles.

The unit begins with "the house of Dibon," but it could easily be emended as "the daughters of Dibon," for we know that in that patriarchal world women were characteristically the professional mourners. However that be translated, the unit is dominated by actions of grief: weep, wail, shorn, wail, melt, with ritual behavior of shorn heads and beards and the wearing of sackcloth. The portrayal is of a community giving itself over completely and without restraint to loss. We are, in the poem, one step removed from the ritual of grief, for this poem simply *describes* such grieving activity. At the same time, however, the poem is performative. It *enacts* grief as a quite public enterprise.

The act of grief continues with the self-investment of the poet (vv. 5–6): "my heart."

15:5 **My heart cries out for Moab;**
    his fugitives flee to Zoar,
    to Eglath-shelishiyah.
    For at the ascent of Luhith
    they go up weeping;
    on the road to Horonaim
    they raise a cry of destruction;
⁶ **the waters of Nimrim**
    are a desolation;
    the grass is withered, the new growth fails,
    the verdure is no more.

Again we notice the verbs: cries out, weeping, raise a cry. Beyond that, however, we also notice more active response to the devastation. War produces refugees. And so the poet presents a scene of fugitives fleeing in fear for their very lives. It may well be that these verses describe a path of escape as they "go up . . . on the road." And even as they come to the more fertile areas of Moab in their flight, everything is in ruins. Even the water supply and the good grazing land are devastated. The poet already knows, long before us, that war works havoc on the environment, so that war refugees are left completely, utterly without resources.

The lament is continued with one new factor (vv. 7–8).

15:7 **Therefore the abundance they have gained**
and what they have laid up
they carry away
over the Wadi of the Willows.
⁸**For a cry has gone**
around the land of Moab;
the wailing reaches to Eglaim,
the wailing reaches to Beer-elim.

The grief and horror of flight are intensified in a vivid portrayal. Now we are told "they carry away . . . the abundance they had gained." This is not simply a flight to survive the battle. This is a complete evacuation. As we read, we can conjure pictures of Rwanda and Bosnia and Serbia and Lebanon, and all those more recent, more available scenes of refugees. They may have taken "their abundances." But characteristically the fugitives have only a small cart and all that can be piled upon it. This is a major, irreversible displacement of people who have no destination, but only "away." And although they may come to safety, they will not soon come to well-being. No wonder the poet's heart cries out! Who except the most rigid ideologue is not moved by the scene!

We have not yet, however, reached the extremity of speech until we arrive at verse 9b.

15:9 **For the waters of Dibon are full of blood;**
yet I will bring upon Dibon even more—
a lion for those of Moab who escape,
for the remnant of the land.

Now speaks for the first time an "I" whom the commentators take to be Yahweh. We learn that it is Yahweh, until now held in abeyance by the poet, who has authored the destruction. This "I" will now do "even more." We may ponder, What more is there? It is to hunt down the escapees, to consume them like a lion until there is no remnant. We are not told why. We only notice the deep tension between the grief of verse 5, offered with no motivation for this tragedy, and the God who is not yet assuaged. There is more—a lion—until there will be no trace of Moab. (This image calls to mind the remnant of Israel in Amos 3:12: "two legs and an ear." One can see the fragments hanging out of the lion's eager mouth.) As it is for Israel in Amos, so it will be for Moab here. Yahweh presses more severely than even this poet had imagined.

"A Throne Shall Be Established
in Steadfast Love!" (16:1–5)

These verses are far from clear. They appear to be a petition for asylum issued by Moab (vv. 1–4a) and a response by Judah (vv. 4b–5).

Moab seeks help from Zion (vv. 1–4a).

16:1 **Send lambs**
      to the ruler of the land,
    from Sela, by way of the desert,
      to the mount of daughter Zion.
  2 **Like fluttering birds,**
      like scattered nestlings,
    so are the daughters of Moab
      at the fords of the Arnon.
  3 **"Give counsel,**
      grant justice;
    make your shade like night
      at the height of noon;
    hide the outcasts,
      do not betray the fugitive;
  4a **let the outcasts of Moab**
      settle among you;
    be a refuge to them
      from the destroyer."

Moab proposes to send lambs from Sela as a gift (protection money) to Jerusalem, in an effort to mobilize Judah's help against the devastator. Hans Wildberger comments that "the poet knew his Bible." In 2 Kings 3:4 Moab was a vassal of Judah and regularly sent "one hundred thousand lambs, and the wool of one hundred thousand rams." Such a tribute ought to purchase a good bit of protection! In initiating the offer, verse 2 adds the motivational statement that the people of Moab are "like fluttering birds, like scattered nestlings," that is, displaced, desperate people. The motivation is followed by a petition for counsel, justice, and protection (v. 3). The request apparently is not for military intervention, but only that Moab's fugitives should be admitted into the haven of Judah for protection, so that Judah should be for Moab,

    [Y]our shade at your right hand. . . .
  [so that] The sun shall not smite you by day,
    nor the moon by night.
                (Psalm 121:5–6)

Judah is apparently capable of such protection, and Moab has enough commonality with Judah to dare to ask for it.

In verses 4b–5, Judah's response to the request of Moab is given.

16:4b **When the oppressor is no more,**
    and destruction has ceased,
  and marauders have vanished from the land,
 5 **then a throne shall be established in steadfast love**
    in the tent of David,
    and on it shall sit in faithfulness
 a ruler who seeks justice
    and is swift to do what is right.

It is an answer less than clear and perhaps deliberately ambiguous. The poem looks past the present crisis. It does not promise intervention to Moab in the present crisis, but anticipates a time when the crisis is "no more . . . ceased . . . vanished." Perhaps as an interim measure, the requested asylum is given, but it is not articulated. Rather, the poem, in good Isaianic fashion, appeals to Davidic theology and in the long term anticipates the establishment of the Davidic throne in steadfast love and faithfulness. Thus, in a future-oriented hope—perhaps eschatological, perhaps messianic—the poem invokes the defining characteristics of the promised good and effective Davidic king, who perhaps stands in contrast to the present shabby occupant of the throne (if this is a preexilic statement). In that coming time, the king will effectively enact the mandate for justice and equity. Thus the grief and the need of Moab are resolved in a characteristic Davidic fulfillment.

It is, however, far from clear how this Davidic assurance touches the Moabite emergency. Otto Kaiser concludes:

> This hope is really of comfort only to Jews. They can look beyond the distress which is coming upon them (cf. 14:24ff.) to the age of salvation. It is of no benefit to the Moabites who beg protection in their need (*Isaiah 13–39*, 73).

But alternatively, Wildberger suggests that the scope of the promise moves beyond eighth-century Isaiah: for Isaiah, the guarantee of salvation is "only for Israel." Here it is also "for the peoples," expressly illustrated in the example of Moab.

The text is not clear. Perhaps the different readings of Kaiser and Wildberger nicely reflect the unresolve of the text and the continuing issue in interpretation concerning, "Who is my neighbor?" That is, who counts in the scope of the promise? Kaiser may be right that the promise is not here extended to Moab. The poem does make clear, nonetheless, that the question is at least upon the horizon of this text-community. The question persists about the ways in which long-term grand promises from God touch down in the concreteness of historic pain. Clearly, we are not finished with this question, even as Judah and Moab were not finished with it. It is promised that after the pain will come steadfast love, faithfulness, justice, and equity; that is, all that this suffering community so passionately yearns for. It is not clear ahead of time, as it never is, who will be included in the generous grant to come. That question endlessly haunts ancient Israel, even as it endlessly haunts the church.

From Blame to Grief (16:6–11)

This lament reiterates the loss, grief, and pathos of 15:1–9a, sounding many of the same themes. However, unlike 15:1–9a, the moods and messages here are more complex. In 15:1–9a, the grief was not toned down by any indictment. Here, however, the lament begins with an accusation that Moab was proud, arrogant, and insolent, suggesting that the suffering is in some way deserved.

16:6 **We have heard of the pride of Moab**
      —how proud he is!—
of his arrogance, his pride, and his insolence;
      his boasts are false.

Oddly enough, the poet makes nothing of this indictment, leaving it unexploited and uncommented upon. What follows is governed by three "therefores," which may be taken as consequences of the accusation of verse 6.

    The first "therefore," articulates a stunning reversal of fortune:

16:7 **Therefore let Moab wail,**
      let everyone wail for Moab.
Mourn, utterly stricken,
      for the raisin-cakes of Kir-hareseth.

   8 **For the fields of Heshbon languish,**
      and the vines of Sibmah,
whose clusters once made drunk
      the lords of the nations,
reached to Jazer
      and strayed to the desert;
their shoots once spread abroad
      and crossed over the sea.

The listener is called to wail with Moab (v. 7). The ground for grief is that the splendor that once was is no more (v. 8). In former time, Moab produced enough wine to satiate "the lords of the nations." Indeed, the vineyards were so abundant and luxurious that they spread even beyond fertile land. They would grow everywhere! But now all is shriveled and ruined; war will do that!

The second "therefore" ruminates on the celebrative sounds of harvest time that are now silenced:

16:9 **Therefore I weep with the weeping of Jazer**
     for the vines of Sibmah;
   I drench you with my tears,
     O Heshbon and Elealeh;
   for the shout over your fruit harvest
     and your grain harvest has ceased.
 [10] **Joy and gladness are taken away**
     from the fruitful field;
   and in the vineyards no songs are sung,
     no shouts are raised;
   no treader treads out wine in the presses;
     the vintage-shout is hushed.

The tradition of Isaiah knows about the unrestrained singing, dancing, shouting, and drinking that belong to a successful harvest (cf. 9:3; Ps. 126:6). But now there is the ominous silence of failure, dismay, and death; the shouting has ceased; joy and gladness are taken away; there are no sounds, no shouts, no treaders; all is hushed. The population is slaughtered, the land is ruined, the vineyards are abandoned (cf. the imagery of 5:5–6).

No wonder we conclude with a third pathos-filled "therefore"!

16:11 **Therefore my heart throbs like a harp for Moab,**
      and my very soul for Kir-heres.

The translation "my heart" and "my very soul" are too tame for the verse; better "my bowels" (cf. Jer. 4:19), my most visceral innards. The deepest instinctive response is one of astonished repulsion. The poet can hardly believe and hardly bear the deep, violent, abusive nullification of all that was Moab. The passion does not cancel out the indictment of verse 6. That accusation, however, provides the poet with no protection from the deeply moving assault of what is seen. One can hardly imagine such a reversal in the historical process, but it happened. And it happens!

Complete Reversal (16:12–14)

The oracle concerning Moab concludes with two devastating prose verdicts.

> 16:12 **When Moab presents himself, when he wearies himself upon the high place, when he comes to his sanctuary to pray, he will not prevail.**

Moab will come to worship in its desperation, surely to its own god. Indeed, Moab will exhaust itself in feverish petition to god for relief. But to no avail. Such vigorous worship cannot and will not produce anything positive. The text passes up the chance to make an Israelite point that a Moabite god cannot save. The accent here is otherwise: Moab's sorry state is hopeless and beyond recall. Nothing will change that. Clearly, this verdict is not compromised at all by the promise of vv. 4b–5.

The second verdict is equally negative.

> 16:13 **This was the word that the LORD spoke concerning Moab in the past.** [14] **But now the LORD says, In three years, like the years of a hired worker, the glory of Moab will be brought into contempt, in spite of all its great multitude; and those who survive will be very few and feeble.**

This verdict is introduced, by a messenger formula, from the very mouth of Yahweh. Notice that this is the first time such an attribution is made in the Moabite material. The reference to Yahweh makes the verdict solemn and beyond challenge. Very soon, in the time it takes a hired worker to work off a debt, *the glory* (*kbd*) *of Moab* will become *contempt* (*qal*). The two contrasting Hebrew words are "weightiness" (*kbd*) and "lightness" (*qal*), that is, triviality. Moab will cease to be a formidable presence and will therefore become a helpless pawn in the drama of power politics. The theme of radical reversal is sounded one more time: The *many* will become the *few*. Oddly, there will be "survivors" (a remnant), against the threat of 15:9. But their exposed, endangered state is no cause for satisfaction. The text itself enacts within our listening the demise of a reputable nation-state. We have heard it happen. Yahweh is twice agent of the demise (15:9; 16:3–4), but the Yahweh reference is subdued. This is the voiced dismay of Judah observing a neighbor and daring to engage the pathos evoked by the relentlessness of lived reality, relentless in its pain. Verse 6 suggests "due cause" for the suffering. Mostly, however, this song of grief is not interested in blame. The costs and hurts are too massive and acute for moralizing.

YET ANOTHER HEAP OF RUINS
17:1–3

17:1 **An oracle concerning Damascus.**

See, Damascus will cease to be a city,
   and will become a heap of ruins.
2 Her towns will be deserted forever;
   they will be places for flocks,
   which will lie down, and no one will make them afraid.
3 The fortress will disappear from Ephraim,
   and the kingdom from Damascus;
and the remnant of Aram will be
   like the glory of the children of Israel,
                              says the LORD of hosts.

This brief oracle concerns Damascus, capital of Syria, Israel's near neighbor and ofttimes enemy. The announcement of destruction of a foreign nation is by this time stylized and routine. This oracle is of interest, however, because in chapters 7—8, eighth-century Isaiah anticipated the destruction of Syria at the hands of Assyria. It may be that this oracle is linked to that portentous crisis. The "description" of the devastation once again employs the imagery of a city now so leveled and emptied of people that it is transformed into a peaceable pasture land (cf. 5:17). The last phrase of verse 2, "no one will make them afraid," echoes the promises of Leviticus 26:6, only now the assertion is used ironically. The assurance is not given to the inhabitants of the city, but to the gentle flocks who now occupy the city in place of its rightful human inhabitants.

Of peculiar interest is the direction taken in verse 3, wherein the disastrous future of Damascus is twinned with the coming disaster of northern Israel. Both Israel and Syria will be devastated. Both will have a lean remnant, and both will lose their glory. It is odd that an oracle against a foreign nation would draw the Israelites into its horizon. The linkage may be designed to reiterate the assurance of 7:7–9 concerning the two nation-states, or it may simply be a harsh polemic made by Judah against its two northern neighbors. Either way, at the end of verse 3 our attention is drawn away from Syria and toward Israel, preparing us for the oracle that follows.

FROM GLORY TO GRIEF—AND BACK AGAIN
17:4–14

It surprises us to find these verses in this larger unit of "Oracles Against the Nations." These verses are concerned with Jacob-Israel. They likely referred first to the Northern Kingdom of Israel, devastated by Assyria in the eighth century. In the book of Isaiah as it stands, however, there can be no doubt that the oracle is reheard in reference to Judah and Jerusalem.

This section of text is put together by an arrangement of smaller independent units. We are able to see the two-phase pattern of *judgment and assurance* that is characteristic of the book of Isaiah. Notice that in verses 4, 7, and 9 there are three introductions of "on that day," bespeaking pivotal turns in Israel's life with Yahweh.

Harvest with a Few Droppings
(17:4–6)

17:4 **On that day**
the glory of Jacob will be brought low,
and the fat of his flesh will grow lean.
⁵ **And it shall be as when reapers gather standing grain**
and their arms harvest the ears,
and as when one gleans the ears of grain
in the Valley of Rephaim.
⁶ **Gleanings will be left in it,**
as when an olive tree is beaten—
two or three berries
in the top of the highest bough,
four or five
on the branches of a fruit tree,
          says the LORD God of Israel.

Here speaks "The Lord God of Israel" (v. 6). It is noteworthy that this is not the characteristic "Lord of Hosts," but the God peculiarly linked to Israel. And now this very God anticipates the nullification of God's beloved people. Verse 4 quickly asserts a reversal in two images, from "glory" (cf. 16:14; 17:3) to "brought low," wherein Israel loses its "umph" in the public process, and from "fat" to "lean," that is, from prosperity to the misery of war.

The dominant image of these verses, however, is the harvest. Although the image of harvest is often used for judgment, that dimension is not accented here. Rather, the point of the figure is that in the process of harvest almost all the fruit will be taken by the reapers; only a little will be left because the reapers cannot reach to the high branches of the trees, for the fruit is "out of reach." The poet easily shifts the image from grain to fruit in order to make the point that "out of reach" produces. Only a few "out-of-reach" folk will be left in Israel as a remnant. The stress, however, is not on the few left, but on the "almost all" taken. Israel is under judgment. It will be massive and comprehensive. The few that will be spared are not worth notice, mentioned only to underscore the totality of the trouble.

An Alternative Look (17:7–8)

> 17:7 **On that day people will regard their Maker, and their eyes will look to the Holy One of Israel;** [8] **they will not have regard for the altars, the work of their hands, and they will not look to what their own fingers have made, either the sacred poles or the altars of incense.**

This section of text abruptly reverses field. There is no doubt—though it is not stated—that Israel's trouble comes from looking away from Yahweh and disregarding Yahweh's governance and Yahweh's requirements. Israel has been excessively preoccupied with its own achievements and mesmerized by its own religious assurances. The oracle names the seductive alternatives to Yahweh: altars and sacred poles. They are not of Yahweh, for they are the products of Israel's own inventiveness. They cannot save and are surely no hope in crisis. They are nonetheless powerfully attractive, and Israel has gazed upon them and counted upon them for too long.

But now, Israel will refocus its gaze, redirect its attention, and bring its eyes and its policies back to "The Holy One of Israel." The theme is repentance and return to Yahweh. We are not told, in this terse utterance, why Israel turned, and we are given no assurance that the turn will avert trouble. Indeed, what strikes one is that verse 9 resumes the tone of verse 6, as if verses 7–8 had not been uttered. The tradition of Isaiah is insistent upon a countertheme that is positive, but that countertheme here scarcely interrupts the utterance of negation.

Coming Incurable Pain (17:9–11)

> 17:9 **On that day their strong cities will be like the deserted places of the Hivites and the Amorites, which they deserted because of the children of Israel, and there will be desolation.**

¹⁰ **For you have forgotten the God of your salvation,**
   and have not remembered the Rock of your refuge;
therefore, though you plant pleasant plants
   and set out slips of an alien god,
¹¹ **though you make them grow on the day that you plant them,**
   and make them blossom in the morning that you sow;
yet the harvest will flee away
   in a day of grief and incurable pain.

Now it is asserted that "their strong cities" will be ruined. The "their" may have been Northern Israel, as in verses 3 and 4–6, but surely it is now intended as the cities of Judah. Long ago, occupying Israel had displaced the predecessor peoples in the land—Hivites and Amorites—and harshly forced them to abandon their cities. What goes around comes around! Now the possessor will be displaced; Judah's cities will be a desolation.

The prose verdict of verse 9 is followed by poetry in verse 10 that seems to give a reason for the coming devastation. It is because Israel has forgotten its God, has not remembered its refuge. In the phrasing of verse 8, it has "looked away." The rhetoric of verse 10 makes clear the characteristic prophetic linkage between *theological commitment* and *military-political policy*. Disregard of Yahweh leads to self-destructive policy. Israel had forgotten its identity and therefore its true support for life in the world. This is poetic language; its reasoning does not fill in all the intermediate steps between *commitment* and *policy*; it simply assumes that they are close and self-evident, even to Israel in its amnesia.

As altars and sacred poles provided an alternative to Yahweh in verse 8, so in verses 10b–11a other religious activity is an attempted alternative to remembering Yahweh. The imagery of planting and growing suggests something like "fertility religion," that is, attempts to harness "the forces of life" by manipulative worship. Nothing, however, is specified. It is only clear that the alternatives cannot produce the desired guarantees because they are remote from Yahweh, Israel's only reliable guarantee.

The outcome is that the harvest of these alternative plantings is nil (v. 11b). They produce nothing, and certainly nothing useful in the face of loss and pain. The poetic imagery is venturesome and suggestive, but the point is a simple one. The devastating end is not in doubt.

From Evening to Mourning (17:12–14)

These culminating verses, quite different from the preceding, now lead us to imagining on a cosmic scale. Structurally these verses offer a positive future, not unlike verses 7–8. But there is a very great difference. Verses 7–8 concern Israel's repentance, which will produce no explicitly positive result. Here the positive turn anticipated is not because of Israel's repentance, but because of Yahweh's massive power that results in rescue.

The rhetoric of this poetic unit clearly marks the decisive turns in the substance of the statement. The oracle begins with "ah," bespeaking great vexation and trouble.

> 17:12 **Ah, the thunder of many peoples,**
> **they thunder like the thundering of the sea!**
> **Ah, the roar of nations,**
> **they roar like the roaring of mighty waters!**
> 13a **The nations roar like the roaring of many waters,**
> **but he will rebuke them, and they will flee far away,**

The vexation is the tumultuous disorder of the nations, churning in vigorous, nonsensical turmoil. Verses 12 and 13a reiterate the same theme in three lines of two parts each. The nations are perhaps portrayed in their aggressive, destructive pose that threatens Judah, though that is not said. More pointedly, they are in feverish conflict with Yahweh's created order; thus they embody the powers of chaos that futilely seek to undermine Yahweh's intention for all of creation. With the mention of peoples and nations, the poem skillfully moves the reality of *political conflict* to the larger arena of *cosmic dispute* between the powers of order and disorder. And because the nations in their vexing, recalcitrant behavior are like the surging primordial waters of chaos, they are said to roar and thunder like those waters.

As emerging Judaism moves toward apocalyptic rhetoric, historical phenomena are shaded toward mythic, cosmic categories. The surging, threatening nations are the concrete embodiment of chaos, which in principle is opposed to the rule of Yahweh. The rhetoric of rebellion is echoed in Psalm 2 (vv. 1–3), where the subject is the nations but the rhetoric is close to cosmic:

> Why do the nations conspire,
> and the peoples plot in vain?
> The kings of the earth set themselves,
> and the rulers take counsel together,
> against the LORD and his anointed, saying,
> "Let us burst their bonds asunder,
> and cast their cords from us."

This portrayal of the churning hostile nations is, however, a foil for the powerful adversative of verse 13b:

17:13b **chased like chaff on the mountains before the wind**
      and whirling dust before the storm.

The creator God will not surrender to the challenging powers of chaos. And so Yahweh *rebukes* the waters, issuing a magisterial command that the unruly waters perforce must obey. At Yahweh's sovereign assertion, the rebellion is ended; the waters return to the proper, tamed place. This is the same rebuke issued to the waters of the Exodus (cf. Psalm 114:3–7). It anticipates, moreover, the utterance of Jesus, who rebukes the primordial waters, which promptly become docile and obedient (cf. Mark 4:35–41). The threat is temporary and has no chance of success against the governance of Yahweh.

The nations (waters) that were so boisterous are no threat, indeed, no force at all in the face of Yahweh. The poet employs metaphors that trivialize in order to rob the nations of all seriousness. They are like chaff, like dust. The lordly creator sovereign need only puff modestly and they are indeed "blown away" and the world is left safe.

The poet then summarizes the deep threat and the sudden transformation.

17:14 **At evening time, lo, terror!**
      Before morning, they are no more.
      This is the fate of those who despoil us,
      and the lot of those who plunder us.

In the first two lines there are no active verbs, only a drastic, hidden, inexplicable turn. In the evening, when Israel went to bed, there was everywhere threat, alarm, and danger—all that has been voiced in verses 12–13a. But then, inscrutably, before dawn the threat has evaporated. The text witnesses to the astonishing reversal but makes no attempt to explain. In the hiddenness of the night, when things are shadowed and out of control, Yahweh works wonders. Thus it is "at midnight" that Yahweh violently worked the liberation of Israel from bondage (Exod. 12:29). It was "early the next day" that the Philistines found their god inscrutably smashed by Yahweh (1 Sam. 5:3). It was at the same "early dawn" that the women found that Jesus was raised to new life (Luke 24:1). The Bible never explains. It only attests in astonishment and gratitude: "Weeping may linger for the night,/but joy comes with the morning" (Psalm 30:5b). While the world is in repose, Yahweh works newness.

The newness, moreover, is not evenhanded. It works for "us." We may take the "us" (used twice) to refer to the beleaguered Israelites under assault from the forces of chaos. In the end, however, after the frantic churnings of disorder, a confident conclusion is drawn by the faithful: "This is the fate . . . " It could not be otherwise; Yahweh is powerful and faithful. Chaos may surge, but it cannot prevail. It finally must yield to Yahweh's governance, and therefore "we" are safe. Yahweh works a radical reversal upon Israel's detractors. The theme is echoed in the affirmation of Jeremiah 30:16:

> Therefore all who devour you shall be devoured,
> and all your foes, everyone of them, shall go into captivity;
> those who plunder you shall be plundered,
> and all who prey on you I will make a prey.

It is no wonder that the intimates of Jesus "were filled with great awe" when they saw the powers of chaos driven back by the command of Jesus (Mark 4:41). Chaos cannot resist such sovereign command. And so "we" are safe.

LOOK, LISTEN!
18:1–7

This oracle again warns against and anticipates Yahweh's devastation, this time concerning Ethiopia. This land is to the south of Egypt; we are not at all sure what role it played in international affairs, though it is evident that Ethiopia is an active player. The oracle is exceedingly obscure, both because of the elusive images that are used and because we do not know enough to grasp any historical allusions that may be offered. On the whole, this oracle has defied the understanding of commentators. For that reason, my own comment will be brief, for a clear understanding eludes me.

18:1 **Ah, land of whirring wings**
beyond the rivers of Ethiopia,
² **sending ambassadors by the Nile**
in vessels of papyrus on the waters!
Go, you swift messengers,
to a nation tall and smooth,
to a people feared near and far,
a nation mighty and conquering,
whose land the rivers divide.

These verses make specific reference to Ethiopia and so begin in standard fashion. The initial "ah" likely anticipates a statement of threat. Verse 2 is greatly problematic. It suggests that Ethiopia is actively engaged in international diplomacy, perhaps with ambassadors in Jerusalem. The primary import of the verse, however, is to characterize the Ethiopians—soon to be devastated—as a formidable, impressive people: swift, tall, smooth, feared, mighty, conquering. The same sort of rhetorical strategy is employed in the tradition of Jeremiah in order to characterize a coming (Babylonian?) enemy (Jer. 5:15–17; 6:22–23) and subsequently the Persians (Jer. 50:41–42). The purpose in enhancing the Ethiopians in this way is presumably to escalate the power of Yahweh, who is about to destroy them.

18:3 **All you inhabitants of the world,**
>   **you who live on the earth,**
> **when a signal is raised on the mountains, look!**
>   **When a trumpet is blown, listen!**
> [4] **For thus the LORD said to me:**
> **I will quietly look from my dwelling**
>   **like clear heat in sunshine,**
>   **like a cloud of dew in the heat of harvest.**
> [5] **For before the harvest, when the blossom is over**
>   **and the flower becomes a ripening grape,**
> **he will cut off the shoots with pruning hooks,**
>   **and the spreading branches he will hew away.**
> [6] **They shall all be left**
>   **to the birds of prey of the mountains**
>   **and to the animals of the earth.**
> **And the birds of prey will summer on them,**
>   **and all the animals of the earth will winter on them.**

In this section of the oracle, all specificity is lost. The horizon turns from the concreteness of Ethiopia and any historical struggle to the cosmic rule of Yahweh. Now the address is to "all the inhabitants of the world," who are summoned to pay attention. The world is to look and listen and notice. Yahweh is about to give military signals so that a major assault will begin whereby Yahweh moves in determination to assert governance in the world (v. 3; cf. 13:2). We may assume, in context, that the campaign concerns Ethiopia, but nothing is said of that.

On the one hand, Yahweh's sovereignty is evidenced by the ominous forcefulness of military imagery. On the other hand, Yahweh's complete control is unmistakable, for Yahweh will watch and wait quietly, biding time until Yahweh is ready. Yahweh will not be hurried or provoked or pressed to any schedule of combat other than Yahweh's own. Yahweh is as

constant as hot sun or a summer cloud—ready, but not to be mobilized by
any force or will other than Yahweh's own.

But the onslaught will happen (v. 5)! It will happen before harvest time.
It is not far away. It is coming soon. And when it comes, it will be devastating. The poet has appealed to agricultural imagery for the time of attack (harvest time; v. 5a), and now the agricultural imagery is continued to
characterize the devastation (v. 5b). The enemy of Yahweh is "shoots" to
be cut off, "branches" to be hewn away. The verbs are powerful and harsh.
The growth is vulnerable and now will be cut and trimmed. The Isaiah tradition regularly speaks, in turn, of devastation and then of modest "remnants" that have escaped the devastation. Here verse 6 apparently reflects
upon the shoots and sprouts now cut. They will be left as food for birds
and animals. Thus the shoots and branches are twice eliminated—first by
Yahweh's own forceful verbs of harvest, and then by animals that devour
until nothing is left. It is of interest that "summer" and "winter" are here
employed as verbs, so that the seasons themselves, as agents of the creator,
work the will of the creator. The Ethiopians are "fodder" to help all the
creatures to live. The devastation is complete.

> 18:7 **At that time gifts will be brought to the LORD of hosts from a people
> tall and smooth, from a people feared near and far, a nation mighty and con-
> quering, whose land the rivers divide, to Mount Zion, the place of the name
> of the LORD of hosts.**

After the soaring imagery of verses 3–6, the oracle offers an addition that
is an intentional reprise on verse 2. In verses 1–2, the Ethiopians are proud
players in international affairs. But the poem has wrought a complete reversal. The Ethiopians are no more "swift ambassadors," but now are reduced to suppliants who come to Jerusalem, not to bargain and negotiate
but to submit. The image is of representatives bringing tribute money, the
losers placating the winners. The power of the reversal is enhanced by the
repeated use of the poignant language of verse 2, only now it is used ironically. They may be "smooth and tall," but now they are defeated and no
longer feared near or far. The oracle culminates with yet another Isaianic
vindication of Zion, the place to which the nations will come in submission to "The Lord of hosts." The God who enacts great military victories
is the God who rightly receives tribute that acknowledges the triumph of
Yahweh (cf. 2 Kings 3:4; 16:7–18; Psalm 2:10–11).

Although verses 1–2, 7 refer to Ethiopia, the main body of the oracle is
not interested in any particular enemy but voices the sovereign power and
will of Yahweh in general terms. The reference to Ethiopia appears to be

only a launching pad for Yahweh's large claim. The nations are invited to look and listen and notice when Yahweh is mobilized. It is for that reason that Wildberger concludes his comment by reference to Isaiah 45:23:

> By myself I have sworn,
>> from my mouth has gone forth in righteousness
>> a word that shall not return:
> "To me every knee shall bow,
>> every tongue shall swear."

What is claimed in Isaiah 45 is on this particular occasion enacted in this oracle. The bowing and swearing are not *pro forma* liturgical activities but are the presentation of military, economic produce now signed over to its proper liege.

EGYPT DEVASTATED AND BLESSED
19:1–25

As an abiding superpower in the ancient world, Egypt is endlessly on the horizon of Judah's geopolitics and is a force in Judah's theological imagination. Through all of the vagaries of international politics, with the rise and fall of many successive powers to the north, Egypt remains an undisturbed constant to the south. Indeed, even in the contemporary situation of the state of Israel, one can notice that as Israel's northern border is endlessly troubled by Syria, Iraq, Iran, and Lebanon, Egypt remains constant in the south.

As a political entity, Egypt was, on occasion, refuge for Israelites out of political favor (cf. 1 Kings 11:40). Indeed, Calvin suggests, with apparent reference to Jeremiah 43—44, that Egypt is also a place for Israelites of distorted faith: "For when they had forsaken God, to whom they ought to have had recourse, they thought that they had no help left to them but the Egyptians" (*Isaiah* II, 48). Egypt is not only haven, but also goad. It was a staple of Egyptian foreign policy to continue to press Israel and Judah to resist the pressures of the northern powers, and therefore to function as a buffer zone for Egypt. To that extent, Egypt is an endlessly destabilizing force in that ancient world.

In addition to refuge and goad, Egypt is also an engine for Israel's theological imagination. Even in the prophetic traditions, it is fair to assume that the Exodus narrative, in which Pharaoh is the quintessential threat to

Israel and adversary to Yahweh, is never far removed from awareness. Thus a useful perspective for the present oracle is to watch for allusions to the themes and motifs of that ancient, treasured tale of emancipation.

Because Egypt looms so large in Israel's imagination and holds down one end of the Fertile Crescent (as does Babylon the other in the tradition of Isaiah), it is appropriate and not surprising that in this oracle Egypt should receive air time commensurate with that of Babylon in chapters 13—14. Chapter 19 roughly divides into two equal parts. The first part is poetry and concerns the devastation of Egypt, as is expected in such oracles (vv. 1–15). The second part consists of five prose utterances, the trajectory of which culminates in an affirmation of and blessing for Egypt (vv. 16–25).

What the Lord of Hosts Has Planned (19:1–15)

Yahweh has planned against Egypt a complete dismantling of Egyptian pride, certitude, prosperity, and security (v. 12). The utterance of this plan, which counters the plans of Egypt (v. 3), is offered in three distinct rhetorical units.

The Lord, the Sovereign, the Lord of hosts is coming to Egypt, and the news is not good for the empire.

19:1 **An oracle concerning Egypt.**

> **See, the LORD is riding on a swift cloud**
> **and comes to Egypt;**
> **the idols of Egypt will tremble at his presence,**
> **and the heart of the Egyptians will melt within them.**
> ² **I will stir up Egyptians against Egyptians,**
> **and they will fight, one against the other,**
> **neighbor against neighbor,**
> **city against city, kingdom against kingdom;**
> ³ **the spirit of the Egyptians within them will be emptied out,**
> **and I will confound their plans;**
> **they will consult the idols and the spirits of the dead**
> **and the ghosts and the familiar spirits;**
> ⁴ **I will deliver the Egyptians**
> **into the hand of a hard master;**
> **a fierce king will rule over them,**
> **says the Sovereign, the LORD of hosts.**

The coming of Yahweh against Egypt is portrayed in the standard mythic image of theophany whereby Yahweh rides on a cloud (v. 1; cf. Pss. 68:33; 104:3). It is plausible that such rhetoric is simply a means to enhance the ominous majesty of Yahweh; but Calvin goes further to suggest that the imagery constitutes a military strategy to soar above Egyptian defenses so that "neither walls nor bulwarks shall hinder his progress." Yahweh is coming and will not be stopped.

Apparently the Egyptians are frightened, and well they should be! Even the Philistines were afraid of Yahweh, for they had heard of Yahweh's savage power against Egypt (1 Sam. 4:6–9). In the dramatic scenario offered here, we are entitled to conclude that the Egyptians remembered Yahweh's previous havoc worked in Egypt under the irresistible leadership of Moses. At that time, "There was a loud cry in Egypt, for there was not a house without someone dead" (Exod. 12:30). The lingering memory would surely produce present-tense panic.

Yahweh's resolve against Egypt is given in three verbs. First, "*I will stir up*" (v. 2). Yahweh's intention is to generate civil dispute, perhaps disorder that escalates into civil war. As is the case with such verbs, the Bible never asks how Yahweh will do this. It is simply affirmed that Yahweh has direct access and can make direct impact upon the political apparatus of a foreign state. The rhetoric does not require us to assume that the poet simply refers to an already existing state of disorder. The rhetoric begins with the resolve and agency of Yahweh.

Second, "*I will confound*" their plans. As Yahweh has robbed Egypt of courage, so Yahweh will rob Egypt of reason (v. 3). Their "plans," that is, their political policies and military designs, will be reduced to ineffective shambles. Egypt "was the workshop of all the liberal arts" (Calvin). That is, Egyptian learning and discernment are enormously advanced. In their confusion and disorder, however, they will abandon their good sense that might have prevailed. Instead of thinking, they will appeal foolishly to phony gods, idols, ghosts, and spirits who of course can tell them nothing useful vis-à-vis Yahweh (v. 4).

Third, "*I will deliver*" Egypt into the hands of a foreign ruler who will be harsh and brutal (v. 4). That powerful king will rule with cruelty. The term "hard" is already known in the Exodus narrative, for Pharaoh imposed "hard labor" on the Israelites (Exod. 1:14). What goes around comes around! Now it is Egypt's turn to be subservient and exploited. If this oracle is indeed from the eighth century, then the anticipated overlord is likely a coming Assyrian, any from Tiglath-pilesar III to Ashurbanipal. And indeed, late in its power in the seventh century, Assyria did extend its governance even into Egypt.

All of this will be done by the Sovereign, the one whom Pharaoh anciently would not acknowledge, but the one finally recognized as overlord even of Egypt (cf. Exod. 5:2; 9:27–28; 12:31–32). Yahweh's strategy is to make Egypt ungovernable and therefore vulnerable. In the end, what is promised is a reversal whereby a superpower is reduced to a vassal state. Israel's prophetic rhetoric does not pause to ponder how this happens. We are given the rhetoric, and it is—so the text accepts—as good as done. The empire cannot resist its true sovereign!

The political disorder effected by Yahweh is matched by the coming catastrophe of the failure of the Nile.

> 19:5 **The waters of the Nile will be dried up,**
>   **and the river will be parched and dry;**
> 6 **its canals will become foul,**
>   **and the branches of Egypt's Nile will diminish and dry up,**
>   **reeds and rushes will rot away.**
> 7 **There will be bare places by the Nile,**
>   **on the brink of the Nile;**
>   **and all that is sown by the Nile will dry up,**
>   **be driven away, and be no more.**
> 8 **Those who fish will mourn;**
>   **all who cast hooks in the Nile will lament,**
>   **and those who spread nets on the water will languish.**
> 9 **The workers in flax will be in despair,**
>   **and the carders and those at the loom will grow pale.**
> 10 **Its weavers will be dismayed,**
>   **and all who work for wages will be grieved.**

Again, we are not told how. We only know that the governor of all history is beyond challenge the lord of creation. The God who destabilizes the empire can nullify the river of life. Later on, the tradition of Isaiah will feature a God who turns deserts into rivers:

> For waters shall break forth in the wilderness,
>   and streams in the desert (35:6).
> I will open rivers on the bare heights,
>   and fountains in the midst of the valleys,
> I will make the wilderness a pool of water,
>   and the dry land springs of water (41:18).

But here it is all negative.

The negation is indeed life-threatening, even more of an emergency than the political disorder just imagined. For the Nile is the mother of

Egypt, the source of life. Without its waters—even now—Egypt is a hopeless, barren wasteland. Everything depends upon the Nile. And it will fail!

According to Israel's representations, it is evident that Pharaoh has never rightly understood the relation between the Nile and Egyptian power. Pharaoh has assumed that the Nile is his property and an instrument of his policy. Thus, in Exodus 1:8–22, Pharaoh foolishly prepares to make the Nile, river of life, into a channel of death by using it as a burying ground for Hebrew boys. And in Ezekiel 29:3, Pharaoh allegedly boasts: "My Nile is my own;/I made it for myself." Pharaoh has not understood that he (and all Egyptian political power) is derived from and dependent upon the Nile, which in turn is a creature and gift of Yahweh, who continues to preside over the river. Ordinarily, Yahweh guarantees the Nile as a source of life. But this is not a time of the ordinary! It is evident in Exodus 7:15–25 that Yahweh is able, in extraordinary circumstance, to halt the life-giving function of the Nile.

Now, in our oracle, that ancient memory will come again to fruition (vv. 5–10). It is striking that in this utterance Yahweh is nowhere named as agent. The verbs are characteristically passive: "will be dried up, will be parched, be driven away." The verbs concerning the same issue are active and direct in Ezekiel 30:12–13:

> I will dry up the channels,
>   and will sell the land into the hand of evildoers;
> I will bring desolation upon the land and everything in it
>   by the hand of foreigners;
> I the LORD have spoken.

> Thus says the Lord GOD:
> I will destroy the idols
>   and put an end to the images in Memphis;
> there shall no longer be a prince in the land of Egypt;
>   so I will put fear in the land of Egypt.

But the effect is the same in both statements. No hearer of the oracle will doubt that this is the work of the creator who will, when needed, undo the life-giving functions and resources of creation.

Verses 5–7 characterize the failure of the river. Verses 8–10 report on the concrete effect the failure will have upon a river-sustained economy, each part of which depends upon the river. The failure will be an economic disaster for the fishing industry and for the textile industry. When these industries fail, moreover, the entire realm is jeopardized. The failed economy now accompanies civil disorder. The mighty Egyptian empire is being brought to a standstill!

The failure of civil order (vv. 1–4) and the failure of the Nile-based economy (vv. 5–10) are now complemented by the failure of Egypt's much-vaunted intellectual power (vv. 10–15).

19:11 **The princes of Zoan are utterly foolish;**
　　　the wise counselors of Pharaoh give stupid counsel.
　　How can you say to Pharaoh,
　　　"I am one of the sages,
　　　a descendant of ancient kings"?
 12 **Where now are your sages?**
　　Let them tell you and make known
　　what the LORD of hosts has planned against Egypt.
 13 **The princes of Zoan have become fools,**
　　　and the princes of Memphis are deluded;
　　those who are the cornerstones of its tribes
　　　have led Egypt astray.
 14 **The LORD has poured into them**
　　　a spirit of confusion;
　　and they have made Egypt stagger in all its doings
　　　as a drunkard staggers around in vomit.
 15 **Neither head nor tail, palm branch or reed,**
　　　will be able to do anything for Egypt.

The Egyptian Empire, old and stable, was indeed a center of vast learning. That vast learning, however, is understood in Israel as a gift of Yahweh. Calvin comments:

> Men have in themselves no understanding or judgment, for whence comes wisdom but from the Spirit of God, who is the fountain of light, understanding, and truth? Now, if the Lord withhold his Spirit from us, what right have we to dispute with him? He is under no obligations to us, and all that he bestows is actually a free gift (*Isaiah* II, 64).

As the Nile is Yahweh's gift that can be withdrawn, so also is wisdom to govern well a gift of God that can be withdrawn. If Yahweh gives, Yahweh can take. And when Yahweh takes back wisdom, the erstwhile wise are reduced to foolishness, stupidity, and delusion. This is not the first time Israel has observed the failure of Egypt's prowess, for in Exodus 8:18 the Egyptian scientists reached the limit of their capacity and could not match the magisterial capacity of Moses.

The test of Egyptian wisdom is to discern what "Yahweh of Hosts" intends against Egypt (v. 12). But of course the Egyptian princes have no clue, so encased are they in their own ideology. As a result of the failure of the wisdom to govern, Egypt is rendered weak, ineffective, helpless, and finally self-destructive. The princes are like drunks (v. 14). All of them, everyone of them, are helpless and impotent (v. 15). None can do anything to save. The sum of the matter is indeed a *March of Folly*, to borrow the title of Barbara Tuchman's book, whereby the mighty empire ends in a feebleness and embarrassing impotence.

Every aspect of Egypt's life has failed, because Yahweh is at work to nullify in every zone of imperial existence. As is by now characteristic, we are not told how the agency of Yahweh operates. Indeed, Yahweh's effective agency is not a conclusion drawn from the data, but a premise from which the data is to be understood. Egyptian history and politics are a part of Yahweh's large enterprise. Other "plans" cannot succeed against the purposes of Yahweh (v. 3).

The Cursed Now Blessed (19:16–25)

At the end of verse 15, without explanation, the text begins an about-face. In five prose utterances, each introduced by "on that day," Egypt is now restored and rehabilitated and welcomed back into the generous governance of Yahweh.

> 19:16 **On that day the Egyptians will be like women, and tremble with fear before the hand that the LORD of hosts raises against them.** [17] **And the land of Judah will become a terror to the Egyptians; everyone to whom it is mentioned will fear because of the plan that the LORD of hosts is planning against them.**

The first utterance in prose, however, is not yet ready for the rehabilitation of Egypt. Indeed, this brief oracle shows Judah committing an act of ideological presumption in two ways. First, it is suggested that although "The Lord of hosts" comes powerfully against Egypt, in fact it is "The Land of Judah" that is the terror of Egypt. What had been a Yahwistic, theological claim is made to be a political assertion for Judah. Judah now reassigns to itself the work of Yahweh. Second, Judah is able to imagine itself, according to the oracle, to be so powerful and menacing as to intimidate Egypt. Judah will be the mouse that roars!

The upshot is that the great macho warriors of Egypt will be "like women" (cf. Jer. 51:30). This sexist slam must have been common parlance in military gossip, whereby "like women" is a code word for cowardice.

The phrase mocks the superpower. In the face of what "The Lord of hosts" plans, Egypt is a pitiful has-been. This brief oracle turns a theological claim into something like political braggadocio in Judah.

> **19:18 On that day there will be five cities in the land of Egypt that speak the language of Canaan and swear allegiance to the LORD of hosts. One of these will be called the City of the Sun.**

This second prose oracle now turns toward positive affirmation concerning Egypt. It is impossible to know what is meant by the reference to "five cities." What is important is that there will be "swearing allegiance to Yahweh": Some in Egypt will embrace Yahwism. It is plausible that this is a reference to communities of Jewish expatriates, such as we know of in Elephantine, who continue to adhere to Yahweh in a perhaps unorthodox form. The following oracles, however, suggest that this oracle concerns the conversion of Egyptians, who are ready to abandon their failed religious commitments. "The language of Canaan" in this context likely means readiness to speak Hebrew. Calvin goes further to suggest that it is a metaphor for "confession"; therefore it is a parallel for "swearing allegiance." In any case, the oracle envisions something Yahwistically positive, for Egypt, erstwhile adversary of Yahweh, is drawn positively into Yahweh's orbit.

> **19:19 On that day there will be an altar to the LORD in the center of the land of Egypt, and a pillar to the LORD at its border. 20 It will be a sign and a witness to the LORD of hosts in the land of Egypt; when they cry to the LORD because of oppressors, he will send them a savior, and will defend and deliver them. 21 The LORD will make himself known to the Egyptians; and the Egyptians will know the LORD on that day, and will worship with sacrifice and burnt offering, and they will make vows to the LORD and perform them. 22 The LORD will strike Egypt, striking and healing; they will return to the LORD, and he will listen to their supplications and heal them.**

This is the longest in this series of prose oracles, and it is extraordinary. It is clear now that the prophet anticipates that not only the Jewish diaspora but the Egyptians will embrace Yahweh. An altar and a pillar are concrete emblems of actual, visible worship. The rhetoric suggests a conversion whereby Egyptians have come to a new faith, having left off their failed practices. It had been promised that Egypt would come "into the hand of a hard master," presumably Assyria (v. 4). Now it is expected that Egyptians will "cry out" under their oppression and be heard by Yahweh (v. 20).

The remarkable fact of this rhetoric is that it replicates the ancient Exodus narrative. Israel in Egypt has been recruited into "hard service" (Exod. 1:14), has "cried out," and has been rescued by Yahweh (Exod. 2:23–25). By the end of the Exodus narrative, moreover, the cry of the slaves has been transferred to the Egyptians (Exod. 12:30; cf. 11:6). Now, in our oracle, the cry of Egypt sounds remarkably like the cry of the ancient Hebrew slaves, perhaps an Egyptian cry continued since Exodus 12:30.

The replication goes further. Not only will Egypt in oppression cry out, as every people in oppression will do. Yahweh will respond: "He will send a savior, and will defend and deliver them" (v. 20). Yahweh will do for Egypt what Yahweh has done for Israel. Israel's Exodus is paradigmatic; it of course pertains peculiarly to Israel, but not exclusively. Yahweh may and will do the same for other peoples who cry out, and now extraordinarily, even for Egypt (cf. Amos 9:7). Kaiser observes: "Yahweh is the God who listens not only to the lamentations of the people but also to those addressed to him by other nations" (*Isaiah 13–39*, 109). Upon crying out and being heard and saved, Egypt will come to *know* Yahweh, *worship* Yahweh, and *make vows* to Yahweh; that is, fully join the community of Yahweh.

The verb "know" of course does not mean to have information about; it means rather to acknowledge fully and embrace as sovereign. For such a prideful state as Egypt to "know Yahweh" is not easy or routine. Indeed, the entire Exodus narrative is driven by Pharaoh's refusal (inability?) to know Yahweh: "Who is the LORD, that I should heed him and let Israel go? I do not *know* the LORD, and I will not let Israel go" (Exod. 5:2). The Exodus narrative is the slow, relentless process by which Pharaoh comes grudgingly to acknowledge Yahweh (cf. Exod. 9:27; 10:16; 12:31–32). But the knowing remains grudging. It is not—until our oracle—a knowing that results in willing worship and the making of vows. Here all the hardhearted resistance of Egypt is overcome. Perhaps it is characteristically overcome only in desperate need and admitted vulnerability, a need and vulnerability in Egypt not known in the Exodus narrative until very late, but evoked by the onslaught of Isaiah 19:1–15.

The oracle is theologically discerning. First there is *cry/deliver*, and only then *know/worship/pay vows*. The oppressed Egyptians did not know and then cry out; rather, they moved from trouble to acknowledgment. That is precisely the sequence in the Exodus narrative concerning Israel: Israel "cried out" (Exod. 2:23–25) and only later "believed" (4:31). The same sequence is reflected in the poignant statement of the psalm: "But there is forgiveness with you,/so that you may be revered" (Psalm 130:4). The salvific act precedes acknowledgment.

This remarkable oracle offers one other noteworthy link to the Exodus narrative. Yahweh is a God who strikes and who heals (cf. Hos. 6:1). There is no doubt that Yahweh has struck (Exod. 5—11) and will strike Egypt

(Isa. 19:1–15). We are not, however, prepared for the assertion that Yahweh will *heal Egypt* (v. 22). Indeed, "healing Egypt" sounds like an oxymoron, a complete contradiction. One of the remarkable assurances of healing by Yahweh is in the Exodus narrative, which requires obedience and which contends with Egypt: "If you will listen carefully to the voice of the LORD your God . . . and give heed to his commandments . . . I will not bring upon you any of the diseases that I brought upon the Egyptians; for I am the LORD who heals you" (Exod. 15:26). Israel is to be healed; Egypt is given over to disease.

In our oracle, in contrast to Exodus 15:26, it is now Egypt who will be healed (v. 22). Egypt has indeed been smitten by Yahweh with disease. But Egypt, as Israel was required to do as a condition for healing, has become obedient to Yahweh. It has "returned to the Lord." And now the God who hears the cry of the slaves hears the cry of oppressed Egypt. The God who is fully known by Israel is now to be fully known by Egypt. The God who healed the Israelite slaves now overcomes "the diseases of Egypt." This is indeed "the healing of the nations" (Rev. 22:2).

19:23 On that day there will be a highway from Egypt to Assyria, and the Assyrian will come into Egypt, and the Egyptian into Assyria, and the Egyptians will worship with the Assyrians.

In the eighth century, Egypt and Assyria are the two superpowers at the ends of the Fertile Crescent. Geopolitically, it is always Egypt to the south, though the northern counterpart may change. These two powers, north and south, endlessly contest for domination. They are inevitably trading partners; in commerce they must traverse the middle territory in which lies Judah. But these major trading partners are at the best uneasy partners. As often as not, they are in hostility, because their spheres of influence overlap. The "King's Highway," the great commercial road connecting the two, is also a military road designed for the movement of troops. Thus the road between is contentious and endlessly in dispute, surely marked by blocks, harassment, toll booths, customs officials, and all that goes with the scramble for domination and the exhibit of domination.

This brief oracle imagines it will be otherwise in time to come. The troubled "connector" will be transformed into a "highway" on which travel is easy, rapid, and unimpeded. (The same term is used in the grand vision of 40:3.) The new road bespeaks a new peaceableness among the nations. A peaceable connector reflects political reconciliation and an acknowledgment of common interests that override enduring hostilities.

It will, however, be more than a commercial connector in time to come.

The two superpowers will "worship" together. The term "worship" is "serve" (*'bd*), the same term used in verse 21. In verse 21, however, the verb is linked directly to cultic activity aimed at Yahweh. Here the verb stands quite alone. But we may import from verse 21 that content, so that this usage means the same—worship of Yahweh. If, however, we stay with the verb itself and take it as "serve," it may suggest that the two superpowers come to peaceableness because they "serve" instead of control. Either way, the oracle suggests that socioeconomic, political, military harmony between old adversaries has as a defining component common worship of the true God whom both had so long mocked and resisted. The oracle speaks about nothing less than the coming "kingdom of Yahweh" on earth, which is not simply a theological *slogan*, but a *practice* in which superpowers will finally engage.

Whereas the first in this series of oracles (vv. 16–17) had introduced Judah's political interest into the equation, there is none of that here. The superpowers are not intimidated by or beholden to Judah, who is absent from this oracle. It is enough that Egypt has cried out and will be healed. Perhaps the same pertains to the northern superpower as well, though that is not stated.

19:24 **On that day Israel will be the third with Egypt and Assyria, a blessing in the midst of the earth,** 25 **whom the LORD of hosts has blessed, saying, "Blessed be Egypt my people, and Assyria the work of my hands, and Israel my heritage."**

Since verse 16, this series of oracles has been moving from "terror" to a vision of reconciliation. In this final oracle, that movement culminates in one of the grandest, most daring hopes of the entire Bible. The speaker knows the map of the Fertile Crescent well. There is Israel in the vulnerable "in-between," precariously between Egypt and the northern superpower, Assyria. This map is saturated with war, blood, hostility, intrigue—even until now. The speaker, moreover, knows about Israel's theological claim as the peculiarly beloved people of Yahweh. All of that is long attested and readily assumed.

In an extraordinarily venturesome maneuver, the oracle engages Israel's best theological claims in order to redefine power relations in the Fertile Crescent. The oracle takes three pet names by which Yahweh characterizes Israel—"my people," "the work of my hands," and "my heritage"—and generously redeploys them across the Fertile Crescent. Israel's long-standing enemies are now renamed and redefined according to pet names now to be used for Assyria and Egypt as well as Israel. Calvin observes:

"Though these titles belonged exclusively to Israel, they shall likewise be conferred on other nations, which the Lord hath adopted to be his own" (*Isaiah* II, 83). By this astonishing renaming, the enemies are renamed as fellow members of the covenant and are invited to accept new identity in the world. But we also notice that to make this possible, Israel must relinquish its exclusive claims and its unrivaled relation to Yahweh and be willing to share the privilege of such identity.

The outcome is an ecumenical vision whereby former enemies are drawn into commonality. Ecumenism inevitably requires giving up one's sense of primacy, exclusiveness, and privilege. Such a maneuver as is here required of Israel would be like the Christian church conceding that God has other chosen peoples as well. Or more parochially, in the Christian community, it would be like rock-ribbed orthodox folk conceding legitimacy as colleagues to those it regarded as outside the fold. Or conversely, multicultural liberals may share legitimacy with those whom they dismiss as narrow and therefore illegitimate. We may celebrate this large, generous vision. We may do so, however, only as we notice the considerable cost to the original "pet" who had been able to monopolize the pet names. Egypt comes home to its true self only as Israel opens its sense of privilege to its adversaries. The God who dismantles Egypt in verses 1–15 is indeed the God who gladly cherishes, welcomes, delivers, and heals all peoples. It is *the world* that turns out to be Yahweh's *chosen people*.

HOW SHALL WE ESCAPE?
20:1–6

20:1 **In the year that the commander-in-chief, who was sent by King Sargon of Assyria, came to Ashdod and fought against it and took it— 2 at that time the LORD had spoken to Isaiah son of Amoz, saying, "Go, and loose the sackcloth from your loins and take your sandals off your feet," and he had done so, walking naked and barefoot. 3 Then the LORD said, "Just as my servant Isaiah has walked naked and barefoot for three years as a sign and a portent against Egypt and Ethiopia, 4 so shall the king of Assyria lead away the Egyptians as captives and the Ethiopians as exiles, both the young and the old, naked and barefoot, with buttocks uncovered, to the shame of Egypt. 5 And they shall be dismayed and confounded because of Ethiopia their hope and of Egypt their boast. 6 In that day the inhabitants of this coastland will say, 'See, this is what has happened to those in whom we hoped and to whom we fled for help and deliverance from the king of Assyria! And we, how shall we escape?'"**

In 19:19–25 we have been offered a brilliant Yahwistic resolution of the geopolitical tensions of the Fertile Crescent. The full rule of Yahweh is interpreted as the source of peaceableness for the entire region. It is, however, a scenario for "that day" not yet realized. In the meantime, in chapter 20 we are plunged back into the geopolitical conflicts of the Fertile Crescent, where the rule of Yahweh is not yet established. This oracle concerns the conquest of the Philistine city of Ashdod and the subsequent defeat of Ethiopia and Egypt. Thus the oracle has important connections to the materials of 14:28–32; 18:1–7; and 19:1–15 concerning respectively Philistia, Ethiopia, and Egypt.

A familiarity with the political-military history of the region is assumed by the oracle. Sargon, the mighty Assyrian emperor who defeated the Northern Kingdom of Israel in 722, is now on the move south. He dispatches his "second" (*tartan*) to defeat southern forces who have conspired against Assyrian rule in 711. The battle is joined at the Philistine city of Ashdod on the Mediterranean Coast, where the coalition is defeated by Assyria and Ashdod is taken. It is probable that the resistance to Assyria was propelled by Egypt (now governed by Ethiopians), who regularly goaded the lesser powers into resistance against Assyria, who regularly promised to support the coalition against Assyria, and who regularly failed to give the support promised. The victory by Assyria in 711 thus is not only a defeat for the coalition but yet another exposé of Egyptian unreliability.

The oracle, however, only assumes such geopolitical data. It is more interested in the odd conduct of Isaiah who, at the behest of Yahweh (we are told), is exposed, naked and barefoot, in Jerusalem for three years. This odd conduct is identified as "a sign and portent"; that is, a gesture commanded by Yahweh in order to assert an intention of Yahweh still hidden but sure to come to fruition. (See examples of such signs in Ezekiel 4:1–17; 5:1–12.) Nakedness is generally taken in the Old Testament as a sign of *exile*, of humiliation, helplessness, and vulnerability when one is given over completely to the power of another (cf. 47:3). Although the sign itself may be a poignant gesture with its intent perhaps well understood, the sign is characteristically accompanied by an interpretive comment. Thus verses 3–4 offer both sign and comment: "Just as [sign] . . . so [meaning]." The linkage between sign and meaning may strike us as far-fetched and unclear, but so it is given.

Here the interpretation of the sign pertains to Egypt and Ethiopia, sources of the resistance at Ashdod and Assyria's primary nemeses. The sign, bespeaking Yahweh's powerful intention, is that Assyria, having defeated the coalition, will defeat Egypt and Ethiopia, will deport these peoples (or perhaps their leaders), and so subject these once grand powers to deep humiliation. The prophet envisions the large, formidable domination of the entire Fertile Crescent by Assyria at the behest of Yahweh, a domination that did briefly prevail in the seventh century.

The narrative account is not finally interested in the large turn of geopolitics nor even in the prophetic sign. In verses 5–6, the accent is upon a response to the portended defeat of Egypt and Ethiopia. "*They*" shall be dismayed and confounded because they had trusted in Egypt and Ethiopia, who had failed them. The next sentences identify the "they." It is "the inhabitants of the coastlands." That is, the bewildered and distraught are citizens of the small states who have been betrayed by Egypt, who now stare massive Assyrian power in the face, and who sense their own great jeopardy. No doubt the oncoming might of Assyria is intrinsically terrifying. It is more so if one has resisted and must now face the cruel consequences of having resisted the winner. What interests us is that it is plausible that the "they" in their bewilderment includes Judah, who may have given credence to Egyptian-Ethiopian promises as a basis for foreign policy. Those promises had now all failed, and now "they" are fully exposed and forlorn.

This artfully drawn narrative focuses this very large geopolitical crisis upon a double acknowledgment filled with acute pathos: "those in whom we hoped and to whom we fled" (v. 6). All hope in Egypt is lost. It turns out to have been uncommonly foolish to trust Egypt, which in that ancient world characteristically had not kept its promises. This sad assessment of circumstance produces the haunting, overriding question, How shall we escape? How shall we escape the threat of Assyria? There the text ends. The community is left without response, to ponder its impossible situation.

No answer is given. But of course the intended answer is everywhere implied in the tradition of Isaiah. The answer to the question of historical rescue is *Yahweh*. That had been the answer much earlier in the Syro-Ephraimite War: "If you do not stand firm in faith,/you shall not stand at all" (7:9).

The circumstances change, but the theological insistence of the Isaiah tradition is constant. Predictably, Calvin comments: "Now, they ought to have looked to God alone. Their wandering levity is therefore censured" (*Isaiah* II, 90). Or as he offered in his great hymn: "Our hope is in no other."

It is a big leap from this vulnerable, ancient folk to Christians who are citizens of a major superpower. The threats are different. Now the threat is not a military one. It is, I suggest, the juggernaut of consumer capitalism that insists upon redefining our common life in deathly ways. As those ancient folk could not imagine themselves outside the grasp of Assyria—

and so were without hope—so we can hardly imagine ourselves beyond the world-defining power of such consumerism. But of course it is the burden of the prophetic oracle to insist, precisely, upon life received beyond the compelling horizon of the superpower. We may from this text be haunted by the same question, How shall we escape? The answer is not changed. It was not easy (or obvious) then; it is not easy (or obvious) now.

"I BRING TO AN END"
21:1–17

Of this passage Kaiser comments: "We would have been grateful to him [the poet] for expressing himself less cryptically" (*Isaiah 13–39*, 125). Indeed, this chapter is extraordinarily enigmatic and elusive and, given our present understandings, almost completely beyond comprehension. I take comfort in the surmise that likely the only people who attend to this poem are those, like myself, who attempt to write a commentary that does not permit skipping over the material.

The chapter consists of an extended oracle anticipating the fall of Babylon (vv. 1–10; cf. v. 9), plus brief oracles concerning Dumah (vv. 11–12), "the desert plain" (vv. 13–15), and Kedar (vv. 16–17). The poetry is tilted toward apocalyptic rhetoric, so that historical references are exceedingly elusive. It is evident that the primary oracle concerns a vast disorder and an ending of power arrangements dominated by Babylon, an ending that is welcome but causes a response of enormous confusion and dismay.

> 21:1 **The oracle concerning the wilderness of the sea.**
>   **As whirlwinds in the Negeb sweep on,**
>   **it comes from the desert,**
>   **from a terrible land.**
>   ²**A stern vision is told to me;**
>   **the betrayer betrays,**
>   **and the destroyer destroys.**
>   **Go up, O Elam,**
>   **lay siege, O Media;**
>   **all the sighing she has caused**
>   **I bring to an end.**

The poem begins with an onslaught that is likened to a huge windstorm off the Negev that is hot, destructive, massive, and irresistible. The "it" of verse 1 still refers to the storm, but in the process of the poetry, "it" is converted into the ominous attacker. "The betrayer" and "the destroyer" may

refer to a historical enemy, but there is enough of an apocalyptic hint here
to suggest that they refer to "the ultimate enemy" who will terminate
everything. The reference to "Elam and Medea" is taken by most scholars
to refer to the Persians under Cyrus who will overcome Babylon. On that
reading, the text is linked to more concrete references to the coming of the
Persians under Cyrus, a reference that is made explicit in chapters 44—45.
Thus the poem employs venturesome rhetoric for this pivotal historical
turn that comes to dominate the tradition of Isaiah. Oppressive Babylon
has caused much sighing and groaning and yearning for relief. And now all
that sighing will end, for relief is about to be given. Although "Medes and
Elamites" are engaged, it is the great "I" of Yahweh who acts. Yahweh has
the authority to terminate all that has been, including oppressive Babylon.

21:3 **Therefore my loins are filled with anguish;**
    pangs have seized me,
    like the pangs of a woman in labor;
I am bowed down so that I cannot hear,
  I am dismayed so that I cannot see.
    ⁴My mind reels, horror has appalled me;
    the twilight I longed for
    has been turned for me into trembling.

In these verses the poet characterizes the deep emotional response to the
news of verses 1–2. Although there may be relief at the end of Babylon,
nonetheless the news is staggering and stunning, because it means the end
of the known world. The poet uses figures of internal bodily responses to
tell how the news is received. Because the language is exaggerated, it seems
as though the poetry looks past the historical crisis and regards the turn as
a world-ending of apocalyptic scope and power. One must imagine an
external event that is commensurate to the internal response of anguish,
pangs, dismay, reeling, horror, and trembling. The coming time evokes
massive upset!

21:5 **They prepare the table,**
    they spread the rugs,
    they eat, they drink.
  Rise up, commanders,
    oil the shield!
 ⁶ For thus the LORD said to me:
  "Go, post a lookout,
    let him announce what he sees.
 ⁷ When he sees riders, horsemen in pairs,
    riders on donkeys, riders on camels,

let him listen diligently,
very diligently."
8 Then the watcher called out:
"Upon a watchtower I stand, O Lord,
continually by day,
and at my post I am stationed
throughout the night.
9 Look, there they come, riders,
horsemen in pairs!"
Then he responded,
"Fallen, fallen is Babylon;
and all the images of her gods
lie shattered on the ground."

This unit of the poem begins with an imagined scene from complacent, opulent Babylon. The political and military leaders are at ease, eating and drinking. But then abruptly, a call to arms! It is as though the early warning system of the empire had failed.

At verse 6 the imagery is abruptly inverted. Now there is no ease or complacency, but the agitation and alarm that belong to invasion. We are transported by the poem to a surveillance post. From there one can observe riders mounted on horses, donkeys, and camels, as though the coming troops have seized upon every possible mode of transportation (v. 7). The sentinel is alert and at his post continually day and night to report on the incessant arrival of more attackers (vv. 8–9a).

In the middle of verse 9, we receive report of the outcome of the battle: "Fallen is Babylon." We are given no detail of the battle, only the arrival of the troops. Now we are able to see where the poem has been heading since verse 1. The "storm" is an assault upon Babylon. The sighing ended (v. 2) is the sighing generated by harsh Babylonian policy. The emotional response of verses 3–4 concerns the loss of Babylon as a fixed point of reference. The "I" of verse 2 causes the end of Babylon. It is Yahweh over Babylon. Babylon for so long had seemed forever. Such an appearance, however, is credible only until Yahweh is mobilized, and then—in an instant, in an utterance—the great empire that had defeated every Jewish hope is terminated.

The fall of Babylon is indeed a historical event. It is a datable, identifiable happening. But because Babylon had completely occupied world opinion, dominated world politics, and preempted world imagination, the occasion of its demise is more than historical. It is a cosmic happening that signifies a revolutionary redefinition of the world. The terse announcement given here is expanded in the gloating relief of the Jewish tradition noted in Jeremiah 50:2:

> Babylon is taken,
>   Bel is put to shame,
>   Merodach is dismayed.
> Her images are put to shame,
>   her idols dismayed.

In this rendering, the military event is transposed into theological combat wherein the Babylonian gods have been defeated and humiliated by the greater power of Yahweh. The defeat of Babylon, surely a historical event, becomes in Israel's imagination a pivotal example of Yahweh's capacity to override the power of evil. In christological reflection in the New Testament, this same model bespeaks Yahweh's capacity to defeat the power of death.

21:10 O my threshed and winnowed one,
   what I have heard from the LORD of hosts,
   the God of Israel, I announce to you.

This poem of the news of a decisive turn of the world comes to its culmination in this pastorally attentive address to Israel. After the swirl of the storm and the bombast of attack, here the people of Yahweh—long in exile—is addressed. The news is from "The Lord of hosts," the powerful God of military capability. The news from that God is peculiarly for Israel, "my threshed and winnowed one." Israel has long been vulnerable, exposed, taken advantage of, abused. The imagery is agricultural, but the allusions are violent. To thresh is to beat; to winnow is to crush enough to get the grain from the sheaf. Israel had long been at the merciless hands of the threshing, winnowing empire, without any protection from Yahweh. And now it is over! The end wrought by Yahweh is an end to such abuse. In subsequent Isaiah (41:15), the tables will be turned:

> Now, I will make of you a threshing sledge,
>   sharp, new, and having teeth;
> you shall thresh the mountains and crush them,
>   and you shall make the hills like chaff.

21:11 The oracle concerning Dumah.

   One is calling to me from Seir,
   "Sentinel, what of the night?

> Sentinel, what of the night?"
> 12 The sentinel says:
>   "Morning comes, and also the night.
>   If you will inquire, inquire;
>   come back again."

This little oracle is completely baffling, in large part because of the super-scription "concerning Dumah." It is possible that "Dumah" is a place (an oasis), a reference to awed "silence," a misspelling of Edom that may be suggested by "Seir" in what follows, or an intrusion that mistakenly divides verses 11–12 from the preceding.

In any case, the double question of verse 11 is put to the sentinel, a guard not unlike the "watcher" in verse 8. The sentinel is the one who watches and waits and listens for word from a battle being fought some-where else. The question in effect means, 'What time is it?' That is, Is the night almost over? The answer is, It is still night, but the day comes soon; ask again later.

If this question and answer are linked to verses 1–10, it may be an in-quiry about the "ultimate" battle against Babylon, for certainly Seir, like Judah, would wait for the defeat of Babylon. It is quite plausible that "night . . . morning" can be understood metaphorically so that "night" refers to the long season of oppression under Babylon and "morning" is the new day of relief and emancipation: "Weeping may linger for the night,/but joy comes with the morning" (Psalm 30:5). On that reading, the inquiry is whether the promises of verses 1–10 have yet come to fruition. The an-swer is, Not yet. Not yet . . . but ask again later. That is, the sentinel does not doubt that good news is coming soon. Here reference may be made to 52:7–8, another reference to a sentinel receiving news of the defeat of Babylon (though with a different word for sentinel). It may also be noted that the verses of our oracle have been appropriated by Christians for Ad-vent, wherein the question concerns the coming of liberation in Jesus, as in the carol "Watchman, Tell Us of the Night."

21:13 **The oracle concerning the desert plain.**

> In the scrub of the desert plain you will lodge,
>   O caravans of Dedanites.
> 14 Bring water to the thirsty,
>   meet the fugitive with bread,
>   O inhabitants of the land of Tema.
> 15 For they have fled from the swords,
>   from the drawn sword,

from the bent bow,
and from the stress of battle.

This brief oracle concerns caravaners who have fled from the horrors of combat and have retreated to safe places in the desert. That is, they are fugitives of war, and like any such fugitives, they are in need of life's necessities: bread and water. If the battle of verses 6–9 is something like an end-time struggle, then these verses may attest to the costly ferocity of the war, which, as is usual in battle, exacts heavy penalties from those who are unfortunately and innocently too close to the action.

> 21:16 **For thus the Lord said to me: Within a year, according to the years of a hired worker, all the glory of Kedar will come to an end; 17 and the remaining bows of Kedar's warriors will be few; for the LORD, the God of Israel, has spoken.**

This final oracle oddly and without explanation asserts the defeat of the desert power of Kedar. It is of interest that here speaks "The God of Israel." This appellation may suggest that Kedar was a vexation to Israel. Insofar as this chapter moves toward an apocalyptic notion of a final battle for the rule of the world, it was perhaps thought appropriate to throw in for good measure all of the powers vexing to Israel, none of whom can withstand Yahweh. The sum of this odd chapter is that an end of the known world of brutality is being wrought by Yahweh (v. 2). That ending is good news for Israel (v. 10), but surely also for Seir, who awaits the dawn (vv. 11–12), and for the caravaners of Dedan who yearn for bread and water (vv. 13–15). The news is that the turn of the world is under way. The exalted ones (Babylon, Kedar) are becoming humble. That is good news for the currently humbled.

PLANNED LONG AGO
22:1–14

We are surprised to find this oracle, formed in a complicated editorial process, placed among the "Oracles Against the Nations." It articulates a harsh judgment against Jerusalem and Judah ("my beloved people"), as harsh as the treatment of any foreign nation (v. 4). And because it is against Jerusalem, it apparently can be linked, at least in some of its parts, to the actual known history of Judah. The most likely locus is the siege of Jerusalem by Sennacherib, the Assyrian, in 701. In that event, Jerusalem was saved. Sennacherib and his armies went home without victory (Isa. 37:36–

38). They did however take home a heavy load of captured booty, as the Assyrian annals indicate. Thus the crisis of 701 was exceedingly costly for Judah, exacting an enormous price, but one that could be misperceived as a great rescue. It is precisely the ambivalent character of an *actual loss* and *a perceived victory* that here is dealt with.

22:1 **The oracle concerning the valley of vision.**

> **What do you mean that you have gone up,**
> **all of you, to the housetops,**
> ² **you that are full of shoutings,**
> **tumultuous city, exultant town?**
> **Your slain are not slain by the sword,**
> **nor are they dead in battle.**
> ³ **Your rulers have all fled together;**
> **they were captured without the use of a bow.**
> **All of you who were found were captured,**
> **though they had fled far away.**

The valley of vision in verse 5 is a place of "tumult, trampling, and confusion," bespeaking loss of control and abuse. The superscription of verse 1 locates this oracle in that "valley of vision." The oracle speaks out of a depth of disarray, which the poet takes with deep seriousness but which goes unnoticed by the community.

The poet, presumably Isaiah, notices that the populace is on the housetops celebrating, perhaps in a wild, out-of-control way as when a city wins a great sports championship (vv. 1–2a). The poet is appalled, for the celebration is completely incongruent with reality. The reality is that many fled the battle, even the rulers who should have stayed to fight. But none escaped! All were captured. There is, as a consequence, no cause for celebration. The celebration is based on a complete misconstrual of reality, driven by an eagerness to deny reality. In 5:20, we have seen Judah's propensity to misconstrue in its denial; here that denial is acted out in a foolish, boisterous crowd scene.

22:4 **Therefore I said:**
> **Look away from me,**
> **let me weep bitter tears;**
> **do not try to comfort me**
> **for the destruction of my beloved people.**

The "shoutings" of the "tumultuous city, exultant town" are set in profound contrast to the mood of the poet, which here, of course, is reckoned to be a correct perception of events (v. 2). The poet is driven, by the same events that produced popular rejoicing, to a deep mood of grief and sadness. The poet sees differently, and what he sees is destruction. He is driven to tears, not only because of what has happened, not only because he knows what will yet happen, but also because of the cynical denial of his contemporaries. Indeed, the poet refuses to be comforted (cf. Jer. 31:15). One may imagine that the use of the term "comfort" (v. 4) is intended precisely as the term is used in Lamentations 1:9, 17, 22. The term sits here unanswered until it is powerfully answered in Isaiah 40:1. That use, however, is far removed from this oracle and comes only late to Jerusalem. In the meantime, this poet sees as the crowd does not, and there is no cause for joy and no ground for comfort.

> 22:5 **For the Lord GOD of hosts has a day**
> **of tumult and trampling and confusion**
> **in the valley of vision,**
> **a battering down of walls**
> **and a cry for help to the mountains.**
> 6 **Elam bore the quiver**
> **with chariots and cavalry,**
> **and Kir uncovered the shield.**
> 7 **Your choicest valleys were full of chariots,**
> **and the cavalry took their stand at the gates.**
> 8a **He has taken away the covering of Judah.**

These verses reflect a quite changed tone. The rhetoric refers to remote enemies (Elam and Kir), so scholars think these verses arise late and move in an apocalyptic direction. That is, the specific crisis of verses 1–4 is now escalated into a cosmic event. "The Lord of hosts" is an exaggerated title, the agent who drives the crisis. And because of Yahweh in full military regalia, the scene is one of massive upheaval. The enemies come strong and well armed, just outside the gates of the city. Judah is exposed and unprotected.

It may well be that verses 1–4, historically based, record an actual prophetic experience. And verses 5–8 are a visionary extrapolation of what is yet coming. The city escaped in 701 with a mixed verdict that could be perceived as vindication of royal policy. In a more visionary act, however, the poet can see more trouble coming. The poet knows enough about Judah's characteristic actions and knows enough, equally well, about Yahweh's characteristic responses, that judgment to come is massive and inescapable.

> 22:8b **On that day you looked to the weapons of the House of the Forest,** 9
> **and you saw that there were many breaches in the city of David, and you**

collected the waters of the lower pool. ¹⁰ You counted the houses of Jerusalem, and you broke down the houses to fortify the wall. ¹¹ You made a reservoir between the two walls for the water of the old pool. But you did not look to him who did it, or have regard for him who planned it long ago.

The poet describes Jerusalem's characteristic response when the heavy-duty negative intervention of Yahweh is underway. Judah responds to the crisis but regards the crisis as if Yahweh were not a factor. The oracle employs two rhetorical patterns in order to make the point. First, the poet describes what the populace saw and did not see. "You looked" to the arsenal of "The House of the Forest." That is, the populace relied on the military resources of the royal establishment to provide protection from the onslaught, for "The House of the Forest" is a royal building (cf. 1 Kings 7:2). There was reliance upon the very monarchy that has foolishly brought on the Yahwistic crisis. The verb "look" is reinforced by "saw" in verse 9. They saw what needed to be done by way of civil defense. This included repairing the city walls so that the enemy could not invade. In order to repair the walls, some houses were torn down to secure stones for the walls. They worked, moreover, to secure the water supply, which is always problematic in the city. To secure walls and water is an act of prudence.

The problem with such emergency measures is that they represent reliance upon conventional measures of human security. What they do not do is *"look to him"* who evoked the crisis. All the pragmatic measures taken are futile because the real problem, so the text insists, is Yahweh. Any reckoning without Yahweh is a foolish, ineffective calculation, because Yahweh had "formed" this action long ago. The text insists, yet again, upon the decisive governance of Yahweh over the destiny of Judah. By now Judah should have known, but it knows nothing. This is indeed a people who listens but does not comprehend, who looks but does not understand (6:9). Indeed, the *wrong looking* in verses 8b–11, that is, looking to pragmatic matters but not to Yahweh, is parallel to the wrong perception of verses 1–2a. The prophet sees clearly the Yahwistic-covenantal dimension of Israel's life and the consequences of the disregard of that aspect of life. His grief (v. 4) is escalated by the obduracy of his people whose horizon is limited to quick fixes that change nothing important (vv. 8b–11) and to fun and games that notice nothing important.

22:12 **In that day the Lord GOD of hosts**
        called to weeping and mourning,
            to baldness and putting on sackcloth;
    ¹³ **but instead there was joy and festivity,**

> killing oxen and slaughtering sheep,
> eating meat and drinking wine.
> "Let us eat and drink,
> for tomorrow we die."
> ¹⁴ The LORD of hosts has revealed himself in my ears:
> Surely this iniquity will not be forgiven you until you die,
> says the Lord GOD of hosts.

The contrasting discernments of poet and populace are reiterated and forcibly summarized. The poet asserts and embraces the summons of Yahweh to weeping, mourning, grieving, and acknowledging loss (cf. v. 4). But what was practiced was precisely the antithesis to the summons of God: joy, festival, extravagance, self-indulgence (cf. Amos 6:4–6). The quotation in the last lines of verse 13 perhaps does not report what was uttered, but it surely reports the statements made through self-indulgent activity. The self-approving verdict parallels Ecclesiastes 7:9, except that here there is a cynical, numbed embrace of death. There is no care for the future, but only a completely undisciplined embrace of an extravagant present tense.

The poet insists that his sense of what is appropriate has been disclosed to him by Yahweh. The prophet has not invented the message. The antithesis being lived out in defiance of Yahweh is indeed a sin so great that it cannot be "forgiven" "covered"). The final word, "die," echoes and reiterates the cynical term of verse 13, as though to say, "Yes, die you will . . . and unreconciled."

This oracle, complex as it is, stands at the core of Isaianic faith. Life reckoned without Yahweh is simply nonsense that will surely lead to destruction. The oracle scarcely requires interpretation for our own situation in the opulent, self-indulgent West, eating and drinking and spending to self-destruction, completely misconstruing the costs. In that ancient day there was this lone prophet in grief; even now, here and there, there are such voices who discern that a deathly future was "formed" by God long ago. Inappropriate rejoicing and self-indulgences such as "eating, drinking, and making merry" lead to a voice in the night that addresses, "Fool" (Luke 12:19–20).

BAD STEWARD, GOOD STEWARD
22:15–25

This portion of text purports to give a glimpse into the internal workings and internal tensions in the royal household. It contrasts two officials who functioned as "chancellor," that is, as in command second only to the king. The narrative contrasts *Shebna*, who is condemned and rejected for unacceptable actions, and *Eliakim*, who is commended and endorsed as a faithful and effective official. The juxtaposition appears to be informed by the historical notes of 2 Kings 18:18; Isaiah 36:3 and 37:2, in which Eliakim is the senior officer and Shebna ranks next in authority. On the face of it, the text concerns the wise and the irresponsible use of public power.

22:15 **Thus says the Lord GOD of hosts: Come, go to this steward, to Shebna, who is master of the household, and say to him:** [16] **What right do you have here? Who are your relatives here, that you have cut out a tomb here for yourself, cutting a tomb on the height, and carving a habitation for yourself in the rock?** [17] **The LORD is about to hurl you away violently, my fellow. He will seize firm hold on you,** [18] **whirl you round and round, and throw you like a ball into a wide land; there you shall die, and there your splendid chariots shall lie, O you disgrace to your master's house!** [19] **I will thrust you from your office, and you will be pulled down from your post.**

In this text, Shebna is identified as the "steward . . . of the household," that is, the one with primary authority for the king's affairs. The text is organized in characteristic fashion as a prophetic speech of judgment:

(a) Through a *messenger formula*, the prophet is dispatched by "The Lord God of hosts" to confront and dismiss the chancellor (v. 15). This authorization is not unlike a CEO sending a second in command to do the firing of a top employee.

(b) The prophet issues an *indictment* that condemns the chancellor (v. 16). The indictment opens with a general (rhetorical) question: "What do you think you are doing?" This is followed by a suggestion that Shebna is disqualified as a foreigner, and then by a critique for having built himself an ostentatious tomb. Apparently the charge is that the chancellor has engaged in self-aggrandizement at the expense of the crown, surely a punishable offense.

(c) The *sentence* following the indictment is dismissal from office (vv. 17–19). It is given in elaborate rhetoric, though the exact image employed is obscure. It is enough to notice that Shebna is dismissed as a "disgrace" to the throne. This exchange is perhaps a characteristic one concerning power struggles in the royal entourage, though it is noteworthy that it is cast in the rhetoric of prophecy. With his Reformed polemic against Romanism, John Calvin finds a contemporary Shebna in the life of Thomas More, who was "a very bitter enemy of the gospel" who was "accused of treason, condemned, and beheaded." I should have thought rather of Cardinal Woolsey, for More operated from a courageously held principle, but Woolsey manifestly did not.

22:20 On that day I will call my servant Eliakim son of Hilkiah, ²¹ and will clothe him with your robe and bind your sash on him. I will commit your authority to his hand, and he shall be a father to the inhabitants of Jerusalem and to the house of Judah. ²² I will place on his shoulder the key of the house of David; he shall open, and no one shall shut; he shall shut, and no one shall open. ²³ I will fasten him like a peg in a secure place, and he will become a throne of honor to his ancestral house. ²⁴ And they will hang on him the whole weight of his ancestral house, the offspring and issue, every small vessel, from the cups to all the flagons. ²⁵ On that day, says the LORD of hosts, the peg that was fastened in a secure place will give way; it will be cut down and fall, and the load that was on it will perish, for the LORD has spoken.

The second part of the text concerns Eliakim, who holds the same office as Shebna and is regarded positively. If we follow the historical notes cited above, then Eliakim *holds the office* but apparently has been *succeeded in office* by Shebna, and then is *restored to office* after the fall of Shebna. Such a sequence would treat verses 20–25 as a historical report that matches the historical narrative of verses 15–19.

I am, however, persuaded of the alternative view of scholars that in contrast to the historical report concerning Shebna, these verses concerning Eliakim are not to be taken as a historical narrative, but are an act of eschatological imagination that envisions the coming of "the good steward" in the future of Jerusalem.

The ground for the judgment that Eliakim is not a historical figure (though appeal is made to a historical figure from 2 Kings 18:18; Isa. 36:3; 37:2) but is a "good type" begins in the judgment that the opening phrase "on that day" does not refer to the day of Shebna's demise in verses 17–19 but is a characteristic Isaianic use about an anticipated future not yet in hand. That is, it is an eschatological formula of a "coming steward" not unlike Jerusalem's long-term hope of a coming good king, a messiah. Moreover, here Yahweh speaks directly and not through a prophetic messenger, as in verses 15–19, so that the genre is indeed promissory oracle. And most important, the rhetoric concerning the coming steward is an echo of the royal, Davidic ideology. As the coming king will be "an everlasting father" (9:6), so the coming steward will be "father to the inhabitants of Jerusalem and to the house of Judah" (v. 21). As the Davidic incumbent will have "a house and a kingdom made sure (*'āmēn*) forever" (2 Sam. 7:16), so the coming steward will be "in a secure (*'āmēn*) place," a "throne of honor to his ancestral house" (v. 23). The rhetoric imagines a coming time when the well-established Davidic officers will have a well-established chancellor, anticipating a pure, perfect, and secure regime. The *ideal* of Eliakim is a complete contrast to the *reality* of Shebna, thus serving "the royal eschatological politics" of the Isaiah tradition.

The promise to the coming Eliakim is a full *investiture of power and authority* in which he is given the emblems of office (v. 21; cf. Joseph in Gen. 41:41–45). Beyond the emblems, moreover, he is given the official key to the royal establishment, so that he has complete control and determines access to the official organs of power (v. 22). Moreover, he will be "the peg," that is, the lynchpin of administrative power, so that everything flows to and depends upon him. This is indeed an empowerment that is awesome and without qualification.

The comment of verses 24–25 construes the metaphor of "peg" differently (mistakenly). It imagines a peg upon which everything royal is hung, so that the weight of it all, even though "in a secure place," will give way. Even the glorious Eliakim cannot last forever. These last verses no longer understand the oracle to be concerned with an ideal figure, but now take Eliakim as a limited historical agent who, like every historical agent, eventually gives way in the political, historical process.

Assuming the correctness of the judgment that Shebna is a historical figure (vv. 15–19) and Eliakim is an eschatological model (vv. 20–23), this completed juxtaposition is a remarkable achievement of Isaianic theology. The completed text takes what must have been a concrete and momentary crisis in the royal entourage and has used it as a vehicle for a theological statement concerning "former time" and "latter time" (cf. 9:1), or what in later Isaiah tradition will be termed "former things" and "new things" (43:18–19). Shebna is the embodiment of "former time, former things" and finishes in *dishonor* for having been disobedient, irresponsible, and self-serving, not attending to the centrality of the king. By contrast, the ideal Eliakim to come is the perfection yet to be received in Jerusalem; he plays his part faithfully, enjoys the "security" ('*āmēn*) of power, and finishes in "a throne of *honor*." Shebna and Eliakim come to be embodiments of old, failed Judah and the coming Judah yet to be given by God. The large, two-stage theology of Isaiah that we have seen elsewhere is embodied in two "historical," named agents, one known and censored, the other anticipated and celebrated.

Finally, we may notice two derivations from this text. First, it is likely that the reference to Eliakim and "the key of the house of David" (v. 22) is replicated in Matthew 16:19, wherein Peter is promised: "I will give you the keys of the kingdom of heaven, and whatever you bind on earth will be bound in heaven, and whatever you loose on earth will be loosed in heaven." This is an enormously powerful authorization, which has been fully and maximally appreciated in the Petrine theory of church authority. Peter holds the office, not unlike Eliakim, second only to the reigning David, Jesus. Peter, like Eliakim, is entrusted with complete oversight of the household of the church. We may extrapolate, as the church always has done, to recognize that immediately after this high investiture of Peter, the very next paragraph in Matthew condemns him as a would-be Shebna who is unfaithful: "Get behind me, Satan! You are a stumbling block to me; for you are setting your mind not on divine things but on human things" (Matt. 16:23). Thus Shebna and Eliakim model the *shame* and *glory* that is always being enacted toward "the second in command" in service to the king.

Second, both Shebna and Eliakim occupy a position of *chief steward* in the royal household. It takes no great imagination to see that the juxtaposition of the two provides a fitting model for *stewardship*, as the church ponders its role as invested by its Lord with massive oversight. Good stewardship concerns faithful care for the household; bad stewardship entails self-advancement at the expense of the realm. Like the Isaiah tradition, the church as steward is always moving between sordid self-promotion and hoped-for faithful administration of the royal trust.

"YOUR FORTRESS IS DESTROYED"
23:1–18

Phoenicia stood at the center of active international commerce in the ancient world. The hub of that Phoenician enterprise, moreover, was Tyre, ancient city kingdom related to Israel since the days of Hiram and his contribution to Solomon's royal splendor (1 Kings 5:1–12). The critical tradition of Yahwism voiced by the prophets had a profound suspicion of such global commercialism, which it regarded as a practice of pride and autonomy in resistance to the intentions of Yahweh. It may well be that the overthrow of Tyre (vv. 1–14) and its subsequent anticipated recovery (vv. 15–18) refer to the actual military and economic events in the ancient world. The commentaries on this passage indicate that although there are many historical linkages that can be made, there is insufficient evidence to be certain about any close connection to actual events.

Without denying that historical realism is operative in this prophetic oracle, we do better to attend to the rhetoric of the passage and understand it as a practice of determined Yahwism. That is, in Israel's frame of reference, both the demise and the recovery of this great commercial center are to be understood in relation to the will and purpose of Yahweh, who governs the horizon of the oracle.

It is clear that Tyre (and Phoenicia) stand at the center of a global economy, for the prophet links the fate of this city to a wide network of other economic centers, with the claim that the fall of Tyre is a matter of moment to other parts of the global economy. Thus the poet alludes to Tarshish, a Spanish port (vv. 1, 6, 10, 14), to Egypt (v. 5), to Cyprus (v. 12), to the Babylonians (Chaldeans) who perpetrate the destruction (v. 13), and to Tyre's sister city, Sidon (vv. 2, 4, 12). The focus on Tyre has in mind an entire world system at whose center is Tyre.

23:1 **The oracle concerning Tyre.**

> **Wail, O ships of Tarshish,**
>   **for your fortress is destroyed.**
> **When they came in from Cyprus**
>   **they learned of it.**
> ² **Be still, O inhabitants of the coast,**
>   **O merchants of Sidon,**
> **your messengers crossed over the sea**
> ³   **and were on the mighty waters;**
> **your revenue was the grain of Shihor,**
>   **the harvest of the Nile;**
>   **you were the merchant of the nations.**
> ⁴ **Be ashamed, O Sidon, for the sea has spoken,**
>   **the fortress of the sea, saying:**
> **"I have neither labored nor given birth,**
>   **I have neither reared young men**
>   **nor brought up young women."**
> ⁵ **When the report comes to Egypt,**
>   **they will be in anguish over the report about Tyre.**

The oracle is *a summons to lament*, as the sailors, traders, and merchants of the Mediterranean world get word of Tyre's demise. Verse 2 characterizes the great activity and massive wealth that was generated by this "merchant of the nations." That wealth, however, is immediately contrasted in verse 4 with the portrayal of "the fortress of the sea" as a bereft, barren woman who has produced no children and therefore has no future. The initial imperative "wail" is echoed by "be still" (v. 2) and "be ashamed" (v. 4). The demise of mighty Tyre is a stunning, completely unexpected turn of affairs, which causes anguish as far away as Egypt, an important trading partner. Perhaps the "anguish" pertains to shock waves in the markets, which reverberated across the Mediterranean.

23:6 **Cross over to Tarshish—**
wail, O inhabitants of the coast!
⁷ **Is this your exultant city**
whose origin is from days of old,
whose feet carried her
to settle far away?
⁸ **Who has planned this**
against Tyre, the bestower of crowns,
whose merchants were princes,
whose traders were the honored of the earth?
⁹ **The LORD of hosts has planned it—**
to defile the pride of all glory,
to shame all the honored of the earth.
¹⁰ **Cross over to your own land,**
O ships of Tarshish;
this is a harbor no more.
¹¹ **He has stretched out his hand over the sea,**
he has shaken the kingdoms;
the LORD has given command concerning Canaan
to destroy its fortresses.
¹² **He said:**
You will exult no longer,
O oppressed virgin daughter Sidon;
rise, cross over to Cyprus—
even there you will have no rest.

The summons to wail continues with a series of imperatives: "cross over, wail" (v. 6), "cross over" (vv. 10, 12). What the world thought would never happen has indeed happened. The new element in this unit of the poem is the reference to Yahweh, who had been notably absent in the first section of the poem (v. 8). The question is raised directly: "Who has planned this?" (v. 7). That is, who is responsible? The question is intensified by the grandiose characterization of Tyre in verse 8 with reference to crowns, princes, and the honored. The traders have become the new royalty. In that ancient world, as in the contemporary world, real leverage and influence are exercised by those with corporate wealth who regularly find ways to manipulate and dominate the political process. This is indeed a "money government."

Given the splendor of crowns, princes, and honors, who has the authority or the clout to intervene negatively? The answer may be unknown to that world of merchants who regarded themselves as autonomous. But the answer is known and expected in Israel: It is the Lord of hosts (v. 9)! It is this massive Agent of power, dismissed in the world system as an irrelevance, who has the capacity to turn pride to defilement, honor to shame, boisterous noise to silence. In this remarkable rhetorical maneuver, the poet has drawn even the world economy into the orbit of Yahweh's rule.

The traders (of Tarshish) are summoned to observe the ruin of Tyre (v. 10). If they look, what they will see is active verbs on the lips of Yahweh, whose speech is effective performance. It is Yahweh who stretched out a hand of destruction over the sea—the same Yahweh who once, by outstretched hand, divided the Exodus waters of liberation. It is Yahweh who has shaken the world of commerce, who has jarred loose all the fixities of that world and created mass confusion, thus breaking up the settled patterns of trade and self-assurance. It is Yahweh who by decree stopped the self-congratulatory rejoicing (v. 12). It is Yahweh—the one not even acknowledged by the world system—who has created an unbearable situation of restless, frantic activity—with no respite (v. 2).

> 23:13 **Look at the land of the Chaldeans! This is the people; it was not Assyria. They destined Tyre for wild animals. They erected their siege towers, they tore down her palaces, they made her a ruin.**
> [14] **Wail, O ships of Tarshish,**
> **for your fortress is destroyed.**

Having said that *it is Yahweh* who has done this, the poet in one verse acknowledges the human agent through whom the work of Yahweh has been enacted: It is Babylon! "This is the people" (v. 13). But of course in this scenario it is Babylon in the service of Yahweh. (Cf. Jer. 25:9; 27:6, wherein Yahweh can refer to Nebuchadrezzar as "my servant.") This modest tilt toward geopolitical reality does not diminish at all the overriding claim made for Yahweh. The conclusion of the primary poem in v. 14 reiterates the opening lines of verse 1, with yet another summons to "wail." The loss is deep and costly. The entire world of self-sufficiency is brought to deep grief.

> 23:15 **From that day Tyre will be forgotten for seventy years, the lifetime of one king. At the end of seventy years, it will happen to Tyre as in the song about the prostitute:**
> [16] **Take a harp,**
> **go about the city,**
> **you forgotten prostitute!**
> **Make sweet melody,**

sing many songs,
that you may be remembered.

Quite unexpectedly, the poet is not yet finished. In this addition the horrific future of Tyre at the hands of Yahweh is pushed beyond immediacy to the long-term horizon of seventy years. The number seventy may be the measure of a lifetime (cf. Psalm 90:10), so that after one generation things will change. It is clear, in any case, that the numeral seventy has become a coded reference for an emerging apocalyptic view of the future (Jer. 25:11–12; Dan. 9:2, 24). However that may be, what interests us is that the oracle now, no doubt belatedly, pushes beyond the devastation of the great city.

In a mocking invitation to recovery, the oracle employs the imagery of an old and forgotten prostitute, surely a patriarchal image to match that of the barren women in verse 4. The image of the prostitute is a poignant one by which to refer to the world system of economics, for that system, like a prostitute, will do anything for money.

But of course, as a prostitute ages she is forgotten and neglected and no longer useful. In this image, the world system, so long forgotten, is now invited to reenter the streets, to sing in the hope of being remembered and perhaps reengaged. Thus the poetry envisions a comeback for Tyre, but it is a comeback less than glorious. Even in the anticipated comeback, the poet does not move past sarcasm to either generosity or celebration.

23:17 **At the end of seventy years, the LORD will visit Tyre, and she will return to her trade, and will prostitute herself with all the kingdoms of the world on the face of the earth.** [18] **Her merchandise and her wages will be dedicated to the LORD; her profits will not be stored or hoarded, but her merchandise will supply abundant food and fine clothing for those who live in the presence of the LORD.**

These verses continue the vision of a recovery and continue to dismiss such trade as prostitution. There is, however, a remarkable turn in this scenario of recovery, well beyond the tone of verses 15–16. Here it is anticipated that the profits that are sure to be generated in this recovered system will be sharply redirected. They will not be accumulated into the surplus wealth that the prophetic tradition so roundly and consistently condemns. Rather, the profits will be "holy to Yahweh"; that is, in acknowledgment of Yahweh's sovereignty, perhaps in gratitude that Yahweh makes such wealth possible or in acknowledgment that Yahweh is the rightful controller of the profits. Even more, the profits will go for rich food and fine clothing for the adherents of Yahweh. The acknowledgment of Yahweh is not simply a theological or a liturgical one; it is a pragmatic, political one whereby adherents to Yahweh, presumably Jews after the Exile, will enjoy the produce of the world system.

This most remarkable turn in the fortunes of Tyre and of the world system is typically Isaianic. It is not doubted, in the tradition of Isaiah, that Yahweh will prevail. The same Yahweh who destroys the system is the Yahweh who will preside over and benefit from its recovery. And of course, in that construal of reality, Yahweh is never alone but always is accompanied by Yahweh's people. Therefore the anticipated recovery of the world economy is not an innocent one, but contains important ideological claims for the "flesh and blood" community of Jews who count on the benefit of Yahweh.

In all of the "Oracles Against the Nations," the tradition of Isaiah thinks large. Nowhere is that more fully true than here. The preceding "Oracles Against the Nations" have mostly focused on single states, including the superpowers of Egypt, Assyria, and Babylon. Here, however, the poetry concerns a world system, a network of economics and commerce in which many states participate in a pattern of mutual interdependence.

A contemporary reader thus might ponder the claim made for Yahweh's decisive governance of a world system of economics. One might think of the GATT treaty, or the collusion of the G-Seven nations, or the unbridled capacity of the World Bank to finance worldwide "development." One might take notice of the "economic government" so well exposited by Charles Reich (*Opposing the System*), its massive production of wealth and its shameless human costs. One might notice that as U.S. readers, we are not positioned as the needful, hopeful Jews of this oracle, but as participants in and beneficiaries of a self-serving system.

Here is imagined nothing less than the conversion of the world system, with the profits made available not for the endless pursuit of obscene wealth but for the enhancement of the world neighborhood. The oracle leaves a haunting question: Have the needy—those who are the recurring wards of Yahweh—grounds for expecting a share in the profits of the world system? Tyre of course never intended so, nor did Sidon or Cyprus or Egypt or Tarshish. Nonetheless, it stands promised—a new horizon for the commerce of the world, perhaps only possible after much "wailing" and "shaking." Tyre's "plan" is opposed by another Plan, and the outcome is not yet.

3. Yahweh's Judgment on the Power of Evil
Isaiah 24—27

In these chapters the book of Isaiah moves into an even larger horizon of concern. I suggest that through chapter 27 the book of Isaiah is roughly arranged in three concentric circles: (1) Yahweh's judgment and promise *concerning Judah and Jerusalem* (chapters 1—12); (2) Yahweh's judgment and modest promise *concerning the nations* (chapters 13—23); and now (3) Yahweh's judgment on the power of evil in *the world system* and the prospect of new well-being for the remnant of Israel (chapters 24—27).

These chapters show Israel's faith pushed to its extremity of need and hope, and a corresponding escalation of the rhetoric of judgment. Scholars characteristically see this material as "apocalyptic." That term means that Israel's traditional, long-established understandings of its life and the way Yahweh works in its life have been pushed to the cosmic, because the truth of God's gospel can no longer be resolved or enacted in what is available of human history. That is, the rhetoric takes flight into more imaginative and mythic categories. As a consequence, this poetry tends to lack historical location or reference, but it can be endlessly resituated and reused in any situation of extremity where it is possible (and necessary) to entertain the termination of all present reality and the abrupt gift of newness given by God.

It is a consensus of critical scholars that these passages are quite late, perhaps as late as 300 B.C.E., so that they are uttered and heard in the midst of an emerging Judaism that was deeply jeopardized in an alien imperial world. The text draws upon the rich resources of the Isaiah tradition—especially its high view of Yahweh's sovereignty—but pushes that tradition into new levels of rhetoric and new extremities of seriousness required by the radical circumstance of faith.

The most characteristic accent of this poetry is the assertion that the present world system—which is arrogant and endlessly exploitative and which creates profound hardship for Jews—is under assault from God and will be brutally nullified. It takes no great imaginative construal in our own time to appropriate such a sentiment as a critique of the ruthless world system of an unfettered market capitalism that endlessly crushes and makes invisible those who are on the margins and without resource or saving connection. (To be evenhanded, in another time and place this poetry would readily yield to an interpretation that heard in these cadences an exposé of the world system of state control [communism] that endlessly crushed and made invisible those who were on the margins and without resource or saving connection.) The poetry not only permits such endless and varied reappropriation but, I suggest, is designed as a script that voices the desperate and resilient hope of every "surplus" people in the face of every exile-producing, humanity-denying system that conducts its high risk game of control in arrogant autonomy.

Along with assault on "the system"—whatever it may be—this literature regularly pauses in order to make utterance about new possibility for the marginalized community of Jews when the world system will have been nullified (cf. 24:14–16a, 23; 25:1, 6–10a, 19; 27:2–6, 12–13). The poetry is indeed able to hope beyond its bitter resentment and rage.

In such a remarkable counterpoint that anticipates newness for the faithful community, special attention should be given to 25:6–10a and 26:19. In these two texts that are without parallel in the Old Testament, the rhetoric of extremity, in remarkable daring, asserts that Yahweh will destroy "the last enemy," death (cf. also 27:1). In 25:6–9 death is "swallowed up." In 26:19, the dead rise, no longer held by death. In both texts, it is asserted that *the cosmic power of negation* no longer has force or authority, and so the community of the faithful may resume its life and its worship of Yahweh.

This claim of renewal is dazzling, even to our Christian ears numbed by familiar Easter clichés. *The cosmic power of negation* is a mythic force that has refused obedience to the true sovereign, Yahweh. That cosmic force may show itself in many guises, not least as socioeconomic-political-military concentrations of power. The news, grounded not in historical data but in the resolve of Yahweh, is that this power of negation is even now at the very edge of nullification.

We imagine a poet saying or writing such claims in an ancient world where imperial power swept all before it. We are aware that the utterance is as lean in its credibility as it is daring. Or we may change the scenery only slightly and imagine such utterance in our time, place, and circumstance, where the world system of economics makes its powerful, destructive way. We notice again, now more poignantly, how lean in credibility the utterance is. But the utterance is all we have and all this faithful community has ever had. As that ancient community clearly treasured the utterance and relied upon it, so we also may cling to it in desperation and in resilient hope.

"THE LORD OF HOSTS WILL REIGN"
24:1–23

All of the themes of judgment against Jerusalem and Judah and against the nations that we have considered thus far in the book of Isaiah are now writ large. The vision is cosmic, concerning all of heaven and all of earth. This poem anticipates a judgment wrought by Yahweh against all of creation. The poem exhibits the creator at the work of undoing and dismantling the creation.

Because of the apocalyptic casting of the poem, it is completely lacking in geographical and historical specificity, except for reference to Israel and Judah (vv. 15, 23). For that reason, one must stay "inside the poem," not seeking external reference but attending to the rhetorical import and emotional intent of the text. That is, the poem tends not to *report* on the undoing of the world but to make that undoing palpably available for the listener.

24:1 **Now the LORD is about to lay waste the earth and make it desolate,**
   and he will twist its surface and scatter its inhabitants.
   ²And it shall be, as with the people, so with the priest;
   as with the slave, so with his master;
   as with the maid, so with her mistress;
   as with the buyer, so with the seller;
   as with the lender, so with the borrower;
   as with the creditor, so with the debtor.
   ³The earth shall be utterly laid waste and utterly despoiled;
   for the LORD has spoken this word.

These verses are bounded in verse 1a and verse 3b by references to Yahweh. It is Yahweh's resolve and Yahweh's decree that produce the effects now to be recited. This is a thoroughly Yahweh-centered statement. The world does not fall apart by happenstance, but even its undoing is a consequence of Yahweh's governance. The whole earth is now to be "scattered" (cf. Gen. 11:1–9). The term "scatter" is characteristically used in these materials to portray Jewish exile. Here the whole of creation is made as vulnerable, exposed, and displaced as were the exiles from Jerusalem. Nothing and nobody will remain in a right place. The poem does not here specify the mode of coming destruction, but in what follows the mode of "laying waste" is variously flood, earthquake, or drought. The broadest designation of disaster is given in verse 1 and reiterated in verse 3. Between these points is a highly stylized unit that enumerates a series of word pairs reflecting a wide range of social roles. *All* are to be scattered, of every class and every stratum and every function of society. Or as the creation tradition might say, "everyone in its kind." None is immune.

24:4 **The earth dries up and withers,**
 the world languishes and withers;
 the heavens languish together with the earth.
 [5] **The earth lies polluted under its inhabitants;**
 for they have transgressed laws,
 violated the statutes,
 broken the everlasting covenant.
 [6] **Therefore a curse devours the earth,**
 and its inhabitants suffer for their guilt;
 therefore the inhabitants of the earth dwindled,
 and few people are left.
 [7] **The wine dries up,**
 the vine languishes,
 all the merry-hearted sigh.
 [8] **The mirth of the timbrels is stilled,**
 the noise of the jubilant has ceased,
 the mirth of the lyre is stilled.
 [9] **No longer do they drink wine with singing;**
 strong drink is bitter to those who drink it.
 [10] **The city of chaos is broken down,**
 every house is shut up so that no one can enter.
 [11] **There is an outcry in the streets for lack of wine;**
 all joy has reached its eventide;
 the gladness of the earth is banished.
 [12] **Desolation is left in the city,**
 the gates are battered into ruins.
 [13] **For thus it shall be on the earth**
 and among the nations,
 as when an olive tree is beaten,
 as at the gleaning when the grape harvest is ended.

These verses suggest that the coming threat to creation is a drought (vv. 4–5a, 7) that causes a desperate failure of vineyards, a shortage of wine, and consequently a silencing of the normal boisterous and joyous functions of social life (vv. 8–9, 11). The entire infrastructure of the community will be disrupted. The poem makes clear how much the taken-for-granted well-being of social life is dependent upon the ecological system of the food chain, a system that is fragile and completely dependent upon the sustenance of the creator. The violation of that ecological system is evident in verse 5: "The earth lies polluted." The "pollution" here is first of all torah violation, though the torah violation no doubt consists in concrete acts of disregard for the creator's intention for creation.

This large vision of coming disaster is articulated in a characteristic prophetic speech of judgment (vv. 5b–6). The indictment is that the people have violated the torah commandments and broken "the everlasting covenant." A remarkable claim is made that all of creation, and therefore all human centers of power, is subject to Yahweh's torah provisions. None is autonomous. None is free to abuse the earth or to violate the intentions of Yahweh the creator. The phrase "the everlasting covenant" apparently refers to the post-Flood covenant with Noah and his sons whereby Yahweh promises "never again" to permit such chaos to be on the loose (Gen. 9:8–17; cf. Isa. 54:9–10). But now all of the threat of that ancient Flood narrative is again under way. The violation of that large and old covenant, as large and old as creation, results in a curse of a magnitude commensurate with the covenant. As the (violated) covenant concerns the whole earth, so the curse threatens the whole earth and all viable life in it.

Indeed, "the city of chaos" is shattered. The poet of course does not identify that city. We may take it to mean every concentration of human power that functions effectively but is rooted in disobedience and defiance of Yahweh. What interests us is that the term "chaos" is the conventional and poignant term used for primordial chaos in Genesis 1:2, before the creator imposed life-sustaining order and to which a dismantled creation may regress (cf. Jer. 4:23–26).

The conclusion of this unit is a summary statement bespeaking an ending of the earth and all its nations (v. 13). The imagery is like that of 17:6, which envisions a harvest that has taken everything except for a few remnants beyond reach. The poet has offered a coming judgment in which nothing will be safe, protected, or immune. The poem strains to be unqualifiedly comprehensive.

These verses and those that follow present a view of *the world as Yahweh's creation*. This view of the world is opposed to most modern notions of the world as a self-sustaining life system without reference to the creator. Thus it makes an important difference if we speak of *creation* rather than *nature*. The point of accent here is that the maintenance of the life system is contingent upon obedience to the covenantal will of Yahweh. This is an old and central conviction in Israel. In Hosea 4:2–3, for example, it is affirmed that violation of Yahweh's commands (which seem to allude to the Decalogue; v. 2) leads to a drought that will take away the core triad of creation—animals, birds, and fish (v. 3). Our poem has taken that prophetic insight and voiced it even more compellingly.

24:14 **They lift up their voices, they sing for joy;**
they shout from the west over the majesty of the LORD.
15 **Therefore in the east give glory to the LORD;**
in the coastlands of the sea glorify the name of the LORD, the
God of Israel.
16a **From the ends of the earth we hear songs of praise,**
of glory to the Righteous One.

These verses sound a counternote in this chapter of massive devastation. The countervoice concerns those who sing for joy at the intervention of Yahweh. We are not told who "they" are, but it is evident that "they" constitute the community of Yahweh, perhaps exiles scattered in the East and the coastlands. They break out into doxology, giving honor and praise to "the Righteous One," the one who will act decisively to impose righteous order on a polluting, disregarding social context.

Taken theologically, this community is so committed to praise of Yahweh that it is willing to see the world system condemned, if that condemnation enhances the splendor of Yahweh. Along with that theological impulse, however, we may allow for a socioeconomic dimension to such praise. If these are the exiled Jews, it may indeed be that they have consistently received, from this buoyant, brutalizing world order only abuse and exploitation. Not only do they not benefit from the system, but they are glad to see it go, given their deep confidence that Yahweh will have for them a better future.

It is probably always a shock (as well as a disappointment) to the key players in the destructive world system to imagine that some will be glad to see it terminated, except that there are always those excluded and not noticed or valued who will not, under any circumstances, benefit from the present order, no matter how successful and comprehensive it becomes. These are the "they" who join in praise and celebration of the destructive potential of Yahweh; it is "they" who wait for a new creation that is always at the edge of this sort of radical rhetoric.

24:16b **But I say, I pine away,**
I pine away. Woe is me!

> For the treacherous deal treacherously,
>   the treacherous deal very treacherously.

> [17] Terror, and the pit, and the snare
>   are upon you, O inhabitant of the earth!
> [18] Whoever flees at the sound of the terror
>   shall fall into the pit;
> and whoever climbs out of the pit
>   shall be caught in the snare.
> For the windows of heaven are opened,
>   and the foundations of the earth tremble.
> [19] The earth is utterly broken,
>   the earth is torn asunder,
>   the earth is violently shaken.
> [20] The earth staggers like a drunkard,
>   it sways like a hut;
> its transgression lies heavy upon it,
>   and it falls, and will not rise again.

The poet, however, will not permit the countertheme of doxology to detract from the primary accent of threat. In verse 16b, therefore, there is an insistent return to the primary theme of verses 1–13. Verse 16 employs the same term "treacherous" four times, an indictment bespeaking exploitative violence. The indictment is not elaborated upon, as it is not in verse 5b. This is enough, nonetheless, to ground the more eloquent threat that follows.

The three terms beginning with verse 17—terror, pit, snare—are a stylized triad as in Jeremiah 48:43. In Hebrew, moreover, they are an alliteration, for all three begin with the letter "p." The three together articulate that no one can escape the coming trouble. Indeed, when one escapes trouble to come, this will only mean a greater trouble to follow (cf. Amos 5:18b–20). The "windows of heaven" are the openings through which the flood waters of chaos are massively released (cf. Gen. 7:11; Job 38:25–27). When these flood waters are released, the earth is completely inundated and shattered. The fourfold repetition of "earth" has the effect of the rhetoric, like the flood waters, beating the earth down to dysfunction and death. The old earth is killed and will stay dead. Creation is nullified.

> 24:21 On that day the LORD will punish
>   the host of heaven in heaven,
>   and on earth the kings of the earth.
> [22] They will be gathered together
>   like prisoners in a pit;
> they will be shut up in a prison,

and after many days they will be punished.
23 Then the moon will be abashed,
    and the sun ashamed;
  for the LORD of hosts will reign
    on Mount Zion and in Jerusalem,
  and before his elders he will manifest his glory.

The introductory formula, as is characteristic in the prophets, bespeaks a massive and decisive intervention of Yahweh in time to come. It is Yahweh, none other, who will actively move against the rebellious. It is the creator who will deal with both the recalcitrant "host of heaven" and the defiant "kings of the earth." All of creation has been in rebellion against Yahweh, but we have not heretofore been told of the former. The refusal of the sun, moon, and stars to obey the creator is a theme known in later apocalyptic literature but is only at the very edge of the Old Testament. The rhetoric is an attempt to exhibit the extremity of wholesale resistance to Yahweh, and so by implication to overstate the threat of Yahweh's coming visitation.

The sentence announced against the rebellious is an imprisonment and then an even more ominous unspecified punishment. We are not told what it will be, but it is clearly not good. The punishment will be a deep humiliation of moon and sun, which have not performed according to the purposes of the creator (vv. 22–23a). We are not even told here about what happens to "the kings of the earth," but if the sun and moon are locked up and detained, what surely follows is the failure of the earthly food chain!

We are scarcely prepared for the astonishing assertion of verse 23b, which is congruent with the hope of verses 14–16a. All of heaven and earth will be undone—except Jerusalem! Jerusalem is the pivot point of Yahweh's newness and the locus of hope for those who are gladly rid of the old system. "The Lord of hosts" will begin a new governance even over the recalcitrant hosts of verse 21. The vision of apocalyptic is profoundly negative, but it is not unrelievedly negative. A new regime begins, and those who now crowd the throne room of Yahweh with joy, well-being, and power are "his elders." The phrase bespeaks an old-fashioned, primitive, low-key community of faith, not beholden in any way to royal expectations or notions of grandeur. "The elders" are perhaps those who lead and sustain vulnerable communities of exiles, who are skilled and cunning about the practice of faith in hostile environments. But they are also the ones who "beheld God" just as "the glory" came down upon the mountain (Exod. 24:1–2, 9–18).

This faithful community, rooted in a deep past, constitutes a decisive and momentous historical exception to the destruction offered in chapter 24. It is the exception because it has been busy in doxology instead of the pollution that brings chaos. Indeed, this community is the new Noah; it will be present and given access to Yahweh as the new governance begins. Apocalyptic thought is uncompromising in its negativity. It imagines that the violators of the creation will lose all that they treasure. That uncompromisingly negative note, however, is not blind to the remnant of those who have not given in. For them the new regime is exceedingly good news.

A SWALLOWING THAT PERMITS LIFE
25:1–12

The vision of chapter 24 is largely one of nullification and destruction, with only the positive assertion of verse 23. Conversely, chapter 25 is largely one of affirmation and confidence, with only the negative assertion of verses 10b–12. And that negation concerns the Moabites and not Israel.

25:1 **O LORD, you are my God;**
I will exalt you, I will praise your name;
for you have done wonderful things,
plans formed of old, faithful and sure.
2 For you have made the city a heap,
the fortified city a ruin;
the palace of aliens is a city no more,
it will never be rebuilt.
3 Therefore strong peoples will glorify you;
cities of ruthless nations will fear you.
4 For you have been a refuge to the poor,
a refuge to the needy in their distress,
a shelter from the rainstorm and a shade from the heat.
When the blast of the ruthless was like a winter rainstorm,
5 the noise of aliens like heat in a dry place,
you subdued the heat with the shade of clouds;
the song of the ruthless was stilled.

The poet breaks out in lyrical, celebrative doxology, overflowing with gratitude, praise, and thanksgiving. The poem is uttered in the midst of the nullification of ordered, "civilized" reality. The poet turns away from what might be loss to the true center of reality, Yahweh. Thus Calvin observes:

When our minds are perplexed by a variety of uneasy thoughts on account of numerous distresses and afflictions which happen daily, we ought immediately to resort to God, and rely on his providence; for even the smallest calamities will overwhelm us, if we do not betake ourselves to him. (*Isaiah* Volume 2, 190)

The poet turns confidently to God and does so in the traditional phrasings of Israel's doxologies. Yahweh has done "wonderful things," that is, transformative miracles that provide a basis for the present moment of anticipation. Israel keeps a ready stock of remembered miracles at hand, ready to recite, reaching all the way back to the Exodus and seeing in present upheavals yet another in that treasured sequence. These miraculous transformations are not happenstance. They have been intended by Yahweh from a long time ago. The qualifier might be translated "true and true," for the terms "faithful and sure" render the same Hebrew term (*'mn;* v. 1). This first verse thus situates the present moment in the context of Yahweh's most trusted, transformative fidelity.

But what is here celebrated as "wonderful things" stuns us (v. 2). The city has been made a ruin (*tel*), and that is the cause of celebration. We are not told what city. As readers of Isaiah, we might imagine it is Babylon (cf. Isa. 13—14; 21:1–10). But here the city moves even beyond Babylon to be the ultimate city of wealth, arrogance, autonomous power, and exploitation. It is every city that is devoted to buying and selling, making money and abusing. Surely some grieved the loss of this city, when the armies marched, the drought came, and the markets collapsed, but not this poet—not this Israelite—not this hoper.

This poet speaks for "the poor and the needy" who are first of all Jews; but in the continuing power of the poem, they are all the poor and all the needy who are crushed by the indifference of urban acquisitiveness (v. 4). It is Yahweh who has intervened against that city, for Yahweh is the only refuge of the resourceless and vulnerable. The psalmist addresses them (Psalm 121:5–6):

> The LORD is your keeper,
> the LORD is your shade at your right hand.
> The sun shall not strike you by day,
> nor the moon by night.

Nor the rainstorm—nor the wintry blasts of the ruthless—nor the coming of brutal intruders.

The mention of the "poor and needy" in verse 4 is surrounded in verses

3 and 4b by the term "ruthless." And as verse 4 is surrounded by the term "ruthless," so in that abusive city the poor are always surrounded by the ruthless who care only for themselves. The poet uses the term "ruthless" three times (vv. 3–5). The "poor and needy" have no chance against the ruthless who are massively present, except that now, even the ruthless must glorify and fear Yahweh because Yahweh has eliminated every other way of living in the world (v. 3). Although the ruthless may gnash their teeth at the loss of the city, this is not their poem. This poem is the voice of the poor and the needy, who regard the demise of exploitative urban civilization as a gain and a gift from Yahweh.

25:6 **On this mountain the LORD of hosts will make for all peoples**
  a feast of rich food, a feast of well-aged wines,
  of rich food filled with marrow, of well-aged wines strained clear.
 7 **And he will destroy on this mountain**
  the shroud that is cast over all peoples,
  the sheet that is spread over all nations;
  he will swallow up death forever.
 8 **Then the Lord GOD will wipe away the tears from all faces,**
  and the disgrace of his people he will take away from all the earth,
  for the LORD has spoken.
 9 **It will be said on that day,**
  Lo, this is our God; we have waited for him, so that he might save us.
  This is the LORD for whom we have waited;
  let us be glad and rejoice in his salvation.
10a **For the hand of the LORD will rest on this mountain.**

These verses push the cause of exultation even further, for now the city and the ruthless have disappeared. Now there is only the wondrous, generous rule of Yahweh. Indeed, these verses bespeak the full coming of Yahweh's rule, the very *Kingdom of God.* This brief unit has two introductory formulae, in verses 6 and 9, that may be separate utterances. Thematically, however, they are of a piece. Special attention might be given to these verses because they are the part of Isaiah 24—27 that frequently appears in the Common Lectionary of the church. The church has seen that these verses offer a most sweeping vision of an attentive world where Yahweh's governance is unqualified. The vision is of "this mountain" (v. 6; cf. v. 10a). The meeting is at Mount Zion, the precise antithesis of the city made a heap (cf. 24:23). "This mountain" is the center of the new governance of God and is here the site of a great feast, the eschatological banquet for "all peoples," a banquet of the richest, most yearned-for food. (The vision of "all peoples" coming is already affirmed in 2:2–4.) Such a welcome feast is already present in the rather more ordinary life of Israel, whereby whenever healing and emancipation happen, a meal for the poor is offered (Psalm 22:26). Moreover, nourishment in the face of enemies is a powerful gesture of support and care (cf. 2 Sam. 17:27–29; Psalm 23:5). This is indeed a new governance! The church imagines out of this a heavenly banquet when the kingdom finally comes on earth (Luke 14:15–24); in the meantime the church intends its regular Eucharistic meal to be an anticipation of this alternative governance (Luke 22:14–20). It is for this reason that the church in the Eucharist recites the tones of Matthew 8:11, thus blending the hope of ultimate well-being with the sacramental gesture of expectation.

The one who offers the banquet as a sign of generosity, well-being, security, and joy also does more. The poet imagines that the earth has over it the pall (shroud, sheet) of death, beset by sadness, loss, and mourning. The world is held in the grip of death and has no power to shake it off. But now, the Lord of life will terminate that mood. The verb "destroy" is in the Hebrew "swallow" (*bl'*), the same verb as in the next verse. The crisis, however, is more than mourning. The crisis is the active power of death that regularly crowds in upon every chance for life. The poet knows, moreover, that vulnerable folk in the city have no capacity to resist the negations of death.

In order to understand fully what is being claimed here, it is important to reflect on what is meant by death. It is not simply the awareness that we are all going to die: "The days of our life are seventy years,/or perhaps eighty, if we are strong" (Psalm 90:10). Death here is rather an active force of negativity that moves to counter and cancel and prevent well-being. So Wildberger nicely observes: "Death is all that circumscribes a life, that limits the life-space of humanity, that diminishes well-being, and that prevents community with human person or God" (*Jesaja* 13–27, 967 [author's translation]). That is who death is; everyone knows about that power of diminishment that we cannot by ourselves resist. And now the news: God will *swallow* death like a great sea monster attacking a smaller fish. God will attack this marauding beast and take it in the jaws, crush it, chew it, reduce it, eliminate it, and perhaps spit it out. It is no wonder that in his Easter lyric, the apostle Paul can quote, "Death has been swallowed up in victory" (1 Cor. 15:54).

From that affirmation it follows that there will be no tears, no cause for sadness, no sense of loss, no occasion for mourning. It is no wonder that this image of wiping away tears endures to be a present comfort and a fervent expectation of the faithful. We read in Revelation 21:4:

"He will wipe every tear from their eyes.
Death will be no more;
mourning and crying and pain will be no more,
for the first things have passed away."

The poet speaks about nothing less than radical, complete transformation. Biblical faith is not a moral system; it is not a mode of holding on or staying in control. It is rather an act of yielding in the present (as this poet does) to the assurances given for God's future. The poet is indeed shrewd and insightful in concluding that the ultimate act of transformation is to remove "disgrace" from this people—the disgrace of being helpless, powerless, and exploited; the shame of being stepped on and not being able to resist the powers of death. It is the humiliation of being, to the bottom of our lives, ultimately inadequate. Now all of that will be overcome.

The work of this God is both positive and negative. The positive is a welcoming feast that signifies the new governance of abundance and well-being. The negative is the elimination of that which threatens and precludes festivals of generosity. This is indeed a newness made possible precisely by the nullification of the deathly city of abuse.

The second formula beginning a subunit of this poem is in verse 9. It is "on that day," the day when these glorious promises will be kept. The beneficiaries of the new governance will be exuberant in testimony. In verse 1, the poet had all alone said, "You are my God." Now the poet is joined by all those who welcome the new regime: "This is our God." This is said with pride, joy, and delight. Those who have believed have waited a long time, seemingly without justification. This brief unit is dominated by the double use of the term "wait" that is here better rendered "hope." This is the community that has hoped in confidence, in the face of every circumstance, never doubting that Yahweh would prevail, never doubting that the city of abuse is a temporary arrangement that cannot be sustained. The hoping is in confidence that Yahweh has the power to save and transform. Therefore the glad rejoicing of verse 1 is here resounded. Indeed, it is the joyous affirmation in verses 1 and 9–10a that provides an enclosure around the city of the ruthless in verses 3–5. The city of abuse cannot escape the God whom Israel trusts and praises. What is old and spent must yield to God's newness. The old city of abuse is being radically displaced by the new city "on this mountain." No wonder the "poor and needy" and "all peoples" are glad to go there. To move from the one city to the other is to move from the shrouded, sheeted environs of death to the rich food and well-aged wine of life. Yahweh's decisive action is indeed "to life," *leḥaîm!*

25:10b **The Moabites shall be trodden down in their place**
        as straw is trodden down in a dung-pit.
  ¹¹ **Though they spread out their hands in the midst of it,**
        as swimmers spread out their hands to swim,
        their pride will be laid low despite the struggle of their hands.
  ¹² **The high fortifications of his walls will be brought down,**
        laid low, cast to the ground, even to the dust.

True to type, the poet returns one more time to the negation that is the
downside of the newness just celebrated. It is not at all clear why the target of negation is Moab. Moab has already received its share of nullification (chapters 15—16), and there is no reason to conclude that Moab
constituted any special focus in this belated period. It is enough to conclude that Moab here is a figure for all detested powers that resist Yahweh
and abuse Yahweh's people. "Moab" will be treated ignobly, humiliated,
and reduced to nothing. The rhetoric follows from the positive claims of
Yahweh; but one can also detect the relish in the utterance of those long
downtrodden and burdened with humongous resentment.

TRUST IN THE
GOD WHO GIVES LIFE
26:1–21

The radical vision of an ending of present world arrangements, already
voiced in chapters 24—25, is here continued. Two matters are evident in
this chapter. First, the capacity to hope for goodness and newness from God
in the face of an *ending* is here voiced with great intensity. Second, this visionary poet is able to use a variety of standard Israelite rhetorical genres in
order to articulate both the *massive judgment* and the *determined hope* that
are on the horizon. In this chapter the preferred genres are a hymn (vv. 1–6)
and a lament that includes a responding "oracle of salvation" (vv. 7–21).

  26:1 **On that day this song will be sung in the land of Judah:**
      We have a strong city;
        he sets up victory
        like walls and bulwarks.
    ² **Open the gates,**
        so that the righteous nation that keeps faith
        may enter in.

> ³Those of steadfast mind you keep in peace—
>   in peace because they trust in you.
> ⁴Trust in the LORD forever,
>   for in the LORD GOD
>   you have an everlasting rock.
> ⁵For he has brought low
>   the inhabitants of the height;
>   the lofty city he lays low.
> He lays it low to the ground,
>   casts it to the dust.
> ⁶The foot tramples it,
>   the feet of the poor,
>   the steps of the needy.

Israel sings in confidence about its future from God, signaled by the antic-ipatory "on that day." The singing is in and about the city of Jerusalem, that is, not "in a foreign land" (Psalm 137:4). Israel at praise is very sure that Jerusalem, "a strong city," will be the locus of God's newness, a theme al-ready voiced in 2:2–4. For that reason, those who sing there are well situ-ated to be "present at creation." The doxology concerns God's "victory" that is yet to be given but that is already sure. The assurance of deliverance yet to come is the ground of faith and the access point to a good and joy-ous future. The imagery of "victory" leads to verse 2, for the poet imagines a great triumphal return in victory, with a processional parade that enters the sanctuary of Yahweh. Thus, in Psalms 24:7–9 and 118:19, Israel had an old liturgical pattern of such "triumphal entries," and now a final proces-sion is to occur. Those who walk in the procession may even include the victorious Yahweh, but the accent is upon the "righteous nation" that has continued to keep faith with Yahweh. In view is the small, vulnerable, post-exilic community that had many opportunities and many reasons to give up on Yahweh, but did not. Because they continued to trust Yahweh in hard times, the Israelites will be the ones most exuberant at the victory parade.

The exuberance expressed in verses 1–2 is transposed in verses 3–4 into a more reflective mood. The actual wording of verse 3 is problematic, but the intention seems to be that Yahweh gives *shalom* to those who trust. To trust means to continue to rely with dogged determination, without re-spect to circumstance. (We will see that this term "trust" becomes focal in the theological disputes of chapters 36—37; cf. Psalm 62:8.) Those who did not "keep faith," who did not stay with Yahweh in dogged determina-tion in spite of circumstance, do not receive the *shalom* God has to offer. "Peace" here likely is to be understood as the antithesis of the *chaos* all around of which this poet speaks so eloquently. Indeed, the world, at the behest of Yahweh, now reverts to chaos. In the midst of such cosmic displacement, however, this little community of relentless advocates of Yahweh knows about assurances and guarantees of order from on high. No wonder the community that trusts wants to sing and dance!

The theme of trust is continued in verse 4, only now it becomes an imperative, summoning a community that may be wavering to reaffirm its confidence in Yahweh. The ground of trust is none other than Yahweh. Two features of this assertion merit attention. First, notice the two temporal terms: "forever, everlasting," that is, in all circumstances, through thick and thin and in every ominous future. Second, the naming of God in the second line of the verse is curious, something like trust in *Yah, Yahweh*. It appears that the poet reiterates the name of God so that the focus of trust is unmistakable. The celebrating community will stake its future, as it has its past, on the powerful reliability of Yahweh.

The reason for such confidence is Yahweh's demonstrated capacity to "bring low" the heights (v. 5). Yahweh's characteristic action that grounds trust is to prevail over every pretentious, arrogant, self-sufficient, exploitative power. This is a recurring theme to eighth-century Isaiah (2:12–17). More than that, however, this inverting capacity of Yahweh is celebrated in these chapters as the capacity to bring down the "lofty city"—perhaps despised Babylon, more likely the figurative city of exploitation, a power that abuses the lowly. Indeed, the "bringing low" is so decisive and so complete that even "the poor and the needy," those who live politically and economically close to the ground, will be able to trample the ruins of the arrogant city. Indeed, this climactic action is so crucial to the argument that the poet uses three parallel lines to make the point (v. 6). The city is trampled by the foot, the feet, the steps. One can imagine a dance of unrestrained vindication and defiance by those long oppressed, now releasing all those pent-up resentments as they trample the holy places and the opulent houses, break store windows, and seize the residue of treasure in the ruins, to which they had no previous access. The "poor and needy" are no doubt the downtrodden community of postexilic Jews, long discounted and forlorn, but now come to a time of enhancement and affirmation. The figure of the triumphant "poor and needy," here surely referring to those Jews, cannot in the generative force of the poem be limited to those Jews. More broadly, the poem invites adherence of all other waiting and hoping diminished peoples, those who live for a time when the lofty are lowered and trampled—they and their urban emblems of smugness and indifference.

This unit of the poem moves from praise to exuberant victory to trust in the God who surely prevails. It contrasts the celebrated "strong city" and the "lofty city" now made low. The *lofty city* is before our very eyes but will be lowered. The *strong city* is still a conjuring of faithful imagination, not yet in hand. It is, however, very sure, as sure as the "everlasting rock."

In a rhetorical juxtaposition that is not uncommon, the *hymn* of verses 1–6 is now followed by a *lamentation* (vv. 7–18). It is not clear how the two elements are related to each other. Perhaps the hymn is intended to motivate Yahweh to act for this lamenting community. Or perhaps the purpose of verses 1–6 is to portray the tough and insistent faith that is practiced even in what follows. In any case, these verses sound the characteristic sounds of Israel's lamentation to Yahweh, a genre especially poignant among exiled, displaced, forlorn people who have not abandoned Yahweh or Yahweh's future.

26:7 **The way of the righteous is level;**
     O Just One, you make smooth the path of the righteous.
 8 **In the path of your judgments,**
     O LORD, we wait for you;
   your name and your renown
     are the soul's desire.
 9 **My soul yearns for you in the night,**
     my spirit within me earnestly seeks you.
   For when your judgments are in the earth,
     the inhabitants of the world learn righteousness.
10 **If favor is shown to the wicked,**
     they do not learn righteousness;
   in the land of uprightness they deal perversely
     and do not see the majesty of the LORD.

The lament begins by asserting that those who speak are "the righteous," who are contrasted with "the wicked," and that the speakers are very sure that God reliably attends to the needs and hopes and prayers of the righteous. "The righteous" are likely to be understood as the most intense torah-keepers and the most passionate trusters in Yahweh in the postexilic community.

This community is confident that Yahweh will make a safe, viable way for the faithful, that is, "A Way Out of No Way." This simple, innocent trust is paralleled in the more familiar cadences of Psalm 23:3: "He leads me in right paths/for his name's sake." This community, moreover, is on that path now (v. 8). It is a path of attentive obedience and complete trust that constitutes the "waiting room" for God's real community. Obedience is the posture for serious hope.

In verses 9b–10, the theme of righteousness is reiterated in something of a didactic tone. Thus it is affirmed, on the one hand, that as Yahweh's decisive work in the world is evidenced, the world will learn righteousness, that is, learn life in response to Yahweh. In verse 10, however, it is asserted that "the wicked" learn nothing and refuse to see Yahweh's powerful performance even when it is evident. Although this latter is perhaps a statement of resentment, it likely also serves as a motivation to Yahweh to underscore the prosperity of the righteous, who stand out in contrast to the obdurate wicked and who deserve Yahweh's positive attention.

These assertions concerning the righteous in verses 7–8a and 9b–10 sandwich a most moving discourse on the faith of the righteous. Righteousness does not consist only in intense moralism or active obedience. Rather, righteousness, as understood covenantly, refers to a life *totally committed to communion with Yahweh*. This middle section is dominated by verbs indicating the urgency of communion (vv. 8b–9a). Thus we *wait* (hope), my life *yearns for*, my spirit *seeks earnestly*. The speaking subject affirms the totality of the community and the totality of the speaking person: soul, spirit = "all of me." The verb "yearn," moreover, is the same root as "desire" in verse 8. This is a profound hunger for communion that cuts deeply beyond contractual obedience. We are here at the core of postexilic spirituality, the kind that permits trust in the face of endless adversity, the very Jewish spirituality mostly unnoticed in Christian caricatures of emerging Judaism.

The hoping, yearning, seeking of Israel for God's intervention echoes the intensity of communion in the Psalter that insists that torah is not simply about *obedience*, but it is about *presence* that sustains:

> One thing I asked of the LORD,
>   that will I seek after:
> to live in the house of the LORD
>   all the days of my life,
> to behold the beauty of the LORD,
>   and to inquire in his temple (Ps. 27:4).
> As a deer longs for flowing streams,
>   so my soul longs for you, O God.
> My soul thirsts for God,
>   for the living God.
>   (Psalm 42:1–2a)

> Whom have I in heaven but you?
>   And there is nothing on earth that I desire other than you.
>   (Psalm 73:25)

In this poetry speaks a voice of faith that refuses to settle for the world that threatens and alienates. At its best, Judaism knows that God is real and available even in such circumstance.

26:11 **O LORD, your hand is lifted up,**
      but they do not see it.
   Let them see your zeal for your people, and be ashamed.
   Let the fire for your adversaries consume them.
  ¹² **O LORD, you will ordain peace for us,**
      for indeed, all that we have done, you have done for us.
  ¹³ **O LORD our God,**
      other lords besides you have ruled over us,
      but we acknowledge your name alone.
  ¹⁴ **The dead do not live;**
      shades do not rise—
   because you have punished and destroyed them,
      and wiped out all memory of them.
  ¹⁵ **But you have increased the nation, O LORD,**
      you have increased the nation; you are glorified;
      you have enlarged all the borders of the land.

The lament continues with a reflection upon Yahweh's dealing with both "your people" (v. 11) and the wicked, who are only referred to as "they" (v. 10). This unit of the poem is dominated by the threefold vocative address to Yahweh (vv. 11, 12, 13). Yahweh, the everlasting rock, deals with the wicked and with the righteous.

Yahweh is about to exercise decisive sovereignty (vv. 11–12). Yahweh's hand is raised in a gesture of authority, but the wicked are so obtuse, resistant, and unnoticing (cf. v. 10). And so the community of the righteous can dare to ask that the enemy, so long abusive, should receive Yahweh's awesome negative treatment. This contrasts with the positive zeal Yahweh has for the beloved community of the righteous. Whereas the wicked are headed to a fire of nullification, the righteous are destined for Yahweh's *shalom* (cf. v. 3). The contrast is total and uncompromising. The poetry states the theological ground for the coming cosmic inversion when Yahweh's beloved community will be vindicated.

This community, in the deft assertion of verse 13, manages to state at the same time its *needy circumstance* ("ruled over") and its *uncompromising faith* ("your name alone"). The lament thus states the contradiction that is at the heart of Israel's characteristic complaint. *Good faith* should receive *good circumstance*. But it has not . . . yet! But it will! Soon!

This confidence that thrives on a sharp contrast now articulates two facets of Yahweh's undoubted sovereignty (vv. 14–15). Negatively, the dead stay dead because that is their punishment and a sign of Yahweh's forceful authority. Conversely, as Yahweh has "deadened" the dead (v. 14), so Yahweh has blessed the community of the faithful with all the abundance of creation (v. 15).

26:16 **O LORD, in distress they sought you,**
they poured out a prayer
when your chastening was on them.
[17] **Like a woman with child,**
who writhes and cries out in her pangs
when she is near her time,
so were we because of you, O LORD;
[18] **we were with child, we writhed,**
but we gave birth only to wind.
We have won no victories on earth,
and no one is born to inhabit the world.

It is evident that in rich and imaginative imagery the entire development of verses 7–15 has as its purpose the drawing of a sharp contrast, with the positioning of the righteous as the special ones of Yahweh, the ones who obey, the ones who yearn, the ones who acknowledge only Yahweh, the ones who have been increased and multiplied. All of this, however, is rhetorical preparation for the complaint of verses 16–17. The complaint begins with yet another abrupt address: "Yahweh!" (v. 16). Now the "they" are not the wicked of verse 11, but they are the desperately needy, the forlorn righteous. They have turned incessantly and trustingly to Yahweh. They have sought and have poured out. They have given themselves passionately over to Yahweh. They have done that even while under the severe pressure of Yahweh. They have not, for any reason, ceased to turn to, rely upon, and trust in Yahweh. But all for nought!

Israel at prayer has been "like a woman with child" (v. 17): vigorous, exercised, crying in pain, and groaning—all this as deep, desperate hope. However, in the end Israel is unlike a woman in labor. The difference is that the woman's pain and effort produce a child that opens the future. But Israel's pregnant anguish produces nothing: no child, no future, no new possibility, no victory, no deliverance, no rescue, no intervention . . . nothing!

The movement and structure of the complaint are enormously artful. The poem has taken a long time to exhibit righteousness, with the unspoken but unmistakable conclusion that Yahweh has not given the victory due such zealous faith. This daring utterance must leave Israel not unlike a woman who has been in labor, now spent and exhausted, but with nothing to show for the long-term effort. And now Israel waits. Israel must always wait when it speaks complaint to (against?) Yahweh, not knowing if the prayer will be heard, if it will offend, if it will be disregarded. The waiting is surely a characteristic liturgical pause. In this context, however, it is more than liturgical. It is cosmic. The picture is of this little passionate community of faith, surrounded by adversaries, having cast its lot with the only alternative power it knows or trusts. So there is a large, awesome, ominous waiting, because Yahweh cannot be coerced or hurried.

26:19 **Your dead shall live, their corpses shall rise.**
       O dwellers in the dust, awake and sing for joy!
    For your dew is a radiant dew,
       and the earth will give birth to those long dead.

And then an answer! The answer is surely beyond anything the righteous could have anticipated, an answer that breaks the categories of all of Yahweh's traditional, available responses. In the conventional, liturgical practice of Israel, complaint characteristically evokes a response from Yahweh, promising presence and intervention (cf. 43:8–13). But now in an unprecedented circumstance, Israel receives from Yahweh an unprecedented response. The dead, the ones done in by the "lofty city" (v. 5), will be raised to life. This response is of uncommon interest because it is one of only two places in the Old Testament where resurrection of the dead is clearly attested (the other is Dan. 12:2). It is conceded, perhaps, that there is no remedy for the troubles of Israel's circumstance "in this life." That, however, will not now be a deterrent to Yahweh's resolve and therefore no ground for Israel to forsake its deep trust in Yahweh. Those who have died will be raised. Those who are asleep will be awakened. Those who are silent will sing. The last line of the verse seems to echo the theme of verse 18, except that the wording is odd. If NRSV is followed, then the prayers of Israel that birthed nothing will now be countered. "The earth," where the dead are buried, will give birth.

This is indeed the ultimate response of Yahweh to the troubles of Israel. It is the ultimate response enacted in the Easter miracle of Jesus. We may, however, pay attention to the context of Yahweh's answer to complaint. This assurance is not a "reasoned" answer arrived at through modern enlightened rationality. It cannot be justified or understood or explained by such reasoning. It is rather an evangelical utterance—news of the gospel whereby the God in whom Israel trusts is indeed powerful enough and willing to deal with Israel's suffering and despair. Kaiser is surely right to say that it is an assertion that is ethical and practical, not speculative or reasonable. It is not a statement about immortality or death as the beginning of new life. It is a statement about God, the God who has swallowed up death (25:8) and knows no boundary beyond which Yahweh will not go in faithful response to faithful people. Kaiser concludes that this assertion is "due less to external influences than to the spelling out of the meaning of faith in God's righteousness to its final conclusion" (Kaiser, *Isaiah 13–39*, 219). Indeed, this gospel assertion has cadence and significance only for those who are righteous, who yearn for and acknowledge Yahweh alone. For all the others who do not yearn and seek and wait, the promise is nonsense. And it is better left so. It is, as Wildberger concludes, the "great Nevertheless" of faith.

26:20 **Come, my people, enter your chambers,**
> **and shut your doors behind you;**
> **hide yourselves for a little while**
>> **until the wrath is past.**
> [21] **For the LORD comes out from his place**
>> **to punish the inhabitants of the earth for their iniquity;**
> **the earth will disclose the blood shed on it,**
>> **and will no longer cover its slain.**

The final summons is yet one more assurance. It appears to be a second response to the lament of verses 16–18, proceeding as if the response of verse 19 had not been given. It is for this reason that some scholars believe verse 19 to be an intrusion in the text. But it is plausible, is it not, that the vigorous and pathos-filled complaint made to Yahweh by Israel might evoke more than one response from God!

Here is an assurance given in quite different imagery. The faithful are urged to take cover, to hide "for a little while." The phrase "for a little while" is an apocalyptic marker. It may mean "briefly," if it is asserted that the great judgment is soon. But it may also refer to a longer time, for a "thousand years are but as a day." That is, it is not a temporal reference but a zone in apocalyptic sequence. The faithful must endure until the raging chaos is over, no matter how long it takes.

The raging chaos that threatens the earth is caused by Yahweh, who comes in resolve and wrath to punish the lofty city, to level all those centers of power that have defied the purposes of Yahweh. The poet does not doubt that such a large trouble is coming. The poet also does not doubt that "in a little while" the trouble will pass, and the faithful will know Yahweh's *shalom*.

The very different responses of verse 19 and verses 20–21 indicate the

vigorous and venturesome interpretive activity to which Judaism is driven.
The violent scenario of verses 20–21 may be offensive to our bourgeois con-
sciousness. But we may take no easy refuge from the harshness in the more
wondrous promise of verse 19, for both assurances are notices of deep, massive displacement. In the end, the resolve of Yahweh matches the yearning
desire of the righteous. The large hope of Israel and the large response of
Yahweh together bespeak a radical destabilizing of the world much treasured then and much relied upon now. Such rhetoric flies against our common readiness to come to terms with the world as it now is. Here faith attests
that even our most stable world is at best penultimate, a condition to be welcomed only by the most serious trusters of Yahweh. We may give Calvin our
final word on this marvelous chapter: "Believers, by fleeing to God, obtain
life in the midst of affliction, and even in death itself" (*Isaiah* II, 237).

BEYOND WRATH
27:1–13

The final chapter of this group of apocalyptic texts continues the twin
themes of judgment and promise. In this chapter, unlike its predecessors,
the theme of promise predominates.

> 27:1 **On that day the LORD with his cruel and great and strong sword will
> punish Leviathan the fleeing serpent, Leviathan the twisting serpent, and he
> will kill the dragon that is in the sea.**

This lone verse is yet another anticipation of "that day" when Yahweh's
sovereignty will be fully enacted. We have already seen how the develop-
ing Israelite tradition anticipates Yahweh's victory over Israel's historical
enemies and then the defeat of the paradigmatic enemy of "the lofty city."
Here the rhetoric is extended one step further, in anticipation of Yahweh's
victory over Leviathan, the great sea monster who embodies the autonomous, recalcitrant force of evil that lies beneath the surface of the
earth and that endlessly threatens the stability of creation.

In order to receive this promise, one must note that the rhetoric here
completely transcends the concerns of historical Israel and engages in old,
pre-Israelite cosmic imagery in order to speak about the force of evil. In
the tradition of Milton's *Paradise Lost*, it suits our habitual moralism to
conclude that evil in the world is simply a consequence of human sin.
There is, however, an alternative tradition in the Bible that explodes such

simplistic moralism and insists that there is loose in the world a real, live, objective power of evil, without regard to human sin or goodness. That power surges against God's ordering of creation and endlessly undermines God's order in the world. On occasion, God may rebuke or repel or domesticate that evil monster, but the text does not claim the final overcoming of evil, at least not yet. And indeed, it is evident in that ancient world, as it is in our own time, that evil is indeed still on the loose. Such diverse voices as Karl Barth in his Calvinism, who speaks of "The Nothingness" (*Das Nichtige*) and Jon Levenson in his attention to biblical myth (*Creation and the Persistence of Evil*) attest to the continuing force of evil in a world that God does not yet fully govern.

As we have seen with the resurrection affirmation of 26:19, so it is with Leviathan here; the matter is not a speculative one, but a deeply felt, lived reality acknowledged in pastoral sensitivity. Even in our world of modern scientific rationality, there is still need for giving poetic name to that force of evil so close at hand, which is beyond our power to control or domesticate. This is evident from the classic of Herman Melville's *Moby Dick* to the more recent fascination with *Jurassic Park*. These artistic expressions make clear the need to name and speak about the threat. It is the same need to name and speak about this threat that propels this remarkable poetry.

This ancient poet gives expression to a sense his contemporaries surely had, that evil is on the loose threatening the very coherence of creation, so that the world is at risk and is not a safe place to inhabit. The poet, however, does more than name the reality. The poet also asserts that in a time soon to come, Yahweh will not only punish and restrain that threatening monster, but will indeed kill, that is, finally eliminate, the threat of objective evil. It is this same hope offered in Revelation 21:1, "the sea was no more."

In my judgment, the contemporary church is excessively preoccupied with guilt as human failure. In our time, or in the ancient context of the poet, the jeopardy of creation is a more elemental pastoral issue than simply human guilt. There is something larger at work than punishment for human violations. And that "something larger" makes us uneasy and profoundly helpless before its raw power. As a result, we may do well to notice not only this naming of evil, but also the daring evangelical expectation that God will indeed fully and finally overcome the power of evil, thereby making creation a genuinely safe home for all creatures as the creator has intended.

27:2 **On that day:**
   A pleasant vineyard, sing about it!

> [3] I, the LORD, am its keeper;
>   every moment I water it.
> I guard it night and day
>   so that no one can harm it;
>   [4] I have no wrath.
> If it gives me thorns and briers,
>   I will march to battle against it.
>   I will burn it up.
> [5] Or else let it cling to me for protection,
>   let it make peace with me,
>   let it make peace with me.
>
> [6] In days to come Jacob shall take root,
>   Israel shall blossom and put forth shoots,
>   and fill the whole world with fruit.

This unit contains two more introductory formulae for the assertion of hope (vv. 2, 6). The formula in verse 2 introduces a new Song of the Vineyard that completely and intentionally counters the Song of the Vineyard in 5:1–7. In that earlier poem, a love song turned sour as the vineyard failed to produce. The love song is there converted into a prophetic speech of judgment. Here, however, the song contains no judgment, but is an oracle of salvation that ushers in God's new propensity toward Israel, who is the well-beloved vineyard. Whereas in the old song Yahweh, the owner, is so provoked at the pitiful produce that the vineyard was abandoned to marauders and left desolate, here Yahweh, the owner, will be attentive, providing water and guarding it day and night to keep it safe. Israel is now—belatedly—chosen, elect, well-beloved, guaranteed, fully protected!

The basis for the assurance is that Yahweh "has no wrath." The wrath is all spent and over with. Now there is only caring attentiveness. In his pastoral eloquence, Calvin portrays God's generous way to Israel:

> God assumes, as we shall see, the character of a father who is grievously offended, and who, while he is offended at his son, still more pities him, and is naturally inclined to exercise compassion, because the warmth of his love rises above his anger. In short, he shews that he cannot hate his elect so as not to bear fatherly kindness towards them, even while he visits them with very severe punishments (*Isaiah* II, 250).

In the earlier song, the vineyard produces "thorns and briers," sufficient cause for God's rejecting anger. By contrast, here, even if "thorns and briers" appear, God will not be provoked but will intervene to root them out, so as to protect the vineyard.

In the earlier song of 5:1–7, "justice and righteousness" were desired by the owner of the vineyard but failed to appear. Here it is all *shalom*. The relation between owner and vineyard is one of *shalom*, so that the vineyard may produce *shalom*. Although these verses are scarcely linked at all to verse 1, it is worth noting that *shalom* is precisely the antithesis to the *chaos* the monster would cause. Thus, in this song Israel's prospects are put on a whole new footing, because Yahweh has determined to be a vigilant, protective presence; for that reason, "no evil shall befall you,/no scourge come near your tent" (Psalm 91:10).

Verse 6 appears to be an addition to verses 2–5 with its promissory introduction. It appeals to the same horticultural imagery and anticipates rootage, shoots, and fruit in rich abundance. It may be noticed that the implied "plenty" is used in the prophets concerning resettlement in the land after exile, thus perhaps anticipating verses 12–13.

27:7 **Has he struck them down as he struck down those who struck them?**
Or have they been killed as their killers were killed?
8 **By expulsion, by exile you struggled against them;**
with his fierce blast he removed them in the day of the east wind.
9 **Therefore by this the guilt of Jacob will be expiated,**
and this will be the full fruit of the removal of his sin:
when he makes all the stones of the altars
like chalkstones crushed to pieces,
no sacred poles or incense altars will remain standing.
10 **For the fortified city is solitary,**
a habitation deserted and forsaken, like the wilderness;
the calves graze there,
there they lie down, and strip its branches.
11 **When its boughs are dry, they are broken;**
women come and make a fire of them.
For this is a people without understanding;
therefore he that made them will not have compassion on them,
he that formed them will show them no favor.

These are exceedingly difficult verses, primarily because the city that is the object of Yahweh's wrath is not easily identified. Commentators have suggested three possible candidates: (1) *Jerusalem*, which is mildly treated by Yahweh and still has a chance in the future; (2) *the "world capital"* of the preceding chapter, which is to be devastated by Yahweh; or (3) *Samaria*, a city devastated by Yahweh, but now to be rehabilitated in a reunified Israel.

The identity of the city makes a decisive difference in interpretation, but none is completely satisfactory. Wildberger makes as good a case as can be made for Samaria, the capital city of the "renegade" Northern Kingdom, destroyed by the Assyrians in 722, an identity that can be usefully pursued.

The point of the awkwardly stated verse 7, whose rhetorical questions are to be answered negatively, is that, no, Yahweh did not strike down Jerusalem/Samaria(??) as severely as Yahweh struck down those who strike against the city. No, Yahweh did not kill the people of Jerusalem/Samaria(??) as Yahweh destroyed the attackers of the city. Yahweh's punishment of Yahweh's own has indeed been harsh, but not as harsh as punishment given to others. This is a cumbersome way to say that Yahweh has not been "too harsh." The assertion is perhaps rooted in the assurances and positive attentiveness of verses 2–6, and has prepared the way for the odd assurance that follows.

To be sure, Yahweh did contend ferociously with the recalcitrant/beloved city (v. 8). Yahweh has not been easy or prematurely forgiving toward the city. Yahweh has countered the recalcitrance of the city by exile, which is like a hot wind that blows away everything in front of it. The development of verses 7–8—whatever the object—exhibits a poet dealing with the vagaries of historical experience whereby Yahweh is positively inclined but not easy, for Yahweh is severe but not too severe. The double message—not too severe (v. 7), not too easy (v. 8)—indicates how problematic it is to link a simplistic notion of Yahweh to the vagaries of history so readily available to the poet.

The harsh "removal" of verse 8 prepares for the surprising "therefore" of verse 9. "Therefore," in the prophets, characteristically asserts a negative juridical sentence. Here, however, the "therefore" is positive (as in Jer. 30:16). There can indeed be "expiation" for Jacob's sin. The reference to Jacob might refer to Northern Israel. This is a good word to the north. The guilt that produced the debacle of 722 when the Northern Kingdom fell into the hands of Assyria will be overcome and the consequence of the sin nullified. But the promised forgiveness is not easy or unconditional. It is "by this," enunciated in the remainder of the verse. The cost of expiation is the crushing removal and elimination of all emblems of false worship. (This assessment of worship in Samaria is in line with the Deuteronomic judgment of 2 Kings 17:7–20.) Moreover, the appeal for transformed behavior on the part of the north to bring it into line with the Yahwistic self-awareness of the south is not unlike the summons to repentance in Jeremiah 3:11–23, culminating in the imperatives of Jeremiah 4:1–4. If this is indeed a condition laid down for future legitimation of the north, then we may understand that it is a requirement laid down by the Jerusalem authorities in their control of emerging Judaism after the Exile. If so, this could suggest a gesture of conciliation toward the north, albeit a gesture with a requirement. If this is a correct reading of the dynamics of this obscure text, it is not unlike the painful "Reconstruction" of the United States, wherein one section dictated the terms of renewal for another section, all couched in pious, uncompromising language with heavy moralistic overtones.

Finally, verses 10–11 reverse field once again and end severely. The fortified city—perhaps Samaria—is seen to be abandoned, with the characteristic scenario of an urban area reverting to idyllic, emptied pastureland. The physical disruption, however, is only a pointer to the theological reality: Because this is a people without "sense," they do not know Yahweh; they do not know who they are or where they belong. The phrasing is reminiscent of the theme statement of 1:2–3. The city is worse than an ox or an ass in forsaking its true owner and master. Inescapably, Yahweh will grant no compassion and show no favor (v. 12). The fate of this fortified, abandoned city, presumably Samaria, is contrasted with Jerusalem, that "pleasant vineyard" blessed with *shalom* (vv. 2–5). History governed by Yahweh is severe and demanding. The poet in any case does not flinch from the way it is and will be in Yahweh's world.

27:12 On that day the LORD will thresh from the channel of the Euphrates to the Wadi of Egypt, and you will be gathered one by one, O people of Israel. ¹³ And on that day a great trumpet will be blown, and those who were lost in the land of Assyria and those who were driven out to the land of Egypt will come and worship the LORD on the holy mountain at Jerusalem.

As a conclusion to this long section of apocalyptic text (chapters 24—27), we are given one more anticipation of "that day"; for the people of Yahweh, the anticipation of "that day" is altogether positive. There will be a "threshing" across the Fertile Crescent. The image bespeaks a process to separate grain from chaff. In context, the process concerns the separation of Jews in exile from the Gentile peoples among whom the Jews live. This promised future, which is only for Jews, is perhaps a step along the way toward the stringent ethnicity of Ezra and Nehemiah.

The good news for Jews (with no counter bad news suggested here for Gentiles) is that the exiles will be gathered, that is, mobilized to come home to Jerusalem. The poet imagines a great festal procession, signaled by a trumpet, that will initiate a dramatic, large-scale process. Though the "trumpet sound" need not be understood so, the signal may be an allusion to the great theme of Jubilee. When the *shophar* is sounded (Lev. 25:9): "It shall be a jubilee for you: you shall return, every one of you, to your property and every one of you to your family" (Lev. 25:10).

That movement is underway in our verses. The Jews will return from Assyria and from Egypt, from the great nemesis states, from the extremities of the Fertile Crescent. They will come to Jerusalem, and there they will worship Yahweh, unfettered and joyous.

Finally, in this utterance of apocalyptic possibility, the poetry moves beyond assault of the world capital and beyond the rhetoric of violence and devastation. The focus now is singular and positive concerning rehabilitation. The culmination of this visionary material is the proper worship of Yahweh in Yahweh's proper place of worship by Yahweh's most serious loyalists. This assertion at the end of the section, however, is only possible because of the claim at the beginning. It is the removal of "the last enemy" (Leviathan) that liberates the world for the true worship of the one God. The world is turned to *shalom*, and so this worship concerns the God of all truth, who is the God of all peace.

4. "The King in His Beauty"
Isaiah 28—33

This portion of the book of Isaiah contains four chapters (28—31) that scholars tend to regard as rooted in the words of Isaiah of Jerusalem in the eighth century. As such, these materials have closest links to Isaiah 1—12 and constitute the core work of the prophet. Chapters 32—33, which most scholars regard as later materials, are filled with more hopeful assertions, tending toward apocalyptic imagination. Taken altogether, these six chapters articulate the characteristic two-stage view of history we have found elsewhere: Jerusalem and Judah will be subjected to a *severe judgment* that will take the form of military attack, issuing in nullification; Jerusalem and Judah will be *restored to full well-being* by the dramatic and glorious reestablishment of the rule of Yahweh, which will permit a peaceable kingdom. Although these two accents are necessarily sequential—first judgment, then restoration—they are to be understood everywhere in the book of Isaiah as a single expression of Yahweh's rule of judgment and grace.

Chapters 28—31 are quite complex poems, largely articulating the coming judgment upon Jerusalem. Each of the four chapters begins with a woe (expressed by "ah," "oh," or "alas"), a rhetorical signal of judgment bespeaking a sure, coming deathliness. Although the woe also includes, at points, the Northern Kingdom of Israel, the rhetoric aims at Jerusalem and Judah. But as we have seen elsewhere in the Isaiah tradition, it is structurally resolved that judgment is not and cannot be God's last word. For that reason, even in these harsh utterances one can notice traces of hope and new possibility given by God (28:5–6, 16–17; 29:5b–8, 17–21, 23–24; 30:15, 18–33; 33:4–5, 8–9), which receive much more extended expression in chapters 32—33. Scholars suggest that 29:1–8 constitutes something of a "key" whereby an announcement of *judgment* is "in an instant, suddenly" turned to *hope*.

Within this general framework of judgment and hope, I will call attention to two particular motifs. First, emphasis is given, from time to time, to "ears and eyes," the capacity to perceive and notice and respond. These references are likely related to the devastating resolve of Yahweh in 6:9–10 that Judah will be smitten with blindness and deafness, and so unable to respond to Yahweh in obedience. Thus the people are in a stupor with eyes closed, dumb, "but not from wine" (29:9–10). It is anticipated in 29:18 that in the coming scenario of well-being wrought by Yahweh, the deaf will hear and the blind will see. It is important to recognize that in the larger strategy of the book of Isaiah, this recurring theme suggests that Jerusalem's obduracy is at the behest of Yahweh, even as is Jerusalem's belated capacity for positive response to Yahweh.

A second theme concerns Jerusalem's readiness for obedience to Yahweh. The obscure text of 28:7–9 indicates resistance to teaching and instruction on the part of the leaders of the community. The "wise and discerning" are to be incapable of discernment (29:14), but in God's new time will come to understanding and an acceptance of instruction (29:24). In 30:9 a rebellious people is resistant to instruction; but in 30:20–21 this same people in the midst of adversity will accept torah teaching and will return to the way of obedience previously rejected. The upshot of the new obedience is that Jerusalem will give up its idols, emblems of arrogant autonomy (30:22; 31:6; cf. 29:16), and return to its proper status as an obedient respondent to Yahweh.

We may notice in these chapters, moreover, a number of remarkable images and poignant phrases suggesting a rhetorical artistry worthy of the theological daring of the text. Among these, I call attention to the following:

- "A covenant with death," an ironic phrasing of negativity (28:15, 18).
- "A precious cornerstone," a metaphor that subsequently comes to carry christological freight in the New Testament (28:16).
- "God's alien work," later to become a way whereby Luther speaks of God's judgment (28:21).
- An agricultural parable concerning Yahweh's wise timeliness (28:23–29).
- A pedagogical chant used satirically to bespeak elemental instruction rejected (28:10–13).
- Use of the image of potter-clay to be taken up later in the tradition (cf. 45:9; 64:8).

All of these uses indicate the powerful force of the rhetoric and the dense complexity of the text. Clearly, the role of Yahweh in the life of Jerusalem is not a simple, straight-line plot, but requires an artistry of articulation that in turn demands our attentiveness.

Chapters 32—33 are clearly a different sort of material. Chapter 32:1 breaks the sequence of beginning woes with "See," calling attention to a positive announcement. To be sure, 33:1 returns with a beginning woe, only now the deathly utterance is against Israel's enemy. On the whole, these chapters are affirmative of Jerusalem, articulating the establishment of a new, positive governance, either through a human, messianic king (32:1–8) or directly through the kingship of Yahweh (33:17–24). Corresponding to the affirmations are heavy, nullifying condemnations of the enemies of Jerusalem.

There can be little doubt that chapters 28—31 and chapters 32—33 constitute different kinds of material. There is good reason that critical scholarship has concluded that chapters 28—31 reflect early Isaiah and chapters 32—33 reflect a much later circumstance and perception. Christopher Seitz nonetheless has made a compelling case to see a *canonical* connection in these materials that anticipates the good king (Hezekiah), who will enact Yahweh's good rule. Such a canonical reading, as Seitz intends, moves us along toward the wondrous affirmations of the later parts of the book of Isaiah (Seitz, *Isaiah 1–39*).

These chapters, taken altogether, reflect a realism about Jerusalem's geopolitical situation. There is a recognition that the Northern Kingdom of Israel is under judgment and on its way to nullification. There is an awareness that Jerusalem's failed leadership has jeopardized the city and all for which it stands. There is an acknowledgment that Egypt is no reliable ally and that even Assyria finally cannot endure.

It is characteristic of prophetic material to pay close attention to lived reality "on the ground." The tradition of Isaiah is clearly no slouch about this matter. In the end, however, prophetic material is not simply social analysis. It is, rather, *Yahwistic imagination.* For that reason, in the midst of acute social analysis, accent is finally upon Yahweh as Jerusalem's most severe adversary and as Jerusalem's only hope. Already in 6:1, it is recognized that when the king dies, the "Real King" becomes visible. Here as well, it is when old recipes for reality are nullified that Yahweh's true governance becomes available. The end point is jubilation in the coming of "The Kingdom of God." That governance, however, comes only through the vagaries of history, here matched by venturesome rhetoric. In prophetic horizon, it is such rhetoric that is the indispensable vehicle for Yahweh's new age.

FRESH PHRASINGS OF TROUBLE
28:1–29

This long and rich chapter articulates, except for verses 5–6, the coming judgment of Yahweh, first on the Northern Kingdom (vv. 1–4) and then upon Judah and its leadership. The theme of judgment is of course a familiar one. What sets this poetry apart is the rich rhetorical freedom that offers both remarkable metaphors and durable phrasings through which the text continues to energize our imagination over the generations.

A Beauty Overwhelmed,
a Beauty Anticipated (28:1–6)

This text includes a vision of destruction—apparently concerning the Northern Kingdom (vv. 1–4)—and a responding vision of coming well-being (vv. 5–6). The two sections may be in substance distanced from each other, but they are rhetorically bound together by common phrasing.

> 28:1 **Ah, the proud garland of the drunkards of Ephraim,**
>   **and the fading flower of its glorious beauty,**
>   **which is on the head of those bloated with rich food, of those**
>   **overcome with wine!**
>   **²See, the Lord has one who is mighty and strong;**
>   **like a storm of hail, a destroying tempest,**
>   **like a storm of mighty, overflowing waters;**
>   **with his hand he will hurl them down to the earth.**
>   **³Trampled under foot will be**
>   **the proud garland of the drunkards of Ephraim.**
>   **⁴And the fading flower of its glorious beauty,**
>   **which is on the head of those bloated with rich food,**
>   **will be like a first-ripe fig before the summer;**
>   **whoever sees it, eats it up**
>   **as soon as it comes to hand.**

This speech of judgment begins with a characteristic woe ("ah") anticipating a condemnation and threat to come. The subject of this oracle is named only in the midst of the indictment of verse 1. It is Ephraim!

The poetry of Isaiah looks northward to anticipate the Northern Kingdom in great jeopardy. The lyrical characterization of Ephraim as "fading flower" suggests a self-indulgent well-being that is on the wane. The indictment concerns a life of self-indulgence, rich food, and wine (cf. Amos

6:1–6). The reference may be literal (that is, irresponsible alcohol), or it may be metaphorical (referring to a life of narcoticized indifference). Either way, Israel to the north has squandered and abused its life and is now subject to a prophetic woe.

The sentence, introduced by an attention-getting "see" (v. 2) is directly from Yahweh. It is Yahweh "who has one." It is generally assumed, given eighth-century history, that the "one" whom Yahweh has is Assyria. This "one" may be precisely Tiglath-pileser III, a most ominous military leader, or one of his successors at the head of cruel Assyria. This utterance, reminiscent of 7:7–9, together with the flood imagery of 8:7–8, anticipates the coming massive, irresistible devastation of Assyria. And in fact, in 725–722 the capital city of Samaria was overrun by the Assyrian armies.

Verses 3–4 are a reprise of verse 1, reiterating the same phrasing concerning the self-indulgent irresponsibility that evokes Yahweh. The new urgency of verse 4b concerns the earliest, most desirable figs, the ones that taste the best. Israel will be "swallowed" (bl') like a tasty fig. The verb *swallow* is used positively in 25:7. Here it is a negative. Assyria will gulp down Israel!

The sequence of warning-threat-outcome offers a daring, albeit characteristic, prophetic scenario. The poet ventures into geopolitics and links Assyrian expansionism to Israel's self-indulgence, a linkage rooted in Yahweh's covenantal requirements. The poem asserts not only the inevitability of Assyria (cf. 10:5–19), but also the large, magisterial governance of Yahweh over the entire international process. Imperial expansionism does not just happen. It reflects the moral agenda of Yahweh, who dispatches the rise and fall of nations.

28:5 **In that day the LORD of hosts will be a garland of glory,**
      and a diadem of beauty, to the remnant of his people;
  6 **and a spirit of justice to the one who sits in judgment,**
      and strength to those who turn back the battle at the gate.

These two verses voice an important variant in this chapter of judgment and doom. As is characteristic of the tradition of Isaiah, it is possible to look beyond the anticipated devastation to a gift of glory not assaulted and a gift of beauty not faded, gifts that are sure to come. These gifts will not be Israel restored, but Yahweh's own presence given to "the remnant." The one given is "The Lord of hosts" in full sovereign power. That is, the gift is after the devastation. The gift is Yahweh's own enhancing self. With Yahweh comes "a spirit of justice" and "strength." It could be that this refers to two officers in the community, judicial and military. Or this part of Isaiah could be anticipation of the coming (Davidic) king who will be endowed (as in 11:1–5) with all that is required for communal well-being. Thus Calvin declares that "in God alone there is enough of riches and glory to supply all earthly defects" (*Isaiah* II, 275).

The turn from condemnation (vv. 1–4) to anticipation (vv. 5–6) bespeaks a major discontinuity. The poetry foresees a deep and costly fissure (exile), after which comes restoration. The condemnation is closely geopolitical; the anticipation has political dimension to be sure, but concerns Yahweh's own investment in the future of "the remnant."

An Alien Tongue (28:7–13)

This enigmatic passage, insofar as we can determine who is speaking which lines, appears to be an assault on the leadership of Judah (vv. 7–8), a defiance of prophetic teaching (vv. 9–10), and an uncompromising reiteration of prophetic judgment as response to the defiance (vv. 11–13).

28:7 **These also reel with wine**
and stagger with strong drink;
the priest and the prophet reel with strong drink,
they are confused with wine,
they stagger with strong drink;
they err in vision,
they stumble in giving judgment.
⁸All tables are covered with filthy vomit;
no place is clean.

This complicated passage takes up the theme of "wine and strong drink" we have already met in verses 1–4. This is, however, a distinct rhetorical unit, and it is probable that the "these also" in verse 7 refers to the priests and prophets in Jerusalem, as distinct from the leaders of the north. In any case, the reference is clearly to someone other than those condemned in verses 1–4. The indictment concerns religious leadership that, because of self-indulgent drinking, has forfeited the powers of discernment whereby they can execute their offices of leadership. As a consequence of such self-indulgence, the prophet fails in visionary leadership, and the priest fails in giving judgment about holiness and cleanness, judgments that are crucial to priestly responsibility (cf. Ezek. 22:26; Hag. 2:11–13). Failure in vision and in judgment, moreover, jeopardizes the entire community that depends upon reliable religious leadership.

In order to reinforce the indictment, the poem adds the vivid imagery of verse 8. The scene is the meeting room of priests and prophets, a place of purity and attentiveness, that now looks like an abandoned barracks after a rowdy, brawling party among soldiers. The stench of vomit is palpable and unbearable. In addition to that, however, the disorder bespeaks a forfeiture of the "cleanness" necessary to divine presence. Religious leadership of this sort, without focus or discipline, can indeed drive Yahweh away, making big trouble for the community.

28:9 **"Whom will he teach knowledge,**
    and to whom will he explain the message?
  Those who are weaned from milk,
    those taken from the breast?
¹⁰ **For it is precept upon precept, precept upon precept,**
  line upon line, line upon line,
  here a little, there a little."

These verses appear to be a defiant response of the priests and prophets, who reject the poetic utterance of prophetic instruction and defy the right and authority of the prophet to speak. It is as though they asked: "Who is he to be instructing us?" These are apparently institutional (tenured?) leaders who think they know everything (or at least enough) and surely resist any instruction that smacks of reprimand. The opening line of verse 9 asks indignantly, "Who?" that implies an answer, "Not us." The second rhetorical question suggests that the prophet will address those who are just weaned, so elemental is his instruction. But, the religious leaders imply, we are not babies and so do not need elemental instruction concerning work, faith, or responsibilities.

The defiance is reiterated in verse 10. The meaning of the lines is obscure, but what is not to be missed, and what is not evident in English translation, is that the two lines consist in four sets of brief terms. The first two are reiterated four times each: saw, saw, saw, saw; qaw, qaw, qaw, qaw. The third element consists of two words and is repeated only once. The NRSV rendering, "precept upon precept, precept upon precept," is much too cognitive. The effect of the lines is more likely concerned with the sound rather than the substance, a sound that reiterates a simple, sharp syllable, delivered in mocking overstatement. Although no one knows what the lines mean, it may be a parody on teaching the alphabet, perhaps not unlike Professor Higgins's repeated sounds to Elisa Doolittle in "My Fair Lady." The effect is of a teacher working with small children on the alphabet or the multiplication tables, with an emphasis on *repetition* of the *elemental*. The sarcasm implies that the poet is a boring repeater of elemental, obvious claims, sounding the a-b-c's of Yahwism over and over, when the prophets and priests are sophisticated and have moved well beyond such elemental data. They will not sit still for such instruction!

The second part of this unit (vv. 11–13) appears to be a prophetic response to the indignation of verses 9–10, reasserting the prophetic instruction, intensifying the threat, and taking up the mocking of verse 10 in order to underscore the weightiness of the message.

28:11 **Truly, with stammering lip**
      and with alien tongue
  he will speak to this people,
    ¹² **to whom he has said,**
  "This is rest;
      give rest to the weary;
  and this is repose";
      yet they would not hear.

The response to the indignation of the critiqued leaders is a firm resolve: Indeed! (*kî*). Now the "he" who speaks is not the prophet who was attacked, but apparently God. God, through the prophet, has invited the people to "rest," but they—both leaders and people—have refused to listen (v. 12). The words attributed to "him" appear to be a quotation. Although we cannot be precise, what Judah had been previously told is perhaps anticipated in 7:9 and more precisely in 30:15: "In returning and rest you shall be saved;/in quietness and in trust shall be your strength." Kaiser opines that this statement is "a summary of Isaiah's preaching." The "rest and repose" offered is given through trust in Yahweh, the very trust that the leaders of verses 7–8 have refused and resisted (cf. Matt. 11:28). Israel's fundamental requirement is to listen (cf. Deut. 6:4). But the invitation of Yahweh has been rejected. Since Deuteronomy, the promise of rest has been conditioned by obedience. As a consequence, there will be another utterance, but this one in an "alien tongue" (v. 11). Although the threat is imprecise and elusive, the offer of an alien tongue likely suggests an invading and occupying army that speaks a foreign language and is ominously inscrutable. When Judah rejects Yahweh's *language of invitation* (v. 12), it is readdressed in the *language of threat* (v. 11).

28:13 **Therefore the word of the LORD will be to them,**
    "Precept upon precept, precept upon precept,
    line upon line, line upon line,
    here a little, there a little";
  in order that they may go, and fall backward,
    and be broken, and snared, and taken.

In this final verse of repudiation, the poet returns to the rhetoric of verse 10. In that verse, the clipped repetitions of instruction had intended to mock the prophet. Now the poem takes up and quotes the mocking and turns it into yet another ominous warning. The elemental instruction of the prophet—the a-b-c's of prophetic faith—will indeed be enacted. Here we are not told what that elemental instruction entails. In a general way, however, the tradition of Isaiah is unambiguous. This community that fails to put Yahweh at its center will be assaulted and exiled. The leaders, by their indifference, self-indulgence, and unresponsiveness, will bring deep trouble upon Judah. The final line names a triad of passive verbs of judgment: "broken, snared, taken" (cf. 8:15). The language is not unlike Hosea 4:9–12: "like people, like priest." There also it is a "stumbling" (Hos. 4:5) linked to "wine and new wine" (4:11). The community is numbed and stupefied, bent on self-destruction.

An Alien Work (28:14–22)

These verses constitute a conventional and characteristic prophetic speech of judgment. The unit is particularly to be noted for the phrases "covenant with death" (vv. 15, 18), "a precious cornerstone" (v. 16), and "alien work" (v. 21), all uses that have a powerful theological afterlife.

28:14 **Therefore hear the word of the LORD, you scoffers**
who rule this people in Jerusalem.
¹⁵ **Because you have said, "We have made a covenant with death,**
and with Sheol we have an agreement;
when the overwhelming scourge passes through
it will not come to us;
for we have made lies our refuge,
and in falsehood we have taken shelter";

The unit begins with a prophetic indictment aimed at the "rulers" in Jerusalem, presumably the priests and prophets of verse 7. They have scoffed at the requirements of Yahweh and at the prophet who speaks for Yahweh. In a characteristic maneuver, the prophet attributes statements to his opponents, statements that evidence their resistance to the prophetic requirement.

The "rulers" claim a "covenant with death" that will make them safe when the "overwhelming scourge" comes. It is possible that "death" here refers to a religious commitment alternative to Yahweh, the god Mot (whose name means "death"). If so, the claim is, in prophetic perception, ludicrous. It is more likely, in my judgment, that this attribution to the rulers is ironic. The covenant they make is with deathly, self-serving, self-indulgent practices, such as those noted in verses 7–8. The only reason they dare imagine their safety in such stratagems is because of their numbed illusion and denial.

The irony is intensified by the ready acknowledgment of "the overwhelming scourge" (cf. v. 2), presumably the coming of Assyria. Thus the attribution is a self-indictment, making clear the ludicrous pretense of well-being in a narcoticized culture that is unable to notice threat. The denial of danger is of course a denial of the cruciality of Yahweh, who dispatches the scourge.

28:16 **therefore thus says the Lord GOD,**
See, I am laying in Zion a foundation stone,
a tested stone,
a precious cornerstone, a sure foundation:
"One who trusts will not panic."
[17]**And I will make justice the line,**
and righteousness the plummet;
hail will sweep away the refuge of lies,
and waters will overwhelm the shelter.

The "therefore" of verse 16 (cf. v. 14) leads us to expect a threat. But before the threat is enunciated, the poem offers an assurance that is most characteristic of the Isaiah tradition. Yahweh provides a reliable alternative to the madness of the leaders. The rhetoric is exaggerated: foundation stone, tested stone, precious, sure. The imagery appeals to the solid reliability of the temple, but the precise reference of the image is uncertain. We know only that it relates to the certitude and reliability of Zion-David theology (cf. Psalm 118:22). The offer, moreover, includes the David-Isaiah term "trust" (*'amen*). Yahweh offers a safe haven from the coming scourge, a sure place of refuge in which to be safe. Most plausibly, this is an invitation to *trust in Yahweh*, given in the imagery of Zion. The summons to faith is the only "safe place" in a world severely under assault.

This imagery is taken up as testimony to Jesus in the early church (Rom. 9:33; 10:11; 1 Tim. 1:16; 1 Pet. 2:4–8). In New Testament faith, it is Jesus who is the sure place of well-being. To be sure, the christological appropriation of the imagery is a daring one. Given that, however, the usage is congruent with that of Isaiah. In both cases, the gift of God is an offer of protection from an unlikely source in a season of acute danger.

In verse 17 the offer of refuge is marked by the characteristic terms "justice and righteousness" that link well-being to covenantal requirements (cf. 5:7; 9:7). This sure place (vv. 16–17a) is contrasted with "the refuge of lies," the self-deception marked as a "covenant with death." Thus the poem offers a radical either/or.

28:18 **Then your covenant with death will be annulled,**
       and your agreement with Sheol will not stand;
     when the overwhelming scourge passes through
       you will be beaten down by it.
   19 **As often as it passes through, it will take you;**
       for morning by morning it will pass through,
       by day and by night;
     and it will be sheer terror to understand the message.
   20 **For the bed is too short to stretch oneself on it,**
       and the covering too narrow to wrap oneself in it.
   21 **For the LORD will rise up as on Mount Perazim,**
       he will rage as in the valley of Gibeon;
     to do his deed—strange is his deed!
     and to work his work—alien is his work!
   22 **Now therefore do not scoff,**
       or your bonds will be made stronger;
     for I have heard a decree of destruction
       from the Lord GOD of hosts upon the whole land.

Now, after the positive interlude of verses 16–17a, the threat signaled by "therefore" (vv. 14, 16) is voiced. The "covenant with death"—whatever it may be—will be no refuge at all. There are no alternatives to Yahweh. The imagery is of a massive rise of flood waters that is completely irresistible, that will sweep away every line of defense. The reference is likely to Assyria, but the imagery of flood waters is sustained on its own terms. The threat is made more ominous by the reiterated "it" in verses 18–19. The recalcitrant, unresponsive leadership now is completely exposed. Jerusalem and its environs could have been safe within the "foundation stone" (v. 16) of faith. When that is rejected, however, there is no place to hide. There is no adequate protective covenant, no high ground (v. 20).

Yahweh is on the move as resolute, invading force. The poetry summons Israel's memory. Yahweh had fought vigorously for Israel against the Philistines (2 Sam. 5:17–25) and at Gibeon (Josh. 10:9ff.). Yahweh's ferocious vigor will be now as it was then. It will be exactly the same—same vigor, same irresistible force, same destructiveness. However, everything is now reversed! Now the ferocious military might of Yahweh is mobilized *against Israel*, and not, as heretofore, *for Israel*. Yahweh has been Israel's

sure protection and defense for a very long time. But not now. Now Yahweh has become adversary and invading foe. So Calvin concludes:

> The Lord formerly performed miracles when he wished to save his people;
> he will now perform them in order to destroy that people: for since the Is-
> raelites degenerated, they shall feel the hand of God for their destruction
> which their fathers felt for their salvation (*Isaiah* II, 299).

It is *foreign* work—the work of a foreigner—foreign to Yahweh's own history and inclination. It is not what Yahweh has characteristically done nor,
we may assume, not what Yahweh would choose to do. But it must be done.
Jerusalem has exhausted all of the kind inclination of Yahweh, and there is
now only devastation. John D. W. Watts observes that the message of destruction contradicted the people's understanding of what they considered
to be Yahweh's real "work" in and through Israel.

The phrase "alien work" became a crucial term for Martin Luther, who
related it to Yahweh's judgment. Luther took the specific, contexted term
of Isaiah and transposed it into a large theological theme. Yahweh's "normal" work is grace. Judgment is foreign work, alien to God's own propensity but unavoidable. Thus the poem nullifies the entire tradition of
Yahweh's care for Israel.

The poem concludes with a summary statement corresponding to the
introduction of verse 14 (v. 22). The term "scoff" is sounded again. "Scoff-
ing" is the verbal, defiant rejection of Yahweh. It is enough to evoke from
Yahweh a decision to destroy. The final phrase uses Isaiah's most powerful term for Yahweh's awesome governance—Lord God of hosts—and
matches the intensity of Yahweh to the scope of the coming assault. The
high God against the whole land! The community that refuses an invitation receives alien work expressed in alien tongue. Even Zion is now not
safe, even though an offer was made.

A Well-Instructed Farmer (28:23–29)

These verses offer a parable that appeals to agricultural imagery. The story
line of the imagery is fairly obvious. What is unclear is the tenor of the
parable; that is, what is the intent beyond the concreteness of the imagery?
Although the subject seems to be taught by God (v. 26), it seems likely that
this is a sapiential reflection on God's own skillful, precise work.

28:23 **Listen, and hear my voice;**
Pay attention, and hear my speech.
24 **Do those who plow for sowing plow continually?**

> Do they continually open and harrow their ground?
> 25 When they have leveled its surface,
>   do they not scatter dill, sow cummin,
> and plant wheat in rows
>   and barley in its proper place,
>   and spelt as the border?
> 26 For they are well instructed;
>   their God teaches them.

The mode of speech is instruction through a series of three rhetorical questions. The first question asks about endless plowing. The second about endless harrowing. The third question is more complex, reflecting the routine sequence of farming in terms of preparing the ground (leveling), scattering and sowing and planting each crop in the right place at the right time.

It is noteworthy that this series of questions makes no historical or theological interpretive connection. It could as well be instruction to the young about what to do when and for how long. The questions are commensurate with my own amazement about farming: Good farmers seem to have an intuitive sense about what to do when—not too soon, not too late.

Because this didactic articulation occurs in this freighted chapter, we are bound to think it pertains now to more than agriculture. If so, it suggests that God knows the right time (cf. Eccles. 3:1–8). However, nothing is said about what time it is. The context suggests that it is punishment time, but that is not said here.

> 28:27 Dill is not threshed with a threshing sledge,
>   nor is a cart wheel rolled over cummin;
>   but dill is beaten out with a stick,
>   and cummin with a rod.
> 28 Grain is crushed for bread,
>   but one does not thresh it forever;
> one drives the cart wheel and horses over it,
>   but does not pulverize it.

In these verses a similar agricultural theme is presented. This time the concern is the match of the tool to the task. The controlling imagery is not unlike using a sledgehammer to kill a fly. The instrument must be proportionate to the task so as not to overdo or crush. Again, no application is made. The theological reference may be that as God knows the right time like a farmer, so God like a farmer knows the right tool. We are told nothing of the tool or the task. In context, we may wonder if the task is destruction and the tool is Assyria. Such an interpretation, however, seems oddly incongruent with the irenic, instructional tone that carries no hint of threat.

28:29 **This also comes from the LORD of hosts;**
          he is wonderful in counsel,
          and excellent in wisdom.

It is only here that the reference to Yahweh as an agent is made, though in verse 26 the instructional tone is linked to Yahweh. In verse 29 the language becomes more lyrical and expansive. Now to be celebrated is Yahweh's wisdom, which knows the right time and the right tool. Taken by itself, this unit lacks specificity and seems only to be a doxological celebration of Yahweh as a good farmer. Taken in context, Yahweh the farmer may conclude that it is time to act, as Yahweh acted toward the vineyard, negatively in 5:1–7 and positively in 27:2–6. The interpreter must decide how intimately to connect the poem to its context, or whether to permit it to stand alone as an affirmation of Yahweh's reliable oversight. The text itself does not tell us how to proceed beyond the foundational assertion of God's wise administration of creation.

A CITY "VISITED"—TWICE
29:1–24

This chapter consists of a series of smaller poetic units that altogether testify to Yahweh's judgment on Jerusalem and Yahweh's rehabilitative concern for the city.

Jerusalem Visited (29:1–8)

This unit asserts the devastation to be wrought by Yahweh (vv. 1–5c) and the resolve of Yahweh to move against the enemies of Jerusalem (vv. 5d–8). This double theme of judgment and deliverance represents Isaiah's characteristic two-stage articulation of Jerusalem's destiny, so much so that Wildberger takes this passage's "theological ambivalence" to be a "key presentation" of the theology of Isaiah (Wildberger, *Jesaja 28–39*, 1110).

29:1 **Ah, Ariel, Ariel,**
          the city where David encamped!
      Add year to year;
          let the festivals run their round.
      ² **Yet I will distress Ariel,**
          and there shall be moaning and lamentation,
          and Jerusalem shall be to me like an Ariel.
      ³ **And like David I will encamp against you;**

I will besiege you with towers
  and raise siegeworks against you.
⁴ Then deep from the earth you shall speak,
  from low in the dust your words shall come;
 your voice shall come from the ground like the voice of a ghost,
  and your speech shall whisper out of the dust.

⁵ But the multitude of your foes shall be like small dust,
  and the multitude of tyrants like flying chaff.

The speech of judgment begins with a woe ("ah"), bespeaking deathly trouble to come. "Ariel" is an enigmatic term for the city of Jerusalem, the pivot of Isaiah's words concerning "the city where David encamped." David's city is, by the time of Isaiah, the great liturgic center (the temple) that preoccupied the royal establishment, that served to guarantee safety under Yahweh's presence, and that seemed to narcoticize establishment Jerusalem against threat. The liturgical-ideological activity of festivals, roundly condemned by Isaiah (1:11–15; cf. Amos 4:4–5) is part of an illusionary world into which the woe intrudes.

Yahweh, the festivals notwithstanding, will move decisively to trouble Jerusalem (vv. 2–3). The threat is a series of first-person verbs with Yahweh as subject: distress, encamp, besiege, raise. The imagery is military. Yahweh will command an assault upon the city as the enemy of "David's city."

The outcome will be "moaning and lamentation" (v. 2). Inhabitants of the city will be reduced to misery, brought low, defeated, and humiliated (vv. 4–5). From such a state of being driven into the ground, the residents of the city will speak. These verses stress speech: "speak, words, voice, speech, whisper." Most likely the speech consists of lamentation and complaint, articulation of loss, hurt, and suffering. The petition to Yahweh, the attempt to mobilize Yahweh, however, will not deter the destruction. At the behest of Yahweh, the destruction will be military activity that will be fierce and unrelenting, so as to reduce Jerusalem to dust and chaff (v. 5a–c). In Isaiah's context, the military reference is likely to Assyria, but that is not specified. The ultimate agent of devastation is Yahweh.

29:5d And in an instant, suddenly,
    ⁶ you will be visited by the LORD of hosts
  with thunder and earthquake and great noise,
    with whirlwind and tempest, and the flame of a devouring fire.
 ⁷ And the multitude of all the nations that fight against Ariel,
    all that fight against her and her stronghold, and who distress her,
    shall be like a dream, a vision of the night.

^{8} **Just as when a hungry person dreams of eating**
   and wakes up still hungry,
or a thirsty person dreams of drinking
   and wakes up faint, still thirsty,
so shall the multitude of all the nations be
   that fight against Mount Zion.

Because of the ferociousness of the assault, we are not prepared for the radical turn in prophetic rhetoric: "In an instant, suddenly . . . !" Abruptly, without a hint, Yahweh of hosts, the great military agent and adversary, will "visit" Jerusalem. The term "visit" is pivotal here and nicely marks the odd turn of rhetoric. The term can imply angry negativity. Thus verses 1–5c are an anticipation of a "visit" from Yahweh. But here the verb is positive. Yahweh will visit Jerusalem in order to fend off assaulting armies. The rhetoric of verse 5 is that of a theophany. The full force of Yahweh's majestic power will be mobilized. Yahweh will come with massive, ominous power. But the rage of Yahweh's incursion is now not against Jerusalem but against the "multitude of all the nations who assault Jerusalem." Yahweh reverses field. We are not told why—except we now know that the tradition of Isaiah cannot countenance the full destruction of Jerusalem. Historically, the Assyrian assault of 701 against the city ended without imperial success. Rhetorically, Assyria is mandated against the city, but goes too far in its autonomy (10:5–19). Later on, Babylon is also sent by Yahweh against the city, but then is promptly rebuked by Yahweh for lack of mercy toward Judah (47:6).

The outcome of this "visitation" is that the assault of the nations will be like a fantasy, as though it had never happened, as though it leaves no enduring effect (v. 7d). The nations will not be satisfied (v. 8). They may seek to "devour" Jerusalem, but at the end of the nightmare of assault they will not have eaten. They may set out to quench their thirsty imperial acquisitiveness, but in the end there will be no quenching. The nations will not be satisfied in this quest, because Yahweh stops them short of Mount Zion, the very city heretofore in jeopardy.

A great deal is here left unsaid. This is an oracle of anticipation, so that we need not seek a linkage to historical events. We are given no rationale for the decisive turn in the poem. Yahweh's protective care for Jerusalem may operate, but it is not justified. All that is said is that the nullification attempted by the nations is not autonomous but is curbed by Yahweh. For whatever reason, the consequence of the turn is the safety of Jerusalem.

An Assurance beyond Understanding
(29:9–12)

These verses seem to reflect an interpretive wonderment about the pre-ceding oracle. Perhaps some asked about the sudden inversion (wanted it explained). The response here to such a wonderment is given in a poetic utterance (vv. 9–10) and a subsequent prose commentary (vv. 11–12).

29:9 **Stupefy yourselves and be in a stupor,**
blind yourselves and be blind!
Be drunk, but not from wine;
stagger, but not from strong drink!
¹⁰ **For the LORD has poured out upon you**
a spirit of deep sleep;
he has closed your eyes, you prophets,
and covered your heads, you seers.

The inquiring community is addressed in a series of six imperatives, all of which bespeak confusion, inability to reason, loss of the powers of discernment. The inhabitants of Jerusalem are urged to be numbed and unresponsive. The rhetoric is reminiscent of 6:9–10, wherein Yahweh anticipates that Jerusalem will never "get it." Perhaps Jerusalem is not supposed to "get it," to understand its own life with Yahweh, because the resolve of its own life is hidden in Yahweh's inscrutable providential power. Indeed, the unresponsiveness of Jerusalem is not a state of mind and heart chosen by Jerusalem. It is rather imposed by Yahweh, who wants Jerusalem not to understand (v. 10). The "deep sleep" is a comalike condition imposed by Yahweh, whereby Yahweh can do inscrutably transformative acts without the knowledge or consent of the object. Yahweh does not want Jerusalem to know or to discern, perhaps an assertion that Yahweh's governance is so sovereign that it is not to be understood or questioned or explained. Moreover, Yahweh has dealt in like manner with Israel's leadership. Prophet and seer, those most likely to discern God's mysterious ways, are prevented from seeing or knowing. Thus the "suddenly" of verse 5 lies completely hidden beyond the ken of Jerusalem. The city will live on terms completely other than its own.

29:11 **The vision of all this has become for you like the words of a sealed document. If it is given to those who can read, with the command, "Read this," they say, "We cannot, for it is sealed." ¹² And if it is given to those who cannot read, saying, "Read this," they say, "We cannot read."**

This prose commentary seems to be subsequent to and only a reinforcement of the oracle of inscrutability of verses 9–10. The language of "vision" suggests that we are drawn here into apocalyptic jargon, a move from uttered oracle to witnessed vision. In like manner, the vision is written and not heard. And it is "sealed," that is, closed off from easy access and available only to the special ones who know "the key." This rhetoric is well known in apocalyptic texts that later on link *sudden intervention* with *specialized knowledge*.

This vision of God's future is completely beyond access by reason of a Catch-22. Those who would understand either can read but cannot open the seal, or can open the seal but cannot read. Either way, an understanding of what is happening is beyond the horizon of Jerusalem, deliberately kept so. The governance of Jerusalem, so it is asserted here, is not to be understood in terms of moral equation or international strategies. It is all hidden in the resolve of Yahweh, who need explain nothing to anyone. The good news, so it seems, is that this hidden resolve on Yahweh's part is a good resolve. The visitation is protective. Yahweh wills good for Jerusalem, even under threat. The assurance, hidden in Yahweh's purpose, happily outruns any rational discernment. It is no wonder that in the end, this tradition can only urge *trust* in the God beyond explanation.

Resistance to the Reality of Yahweh (29:13–16)

These verses comprise two distinct poetic units, each of which indicates Jerusalem's negation of Yahweh's governance.

29:13 **The Lord said:**
> **Because these people draw near with their mouths**
>> **and honor me with their lips,**
>> **while their hearts are far from me,**
> **and their worship of me is a human commandment learned by rote;**
> ¹⁴ **so I will again do**
>> **amazing things with this people,**
>> **shocking and amazing.**
> **The wisdom of their wise shall perish,**
>> **and the discernment of the discerning shall be hidden.**

These verses are arranged as a standard prophetic speech of judgment. The indictment of verse 13 condemns "these people" because their ostensible devotion to Yahweh, expressed in pious utterance and visible worship, is lacking in true devotion or sincerity. They are merely going through the motions with no serious intent and no serious consequences.

The phrase "human commandment" indicates that they follow the rules and regulations of prescribed piety that is lacking in the serious commitment of the heart, whereby the intentions of life correspond to the appearances of worship. Later on in the Isaiah tradition, a like condemnation of worship will be issued (58:1–5). The gospel narrative indicates, moreover, that Jesus quotes this text as a critique of the punctilious legalism of his opponents, who "abandon the command of God and hold to human tradition" (Mark 7:6–8). The problem of connecting worship to life is a recurring one for the people of Yahweh.

The prophetic sentence that is Yahweh's punishment for the phoniness of Israel's commitment is voiced in verse 14. The first two lines of this verse offer a play on the term *pela'* that is used three times, translated "amazing, shocking, amazing." The governing verb "do again" shows that Israel has a ready memory of Yahweh's "amazing, shocking deeds" from its past. Indeed, the term "amazing deed" refers characteristically to Yahweh's mighty deeds of rescue and transformation in behalf of Israel, as in a birth to barren mother Sarah or the Exodus from Egypt. In Psalm 105:5, for example, this is the term rendered "miracle," featuring a standard recital of Yahweh's deeds in behalf of Israel. As we have seen, the term "visit" in verse 6 is a term to be read both positively and negatively; so here the poet appeals to past *positive* miracles in order to articulate a present *negative* miracle. The line intends irony, for a sense of grateful amazement is here transposed into an ominous anticipation.

The second two lines of verse 14 specify what dreadful things Yahweh will now do as a result of Jerusalem's bad faith. The two lines reiterate the main terms "wisdom-wise, discernment-discerning," thus imitating the triple use in the first two lines. The miracle that Yahweh will now work against Jerusalem is to deny (to its leaders) the capacity to understand and discern, to plan shrewdly and decide knowingly. The public life of Israel will be one of dismay, because the leadership will now act foolishly and destructively.

29:15 **Ha! You who hide a plan too deep for the LORD,**
　　　whose deeds are in the dark,
　　　and who say, "Who sees us? Who knows us?"
　　 16 **You turn things upside down!**
　　　Shall the potter be regarded as the clay?
　　Shall the thing made say of its maker,
　　　"He did not make me";
　　or the thing formed say of the one who formed it,
　　　"He has no understanding"?

These verses articulate as threat only one word, "woe." That thin judgment of course entails all of the threats of verses 1–5c as well as verse 14.
It put Jerusalem on notice that it is under death sentence. The bulk of these
verses, however, is an indictment. The false worship of verse 13 (which
amounts to self-worship) here is matched by an arrogant autonomy that
Kaiser treats as "atheism." The arrogant autonomy of Jerusalem is to make
plans (and therefore policies) that are kept remote and hidden from Yahweh, not reliant upon Yahweh but conducted so that Yahweh may not correct, discipline, or overrule. The two rhetorical questions—Who sees us?
Who knows us?—on the lips and in the acts of the defiant expect a negative response. No one sees, no one knows, and so Jerusalem takes itself to
be completely free to do what it wants. The poet anticipates Dostoyevsky:
"Without God, everything is possible."

Such a practice of autonomy of course upsets and inverts the long-
affirmed conviction of Jerusalem that its people (and leadership) are subject to the governance of Yahweh. The imagery of potter and clay (used in
similar fashion in 45:9 and pleadingly in 64:8) asserts that Yahweh is the
initiative-taker and decider in this relation, and Jerusalem is the pliable, responsive product of Yahweh's work (see also Jer. 18:1–6). In its practices
for which it is here indicted, Jerusalem has inverted the normal, proper relation of God and people. Contrary to "reality," it is as though the potter-
God is treated as supple clay, pliable and to be shaped according to the will
of Jerusalem, whereby the clay rejects its derivative position and concludes
that Yahweh has no "understanding."

Although verses 13–14 and verses 15–16 are distinct poetic units, they
work with parallel themes, namely, the drastic, arrogant rejection of Yahweh. Moreover, both units end with a comment on discernment. In verse
16, Jerusalem concludes that Yahweh has no "discernment" and need not
be obeyed; in verse 14, Yahweh will take discernment away from Israel.
The two units together underscore the accents of verses 9–12. In those
verses it is claimed that Yahweh is beyond understanding by Jerusalem;
here, Jerusalem no longer seeks to understand or come to terms with Yahweh, but proceeds according to its own way in the world, a way that leads
to the "woe" of death. Positively, verses 9–12 assert Yahweh's inscrutability, which may produce good. Negatively, verses 13–14 and
15–16 identify Jerusalem's arrogance, which will produce death. The several articulations of verses 9–16 raise deep and complex issues about *faith
and knowledge*. Isaiah, prophet of faith, views Jerusalem's autonomous
knowledge as an invitation to disaster, disaster that is one of Yahweh's great
"amazements."

A Coming Transformation (29:17–24)

29:17 **Shall not Lebanon in a very little while**
    become a fruitful field,
    and the fruitful field be regarded as a forest?
18 **On that day the deaf shall hear**
    the words of a scroll,
    and out of their gloom and darkness
    the eyes of the blind shall see.
19 **The meek shall obtain fresh joy in the LORD,**
    and the neediest people shall exult in the Holy One of Israel.
20 **For the tyrant shall be no more,**
    and the scoffer shall cease to be;
    all those alert to do evil shall be cut off—
21 **those who cause a person to lose a lawsuit,**
    who set a trap for the arbiter in the gate,
    and without grounds deny justice to the one in the right.

Verse 17 announces an abrupt, positive transformation. The governing term is "in a very little while," bespeaking a sudden transformation that hints of a move in an apocalyptic direction. Indeed, "in a very little while" functions rhetorically like "in an instant, suddenly" in verse 5. The scope of the transformation is large, concerning not only political circumstances but the condition of creation. Devastated Lebanon will be made into a "fruitful field" (Carmel); that is the good news. The land will be made as fruitful as creation is intended to be. Conversely, the bad news is that what is now a fruitful field will be made into a wooded (uninhabited) forest. The claim is that Yahweh will act sovereignly to renovate and reshape the circumstance of all of life.

Verse 18 is introduced, once again, with an abrupt, promissory formula, "On that day"—the day of Yahweh's decisive intervention. Whereas verse 17 uses vocabulary of fruitful creation, verses 18–19 concern four classes of marginalized, disabled people who suffer at the hand of a wrongly ordered society. Because of Yahweh's intervention: the deaf will hear; the blind will see; the meek will rejoice; and the neediest will exult in Yahweh.

To be sure, the two pairs of terms are different. The first pair—deaf and blind—refer to the physically disabled; these terms are also used in Isaiah to characterize the undiscerning and unresponsive. The second pair of terms—meek and needy—more directly pertain to poverty and an exploitative economy. But all four terms—both pairs—bespeak a radical renewal of society made possible by Yahweh's transformative action.

The transformation of verses 18–19 is made possible by the expelling action of verses 20–21. Three terms—tyrant, scoffer, evildoer—are employed to characterize those who prey upon those named in verses 18–19. It is most plausible that these appellations are not concerned with "foreigners" (cf. vv. 7–8), but with internal exploitation in the society of Judah (as in Nehemiah 5).

The blind-deaf-meek-needy are in their present state because of the tyrant-scoffer-evildoer. Indeed, the poet identifies the specific actions whereby the first groups are diminished. The language of verse 21 echoes the accent of Deuteronomy and the early prophets concerning the court. It is in the court that the powerful can (legally?) ruthlessly exploit. It is at "justice in the gate" that the powerful distort questions of innocence, so that the powerless never have a chance. Prophetic rhetoric here imagines that God attends to the proper maintenance and correction of public institutions, whereby a visible communal life is made possible. Indeed, the transformation of creation is to little positive effect unless it is accompanied by a rehabilitation of public institutions that guarantee communal life. In this oracle, both creation and public institutions will be restored to right function "in a very little while."

> 29:22 **Therefore thus says the LORD, who redeemed Abraham, concerning the house of Jacob:**
>> **No longer shall Jacob be ashamed,**
>>> **no longer shall his face grow pale.**
> 23 **For when he sees his children,**
>> **the work of my hands, in his midst,**
>> **they will sanctify my name;**
>> **they will sanctify the Holy One of Jacob,**
>>> **and will stand in awe of the God of Israel.**
> 24 **And those who err in spirit will come to understanding,**
>> **and those who grumble will accept instruction.**

This final promise begins with a most distinctive introductory formula. The initial "therefore" likely begins a new oracle. In its present place, however, it suggests that the following promise is a consequence of the assurance of verses 17–21. The conventional reference to the "house of Jacob," moreover, is intensified by the peculiar reference to "Abraham redeemed." This reference plunges us into the memory of the ancestral narratives of Genesis and the recurring problem of securing an heir and therefore a future.

The double "no longer" suggests that Israel is now a community ashamed and grown pale. Within the imagery of the ancestral narrative, the cause of shame and paleness is lack of an heir, and therefore no assurance of a future. The imagery here anticipates that of 54:1–8 wherein childlessness produces shame. That present circumstance is overcome, in this oracle, in a way that matches "in an instant, suddenly" (v. 5) and "in a very little while" (v. 17). The meaning of "Abraham redeemed" in the narrative world of Genesis is to have an heir, and so the future is open.

Indeed, this is the substantive assurance of verse 23a: Abraham—Israel in loss—will see "the work of my hands," that is, the gift of children. Hopelessness is turned to possibility. Curse is overcome in blessing. The response of grateful, reassured Israel is to embrace Yahweh's holy name and to accept a holy identity as its own, that is, to reembrace identity as Yahweh's own people in the world.

The "new start" here enacted has practical consequences (v. 24). We have already noticed stupefication (v. 9) and loss of wisdom and discernment (v. 14). Now, in this wondrous rehabilitation, the condition of dysfunction is reversed. Those who "err" will come to "understanding." Those who complain will be instructed. The reference to "understanding" here inverts the loss of discernment in verses 14 and 16. This promissory oracle envisions a rehabilitated community of faith, able to see clearly, to act wisely, to be the faithful, responsible people of Yahweh.

This chapter, with a jerky movement through a series of independent literary units, transverses the course of Israel's life through loss to restoration. As such it is an epitome of the two-stage portrayal characteristic of the Isaiah tradition: Jerusalem will indeed be *ended* and *begun again*. The adherents of "practical atheism" (vv. 13, 15–16) are restored to good sense concerning their true identity. The restoration, however, is through a process of enormous "distress" (vv. 2, 7).

A CHOICE BETWEEN TWO PLANS
30:1–33

This long chapter is constituted by a series of smaller rhetorical units. Its larger movement, however, concerns the contradiction between *plans:* (a) the plan of Yahweh for the well-being of Judah, and (b) Judah's own autonomous plan for well-being that cannot succeed. As is characteristic of the Isaiah tradition, God's dealings with Judah are situated within a large geopolitical scope. The interpreter must pay attention to what seem to be the concrete issues facing Judah, here specifically the power realities of Egypt and Assyria. At the same time, however, it is important to recognize that these specific geopolitical references cannot finally be held to historical concreteness but have become "talking points" for the larger theological issue concerning Yahweh's sovereignty over the nations and Yahweh's goodwill for Judah.

Judah's Rejected Plan of Autonomy (30:1–14)

The characteristic situation of Judah, and certainly the situation of Judah in the particular time of Isaiah, is to be caught between the power of Egypt and the more aggressive power to the north, in this case Assyria. Because of the aggressiveness of Assyria, Judah was inclined to seek succor and support in an alliance with Egypt, a policy that is regarded in this prophetic tradition as a rejection of Judah's proper reliance only upon Yahweh.

30:1 **Oh, rebellious children, says the LORD,**
    who carry out a plan, but not mine;
    who make an alliance, but against my will,
        adding sin to sin;
  2 **who set out to go down to Egypt**
      without asking for my counsel,
    to take refuge in the protection of Pharaoh,
      and to seek shelter in the shadow of Egypt;
  3 **Therefore the protection of Pharaoh shall become your shame,**
      and the shelter in the shadow of Egypt your humiliation.
  4 **For though his officials are at Zoan**
      and his envoys reach Hanes,
  5 **everyone comes to shame**
      through a people that cannot profit them,
    that brings neither help nor profit,
        but shame and disgrace.

This unit begins with a characteristic woe ("Oh"), indicating that the action here described and condemned is one sure to end in disaster. The community is identified as "rebellious children," echoing the thematic indictment of 1:2. In that verse, the trouble is that, unlike donkeys and oxen, Judah fails to remember that it belongs to and relies upon Yahweh. Here as well, Judah operates independently of Yahweh by implementing its own plan (foreign policy) of reliance upon Egypt as a protection against Assyria. Such a plan, however, is here taken to be against Yahweh's intention and will certainly end in destruction.

The prophetic sentence of verse 3 ("therefore") identifies Egypt as "a people that cannot profit" (v. 5), that is, a state that cannot do anything helpful or reliable and surely will not make Judah safe. The inference to be drawn is that reliance upon Egypt is foolishness, because it will not be an adequate defense against the power of Assyria.

It is important, in the prophetic rejection of this policy, to be as clear as we are able about the "foreign policy" advocated in the tradition of Isaiah. Rejection of Egyptian alliance does not imply that the tradition recommends easy submission to Assyria. Nor does it urge withdrawal from international politics into seclusion and passivity, or even pacifism. Rather, foreign policy must begin at a different point, namely, reliance on Yahweh. Such a policy would emerge not from cowardice or anxiety or intimidation or weakness or naiveté, but from *confidence* (trust) that will permit a different perspective on policy. It is not possible to envision what such a foreign policy would look like for readers in the United States, a superpower. It is clear, nonetheless, that the intoxicating reliance upon military might and military budgets in the recent Cold War caused an endless miscalculation concerning true na- tional interest and national possibility. Such military commitments then and now, it is clear, generate only more anxiety and insanity. Even if we ac- knowledge that the parallels are only remote, we are able to see enough of a connection to observe that autonomous madness is scarcely adequate in the contemporary world, as it was not in that ancient world.

> 30:6 **An oracle concerning the animals of the Negeb.**
> **Through a land of trouble and distress,**
>   **of lioness and roaring lion,**
>   **of viper and flying serpent,**
> **they carry their riches on the backs of donkeys,**
>   **and their treasures on the humps of camels,**
>   **to a people that cannot profit them.**
> ⁷ **For Egypt's help is worthless and empty,**
>   **therefore I have called her,**
>   **"Rahab who sits still."**

These verses constitute an independent unit and offer a comment on a "for- eign territory" not unlike those we have considered in chapters 13—23. The Negev consists of the desert land toward the Sinai Peninsula. Although this is an independent oracle dealing with an independent topic, its context here is that it is the territory to be traversed en route to Egypt. Thus it functions only as a subset of verses 1–5. The desert land is portrayed as ominous and hazardous, filled with threats that are characterized in hyperbolic terms. The primary accent of the oracle is that Judah's crossing of the desert en route to Egypt is especially demanding because of the huge cargo carried—tribute money and cargo on donkeys and camels in order to buy protection. The scenario offered is ironic, however, because the poem intends to mock the foolishness of Judah in investing so much, carrying such a heavy burden, and running such risks for an alliance that cannot deliver. What Judah wants from Egypt it cannot give, and in any case, money cannot buy. In the last line of verse 6 and in verse 7, Egypt is scorned as useless. The tag phrase, "a people that cannot profit" is repeated from verse 5. Egypt is dismissed as "worthless and empty," an embodiment of complete futility.

Beyond *the theological accent* of Judah's dependence upon Yahweh and the *geopolitical stress* on wise policy, it is likely that the subtext of these verses, unmentioned but surely recognized by Jewish listeners, is the ancient Exodus narrative and the tale of the risky sojourn in the wilderness (Negev) under Moses. In order to depart slavery, travel with Yahweh, and reach the land of promise, Israel had to traverse the wilderness. Now the story is foolishly reversed. Israel is reenacting its story of rescue backward! In the end, Egypt is *Rahab, the destructive, cosmic power of chaos* (Psalms 87:4; 89:10). What appears to be sanctuary is disorder, and the journey through the perilous Negev is a path as filled with chaotic threat as is the goal of Egypt.

30:8 **Go now, write it before them on a tablet,**
    and inscribe it in a book,
  so that it may be for the time to come
    as a witness forever.
  ⁹ **For they are a rebellious people,**
    faithless children,
  children who will not hear
    the instruction of the LORD;
 ¹⁰ **who say to the seers, "Do not see";**
    and to the prophets, "Do not prophesy to us what is right;
  speak to us smooth things,
    prophesy illusions,
 ¹¹ **leave the way, turn aside from the path,**
    let us hear no more about the Holy One of Israel."
 ¹² **Therefore thus says the Holy One of Israel:**
  Because you reject this word,
    and put your trust in oppression and deceit,
    and rely on them;
 ¹³ **therefore this iniquity shall become for you**
    like a break in a high wall, bulging out, and about to collapse,
    whose crash comes suddenly, in an instant;
 ¹⁴ **its breaking is like that of a potter's vessel**
    that is smashed so ruthlessly

that among its fragments not a sherd is found
  for taking fire from the hearth,
  or dipping water out of the cistern.

The assertion of verses 1–7 is "against the stream," contradicting the assumptions of policy of all those who think pragmatically about public power. For that reason the poem wants to be "on the record," anticipating in time to come a vindication. To assure "the record," as in 8:1–2, the poet inscribes his counterurging in a permanent document. Soon or late, he avers, the foolishness of pragmatic international policy will be manifest. Soon or late, the cruciality of Yahweh for public life will be made evident. Judah is on notice! And we belated readers are on notice along with ancient Judah.

As a reprise on verses 1–7, verses 9–14 offer once more a prophetic speech of judgment. The indictment names Judah yet again a "rebellious people" (v. 9; cf. v. 1). The rebellion consists in a refusal to *listen to torah*, thus echoing the cadences of Deuteronomy. More specifically, Judah is criticized for refusing "seers and prophets" who would teach torah requirements, preferring illusions to the heavy demands of Yahweh. What these "rebellious children" want is to be cut loose, on their own, free to discount the reality of Yahweh. In verse 12, the failure of Judah is located around the word *trust*, a term that is important in later chapters. Judah has invested its most elemental commitment, not to Yahweh, but to *oppression and deceit*. It would be difficult to imagine a way of life more antithetical to the way of Yahweh!

The prophetic sentence, introduced by "therefore," employs a vocabulary of violence: collapse, crash, bulge, break (vv. 13–14). Judah will be assaulted and nullified, though the prophet does not say how. The most sustained image of destruction is that of a broken pot. The metaphor of Yahweh as potter and Judah as clay is a recurring one, indicating that the potter has full freedom over the clay. Here that freedom will be to "smash ruthlessly" into fine pieces, with not a piece of ceramics left large enough to scoop up ashes or water—complete nullification. The beginning in an analysis of bad policy (vv. 1–5) has now moved to "bad faith." How Judah orders its public life matches its life with Yahweh. And the news is not good.

Yahweh's Plan Offered and Rejected (30:15–17)

30:15 **For thus said the Lord GOD, the Holy One of Israel:**
  In returning and rest you shall be saved;

> in quietness and in trust shall be your strength.
> But you refused [16] and said,
> "No! We will flee upon horses"—
>   therefore you shall flee!
> and, "We will ride upon swift steeds"—
>   therefore your pursuers shall be swift!
> [17] A thousand shall flee at the threat of one,
>   at the threat of five you shall flee,
> until you are left
>   like a flagstaff on the top of a mountain,
>   like a signal on a hill.

We now encounter one of the focal declarations of the theology of Isaiah, and therefore special attention needs to be paid to these verses. We may identify three elements in the unit. First in verse 15, in the awesome mouth of "the Holy One of Israel," the poet enunciates the core insistence of the tradition in a text comparable in substance and importance to 9:7. Israel will be *saved and strong* when it lives in *trust*, that is, in returning, rest, and quietness. *The four terms bespeak attentive adherence to Yahweh.* The terms are all rough synonyms for Isaiah's notion of *faith*, utter reliance upon and complete devotion to Yahweh. This assertion clearly intends to contradict the activities of feverish anxiety for which Judah has been condemned in verses 1–14. Judah's *shalom* depends upon and stems from *life with Yahweh*. Wildberger judges:

> The politics of faith is not the politics of weakness but of power, not defeatism but an uncompromising will to endure, not capitulation but the overcoming of opposition because "our faith is the victory which has overcome the world" (1 John 5:4), but not a victory of power as the world regards it (*Jesaja 28–39*, 1118 [author's translation]).

But alas! Almost in the same breath, at the end of the verse is recorded: "You refused." The Hebrew is, "You were not willing," the same phrase as in verse 9 (see Luke 13:34, "you were not willing"). Judah, without any reflection and without apology, refuses the simple Yahwistic option of well-being. Calvin observes:

> By the distinct reply *No*, he shews how obstinately they refused to comply with the advice which was given to them by the prophets, and chose rather to provide for their safety in another manner (*Isaiah* II, 364).

Thus the second point is the refusal. The prophets frequently put into the mouth of their opponents what they say by their actions. By its foolish foreign policy of military treaties, Judah directly contradicts the offer of Yahwism: "No! We will flee upon horses . . . We will ride upon swift steeds" (v. 16). "Horses and steeds" reflect the arms program in which Judah has been engaged since Solomon. It is an ostentatious, expensive way to self-security. Judah prefers autonomous military policy as a way to *shalom*, a way here shown to be the antithesis of trust.

Third, Judah is given over by the prophet to the outcomes of its ill-chosen policy. Judah will suffer the outcomes of its foolish militarism. It wants "flee and swift." It will get "flee and swift" from its enemies who will prevail. Calvin comments:

> It is proper also to observe how unhappy is the end of those who rely more on outward aids than on God; for everything must be unsuccessful and contrary to their expectation. . . . For what avail arms and a vast multitude of men? What avail fortresses and bulwarks, when men's hearts fail and are dismayed? (*Isaiah* II, 364–365)

Specifically, Judah cannot beat Assyria at its military game. Generally, militarism is no way to peace. And so Judah, given its military commitments, will end in deep anxiety, fearful of every threat, frantic at every hostile posturing, undone by adversaries, until it ends hopelessly isolated and without resources. The choice could not be made more clear. The consequence could not be more ominous.

Yahweh's Plan Reiterated (30:18–33)

According to the tradition of Isaiah, Yahweh's harsh judgment upon Judah's rejection in verses 16–17 is not the end of the matter.

30:18 **Therefore the LORD waits to be gracious to you;**
   therefore he will rise up to show mercy to you.
For the LORD is a God of justice;
   blessed are all those who wait for him.

This single verse reiterates the main positive intention of Yahweh. The verse is organized around the double use of the term "wait" (hope). At the outset, Yahweh waits in expectation for a time to be kind to Judah. At the conclusion, Judah is enjoined to "wait" for Yahweh, to expect its peaceable future from Yahweh. The waiting of Yahweh points to Yahweh's firm resolve to do good for Judah. The waiting of Judah is an alternative to its feverish, self-asserting military activity.

The double use of "wait" in the verse brackets three pivotal terms. The words "gracious" and "mercy" are very old in Israel's tradition (cf. Exod. 34:6) and voice the quintessence of Yahweh's good intention to love Israel freely and without restraint. It is this vocabulary that makes unmistakable that the God of the Old Testament is *a God of grace*. The two terms, moreover, are here active verbs: "to grace you," "to mercy you," that is, to intervene actively in behalf of Judah. These terms are matched by the word "justice." God's governance of historical reality is to maintain conditions for a full communal life. That is, Yahweh will not permit Judah to be hurt or exploited but will prevent the public process from being a barbarous one. In this single, deeply freighted verse, Judah is shown the route whereby it may be blessed. It need only count decisively on Yahweh, who makes all the difference. It is plausible to suggest that verses 19–33 are an exposition of this remarkable utterance in verse 18.

> 30:19 **Truly, O people in Zion, inhabitants of Jerusalem, you shall weep no more. He will surely be gracious to you at the sound of your cry; when he hears it, he will answer you. 20 Though the Lord may give you the bread of adversity and the water of affliction, yet your Teacher will not hide himself any more, but your eyes shall see your Teacher. 21 And when you turn to the right or when you turn to the left, your ears shall hear a word behind you, saying, "This is the way; walk in it." 22 Then you will defile your silver-covered idols and your gold-plated images. You will scatter them like filthy rags; you will say to them, "Away with you!"**

The first expository comment is addressed to Zion. But it appeals to theological cadences that are older than Jerusalem and are not especially rooted there. First, it is asserted that if Jerusalem "cried out" for help, Yahweh would hear and answer. This simple statement reflects the oldest structure of Israel's prayers in which God is the decisive, active answerer of prayers. This structure is exhibited in the "case studies" of Psalm 107, where Yahweh answers "cries." But it also stands at the beginning of the Exodus narrative (Exod. 2:23–25). Yahweh is attentive to Israel and is prepared to intervene. Characteristically, however, needy Israel must make a first move by a cry, thus acknowledging need and trust.

The other ancient theological cadence to which appeal is made concerns torah instruction (vv. 20–22). Verse 20, which appears to acknowledge the reality of suffering, is perhaps a retrospective on destroyed Jerusalem. Certainly the citizens of Jerusalem knew about the vagaries of this historical process. The main claim, however, is that in the midst of hardship there will be a torah teacher. The identity of this teacher is not clear. The NRSV capitalizes "Teacher," suggesting that God is the teacher of torah. The term here may, however, refer to the prophetic tradition or to an unnamed figure. What is important is that Israel will be attentive to instruction with eyes to see and ears to hear. This scenario of effective instruction is the counterpoint to the recalcitrance of verses 9–11, in which Israel refuses to hear and prefers illusions. Now, however, the teacher will instruct in *the way of the Torah*. Whereas Israel in verse 11 intends to "leave the way," here Israel walks in the way. Thus the text anticipates a radical reorientation and a new attitude, not unlike Jeremiah 31:33, wherein all shall know the Torah. Positively, the Torah consists in attentiveness to Yahweh. Negatively, right at the first commandment, torah obedience consists in the scuttling of all idols (v. 22). In time to come, Judah will be completely reconstituted, ready and eager for obedience.

> 30:23 **He will give rain for the seed with which you sow the ground, and grain, the produce of the ground, which will be rich and plenteous. On that day your cattle will graze in broad pastures;** 24 **and the oxen and donkeys that till the ground will eat silage, which has been winnowed with shovel and fork.** 25 **On every lofty mountain and every high hill there will be brooks running with water—on a day of the great slaughter, when the towers fall.** 26 **Moreover the light of the moon will be like the light of the sun, and the light of the sun will be sevenfold, like the light of seven days, on the day when the LORD binds up the injuries of his people, and heals the wounds inflicted by his blow.**

In yet a very different comment on verse 18, these verses indicate that Yahweh's "graciousness and mercy" entail a freshly functioning creation. Israel's life is set in an arid climate. The generous response of Yahweh to a creation needful of water is to provide life-giving water in abundance— rain and brooks that activate the earth and cause pasturelands and cattle and all of creation to produce in fruitful abundance. The text grows lyrical, for not only will there be water, but sun and moon will luxuriate in ways that will banish all darkness. Indeed, there will be perpetual light to match abundant rain, so that every threat to life is eliminated. The culmination of this vision is that there will be a healing of Judah (v. 26), of creation, of drought, of darkness—a complete transformation to full *shalom*. Moreover, the healing is of the wounds inflicted by Yahweh. The wounds are not accidental, not caused by a foreign power, but are enacted by Yahweh on the face of Judah's recalcitrance. In the word pair "inflict/heal," we again see Isaiah's two-stage rendering of Judah's history. The "inflicting" is the loss of Jerusalem; the "healing" is its restoration.

30:27 **See, the name of the LORD comes from far away,**
      burning with his anger, and in thick rising smoke;

> his lips are full of indignation,
>   and his tongue is like a devouring fire;
> 28 his breath is like an overflowing stream
>   that reaches up to the neck—
> to sift the nations with the sieve of destruction,
>   and to place on the jaws of the peoples a bridle that leads them
>   astray.

Now the vision of the future turns negative. As the poet has dismissed Egypt as a futile ally (vv. 1–7), so now the enemy of Israel is assaulted (though not named). The language is theophanic, hyperbolic rhetoric that portrays the cataclysmic, ferocious coming of Yahweh. This comment is abrupt, without introduction beyond the attention-getting "see." Yahweh comes (as at Sinai) with fire, smoke, and steam. The "hot God" comes to deal with the nations and to move them to destruction. These verses are completely lacking in specificity, with no reference to Judah and no naming of the nations. The rhetoric simply puts the nation (and us) on notice about a sovereignty that cannot be evaded or overcome.

> 30:29 **You shall have a song as in the night when a holy festival is kept; and gladness of heart, as when one sets out to the sound of the flute to go to the mountain of the** LORD, **to the Rock of Israel.** 30 **And the** LORD **will cause his majestic voice to be heard and the descending blow of his arm to be seen, in furious anger and a flame of devouring fire, with a cloudburst and tempest and hailstones.** 31 **The Assyrian will be terror-stricken at the voice of the** LORD, **when he strikes with his rod.** 32 **And every stroke of the staff of punishment that the** LORD **lays upon him will be to the sound of timbrels and lyres; battling with brandished arm he will fight with him.** 33 **For his burning place has long been prepared; truly it is made ready for the king, its pyre made deep and wide, with fire and wood in abundance; the breath of the** LORD, **like a stream of sulfur, kindles it.**

Finally in verse 31, *Assyria* is named. It is likely that "Assyria" here is a cipher for any resented foreign power. Assyria will be assaulted by Yahweh's own effort, with devastating power and destructiveness (vv. 31–33).

The counterpoint to Assyrian devastation in the service of Yahweh's sovereignty is that there will be festal singing, gladness, and instrumental music (vv. 29–30). Indeed, every blow struck against Assyria is marked by "the sound of timbrels and lyres." We are not told who makes the music. The rhetoric nonetheless suggests that Yahweh's attack on Assyria is a liturgical enterprise whereby each blow becomes a fresh occasion for celebration and exultation in Yahweh. The interplay of *celebration* and *terror* suggests that Yahweh, as The Equalizer, stands between hated, oppressive

Assyria and desperate, needful Judah. The text itself leaves much unsaid. We are led to conclude, nonetheless, that this final text is one more fruit of Yahweh's "graciousness and mercy." Penultimately, Yahweh requires trust as a condition of rescue (v. 15). Ultimately, Yahweh acts for Judah in any case, creating a newness Judah is not capable of choosing for itself.

TRUE AND FALSE HELP
31:1–9

This brief chapter reiterates themes and accents with which we are now familiar: Egypt is an unreliable ally (vv. 1–3), and Assyria's days are numbered (vv. 8–9). The only true hope is Yahweh, who will fight for Judah from Mount Zion (vv. 4–5). Return to Yahweh is the single requirement for well-being (vv. 6–7).

31:1 **Alas for those who go down to Egypt for help**
      and who rely on horses,
   who trust in chariots because they are many
      and in horsemen because they are very strong,
   but do not look to the Holy One of Israel
      or consult the LORD!
   ² **Yet he too is wise and brings disaster;**
      he does not call back his words,
   but will rise against the house of the evildoers,
      and against the helpers of those who work iniquity.
   ³ **The Egyptians are human, and not God;**
      their horses are flesh, and not spirit.
   When the LORD stretches out his hand,
      the helper will stumble, and the one helped will fall,
      and they will all perish together.

Like chapters 28, 29, and 30, this chapter begins with a woe ("alas"). This ominous note pertains to those who turn to "Egypt" as a protective ally. These verses are dominated by the term "help," the word occurring four times. The paramount issue is, *Who can help?* The simple, negative assertion is that Egypt cannot help. "Egypt" no doubt refers to an actual political power. But it has also come to be a metaphor for military might (horses, chariots), which in the end amounts to self-deception that cannot give security. The reason Egypt cannot save is that Egypt is "human" and not "God," "flesh" and not "spirit" (v. 3). That is, Egypt has no intrinsic power or authority to generate newness. Unlike God, who has generative power, Egypt

(military power) is derivative and reactive and cannot produce life. In quite
a local setting, the prophet issues a massive and fundamental critique of the
ideology and idolatry of military power, an illusion that can only bring death.

The alternative to Egypt, of course, is Yahweh. Yahweh, the true subject of Israel's recurring doxology, is *true help:*

> Happy are those whose help is the God of Jacob.
>   whose hope is in the LORD their God,
> who made heaven and earth,
>   the sea, and all that is in them.
>   (Psalm 146:5–6)

Yahweh's capacity to "help" is in contrast to "princes" who cannot help:

> Do not put your trust in princes,
>   in mortals, in whom there is no help.
> When their breath departs, they return to the earth;
>   on that very day their plans perish.
>   (Psalm 146:3–4)

Yahweh is wise, resolved, and irresistible. And when Yahweh acts, Egypt
cannot prevail. As a consequence, Egypt and Judah—the helpers and those
helped—will all perish together. Egypt will go down. And Judah will go
down with Egypt unless it extricates itself from the militarism of Egypt.
Judah is on notice and must choose.

> 31:4 **For thus the LORD said to me,**
>   **As a lion or a young lion growls over its prey,**
>   **and—when a band of shepherds is called out against it—**
>   **is not terrified by their shouting**
>   **or daunted at their noise,**
>   **so the LORD of hosts will come down**
>   **to fight upon Mount Zion and upon its hill.**
> 5 **Like birds hovering overhead, so the LORD of hosts**
>   **will protect Jerusalem;**
>   **he will protect and deliver it,**
>   **he will spare and rescue it.**

Now speaks Yahweh as an alternative to Egypt. These verses are organized
around two metaphors, of lion and bird. The rhetoric is structured as (a) "as
. . . so," (b) "like . . . so." Yahweh is assigned the qualities of the metaphorical figure. Like a lion, Yahweh will fight ferociously and will not be turned

away or intimidated by those who try to detract. Moreover, the imagery of
the lion concerns Mount Zion. Yahweh is rooted there and will make a
stand there. Thus the metaphor becomes a means of voicing Zion theology, for it is from Zion that God "will roar like a lion" (Amos 1:2). Jerusalem is Yahweh's place from which Yahweh will come to assault the
enemies of Yahweh who threaten Judah. The second metaphor—birds—
moves in the opposite direction. Yahweh is a lion who assaults; now Yahweh is a bird who protects. The poetry employs four verbs to make the
affirmation about the bird: "protect, deliver, spare, rescue." The lion-bird
has qualities of tenacity and durability that no enemy of Zion can withstand.

31:6 **Turn back to him whom you have deeply betrayed, O people of Israel.**
⁷ For on that day all of you shall throw away your idols of silver and idols of
gold, which your hands have sinfully made for you.

Judah must "turn back." Judah must reverse course, abandon its reliance
upon Egypt and its devotion to military might as a mode of security. The
summons to repent is insistent and massive. It is a call that Judah must
completely redefine its genuine source of security and well-being. A turn
to Yahweh, moreover, is a re-turn. Yahweh was previously Judah's true
support and true love. In opting for military defense via Egypt, Judah has
wrenchingly abandoned Yahweh and must now recommit.

The specific form of return and repentance is the abandonment of idols
(cf. 30:22). We must not, however, regard the idols simply as religious alternatives and seductions. They are made of silver and gold and so function
as part of a general commodity fetishism, a deep, systemic notion that *things
can secure.* Thus we must connect the *spiritual force* of silver and gold idols
with the *material appeal* of horses and chariots as modes of security. The linkage between *economic control* and *military security* is a deep one. The linkage
is already reflected in 2:7–8 wherein the idols of silver/gold and horses/
chariots are seen to be all of a piece. And in the Deuteronomic stricture of
Deuteronomy 17:16–17, which curbs the accumulation of silver and gold,
horses and chariots, all are construed as violations of torah obedience. The
summons of our verse is that all of these destructive seductions must be discarded. The imagery echoes that of 2:19–21 wherein Judah desperately scut-
tles its fetishes in a mad, humiliating dash to the caves. The prophetic oracle,
in context, shrewdly understands the linkage of military mesmerization and
religious self-deception, and calls for a complete reorientation of policy.

31:8 **"Then the Assyrian shall fall by a sword, not of mortals;**
and a sword, not of humans, shall devour him;

he shall flee from the sword,
    and his young men shall be put to forced labor.
⁹ **His rock shall pass away in terror,**
    and his officers desert the standard in panic,"
says the LORD, whose fire is in Zion,
    and whose furnace is in Jerusalem.

These verses, which assume a reorientation of Judah to Yahweh, are presented as the utterance of Yahweh. Here speaks Yahweh, who is in Zion/Jerusalem with fire as in a furnace (v. 9). Here speaks the cosmic devastator who, in defense of Jerusalem, is about to move against all would-be rivals.

The utterance of Yahweh concerns the quick, hard disposal of Assyria, the superpower that arrogantly offered itself as an alternative and rival to Yahweh. The threat uttered against Assyria is dominated by a threefold use of "sword." The devastation of Assyria will be by military assault. It will not be, however, a human sword, but Yahweh's own ferocious intervention. Geopolitically, Assyria was subsequently defeated by Babylon. Theologically, however, Babylon is only an instrument of Yahweh (cf. Jer. 25:9; 27:6). Assyria's failure is not a military, political one. It is a *theological* default, because in its self-presentation Assyria took itself to be a competitor and replacement for Yahweh. In conducting itself in this way, Assyria replicated the earlier claim of autonomy on the part of Egypt. See Isaiah 36:4–10, 13–20 for Assyria's characteristic utterance of hubris.

Assyrian pretention, however, is futile and foolish in the face of Yahweh. As a consequence, Assyria's chosen young men, the cream of its military might, will be reduced to forced labor, to humiliating, menial service at the behest of another. Its best officers, in the panic that is sure to come soon, will become deserters. Thus its proud military supremacy will evaporate in the coming crisis. An unexpressed outcome is that Judah and Jerusalem will be delivered when the imperial threat evaporates.

This brief chapter exhibits a firm grasp of geopolitics. It also reflects discerning psychological insight into the way in which militarism takes on a life of its own as a theological reference point. Our reading must pay close attention to both the geopolitical and psychological distinctions that are operative. Both, however, are finally in the service of theological affirmation. In the end, with due attention to detail, Judah, Egypt, and Assyria—every part of the map—must come to terms with "the Holy One of Israel" (v. 1). There is no viable alternative. Every attempt at an alternative ends, inevitably, in humiliating disaster.

THE NEW AGE:
ITS THREAT AND ITS PROMISE
32:1–20

This chapter interrupts a series of chapters, all of which begin with a woe (28:1; 29:1; 30:1; 31:1; 33:1). Unlike all of those utterances, this one begins with "See," a dramatic summons to attention for an important announcement, a harbinger of a radical newness from God. The coming gift of God positively anticipates a coming new governance of justice and righteousness. The predominant note here is positive. At the beginning, it is expected that a coming new king and a coming new governance will usher in a new viable society (vv. 1–8). At the end, it is anticipated that God's spirit will come upon the earth and make all things new, a peaceable society dominated by God's righteousness (vv. 15–20). Between these two positive anticipations, verses 9–14 sound an ominous warning. Old patterns of comfort and complacency will be savagely disrupted. The new age will make no compromise with old ways, and therefore the old must be deeply grieved and finally relinquished. The exaggerated rhetoric voices a deep either/or, at the center of which stands Yahweh's determination to begin again.

A New Society Marked by
Justice and Righteousness (32:1–8)

32:1 See, a king will reign in righteousness,
       and princes will rule with justice.
  ² Each will be like a hiding place from the wind,
       a covert from the tempest,
    like streams of water in a dry place,
       like the shade of a great rock in a weary land.
  ³ Then the eyes of those who have sight will not be closed,
       and the ears of those who have hearing will listen.
  ⁴ The minds of the rash will have good judgment,
       and the tongues of stammerers will speak readily and distinctly.
  ⁵ A fool will no longer be called noble,
       nor a villain said to be honorable.
  ⁶ For fools speak folly,
       and their minds plot iniquity:
    to practice ungodliness,
       to utter error concerning the LORD,
    to leave the craving of the hungry unsatisfied,
       and to deprive the thirsty of drink.

⁷ **The villainies of villains are evil;**
   they devise wicked devices
 to ruin the poor with lying words,
   even when the plea of the needy is right.
⁸ **But those who are noble plan noble things,**
   and by noble things they stand.

The opening parallel lines announce the substance of Davidic hope, a new king committed to righteousness and justice. The core claim of royal ideology in Jerusalem is that some future king of the family of David—the next king?—will surely come to initiate a new world of *shalom*. The substance of that new *shalom* is already known in the Isaiah tradition, as in 5:7 and 9:7. The substance of "justice and righteousness" as guidelines for royal governance is articulated in Psalm 72, a royal Psalm that identifies the role of the responsible king as defender and protector of the poor and the needy against all rapacious, exploitative power. In this oracle, the new king is characterized by a series of metaphors (v. 2). The king will be a *refuge* from danger, a *stream of water* to nourish life, a *rock* of safety in an exhausted society. That is, the king is the guarantor of human well-being in every phase of social existence.

The identity of the new king is not given. Calvin thinks it is Hezekiah, a later, good king in the Isaiah period. Given his christological propensity, Calvin asserts that what was "shadowed out by Hezekiah" is fully actualized in Christ (*Isaiah* II, 404–405). On critical grounds, Christopher Seitz sides with Calvin in seeing Hezekiah as the good, coming king (see Isaiah 36—39), even as Ahaz is the known, bad king in Isaiah 6:1–9:7. However that may be, the oracle anticipates a better king to come.

In that new governance, everything will be changed. The eyes and ears of Jerusalem, perhaps especially those of its leaders, that have been so long dysfunctional, will now become attentive and discerning. There will now be listening, the very responsiveness so long resisted in Jerusalem (see 30:9). A whole new set of social relationships now becomes possible. Verse 5 suggests that society has so disintegrated, norms have so collapsed, self-deception become so pervasive that *fools and villains* have come to be regarded as respectable, honorable people.

It is as though with the coming of a new governance, a new public morality becomes assured. Watts thinks these verses constitute a "civics lesson." This does not portend that fools and villains will cease to be. Rather, they will be seen for what they are, without illusion or euphemism.

Fools are seen as those who treat society with contempt. The lines of verses 5–7 seem to draw on something like the teaching of the book of Proverbs. It is clear that "fools" are not just stupid people. Rather, they embody and practice a fundamental moral indifference and disorder that inevitably works damage to the social fabric. Thus fools are not the ignorant but the wheeler-dealers who are always cutting deals, and taking advantage of others, and acting in self-serving ways without contributing to social well-being. Because they misconstrue Yahweh, they inevitably misconstrue neighborly relations. Specifically, they do nothing for the hungry or the thirsty; they are inattentive to the needy for whom the community has inalienable responsibility. Calvin observes:

> When men are so brutalized that they are not affected by the misery of others, and lay aside every feeling of humanity, they must be worse than the beasts themselves, who have some sort of pity for the wants of their own kind. (*Commentary* VII, 411–12)

In the same way, the "villain" acts destructively toward the community (v. 2; cf. Mic. 2:1–2). The arena of exploitation suggested here is the court. When the poor go to court (a venue over which the king presides) in order to seek just treatment and redress, these crafty and uncaring people manage to distort justice and so to cheat the poor of their just claim. The new "justice and righteousness" of the king will expose such operators for what they are, even though in a season of social pathology they had become accepted, normative operators.

This unit offers in verse 8 only a brief positive alternative to "fools and villains"—the *noble ones*. This verse uses the root word "noble" three times but provides no content to the term. The most we can determine is that they are to be understood as an antithesis to the fool, and therefore are what the sapiential traditions may term "the wise" and "the righteous." If we work from verses 6–7, we conclude that "the nobles" practice theological virtue, speak truth about Yahweh, feed the hungry and nourish the thirsty, and care for the poor, even intervening in judicial processes in their behalf. These are they who care for the upbuilding of the community, who implement and embody the justice and righteousness of the king. We may mention two textual portrayals that likely reflect the same notion of responsible membership in the community. In Psalm 112, the fearers of Yahweh are "gracious, merciful, and righteous" (v. 4); they deal generously and practice justice (v. 5), have steady hearts (v. 8), give to the poor, and are honored (v. 9). In Job 31, we are offered a parallel presentation of an honorable, caring, generous, responsible moral agent who enhances the

community. All this will become practical, valued, and in vogue in God's
coming rule.

A Warning to a Narcoticized Society
(32:9–14)

32:9 **Rise up, you women who are at ease, hear my voice;**
    you complacent daughters, listen to my speech.
  10 **In little more than a year**
    you will shudder, you complacent ones;
  for the vintage will fail,
    the fruit harvest will not come.
  11 **Tremble, you women who are at ease,**
    shudder, you complacent ones;
  strip, and make yourselves bare,
    and put sackcloth on your loins.
  12 **Beat your breasts for the pleasant fields,**
    for the fruitful vine,
  13 **for the soil of my people**
    growing up in thorns and briers;
  yes, for all the joyous houses
    in the jubilant city.
  14 **For the palace will be forsaken,**
    the populous city deserted;
  the hill and the watchtower
    will become dens forever,
  the joy of wild asses,
    a pasture for flocks;

The news of verses 1–8 is good news. Those who cling to the old ways of
satiation and indulgence do not welcome the newness. Indeed, they do not
even notice its coming. And so the text voices a jarring summons to those
who are three times said to be "complacent" and twice "at ease." They represent a body of society that is safe, secure, affluent, and comfortable, who
take no notice of need and who can never imagine that their wondrous way
of life will not last forever.

We do not know why the warning is issued to women. It is perhaps because women may be the primary exhibitors of affluence, or because they
are the least exposed to the risk and danger when the threat does come.
Most likely the address to "the women" is a rhetorical strategy aimed at
the entire community. The address and warning are not unlike Amos's fa-
mous address to "the cows of Bashan" (4:1) or the "daughters of Zion" who

are mocked in their affluence and self-indulgence (Isa. 3:16–26). We must, however, note an important difference in tone. In Amos 4 and Isaiah 3, the tone is one of savage assault about the threat to come. Here the tone is not threat as much as an invitation to grief. The mood is not one of assault but of loss and death, of the ending of a world deeply treasured and taken for granted. Thus the genre is a summons to a death lament, with a series of summoning imperatives: rise up, hear, listen, tremble, shudder, strip, make yourselves bare, put on, beat (vv. 9–12). The urging is to "face the music" that is a dirge, to be equipped for grief work.

The reason for grief is that the vineyards will fail (v. 10), the vines will turn to briers and thorns (vv. 12–13; cf. 5:7); the fortress, the city, and the watchtower will all be abandoned. The land will be emptied of life and of resources for life. The mighty inversion to come will reduce the city to a pastureland for donkeys and sheep. The double use of "joy" makes the point poignantly. What was the *joy of houses* will become, in short order, *the joy of wild asses*.

The summons to grief and loss is stated without reason. The reason may be implied in the conduct of fools and villains (vv. 5–7), but no explicit connection is made. There is no motivation for loss in either the disregard of God or the disregard of neighbor. Much may be inferred, but nothing is stated. All the women know is that grief is now appropriate for a happy world that was and will be no longer.

A Spirit-Bestowed Newness
(32:15–20)

32:15 **until a spirit from on high is poured out on us,**
          and the wilderness becomes a fruitful field,
          and the fruitful field is deemed a forest.

16 **Then justice will dwell in the wilderness,**
          and righteousness abide in the fruitful field.
17 **The effect of righteousness will be peace,**
          and the result of righteousness, quietness and trust forever.
18 **My people will abide in a peaceful habitation,**
          in secure dwellings, and in quiet resting places.
19 **The forest will disappear completely,**
          and the city will be utterly laid low.
20 **Happy will you be who sow beside every stream,**
          who let the ox and the donkey range freely.

The summons to grief is abruptly broken by "until" (v. 15). The following verses play against verses 9–14 but now turn in a marvelously positive direction. There is nothing here of loss or grief because a spirit is given that generates newness. In the rhetoric of the Fourth Gospel, this is "the comforter" (John 15:26; cf. Isa. 40:1) who will move the community beyond loss and grief. This is the same "spirit," let us imagine, who moved against chaos to make life possible at the outset (Gen. 1:2). The spirit here is not to be reified in the subsequent dogmatic language of the church but is "the force of God" that enlivens and transforms God's creation. The wondrous outcome of the work of this spirit is inversion, whereby wilderness becomes "fruitful land," and "carmel," that is, garden land, becomes thicket. The "fruitful land" is restored creation that will burst with vitality and generativity to create well-being and prosperity.

The consequence of this new gift of the spirit is the production of a viable place for life. Verses 16–18 teem with Israel's rich vocabulary of well-being. The justice and righteousness of the king from verse 1 is here matched (trumped?) by the justice and righteousness of creation, whereby the wilderness and the fruitful land of verse 15 are both marked by God's full well-being. The outcome of righteousness wrought by God is *shalom*. Or, said in parallel, the consequence of righteousness is quietness and trust, the gift generously offered in 30:15 and firmly rejected in 30:16. Here those gifts are given without any conditionality. "My people" will now be situated, not in a contested, risky political place, but in a habitation of *shalom*, a place of restful confidence and serene trustfulness. All of the old covenant blessings are now offered as God enacts the new age of well-being. That new age may be governance by the Davidic king of verse 1, except that in verses 15–20 there is no historical agent. The newness is a gift from God.

Verse 19 constitutes something of an enigma. The verse perhaps refers back to the devastation announced earlier in the chapter. Or perhaps, as Kaiser suggests: "The 'forest' refers to the enemy army that causes the devastation, 'the city' is the world capital (Nineveh, Babylon) from which comes the destruction" (Kaiser, *Isaiah 13–39*, 335–336). Either way, the verse develops the linkage of verses 18 and 20.

Calvin ingeniously and unconvincingly proposes that the verse imagines cities being safely built in valleys where they are safe without fortification (not unlike the Cathedral of St. David in Wales) (*Isaiah* II, 424–425).

The final verse appears to be an add-on of a wisdom saying, envisioning a simple, pastoral existence that is perhaps pre-urban. It envisions an idyllic state of small agriculture, where one sows beside a stream (cf. Psalms 1:3; 23:2), where ox and donkey ("deer and antelope"?) play. This is an untroubled social context in which none is threatened and none is threatening. The Bible offers, at times, urban scenarios of *shalom*. Here it is a pastoral scene. Here there are no fools or villains, and there is no need for women to shudder or tremble. Or perhaps we may conclude that modestly farming beside a stream with one donkey and one ox is a precondition for *shalom*. More than that seemingly requires military force, whereby the vicious cycle of exploitative violence begins again. Attention might be paid, in this connection, to the scenario of Isaiah 2:2–4, which in the parallel version of Micah 4:1–4 is even more pre-urban. In this vision the vicious cycle of militarism, and all that goes with it, is broken. We are close here to "the kingdom of God," to Yahweh's peaceable governance.

THE COMING KINGDOM OF GOD
33:1–24

The broad outline and plot of this chapter are not difficult to discern. It is the assertion that the unnamed, threatening world power will be defeated by Yahweh; in its place Yahweh will establish a new governance of well-being that will bring joy and solace to God's people. That much is clear. Beyond that the chapter is complex and obscure, for at least two reasons. First, there are no historical "markers" to identify "the enemy" or the situation of expectation. There is a rough scholarly consensus that the text is from the latter part of the first millennium B.C.E. and reflects an apocalyptic, transhistorical mode of hope. Against that consensus Seitz makes a case that the text refers to Isaiah's eighth century and stands between the materials of chapters 28—31 and the narrative of Hezekiah in chapters 36—39, thus pointing to the deliverance of 701. The second problematic is that the text consists of a series of short units, many of which are allusions to or quotations of older liturgical material. It is by no means clear how these units are related to each other or come in sequence. It is the task of the interpreter to see how these small textual elements may relate to the larger assertion of hope.

Yahweh Rescues Zion (33:1–6)

33:1 **Ah, you destroyer,**
       who yourself have not been destroyed;

you treacherous one,
    with whom no one has dealt treacherously!
When you have ceased to destroy,
    you will be destroyed;
and when you have stopped dealing treacherously,
    you will be dealt with treacherously.

²O LORD, be gracious to us; we wait for you.
    Be our arm every morning,
    our salvation in the time of trouble.
³At the sound of tumult, peoples fled;
    before your majesty, nations scattered.
⁴Spoil was gathered as the caterpillar gathers;
    as locusts leap, they leaped upon it.
⁵The LORD is exalted, he dwells on high;
    he filled Zion with justice and righteousness;
⁶he will be the stability of your times,
    abundance of salvation, wisdom, and knowledge;
    the fear of the LORD is Zion's treasure.

This passage begins—like 28:1; 29:1; 30:1; 31:1—with a woe that bespeaks loss and death. Unlike those uses, however, here the woe is spoken against an unnamed, destructive enemy of Judah. Here Yahweh announces coming death to the enemy of Judah. The first verse is a remarkable poetic achievement, using both the terms "destroy" and "treacherous" four times, thus strongly accenting the negative character of the enemy and assuring that it will receive in full measure what it has given out to others. The oracle is a lordly assertion that sets the tone for what follows.

Abruptly, tone and address are changed. Verse 2, on the lips of Judah, is a petition for rescue that seeks to mobilize Yahweh, who is indeed a God of graciousness. Judah voices its hope ("wait"), perhaps suggesting that Yahweh does indeed have an obligation to act for Judah. Yahweh's "arm" bespeaks Yahweh's power (military power) that has been an instrument of rescue for Israel since the days of the Exodus narrative (Deut. 26:8). "The enemy" cannot withstand the powerful arm of Yahweh.

After the petition of verse 2, verses 3–6 are a lyrical articulation of Yahweh's mighty power against the enemy. The rhetoric is presented as a characterization of what has already happened. In light of the "wait" of verse 2, we may conclude that the past tense is in fact anticipation of what Yahweh will yet do. When Yahweh's great sovereign majesty begins to move against the nations—as it surely will in response to Judah's petition—none can withstand the incursion. The peoples will flee; the nations will be scattered in confusion, fear, and retreat. Yahweh, however, will seize plunder and booty from the enemy the way locusts or caterpillars ravage the land. Yahweh will pursue a "scorched earth" policy against "the destroyer," and none can resist.

This scenario is like a royal procession in which Yahweh moves through the land and finally arrives at the goal that is Zion. There Yahweh's new governance is established, marked by "justice and righteousness" and "stability." This latter term renders *'amûnah*, a reference to order, safety, security, and reliability. The term is from the same root as "faith" in 7:9 and serves as a tag word for Isaiah's royal theology. The cluster of positive terms in verses 5–6 that characterize the new rule of Yahweh indicates that Judah's long wait is over. This is indeed the establishment of the *new kingdom* that has now completely displaced the reign of destruction and treachery.

An Offer to Covenant Keepers
(33:7–16)

33:7 **Listen! the valiant cry in the streets;**
    the envoys of peace weep bitterly.
  8 **The highways are deserted,**
    travelers have quit the road.
  The treaty is broken,
    its oaths are despised,
    its obligation is disregarded.
  9 **The land mourns and languishes;**
    Lebanon is confounded and withers away;
  Sharon is like a desert;
    and Bashan and Carmel shake off their leaves.

  10 **"Now I will arise," says the LORD,**
    "now I will lift myself up;
    now I will be exalted.
  11 **You conceive chaff, you bring forth stubble;**
    your breath is a fire that will consume you.
  12 **And the peoples will be as if burned to lime,**
    like thorns cut down, that are burned in the fire."

  13 **Hear, you who are far away, what I have done;**
    and you who are near, acknowledge my might.
  14 **The sinners in Zion are afraid;**
    trembling has seized the godless:

"Who among us can live with the devouring fire?
    Who among us can live with everlasting flames?"
15 Those who walk righteously and speak uprightly,
    who despise the gain of oppression,
who wave away a bribe instead of accepting it,
    who stop their ears from hearing of bloodshed
    and shut their eyes from looking on evil,
16 they will live on the heights;
    their refuge will be the fortresses of rocks;
    their food will be supplied, their water assured.

It is likely that the petition of verse 2 is one element of a larger song of complaint. A second element of that larger rhetorical pattern is evidenced in verses 7–9, which are a complaint proper. The intended function of the complaint is to rouse Yahweh to new action on the assumption that the present vexation at the hands of the enemy has come about because of Yahweh's temporary disengagement. The remedy, then, is to urge Yahweh's immediate reengagement.

The complaint is a characterization, perhaps in exaggerated terms, of the sorry state of affairs. The first emphasis is that social relations are in a state of disorder and dismay. Those who work for *shalom* are in disarray and despondency. Traffic has ceased because the roads are not safe; and if traffic ceases, the economy surely comes to a standstill. Moreover, the "social contract" that makes social life possible has disintegrated. More than likely, these articulations concern the internal life of Judah. But that internal life and its breakdown are perforce a function of the larger context of "the destroyer," the pressure of which has made internal relationships deeply problematic. The triad of broken treaties, despised oaths, and disregarded humanness indicates that life in the community has failed.

There is, however, an even more massive subject for complaint. The imagery of verse 9 concerns a deep drought. "Lebanon" refers to the lush mountainous regions, and Sharon-Bashan-Carmel are rich agricultural areas. Everything is dried up, so that the trees shrivel and lose their leaves. No particular connection is here made between communal disorder and the drought, that is, between the "historical" and the "natural" crises. The poem simply affirms that both crises wait upon the attentiveness of Yahweh, and that they are surely interrelated in that regard. The prophetic tradition is relentless in its insistence that violated justice disturbs the environment. The complaint is about the loss of *shalom* in every dimension of life. In such a fix, Judah has nowhere to turn except to Yahweh. It does so in intense hope.

The purpose of such complaint is to motivate Yahweh to renewed action. In this case, the complaint is effective. Yahweh announces a new resolve to act and to be exalted (vv. 10–12). Although it is the glorification of Yahweh that is central, such glorification can happen only by a powerful restoration of healthy order, precisely the good order for which Judah has prayed in verse 2. Such a restoration is the only way in which Yahweh can demonstrate effective sovereign governance.

Yahweh's resolve to reassert order and power appears to have two consequences. First, in verses 11–12 Yahweh's grand majesty is directed against the "peoples." These verses are dominated by an image of fire that easily burns chaff and stubble, so that the peoples—presumably the destroyer—will be burned the way in which a farmer burns the refuse of thorns and briers. The land will be cleansed of outside forces that work harm and havoc.

But second, the poetry also addresses internal disorder in the community. The phrasing of "near and far" (v. 13) might be geographical, referring to Israelites in Jerusalem and those scattered elsewhere. It might more likely refer to those who stand in varying relationships to the cultic presence of Yahweh available in worship. All are now called to pay attention and to acknowledge what Yahweh is doing, because the threat of Yahweh's "fire" pertains not only to oppressor nations but applies equally to members of the covenant community who are "godless" (see 32:6). Likely the terms of verse 14 reflect moral, covenantal distinctions in the community not unlike those of Psalm 1 concerning the righteous and the wicked.

In verses 14b–16, after the harsh warning of verses 13–14a, rhetoric of a "Torah-entrance liturgy" is voiced that appears to echo Psalms 15 and 24. In those Psalms, a question is asked about who can enter the holy place for access to God and to God's goodness (Psalms 15:1, 24:3). Here the question is, Who will survive the threatening fire of Yahweh? It is the same question as in the Psalms, only harshly escalated, because failure to enter the holy place and the presence of God is a mighty negative judgment. In the Psalms, the priestly answer details the ethical requirements of covenantal obedience (Psalms 15:2–5; 24:4). Here also the answer in verse 15 begins with a programmatic urging of righteousness and uprightness, that is, devotion to the stability and well-being of the community (see 32:8). This is then detailed with a rejection of ill-gotten gain, bribes, and engagement in community-destroying evil. This verse may be regarded as one of the classic summaries of ethics in ancient Israel, no doubt originally formulated in a liturgical setting.

Thus all "outsiders" will be destroyed by "the fire" (vv. 11–12). Insiders will be destroyed by the fire unless they act covenantly toward the community (vv. 14–15). Only those who act responsibly will be safe. Those latter ones are given a sweeping assurance in verse 16, not unlike the assurances of Psalms 15:5b and 24:5–6.

It is to be noted that the key accent of verses 7–16 is in considerable tension with the affirmation of verses 2–6. In the earlier text, the gift of *shalom* is given unconditionally by Yahweh, who will enact righteousness and justice. In verses 7–16, however, the offer of well-being is conditional, depending upon the human enactment of an uncompromising covenantal ethic that upbuilds the community. This tension of course runs throughout the faith of Israel. This text refuses to relax or concede either emphasis.

The Coming King (33:17–24)

33:17 **Your eyes will see the king in his beauty;**
        they will behold a land that stretches far away.
  [18] **Your mind will muse on the terror:**
        "Where is the one who counted?
        Where is the one who weighed the tribute?
        Where is the one who counted the towers?"
  [19] **No longer will you see the insolent people,**
        the people of an obscure speech that you cannot comprehend,
        stammering in a language that you cannot understand.
  [20] **Look on Zion, the city of our appointed festivals!**
        Your eyes will see Jerusalem,
        a quiet habitation, an immovable tent,
      whose stakes will never be pulled up,
        and none of whose ropes will be broken.
  [21] **But there the LORD in majesty will be for us**
        a place of broad rivers and streams,
      where no galley with oars can go,
        nor stately ship can pass.
  [22] **For the LORD is our judge, the LORD is our ruler,**
        the LORD is our king; he will save us.

  [23] **Your rigging hangs loose;**
        it cannot hold the mast firm in its place,
        or keep the sail spread out.

      Then prey and spoil in abundance will be divided;
        even the lame will fall to plundering.

**²⁴ And no inhabitant will say, "I am sick";
the people who live there will be forgiven their iniquity.**

With the defeat of "foreign destroyers" and with the purgation of "sinners" from the community of Judah, we are now prepared for the emergence of "the king in his beauty" (v. 17). This assertion refers to *Yahweh as king* and to no human messiah. The rhetoric here perhaps appeals to the vision of "the king" in 6:1–8 and likely draws upon the hymnody of the divine king who appears in the midst of the liturgy in regal procession. This assertion is the full resolution of the petitionary bid of verse 2. Judah had waited and prayed, and now the prayer is answered. Yahweh has come to power, and with that new rule a full gift of ordered, fruitful, safe, prosperous communal life is assured.

The coming of king Yahweh establishes a vast governance over an extended territory (v. 17b), from which have been eliminated all occupying armies. The wistful hope of this oppressed people is answered, according to this scenario, by a large, safe land from which every threat has been removed. The delight of such emancipation is first voiced negatively, relishing the absence of occupying forces (vv. 18–19). Verse 18 poses a threefold rhetorical question: Where is the one who counted? Who weighed? Who counted? The reference is to the rapacious practice of occupiers who seized and confiscated, taxed and devoured all the resources of Judah. That of course is one of the primary purposes of occupation, long practiced by imperial forces—to take over the wealth of the land. Every such power does it, and certainly they did it to Judah! Verse 19 supplies a triumphant response to the rhetorical question of verse 18. Where are they? Answer: *Nowhere*, gone, out of sight, banished. Judah will no longer see arrogant occupiers who speak a strange, arrogant, intimidating language. The land is freed now for the cadences of Yahweh. The language of faith—Judah's "mother tongue"—is now the only sound heard.

The negation of verses 18–19 clears the ground. Now, in verses 20–22, the positive portrayal of the rescued city is exultantly offered. Zion is now an exuberant place of unending festival. The festival is not a narcotic for the unaware, as it was in 32:9–11a, but is now a true discernment of a new reality. Zion is one long doxology. The city is now, with the new governance, precisely the place of quietude and well-being anticipated in 30:15, only to be tersely rejected. The imagery of stability anticipates 54:1–4, wherein the stakes and ropes are strong and will not be disturbed.

Verse 21 offers a reassuring image and then takes that image in an unexpected direction. Yahweh's own presence will be a place of rivers and streams. The text does not say Yahweh gives water, but is the sustaining water for Jerusalem (see Ezek. 47:1–12; John 4:13–14). This imagery perhaps reflects the old Zion song of Psalm 46:4 and perhaps alludes to the "gentle river" of Isaiah 8:6. Moreover, we are mindful of the endless need for water in an arid climate: for example, the drought of 33:9 and the promise of 35:6–7. It is a guarantee of life for the city, overcoming all the thirsts that are so foreboding.

In verses 21b and 23, however, the imagery of a river in the city is turned negative. The poem seems to envision foreign ships coming to the city, either to confiscate goods or to assault. In any case, they are a threat sailing up the river, and that threat will not be blocked. The imagery is odd, because Jerusalem is clearly landlocked. Nonetheless the poet employs the imagery in order to state, yet again, that Yahweh has secured the city against foreign invasion. The imagery is continued in verse 23 to assert that these intrusive vessels cannot succeed in their approach to the city.

After that odd imagery in verses 21 and 23, the poem concludes in verses 22 and 24 with a ringing assertion of Yahweh that refers back to the opening declaration of verse 17. In verse 22, the name of Yahweh is celebratively uttered three times, each time with a royal office: judge, ruler, king. In those offices, Yahweh works powerfully for the good of Jerusalem. The threefold acclamation, moreover, ends with the same Hebrew term ("salvation") used in the prayer of Israel in verse 2.

The concrete implementation of this royal acclamation is envisioned in verses 23b–24. Yahweh had seized the booty of the enemy (v. 4). That booty is now boisterously distributed among eager hands for long disadvantaged and deprived. The distribution is conducted in shameless delight, taken as the rightful reward of Yahweh's great triumph. The last line of verse 23 asserts that there is so much booty that even the lame, who must wait at the back of the line, will benefit. This is indeed a complete reversal of fortunes, authorized by Yahweh's rule but given passion by long and deep resentments now given free rein.

Whereas verse 23 mentions the lame who benefit, verse 24 overrides even that good news with the more sweeping assurance that there will be no lame people in the new governance. All disability will be overcome! The new rule of Yahweh will be one of complete health, utter forgiveness, full reconciliation, total rehabilitation, life as dreamed by Judah, life as willed by the creator God.

It is no wonder that in the later messianic hope of Jews and in the celebration of Jesus by Christians, this imagery prevails. The full coming of God's kingdom will mean a total elimination of all that is negative. It is as yet a vision and a hope in this poem, but it is one held to passionately as the only alternative to endless savagery, resentment, and despair.

This complex chapter traverses the entire panorama of Judah's lived experience. It begins in the midst of the destroyer before whom Judah can only pray and wait. In due course, so the poem affirms, the prayer of Judah to Yahweh is heard. The waiting is vindicated. The city receives its true governance; the world begins again, free, pure, innocent, glad, without disability or lack. Zion is indeed, at long last, a "quiet habitation" where converge all the "hopes and fears" of this text-making community.

5. The New Governance of Harshness and Joy
Isaiah 34—35

These chapters are the negation (34:8) and the affirmation (35:4) of God's right-wising vindication, recompense, and vengeance. God will not leave the world as it is, in bondage, drought, and oppression, but will bring it right. Here that rehabilitative transformation, which pivots on the gospel "Here is your God" (35:4), is focused on the restoration of displaced Israel. But before the lyrical affirmation of chapter 35 is possible, God must clear the ground of hostile forces, the ominous work of chapter 34.

In chapter 35, the ultimate theme is homecoming. The chapter is arranged, however, to juxtapose the problem of drought (vv. 1–2) and human disability (vv. 3–6a), in turn rectified by water (vv. 6b–7) and by homecoming (vv. 8–10). The poet seeks, with every possible image, to voice the newness that outruns all conventional categories. So the poem moves easily between "nature" and "history," between "creation" and "redemption," because what is asserted and celebrated is God's new governance over every zone of reality.

The judgment-grace pattern of chapters 34—35 is an anticipatory overture for the larger assertion of chapters 40—55, wherein Babylon (like Edom here) is eliminated as a threat so that God's people may come home. Thus chapters 34—35 assert themes that will dominate much that is yet to come in the tradition of Isaiah. Beyond that, this double affirmation about the defeat of evil and the coming of God's new governance becomes pivotal for Christian hope. Chapter 35 occupies an important place among the Advent texts of the church, texts that announce nothing less joyous or less modest than God's full coming kingdom. Such large hopes sit exuberantly upon the lips of such poets as this one.

A DAY OF VENGEANCE
34:1–17

This chapter is intimately tied to chapter 35. The two chapters together articulate *Yahweh's savage defeat* of "the enemy" and *Yahweh's powerful re-*

habilitation of Israel. The exaggerated negativity of chapter 34 needs to be seen in the context of the positive, exuberant counterpoint of chapter 35.

34:1 **Draw near, O nations, to hear;**
     O peoples, give heed!
   Let the earth hear, and all that fills it;
     the world, and all that comes from it.

The text begins as a great international summons for all peoples to come and observe. It imagines a court case in which Yahweh will adjudicate the affairs of all nations. The unspoken assumption is the sovereignty of Yahweh, who is able to exercise unqualified oversight of all nations. The sense of this summons is amply reflected in chapters 13—23 and is the pervasive affirmation of the Isaiah tradition. Yahweh governs all peoples.

34:2 **For the LORD is enraged against all the nations,**
     and furious against all their hoards;
     he has doomed them, has given them over for slaughter.
   ³ **Their slain shall be cast out,**
     and the stench of their corpses shall rise;
     the mountains shall flow with their blood.
   ⁴ **All the host of heaven shall rot away,**
     and the skies roll up like a scroll.
   All their host shall wither
     like a leaf withering on a vine,
     or fruit withering on a fig tree.

Immediately, the verdict of Yahweh is announced. It is a negative verdict that pertains to all nations. The premise for all that follows in this chapter is that Yahweh is "enraged . . . furious." We are not told why. There is an unresolved abrasion between Yahweh and Yahweh's rightful realm of governance. We may extrapolate from elsewhere that the nations operate with arrogant autonomy, thus defying Yahweh. But we are not told that here.

We are given only a sentence, without any specific indictment. The sentence is massive, total, and uncompromising. It entails a devastation of "the host of heaven" (v. 4a) and a withering drought on the earth (v. 4b). All of heaven and earth will be nullified. The most important term in this general decree of destruction is the term "doomed" in verse 2. This is a rendering of the Hebrew *ḥerem*, which means to be totally destroyed, totally sacrificed to Yahweh without any element of preservation or restraint. By using this term, the poem appeals to the ancient war ideology of Deuteronomy 20:10–18, whereby nations that resist Yahweh and threaten Israel are to be "devoted." The principal "case study" is that of Amalek in 1 Samuel

15:4–33, wherein Amalek is totally destroyed as Israel's enduring enemy and Yahweh's unforgiven adversary (see also Exod. 17:8–16). The use of the term "doom" (*ḥerem*) is one of a universalizing ideology that appears not to trouble with detailed evidence. That is, all the nations are held summarily to be in defiance of Yahweh, and so all must be devastated.

34:5 **When my sword has drunk its fill in the heavens,**
   lo, it will descend upon Edom,
   upon the people I have doomed to judgment.
 6 **The LORD has a sword; it is sated with blood,**
   it is gorged with fat,
   with the blood of lambs and goats,
   with the fat of the kidneys of rams.
 For the LORD has a sacrifice in Bozrah,
   a great slaughter in the land of Edom.
 7 **Wild oxen shall fall with them,**
   and young steers with the mighty bulls.
 Their land shall be soaked with blood,
   and their soil made rich with fat.

With the sweeping international vista of verses 1–4, we are scarcely prepared for the abrupt focus upon Edom, which in this chapter turns out to be the focal recipient of Yahweh's destructive rage. In the midst of the superpowers of Assyria and Egypt, and later Babylon, it is curious that Edom receives such intense, ignominious attention. It may be that Edom was a co-conspirator with mighty Babylon against Israel in the sixth century. Later on, the kingdom of Edom to the east continued to vex and encroach upon the vulnerable community of Judaism, and so to evoke great resentment (as in the book of Obadiah). Whatever may be the historical occasion for such negative sensibility toward Edom, in this chapter Edom plays a representative role, standing in for all peoples who resist the purposes of Yahweh and who consequently become an enemy to Judah.

The general tone of these verses again pivots on the term "doom" in verse 5, which translates *ḥerem*. That ancient ideological word connoted offering the enemy as a sacrifice to Yahweh, as a burnt offering. (Notice in our own time the use of the term *holocaust*, which was a term used for "whole offering" and now is employed for the violent devastation of the Jewish community in the twentieth century. This technical term for liturgical activity became transferred to violent social policy and behavior.) As a result, these verses teem with the language of *sacrifice* as a liturgical activity. Their concrete import, however, concerns violent historical experience. The intention of the rhetoric is the complete devastation of Edom, here the unqualified enemy of Judah and of Yahweh.

34:8 **For the** LORD **has a day of vengeance,**
a year of vindication by Zion's cause.
⁹ **And the streams of Edom shall be turned into pitch,**
and her soil into sulfur;
her land shall become burning pitch.
¹⁰ **Night and day it shall not be quenched;**
its smoke shall go up forever.
From generation to generation it shall lie waste;
no one shall pass through it forever and ever.
¹¹ **But the hawk and the hedgehog shall possess it;**
the owl and the raven shall live in it.
He shall stretch the line of confusion over it,
and the plummet of chaos over its nobles.
¹² **They shall name it No Kingdom There,**
and all its princes shall be nothing.
¹³ **Thorns shall grow over its strongholds,**
nettles and thistles in its fortresses.
It shall be the haunt of jackals,
an abode for ostriches.
¹⁴ **Wildcats shall meet with hyenas,**
goat-demons shall call to each other;
there too Lilith shall repose,
and find a place to rest.
¹⁵ **There shall the owl nest**
and lay and hatch and brood in its shadow;
there too the buzzards shall gather,
each one with its mate.

We may take verse 8 as the theological pivot of the chapter. The devastation here anticipated is Yahweh's act of vengeance, with both military and judicial components. It is as though Edom, surrogate for the rebellious nations (as in Psalm 2:1–3), has long defied Yahweh, and now comes the inescapable consequence of that defiance. The term "vengeance" here may reflect (a) an *elemental yearning on the part of Jews*, who insist on retribution for exploitation that has gone on too long, (b) an insistence upon *Yahweh's sovereignty* that will not be mocked, or (c) an insistence that *the world is just*, and therefore in the long run accounts must be settled. Indeed, it is likely that these several motifs converge into one great rhetorical effort at a recovery of equity in a situation too long skewed.

The extended central section of this chapter is a characterization of what happens to the land of Edom when Yahweh's justice begins to be enacted, as it soon will be. The initial devastation concerns the "fire and brimstone" of Sodom and Gomorrah (vv. 9–10, as in Gen. 19:24–25). When the land is devastated and emptied of viable habitation, moreover, it will not remain empty but will promptly be occupied by low-life creatures who are unclean and incompatible with human habitation. In alluding to verse 16, wherein God's spirit has gathered all the animals, Calvin likens the scene to the work of God mobilizing all of the animals at the flood (Gen. 7:15). And Seitz suggests that the presentation of animals in obedience to Yahweh offers a situation not unlike the post-Flood in which only animals are present, all of whom are obedient to Yahweh. Thus the land is not finally emptied but is peopled with agents of antilife. Worth noting is that the end of verse 11 uses a characteristic word, "chaos," a word best known from Genesis 1:2 to characterize the pre-creation seething disorder of unshaped reality. The land of Edom is returned to a pre-creation formlessness in which real life, as willed by the creator, is impossible.

Indeed, the creator God intends that real life should here be impossible. As verse 12 indicates, it is a "no life" place, with no identifiable political order, no functioning rulers, all reduced to disorderly anarchy and death. This political reference is reinforced in verses 13–15 with a rich inventory of negativities, including thorns and thistles, scavenger animals, creatures of the night, and ominous, ill-defined demonic forces. We note here the single mention in the Old Testament of Lilith, a type of demonic power. The intention of the exaggerated rhetoric is to exhibit the land of Edom as an ominous, dangerous, seething, death-filled place in which human habitation is impossible. The sense of the place strikes me as being parallel in our time to an abandoned nuclear plant, still filled with lethal condemnation, where no human agent could risk to go. This poetry is not reasoned discourse. It intends rather to evoke a deeply felt sense of the elimination of Edom as an identifiable reality in the world of Jewish faith. This exaggerated devastation carries with it two awarenesses. One is that the way is now cleared for Jewish well-being, a theme taken up in chapter 35. The other is that Yahweh is sovereign. Yahweh is not to be trifled with, for Yahweh's vengeance is massive and unrelenting. The creator God will either rule creation or will make life impossible. There is no third alternative.

34:16 **Seek and read from the book of the LORD:**
    Not one of these shall be missing;
    none shall be without its mate.
For the mouth of the LORD has commanded,

and his spirit has gathered them.
[17] **He has cast the lot for them,**
his hand has portioned it out to them with the line;
they shall possess it forever,
from generation to generation they shall live in it.

After the exaggerated spree of verses 9–15, we are taken aback by the sobered discipline of these verses. The writer is aware that he is "making text." This is not mere emotional venting. The writer acknowledges that the task is to build an enduring textual record, as warning to any would-be Edom, as enduring assurance to Jews who are vulnerable, and as persistent celebration of Yahweh, who will not be mocked but who will prevail. Already in 8:16 and 30:8, we have seen that the Isaiah tradition is self-conscious about constructing the testimonial scroll that is en route to becoming *canonical evidence* about the reliability of prophetic utterance and about the reliability of the larger theological claim of Yahweh's governance. All of the new inhabitants of the land of Edom—all of the threatening, ominous forces of chaos—will stay in place for all time to come. Not one will be absent. The linkage between the inventory of threat in verses 9–15 and the canonical assurance in verses 16–17 is evident in the reiteration of "each with its mate" from verse 15 in verse 16. Yahweh has assigned each such agent its proper place to occupy for all time. The rhetoric of possession and apportionment is the same rhetoric used in the older traditions to guarantee Israel its place for all time in "the land of promise." Thus the usage here is somewhat ironic. The God who guarantees land to Israel is the God who guarantees the land of Edom to the forces of death "forever, from generation to generation" (v. 17). Calvin observes:

> If he keeps wild beasts in possession of the place which he has allotted to them, how much more will he preserve men, for whose sake he created heaven, earth, the seas and all that they contain? (*Commentary* VIII, 59)

The plotline of this chapter is not difficult to trace. Interpretation may more usefully focus on the problematic of a God who decrees such a violent fate, seemingly undertaken in rage. The beginning point is in verse 8—to recognize that the God of this text is a powerful, uncompromising agent who in the end will not tolerate challenge to right rule. In a soft, therapeutic, theological context like our own, such "starchiness" is not easy to accept. But it is there. God will not be mocked! God will not be mocked in the public process. God will not be mocked because God's sovereignty is serious business. God will not be mocked because creation and all of its creatures must give answer to the creator.

To be sure, this core theological claim has mixed with it the deep yearnings and resentments of a people too long oppressed and vexed. We cannot, moreover, sort out what is high theology and what is raw resentment. That yearning and resentment give rise together to extravagant rhetoric that may run beyond reasoned faith, the sort of rhetoric unleashed in therapy, when the floodgates of resentment too long closed are finally opened on the raging silence and everything is grossly overstated. There is, to be sure, something of *wish* in this rhetoric of faith, a needy people wishing powerfully against seemingly unchallengeable historical reality. Perhaps the grasping for retaliation is childish expectation and self-indulgence. However, such a wish is deeply linked to hope, and hope is "the assurance of things not seen." In this poetry Israel counts upon God—God savage, God resolved, God attentive—to move against the hurts and injustices of the public process. Such childish wish-become-serious-hope is permitted exaggeration, because the overstatement makes buoyancy possible against great odds. Kaiser suggests:

> A modern sociologist would perhaps categorize it among the poetry of the oppressed. Oppression often produces fine expressions of longing, but also liberation which takes its tone solely from the glow of vengeful passion. It should be noted that the poet places his hope in God and not in his people's sword (*Isaiah 13–39*, 355).

The exaggeration of faith is a crucial antidote to despair among those who have no way out. The same rhetoric is a wake-up call to those who become jaded in their domination, invited to reimagine a world made right, wherein unjust power is reduced to deathly nullity.

In the end, the world is not in the hands of any oppressive power. It is in the hands of the God who makes "a way out of no way." That way out for God's people is celebrated in the next chapter.

VENGEANCE AS HOMECOMING JUBILATION
35:1–10

Chapter 34 had imagined that Yahweh would nullify every threat from the world of Jerusalem. God would come in vengeance to vindicate Zion (34:8). Having cleared the ground of all such threats by reducing Edom to nullity, now in chapter 35 God's vengeance and recompense receive positive content (35:4). The chapter consists of a lyrical anticipation of a coming time when all creation will be restored to well-being (vv. 1–2, 6b–7) and the faithful will be healed (vv. 3–4) and brought home safely and joyously (vv. 8–10). The theme is that the coming governance of Yahweh will radically transform both bereft "nature" and disabled "history." There is no doubt that this chapter is intimately joined to the vision of homecoming in chapters 40—55 and contains many parallels in wording and phrasing. The intention is to invite Jewish listeners to joyous anticipation that God is about to begin again, for the sake of Jerusalem's well-being.

35:1 **The wilderness and the dry land shall be glad,**
  the desert shall rejoice and blossom;
like the crocus [2] **it shall blossom abundantly,**
  and rejoice with joy and singing.
The glory of Lebanon shall be given to it,
  the majesty of Carmel and Sharon.
They shall see the glory of the LORD,
  the majesty of our God.

The vision of well-being begins with the large vista of creation and anticipates radical transformation. The rhetoric is organized as "before" and "after." The "before" is voiced in a triad: wilderness-dry land-desert. Although these terms clearly reflect an intensely arid climate, the theological point is that the creator's intention of full fruitfulness has not been implemented. It is as though Yahweh the creator has lacked intensity, which portends that creation will not "measure up" as a fruitful system. This triad of deathliness, however, is immediately answered by a triad of fertility: Lebanon-Carmel-Sharon. The poet names the richest, most fertile areas of agriculture to exhibit the full generativity of creation. The gospel announcement made here is that wilderness-dry land-desert will abruptly become, by the intention of Yahweh, Lebanon-Carmel-Sharon. As a result, the arid soil will astonishingly produce vegetation and flowers, so much so that the land itself will break out in singing. The imagery concerns a personalized creation that has languished in despair, but now, by the power of Yahweh, is raised to new life and therefore must sing praise to Yahweh the giver of life. These verses explicate the theme already noted in 29:17; 30:23–25; 32:15. The practical reference may be to rain that reenlivens creation. But the theological claim is that such restoration exhibits Yahweh's glory, Yahweh's impressive capacity for regal governance. The rehabilitation of creation is evidence that Yahweh has resumed authority and has made clear who is in charge.

35:3 **Strengthen the weak hands,**
  and make firm the feeble knees.
  [4] **Say to those who are of a fearful heart,**

"Be strong, do not fear!
Here is your God.
He will come with vengeance,
with terrible recompense.
He will come and save you."

⁵ Then the eyes of the blind shall be opened,
and the ears of the deaf unstopped;
⁶ᵃ then the lame shall leap like a deer,
and the tongue of the speechless sing for joy.

Now the imagery shifts abruptly. The subject is no longer arid creation, but it is disabled humans, or more precisely, enfeebled Judaism. The ones with "weak hands" and "feeble knees" are not unlike wilderness-dry land-desert. They also are unable to function and to live according to their God-given potential. The subject would seem to be the physically disabled, though we can imagine that the rhetoric also concerns those immobilized by despair. To those addressed the poet speaks a word of comfort surely as vigorous as the "comfort" of 40:1. The verbs "strengthen, make firm, say" are imperatives. We do not know who is compelled to speak, but it would seem to be some agent or messenger as in 40:1, 9–11; 52:7, who is to assert to needful Jews the restoration of Yahweh's good rule. The imperatives are to effect transformation, not unlike the renovation of creation in verses 1–2. The "before" is weak hands and feeble knees. The "after" is strength and well-being. It is worth noting that this imperative of comfort is echoed in Hebrews 12:12, wherein the text makes a bid that Christians should become more faithful in a situation of great risk.

The turning point for the disabled is the utterance of verse 4a, which is a gospel announcement, the assertion of a newness from God. The assertion consists in two imperatives: "Be strong, do not fear!" The latter is an oracle of salvation, an utterance of assurance that is situation changing, characteristically offered in response to a complaint (see Isa. 41:8–13; 43:4–5). The ground for such strength and fearlessness is "behold your God" (see 40:9–11). God had been absent to Jews in their weakness, as God was absent to creation in its aridity. Now God is again visible, active, available, decisive. Everything depends on this voicing of God now reentering reality in sovereign ways.

The problem of "weak hands . . . feeble knees" has as its antidote the actualization of God. God is announced, made visible, and will come and save. The poet voices an active, insurgent, powerful God who comes with a great intention. God now comes into a situation of disability, as into a

situation of drought, in order to work vengeance (see 34:8). The term
"vengeance" includes a quite negative connotation that we readily assign
to it. But it also includes the positive dimension that God will come to right
wrong, to order chaos, to heal sickness, to restore life to its rightful order.
Thus Israel could anciently have God assert:

> Vengeance is mine, and recompense . . .

> Indeed the LORD will vindicate his people,
>   [and] have compassion on his servants,
> when he sees that their power is gone.
>   (Deut. 32:35, 36)

In an act of hope, moreover, Israel could pray:

> O LORD, you God of vengeance,
>   you God of vengeance, shine forth!
> Rise up, O judge of the earth;
>   give to the proud what they deserve!
>   (Psalm 94:1–2)

The redress of negative circumstances includes (a) the restoration of God's
honor and (b) the rehabilitation of God's people. The two cannot be separated from each other.

The antidote of God's activity in verse 4 with the powerful concluding
verb "save" produces the good consequences of verses 5–6a, introduced by
a double "then." Then—as a consequence—the disabilities of verse 3 will
be abruptly overcome:

> The blind will see!
> The deaf will hear!
> The lame will leap!
> The dumb will sing!

The power of death and dysfunction will be broken! It is no wonder that
God's *recompense* is received as transformative *compassion*. We may suggest
three lines of fruitful interpretation. First, the reference to blind, deaf, and
dumb may, within the larger context of Isaiah, allude back to the disabling
verdict of 6:9–10. If such a connection is made, then we are here in Isaiah's
"second stage," when the judgment motif is overcome in grace. Second, if
this text is situated among exiles, then these several disabilities may be a
large metaphor for the life-denying situation that is now broken for the re-
sumption of life. Third, it is important to notice the linkage made in Luke

to the ministry of Jesus. Thus it is attested, that where Jesus is present: "The blind receive their sight, the lame walk, the lepers are cleansed, the deaf hear, the dead are raised, the poor have good news brought to them" (Luke 7:22). The claim is made that in the ministry of Jesus, God's new governance is effected, the new governance for which Judaism has long waited.

35:6b **For waters shall break forth in the wilderness,**
        and streams in the desert;
    7 **the burning sand shall become a pool,**
        and the thirsty ground springs of water;
    the haunt of jackals shall become a swamp,
        the grass shall become reeds and rushes.

In these verses, we are returned to the "environmental" imagery of verses 1–2. The crisis has been one of drought and aridness. Now, because God has come, that crisis—like the crisis of human disability—is ended. In place of the triad of verse 1, we now have a catalogue of four elements characterizing deathly dryness: wilderness-desert-burning sand-thirsty ground. As in verses 1–2, that condition is now completely altered. In its place come waters . . . streams . . . pools . . . springs. Creation that had sunk into dysfunctional, deathly chaos is now rejuvenated for fruitfulness and generativity. The poet has almost no comment upon how this happens, except for the two abrupt verbs "break forth" and "become." One is struck by the lack of complete sentences. The reversal is terse; we are to understand that the assertion of Yahweh in verse 4 explains everything.

The outcome is that the place of scavenger animals (jackals) now has adequate water holes. The parched grassland is now luxurious. The life of the animal world can resume. Surely, the contrast is intentional between the jackal-land of 34:13 that is deathly and the jackal-land that here comes to new life.

35:8 **A highway shall be there,**
        and it shall be called the Holy Way;
    the unclean shall not travel on it,
        but it shall be for God's people;
        no traveler, not even fools, shall go astray.
    9 **No lion shall be there,**
        nor shall any ravenous beast come up on it;
    they shall not be found there,
        but the redeemed shall walk there.
    10 **And the ransomed of the LORD shall return,**

and come to Zion with singing;
everlasting joy shall be upon their heads;
they shall obtain joy and gladness,
and sorrow and sighing shall flee away.

Again with a change of subjects, the poem returns to the human community, as in verses 3–6a. Whereas verses 3–6a likely referred to Israel, the human references are generic. Now they become quite explicitly Israelite. The imagery, more familiar to us in 40:3–6; 43:19; 49:11, is of a highway built across the wilderness land, so that God's beloved people, so long displaced, can return home in triumphant procession. It will be "the Holy Way," that is, the road upon which the Holy People of the Holy God return to the Holy Land. The imagery is a move to be made through the very hearing of the poem, from the old, failed world of exile—a world of drought and disability—to the new world of God's governance, a world of rich fertility and of healed humanity.

These lyrical lines then characterize the road and the journey now anticipated. Attention is paid to the safety of the road and the identity of those who travel on it. The road will be completely safe. There will be no dangerous or threatening animals along the way, even though the journey must be made through dangerous land. The road assures a "safe conduct" (see Psalm 91:14). The ones who travel there will be God's people. We may notice four qualifying marks about this road, two negative and two positive:

1. No *unclean* people will be on it. The term "unclean" refers to the ritually defiled or disqualified, the antithesis of the term "holy" just preceding it. It is anticipated that the restored community of Jews will indeed be a holy people, not contaminated but purified sufficiently to be confident in the presence of the holy God. The line indicates the priestly tilt of recovering Judaism. See the notion of "washed away, cleansed," in 4:4, another vision of restoration, and notice the awareness of "uncleanness" (with the same word) in 6:5. Moreover, the lepers are cleansed, akin to what we hear in Luke 7:22. That is, it may be that the unclean are excluded in order to protect the clean. Or it may also be that they also are cleansed and healed and made pure, and thereby qualified afresh.

2. No fools will there go astray. Although the line is not unambiguous, it apparently asserts that there will be no "fools" on the road, fools being the impious who do not seriously embrace torah disciplines and so practice Yahweh. "Fools" are like "sinners" (see 33:14) who violate torah and endanger the community. The new community will exclude such risk-engendering folk.

3. The "redeemed" will be on the road. The term refers to the beloved

kin of Yahweh. The notion of redemption has to do with family solidarity wherein a strong, resourceful member of the community intervenes in behalf of the weak and jeopardized members of the community in order to assure their safety, well-being, and honor. The later poetry of Isaiah will speak much about Yahweh as redeemer of Israel in exile as a great assurance: "I have redeemed you;/I have called you by name,/you are mine" (43:1). The ones on the road are guaranteed and know with whom and to whom and for whom they belong.

4. The "ransomed" are the company returning. The verb "ransom" is parallel to "redeem." However, as "redeem" bespeaks an orbit of family solidarity, the notion of "ransom" is an economic transaction whereby a price is paid, the subject is purchased and now belongs to the one who pays. Thus Israel "belongs" to Yahweh. It is likely that too much of a distinction should not be made between the two terms. Both here assert that Yahweh takes full responsibility for Israel, that Israel is singularly oriented to Yahweh and is thereby guaranteed safe passage.

It is no wonder that the *clean-wise-redeemed-ransomed* of Yahweh are on their way rejoicing (v. 1). They are on their way to a new Zion, now fully guaranteed, watered, healed. The homecoming, *dominated by joy*, is in total contrast to the plight of Edom in chapter 34. The land *rejoices* in verse 2; the blind-deaf-lame-dumb *rejoice* in verse 6. Now all the redeemed-ransomed *rejoice* in verse 10. Zion is a recovered, restored place of pure, undiminished, unqualified well-being.

There is left over no trace of the old sorrow of displacement or the old sighs of dysfunction. It is no wonder that Frederick Buechner can conclude:

> Joy is home . . . God created us in joy and created us for joy, and in the long run not all the darkness there is in the world and in ourselves can separate us finally from that joy, because whatever else it means to say that God created us in his image, I think it means that even when we cannot believe in him, even when we feel most spiritually bankrupt and deserted by him, his mark is deep within us. We have God's joy in our blood (*The Longing for Home*, 128).

What Buechner says lyrically and generically about the human endowment, Israel here knows concretely, particularly, on the ground.

6. The Career of the Good King
Isaiah 36—39

These four chapters constitute a distinctive unit in the book of Isaiah. From the perspective of biblical literature, they are of special interest because they stand in close relationship to 2 Kings 18—20, traversing the same material with only slight variation. It is probable that the two texts reflect historical reality: the threat of Assyria, the emergence of Babylon as a new power, and the important, complex interaction of king and prophet.

There is no doubt that the Assyrian threat is acute and reflects the actual circumstance of eighth-century Judah. And surely the earlier materials of the book of Isaiah and the prophet of the eighth century are preoccupied with the Assyrian threat. The three taunting speeches of 36:4–10; 36:13–20; 37:6–13 make clear both the arrogance of the empire and the theological ways in which the prophetic tradition casts the threat. Although the text is, in its present form, far removed from political reality, the biblical tradition focuses theologically on (a) the competition between Yahweh and the Assyrian gods, and (b) the sure supremacy of Yahweh. Thus the effective response to the arrogant military threat of Assyria is in the prayer of the pious king (37:16–20) and in the oracle of Isaiah, who brings Yahweh to powerful speech whereby Assyrian power is overcome (37:22–29). In the end, everything turns on the prophetic oracle concerning the failure of Assyrian power and the sure resolve of Yahweh to save Jerusalem. The high drama of chapters 36—37 culminates in what can only be taken as a miraculous, inexplicable rescue of Jerusalem in the face of impossible imperial odds (37:33–38). This rescue becomes a vindication of Zion theology and a pivot point for the emerging Isaiah tradition.

In chapters 36—37, Hezekiah is presented as the perfectly pious king who relies completely upon Yahweh and who is willing to have policy guided by prophetic utterance. In chapters 38—39, the prominence of the pious king, who is characteristically addressed by prophetic oracle, is further narrated. In chapter 38, the illness and recovery of the king evoke a song of thanksgiving and may be understood in larger Isaianic scope as the illness and healing, loss and recovery, of the city of Jerusalem. That is, the king's loss and recovery of health may embody of the destiny of Jerusalem as construed in this prophetic, two-stage tradition.

The glad, celebrative narrative of chapter 38 is placed in telling juxtaposition to the more ominous chapter 39. Here the illness and recovery of the king are acknowledged (39:1), so as to link the two chapters that were likely independent of each other in their origin. Now, however, perhaps because of royal conduct and certainly because of prophetic declaration, the city and the dynasty are in deep trouble. It may be that Hezekiah, the pious king, is only obedient in 39:8. However that may be, the city is about to enter into a deep sickness through the assault of Babylon, the new enemy who has here preempted the characteristically threatening role of Assyria.

In interpreting this section of the text, we may be mindful of three forces at work. First, there is no doubt that this narrative text is *grounded in historical happening*, even if the facts of the case are difficult to discern. There seems to be no doubt that Assyria put enormous military pressure upon Jerusalem and that the city was oddly—miraculously—rescued from Assyrian devastation. It is clear, moreover, that this odd rescue became a defining datum of emerging Zion theology that assumed Jerusalem would be forever secure, an emerging theology that served Judah ill a century later in the Babylonian crisis.

Second, it is clear that whatever there is of historical grounding here has been totally reshaped and stylized as *theological material*. Thus the text needs to be approached not as documentation but as theological testimony, threat, and invitation. With reference to the royal perspective of the book of Isaiah, Hezekiah is clearly offered as "the good king" in contrast to his father Ahaz (see chapter 7). It is this accent that makes a negative reading of the final verse problematic (39:8). Beyond the good king, the text keeps the prophet Isaiah prominent. The narrative is not interested in his person or even in his office, but in his message. And his message is *faith*, reliance on Yahweh in situations of acute jeopardy. This entire unit of chapters 36—39 functions to *summon Israel to faith* in a circumstance that bespeaks doubt, timidity, and fear.

Third, there is no doubt that in the final form of the text, the prophetic literature addressed to the Assyrian crisis has been redeployed and transposed into a commentary concerning *the Babylonian crisis* a century later. This redeployment is accomplished, most transparently, by the introduction of Babylon in chapter 39 and the prophetic oracle in 39:5–7 that culminates the unit and peers over into the abyss of displacement dominating the final form of the text of Isaiah. The centrality of Babylon, moreover, is reinforced by the placement of this "Hezekiah oracle" (39:5–7) right up against the beginning of Second Isaiah in chapter 40. As it is given to us, the book of Isaiah has now no interest in historical sequence but moves beyond Hezekiah to the devastation a century later. The book is arranged to make clear that the destruction of Jerusalem anticipated in chapter 39 is "the old thing" and the announcement of rescue in 40:1–2 is "the new thing." Thus the materials are arranged and placed to serve the two-stage theology of Isaiah, stages of judgment and grace. These two stages refer to Jerusalem that is in turn *devastated* and then *restored*. But the book of Isaiah is finally not even about Jerusalem; it is about Yahweh. It is Yahweh who does "alien work" (28:21) and then proper work. The first stage is inescapable, given the vagaries of history and the covenantal failure of Judah. The glorious second stage, however, is the exuberant focus of the gospel of the book of Isaiah. This material moves from the first toward the second stage of life with Yahweh. The move is not easy or facile or painless. The cost is asserted by the prophet and is enacted by Assyria (now become Babylon). It is endured by kings for whom Hezekiah is representative. Prophet, foreign nation, and king are all testimonies to the rule of Yahweh, in turn costly and joyous.

ISRAEL TAUNTED FOR FAITH
36:1–37:20

This material presents a remarkable confrontation between massive, arrogant Assyrian power and the fearful, Yahwistic faith of Jerusalem embodied by King Hezekiah. Scholars have spent a great deal of energy seeking to sort out the historical particularities behind the text. There is no doubt that Assyrian armies in the time of Sennacherib came against Jerusalem. This much is attested in the Assyrian royal documents. Moreover, it is clear that a major siege of the city of Jerusalem took place in 701, when the city was miraculously, inexplicably rescued from the threat of Assyria. There is some suggestion of a prior assault against the city in 705, but that is not clear.

It seems increasingly evident, in any case, that detailed deciphering of historical backgrounds for this material will not help us read this text more knowingly, because the text itself is not and does not intend to be historical documentation. It is rather a major and intentional theological statement that gives play to major accents of the Isaiah tradition. That is, the text is closer in genre to *sermon* than it is to *chronicle*. We may identify four prominent themes that serve the larger purposes of the book of Isaiah: (1) This text is a major study in *Zion theology*. The well-being and danger of the city of Jerusalem is a core preoccupation of the tradition. (2) As we have seen, especially in 7:9; 30:15, the key religious obligation of the Isaiah tradition is *faith*, a capacity to trust in Yahweh in situations of risk. (3) The prophetic figure of Isaiah (see 37:5–7) is a key player in the drama of faith. (4) King Hezekiah is a principal reference point for the presentation and is likely presented as a type of "the good king who trusts" as contrasted with Ahaz his father, who is "the bad king who fears" (6:1–9:7).

After the introductory notice of 36:1–3, this unit consists of three speeches of challenge by the voice of Assyria (36:4–10; 36:13–20; and 37:8–13), together with three responses to the Assyrian speeches from the royal household. The responses consist of a request (36:11–12), silence (36:21–22) followed by announcements by the king (37:1–3) and the prophet (vv. 5–7), and a prayer of the king (37:14–20). The interpreter will notice that this material is peculiarly rich and suggestive for theological exposition.

> 36:1 **In the fourteenth year of King Hezekiah, King Sennacherib of Assyria came up against all the fortified cities of Judah and captured them.** 2 **The king of Assyria sent the Rabshakeh from Lachish to King Hezekiah at Jerusalem, with a great army. He stood by the conduit of the upper pool on the high-way to the Fuller's Field.** 3 **And there came out to him Eliakim son of Hilkiah, who was in charge of the palace, and Shebna the secretary, and Joah son of Asaph, the recorder.**

This notice seeks to situate what follows historically. As indicated, the chronological placement of the siege and encounter is uncertain. The date itself, the fourteenth year, situates the reign of Sennacherib, whose dates of leadership are 704–681. The "Rabshakeh" is an Assyrian imperial officer and refers to an official representative of the imperial government. Three high officers of Hezekiah's court are named, perhaps constituting a negotiating delegation. We have seen in 22:15–25 that our present text may have suggested the names for what appears to be the contrived juxtaposition of Shebna and Eliakim in chapter 22. The placement of the negotiations at "the conduit of the upper pool," an echo of 7:3, may suggest that this was the normal, conventional place for such meetings in time of crisis. Or it may refer to the royal sense of crisis, for the royal delegation is near to the waterworks upon which depends the safety of the city. In the editorial enterprise of the book of Isaiah, it is more likely, in my judgment, that the identical location for the conversations of chapters 7 and 36 is to call attention to the parallel between the *doubt of the bad king* and the *faith of the good king*, two models of faith between which Israel must always choose. The locus of the conversation, in this judgment, has a theological intentionality.

36:4 **The Rabshakeh said to them, "Say to Hezekiah: Thus says the great king, the king of Assyria: On what do you base this confidence of yours?** [5] **Do you think that mere words are strategy and power for war? On whom do you now rely, that you have rebelled against me?** [6] **See, you are relying on Egypt, that broken reed of a staff, which will pierce the hand of anyone who leans on it. Such is Pharaoh king of Egypt to all who rely on him.** [7] **But if you say to me, 'We rely on the LORD our God,' is it not he whose high places and altars Hezekiah has removed, saying to Judah and to Jerusalem, 'You shall worship before this altar'?** [8] **Come now, make a wager with my master the king of Assyria: I will give you two thousand horses, if you are able on your part to set riders on them.** [9] **How then can you repulse a single captain among the least of my master's servants, when you rely on Egypt for chariots and for horsemen?** [10] **Moreover, is it without the LORD that I have come up against this land to destroy it? The LORD said to me, Go up against this land, and destroy it."**

The diplomatic message of the great empire to this small, intimidated state is in fact an ultimatum that seeks to establish that Jerusalem in fact has no alternative except to surrender to awesome Assyrian power (see 2 Kings 18:14–16). Clearly, so says Assyria, Judah has no resources for resistance. Although this is a political-military challenge, as a piece of Isaiah tradition it is saturated with issues of faith. The governing term *bṭḥ* dominates this speech and occurs six times (vv. 4, 5, 6, 6, 7, 9), variously rendered as "rely," "confidence." The speech, ostensibly by an Assyrian, is Isaianic theology summoning Judah to the risk and danger of bold faith in Yahweh as the only alternative to life on the harsh, demanding terms of the empire.

The speech begins with the audacious, self-authorizing claim of the "great king," parallel to the usual prophetic, "Thus says the Lord." The formula itself is a sweeping claim of authority. The beginning of the speech contains three rhetorical questions (though one in Hebrew may not be a question): "On what? . . . Do you think? . . . On whom?" The purpose of the questions is to establish Judah's situation as precarious and Judah's resources as intolerably thin. The only named resource in these questions is "strategy and power for war" (v. 5). Judah's military capacity is modest indeed, and everyone knows it.

The speech then names two alternative resources other than Judah's own military capacity. First, verse 6, again with the word "rely," dismisses Egypt as a possible resource. We have already seen that the tradition of Isaiah rejects the Egyptian option on both pragmatic and theological grounds (30:1–4; 31:1–3). Here Egypt is said to be a "broken reed," with sharp points that will only hurt those who draw close to it (see 42:3). The imagery suggests that Egypt is a failed ally. Second, the speech considers Yahweh as an ally. According to this rhetorical strategy, Egypt and Yahweh are grouped together as failed resources. Yahweh is "guilty by association" with Egypt, equally unreliable. Verse 7 apparently alludes to Hezekiah's reforming activity (2 Kings 18:4; 2 Chron. 31:1), whereby the king closed a number of Yahweh shrines. The speech suggests that such "reform" would have offended Yahweh, even though the act is elsewhere taken as an act of jealous fidelity to Yahweh. We may imagine that the speech is constructed by the tradition of Isaiah in order to show, deliberately, that Assyria cannot penetrate the peculiarity of the God of Israel. Here, the Assyrian could not comprehend that Yahweh might regard Hezekiah's actions as faithful reform and not hostility. The speech lingers no longer over Yahweh than it does over Egypt; both are inadequate for the present crisis, according to an Assyrian perspective.

Now the speech returns, mockingly, to military capacity (v. 8). Judah lacks manpower to withstand Assyria. In an act of patronizing humiliation, Assyria offers to provide, as a sporting gesture, horses to arm Judah, if only Judah can supply the riders. But it is known before the offer is made that Judah lacks the people power to mount such horses. Indeed, Judah's situation is so desperate that it depends upon Egyptian horses and riders in order to make any show of military power. (Egypt in this crisis is to Judah as was the United States to South Vietnam in a later crisis!) So we have come full circle. Judah depends upon Egypt, a failed resource . . . over . . . and over . . . and over . . . a failure.

The final assertion, sure to rob Judah of its confidence and buoyancy, is the daring claim that the armies of Sennacherib have come against Judah *at the behest of Yahweh* (v. 10). Yahweh, so it is claimed, is allied to Assyria against Judah! There are two grounds for such a claim. First, it is not unprecedented that conquerors claim to be deliverers in the name of the local god who has rejected the local regime. This could be part of rather routine propaganda. Second, the prophetic tradition of Israel is not averse to identifying invaders of Judah as tools of Yahweh's judgment. Indeed, in Isaiah 10:5–19, Assyria itself is so identified in the tradition of Isaiah. Thus the claim is congruent with one element of prophetic faith.

The speech is exceedingly deft in its rhetorical development, present-ing Judah's situation as completely hopeless, one by one considering and rejecting alternatives to surrender. In the end, Judah is completely caught in the Assyrian web, with no way out!

36:11 Then Eliakim, Shebna, and Joah said to the Rabshakeh, "Please speak to your servants in Aramaic, for we understand it; do not speak to us in the language of Judah within the hearing of the people who are on the wall." 12 But the Rabshakeh said, "Has my master sent me to speak these words to your master and to you, and not to the people sitting on the wall, who are doomed with you to eat their own dung and drink their own urine?"

The first response by Hezekiah's three officers is no response at all. They can only appeal for the discreetness of diplomatic language (Aramaic) in-stead of common language (Hebrew), thus failing to address any substan-tive issue of the challenge. They only hope for containment that will prevent popular awareness of Judah's hopeless situation.

But of course, Assyria will have none of it. Part of the "war effort" is a campaign of propaganda. The rhetoric is designed to rob the crown of public confidence and therefore public support. Israel has known forever that fearfulness undermines the war effort (see Deut. 20:8). Indeed, even the Assyrian response to the request of Judah is more propaganda. Those outside of officialdom who hear are those who will suffer the consequences of siege, war, famine, and defeat, enough to be reduced to dependence upon the nourishment of bodily waste. The Assyrian response to Judah's objection continues the steady assault in a war of nerves.

36:13 Then the Rabshakeh stood and called out in a loud voice in the lan-guage of Judah, "Hear the words of the great king, the king of Assyria! 14 Thus says the king: 'Do not let Hezekiah deceive you, for he will not be able to deliver you. 15 Do not let Hezekiah make you rely on the LORD by saying, The LORD will surely deliver us; this city will not be given into the hand of the king of Assyria.' 16 Do not listen to Hezekiah; for thus says the king of As-syria: 'Make your peace with me and come out to me; then everyone of you will eat from your own vine and your own fig tree and drink water from your own cistern, 17 until I come and take you away to a land like your own land, a land of grain and wine, a land of bread and vineyards. 18 Do not let Hezekiah mislead you by saying, The LORD will save us. Has any of the gods of the nations saved their land out of the hand of the king of Assyria? 19 Where are the gods of Hamath and Arpad? Where are the gods of Sephar-vaim? Have they delivered Samaria out of my hand? 20 Who among all the

gods of these countries have saved their countries out of my hand, that the LORD should save Jerusalem out of my hand?' "

The second speech of Assyria, in precise defiance of the request of verse 11, is addressed to the populace and is in Hebrew, "the language of Judah." The empire goes over the head of the crown to the populace in order to split them off from the official policies of the crown, to undermine confidence in the war policies of Hezekiah. Hezekiah, "the good king," relies upon Yahweh. We have already seen in the first speech the assertion that Yahweh is no more reliable than is Egypt. Now the Assyrian seeks to refute the reliability of the king.

The speech is in three parts. First, in verse 15 there is an opening assertion of Yahweh's unreliability, directly challenging the primary claim of Zion theology that Yahweh will protect Jerusalem. Second, the Assyrian makes a positive counter offer (vv. 16–17). Judah is invited to "make your peace with," that is, *surrender!* The euphemism does not hide the reality. The surrender is a two-stage affair, stated in positive terms, but surely a threat. There will be an interim period of peace, with vine, fig tree, and water at home. The temporary arrangement is not unlike the modest, idyllic picture of Micah 4:2–4. But the long-term policy is deportation, in which the Assyrians are specialists. The people of Judah will be "taken away," removed from their own land, a policy to prevent rebellion against the empire after subjugation. The offer of *exile*, here mouthed as a generous offer of peace, is to a good land of grain, wine, bread, and vineyards. Such a vision of abundance, however, fails in its primary assumption. For the people of Judah, lands are not replaceable parts. No land could ever be an equivalent of this land. What is offered is nothing but exile, no matter how well it is voiced. Surely, any people would resist deportation away from its own land; but surely *this people*, heirs to *this land*, must refuse. Notice that the tradition, by this speech on the lips of a foreigner, has insinuated the threat of exile into the policy-making arena of Judah. The offer is a threat. The tradition knows where the destiny of Judah lies!

Now the Assyrian returns to the dismissal of Yahweh noted in verse 15 (vv. 18–20). Verses 18–20 are dominated by the verbs "deliver" and "save." Yahweh is a God who delivers, who saves, so Judah claims. But really! One cannot imagine a god who can deliver from Assyria, because Assyria is too strong, too brutal, too formidable. The speech proceeds by appeal to parallels. Assyria has a long record of conquering, and no god of any conquered people has withstood the empire—not Hamath, not Arpad, not Sepharvaim. And now surely not Samaria! The Assyrian has misunderstood the distinctiveness of the *land of Judah* in verse 17, imagining it like any other fertile land. And now the same speech misunderstands the distinctiveness of the *God of Judah*, who is like no other god. In the end, the parallels are worthless, because Yahweh is not comparable to the others. But the Assyrian does not know that. So far the text itself yields no hint of Yahweh's distinctiveness. The second speech draws the same conclusion as the first speech. Judah has no option—not a military one, not a Yahwistic one. The world must be accepted on demanding Assyrian terms.

> **36:21** But they were silent and answered him not a word, for the king's command was, "Do not answer him." **22** Then Eliakim son of Hilkiah, who was in charge of the palace, and Shebna the secretary, and Joah son of Asaph, the recorder, came to Hezekiah with their clothes torn, and told him the words of the Rabshakeh.

> **37:1** When King Hezekiah heard it, he tore his clothes, covered himself with sackcloth, and went into the house of the LORD. **2** And he sent Eliakim, who was in charge of the palace, and Shebna the secretary, and the senior priests, covered with sackcloth, to the prophet Isaiah son of Amoz. **3** They said to him, "Thus says Hezekiah, This day is a day of distress, of rebuke, and of disgrace; children have come to the birth, and there is no strength to bring them forth. **4** It may be that the LORD your God heard the words of the Rabshakeh, whom his master the king of Assyria has sent to mock the living God, and will rebuke the words that the LORD your God has heard; therefore lift up your prayer for the remnant that is left."

The response to the first speech was brief and subdued (vv. 11–12). Now the second speech draws closer home, and so the response is more elemental. It is made in three parts. First, the three royal officials are reduced to silence. The silence may be characteristic diplomatic discretion. More likely, they can think of nothing to say. The officials experience the dismissal of Yahweh as unanswerable, lacking as they do any ground for stating that Yahweh is unlike the other gods (vv. 21–22). They can only return to report to the king. They do so as defeatists, already dressed as grievers who have capitulated.

The second response to the second speech is made by the king himself (37:1–4). He shares with his advisers a sense of dismay. He also dresses himself for grief and defeat. But he does something more than his advisers do. He goes to the house of Yahweh. He is indeed the model of faith, for he refers the crisis to Yahweh. He does not accept that Yahweh is driven from the field as one of the other gods of the second speech. Rather,

Hezekiah continues to act in faith that acknowledges Yahweh as a continuing major player. He does not deny the seriousness of the crisis, and surely he also can see no way ahead. But he acts in faith that keeps Yahweh as his reference point.

His faith in Yahweh is not only a formal temple gesture. His faith more concretely extends to the prophetic. He dares to entertain the possibility that the prophet Isaiah can make a difference in a state crisis of staggering proportion. For him, the world is not closed against faith's impingement upon public reality. The hope now voiced is for the remnant. The remnant is the small piece of Judah not yet taken by Assyria. In the larger context of the book, the remnant is Judaism, surviving after exile and into the future. The God who has been mocked may move to act for the remnant. But such a move will take intercession. It will take prophetic intercession. Royalty depends on prophecy. Hezekiah must have Isaiah! Political realism finally yields, in this scenario, to prophetic faith!

> 37:5 **When the servants of King Hezekiah came to Isaiah, ⁶ Isaiah said to them, "Say to your master, 'Thus says the LORD: Do not be afraid because of the words that you have heard, with which the servants of the king of Assyria have reviled me. ⁷ I myself will put a spirit in him, so that he shall hear a rumor, and return to his own land; I will cause him to fall by the sword in his own land.'"**

The third response then is that of Isaiah (37:5–7). The response is to the needful petition of Isaiah, but it is as well a response to the Assyrian misconstrual of Yahweh. It is stunning that the prophet does not, as Hezekiah requests, utter a prayer. It is as though the prayer has already been uttered, and now the prophet speaks to the king Yahweh's *answer to prayer.* The divine answer to royal prayer given in prophetic utterance is a salvation oracle. The salvation oracle is characteristically an answer to complaint. So it is that verses 5–7 respond to verses 3–4, to dismiss the fear of the king and to bring the troubled king to confidence. Isaiah utters the most fundamental gospel words: *Do not fear.* The assurance of Yahweh overpowers the threat of the empire in this speech. Do not fear the policy or the speech of Assyria. Yahweh knows about the reviling, by being treated like other gods. Yahweh will not stay reviled. Yahweh will be Yahweh's incomparable self, good news for Hezekiah.

Now in a first-person utterance, the kind of first-person utterance none of the other gods could ever speak, Yahweh promises the complete nullification of the Assyrian threat: "I will put a spirit . . . I will cause him to fall" (v. 7).

The assertion ends with the dual refrain "his own land." The end of Sennacherib will not be in Judah but in Assyria. Sennacherib will hear a "rumor" and will rush home to trouble. There he will be killed. As is usual, the prophetic promise explains nothing, tells nothing about how this will happen. The details come later. Now all that is given is *divine resolve*. That, however, is enough. The king now knows about the *living God*. The living God has been mocked and knows it. The living God will not tolerate rivalry. The living God will move in decisive ways to recover honor. The living God will do exactly what Assyria had imagined could not happen. This Yahweh is no fiction of propaganda. The king and prophet rest upon a reality to which Assyria has no access. It is the world in which faith trumps fear. The Assyrian speeches intend to evoke fear. Now the hemorrhaging has stopped. The prophet provides the king an alternative basis for policy. Assyria, the great empire, cannot have its way.

37:8 **The Rabshakeh returned, and found the king of Assyria fighting against Libnah; for he had heard that the king had left Lachish.** [9] **Now the king heard concerning King Tirhakah of Ethiopia, "He has set out to fight against you." When he heard it, he sent messengers to Hezekiah, saying,** [10] **"Thus shall you speak to King Hezekiah of Judah: Do not let your God on whom you rely deceive you by promising that Jerusalem will not be given into the hand of the king of Assyria.** [11] **See, you have heard what the kings of Assyria have done to all lands, destroying them utterly. Shall you be delivered?** [12] **Have the gods of the nations delivered them, the nations that my predecessors destroyed, Gozan, Haran, Rezeph, and the people of Eden who were in Telassar?** [13] **Where is the king of Hamath, the king of Arpad, the king of the city of Sepharvaim, the king of Hena, or the king of Ivvah?"**

The third speech of the Assyrian traverses much of the same ground as the first two speeches. We may, however, notice three important differences. First, the apparently historical notice of the mobilization of Ethiopia against Assyria is perhaps designed to intensify Assyria's felt urgency. Second, the prophetic oracle of verses 5–7 perhaps permitted a different hearing of Assyrian taunting on the part of Judah, one with less fear. Assyria of course knows nothing of the oracle and would not in any case countenance it. Even if Judah hears differently, Assyria continues in its shameless bombast. Third and most important, the point of the third address is different. The second speech (36:13–20) is addressed to the populace and enjoins it not to be deceived by the king. Now in the third speech, the matter is escalated. It is addressed to the king, who is warned against the deception of Yahweh. This third speech concerns theological misrepresentation. Now the issue is *the character of Yahweh*, whom Assyria massively misperceives.

In this oracle we meet the recurrence of "rely" (v. 10), which dominated the first speech, and "deliver" (vv. 14, 15), which dominated the second speech. Again, by appeal to comparisons, the argument is that Judah has no more chance against Assyria than had Assyria's other enemies, because Yahweh is no more an effective god than the other gods who have been summarily defeated and humiliated.

This speech, unlike its predecessors, is aimed precisely at the king. Whereas the second speech asked defiantly, 'Where are the other gods?' now the question is, 'Where are the other kings?' And the answer is "nowhere." But of course Judah, in its listening, knows something Assyria does not. Not only is *Yahweh incomparable*, the answer to the second speech; the answer to the third speech is that Yahweh *has made promises to the house of David*. Hezekiah is left to ponder the difficult question: Does that promise persist? Can it be trusted? Is it operative in this crisis? Hezekiah must now decide, as must the reader.

37:14 **Hezekiah received the letter from the hand of the messengers and read it; then Hezekiah went up to the house of the LORD and spread it before the LORD. ¹⁵ And Hezekiah prayed to the LORD, saying: ¹⁶ "O LORD of hosts, God of Israel, who are enthroned above the cherubim, you are God, you alone, of all the kingdoms of the earth; you have made heaven and earth. ¹⁷ Incline your ear, O LORD, and hear; open your eyes, O LORD, and see; hear all the words of Sennacherib, which he has sent to mock the living God. ¹⁸ Truly, O LORD, the kings of Assyria have laid waste all the nations and their lands, ¹⁹ and have hurled their gods into the fire, though they were no gods, but the work of human hands—wood and stone—and so they were destroyed. ²⁰ So now, O LORD our God, save us from his hand, so that all the kingdoms of the earth may know that you alone are the LORD."**

The third speech to Judah by Assyria is in fact a letter, a formal diplomatic communique. Hezekiah's response is not directed to Assyria. Rather, as in verse 1, his response is to worship in the temple, a model of faith. Whereas in verse 4 the king had asked the prophet to pray, here he prays his own prayer. It is a characteristic prayer, a model case of true faith being brought to voice.

The prayer proceeds in three quite discrete, easily identified elements. It begins in *doxology* (v. 16). Praise is the foundation and context of faith. The doxology consists of a most formal title for Yahweh, bespeaking both

Yahweh's immense power and peculiar linkage to Israel. Moreover, it connects Yahweh directly to the Jerusalem temple, for "enthroned above the cherubim" is a reference to temple decor (see 1 Kings 6:23–28), and it then asserts that the powerful creator and governor of the world has no rivals and no competitors, and is indeed incomparable. It is of course this point that the Assyrians have failed completely to comprehend. The doxology as formal address to Yahweh functions as a motivation to Yahweh. In what follows, Yahweh is asked to act in the role of the unrivaled governor.

Second, the core section of the prayer is a *complaint* that describes in detail for God the negativity that Judah now endures. The doxology makes clear that Yahweh's power is not in doubt. What is always uncertain for Israel is Yahweh's attentiveness to the particular crisis, so that Yahweh can be mobilized to act. For that reason, a series of five imperatives urge Yahweh's attention: incline, hear, open, see, hear.

Yahweh is to focus upon Sennacherib, the real speaker of these three intolerable speeches. In these speeches, Assyria has mocked the living God (see v. 4) by failing to acknowledge Yahweh's incomparable capacity to act and generate life; that is, by failing to acknowledge the very claims made in the doxology of verse 16.

Assyria's affront, however, is not only mocking speech. The mocking speech is matched by violent military policy that has ravaged the entire world of the Fertile Crescent, devastating peoples and destroying gods. This part of the complaint is remarkable on two counts. First, it is readily assumed that "laying waste" the nations is indeed a concern to Yahweh, who is God "of all the kingdoms of the earth." What offends Yahweh is not only harsh treatment of Judah, but harsh treatment of other peoples, who are also Yahweh's peoples in Yahweh's care. The prayer thus circles back to the doxology and gives Yahweh's sovereignty world scope. But second and even more astonishing, the complaint describes for Yahweh the brutal destruction of the gods of the peoples. In many circumstances in the Old Testament, Yahweh would be glad to have these gods destroyed, but not here. Perhaps the prayer strains for data and so overstates the case against Assyria. But if the complaint is a serious one, then we are led to conclude that Yahweh is affronted by the destruction of the other gods, perhaps because an assault on any god, an assault on every god including Yahweh, is a blasphemous disregard of spiritual power. Or perhaps it may be suggested that the other gods are secondhand representations of Yahweh in those other lands—what might be called, after Karl Rahner, "latent Yahwism." The text itself is not reflective on the point; the petition is a strange one, inviting our own continued reflection.

The prayer concludes, third, with the *petition* for which *doxology* and *complaint* have prepared the way (v. 20). The petition is dominated by the imperative "save"; that is, act in power to make us safe. The prayer indicates that the intimidation attempted by Assyria has not worked. The king, a model of faith, does indeed rely upon Yahweh, for Yahweh is not to be slotted along with gods who have elsewhere failed. This God is the only God, the only one of its kind, the only God who can be addressed by faith with an imperative, the only God with force enough to counter the empire.

The king knows, already in verse 16, that Yahweh *alone* is God, no rivals, no competitors, no comparisons. If Jerusalem is saved from Assyria, however, then the kingdoms of the earth will also come to know and acknowledge Yahweh. The nations are already governed by Yahweh, but they do not know it or acknowledge it. Thus the petition is surely on behalf of Judah and the dynasty. More than that, it also serves the "evangelism" of Yahweh. Thus the last phrase, in looking back to the doxology, functions as an additional motivation for Yahweh. Along with *Judah's well-being* will come *Yahweh's enhancement*. Such a "knowing" among the nations might halt arrogant speeches like those of Assyria and might impede brutalizing policies like those of the empire. The rescue of Judah is a maneuver in bringing the whole world to the rule of Yahweh. So speaks insistent faith.

I PLANNED FROM THE DAYS OF OLD
37:21–38

These verses, which present a prophetic response to the royal prayer of verses 16–20, are in fact a continuation of the rich exchange of 36:1–37:20. I have treated them in a distinct section, partly so that the section is not too long to manage, but primarily because the prophetic response beginning in verse 21 marks a decisive turn in the discourse. No longer does Assyria speak, and no longer is Yahweh mocked. Now a turn has been made so that Yahweh is from this point on in the chapter the single, dominating voice of sovereignty. In 37:5–7 the prophet had already delivered to the king the decisive promise of a salvation oracle that assured that Sennacherib, the Assyrian king, would not prevail over Jerusalem. In the present verses, we are given three prophetic responses in sequence: an extended poetic oracle addressed to Sennacherib (vv. 22–29), an announcement of a sign concerning the future well-being of Jerusalem (vv. 30–32), and a remarkable oracle guaranteeing the well-being of Jerusalem (vv. 33–35). These three assurances are quite distinct units and had no original relation to each other. They do, nonetheless, in their present arrangement offer a unified affirmation. The whole of the prophetic assurance is confirmed in the historical notice of verses 36–38.

Yahweh as the God of the Assyrians (37:21–29)

> 37:21 Then Isaiah son of Amoz sent to Hezekiah, saying: "Thus says the LORD, the God of Israel: Because you have prayed to me concerning King Sennacherib of Assyria, ²² this is the word that the LORD has spoken concerning him:
>
>> She despises you, she scorns you—
>>> virgin daughter Zion;
>> she tosses her head—behind your back,
>>> daughter Jerusalem.
>
>> ²³ Whom have you mocked and reviled?
>>> Against whom have you raised your voice
>> and haughtily lifted your eyes?
>>> Against the Holy One of Israel!
>> ²⁴ By your servants you have mocked the Lord,
>>> and you have said, 'With my many chariots
>> I have gone up the heights of the mountains,
>>> to the far recesses of Lebanon;
>> I felled its tallest cedars,
>>> its choicest cypresses;
>> I came to its remotest height,
>>> its densest forest.
>> ²⁵ I dug wells
>>> and drank waters,
>> I dried up with the sole of my foot
>>> all the streams of Egypt.'
>
>> ²⁶ Have you not heard
>>> that I determined it long ago?
>> I planned from days of old
>>> what now I bring to pass,
>> that you should make fortified cities
>>> crash into heaps of ruins,
>> ²⁷ while their inhabitants, shorn of strength,

are dismayed and confounded;
they have become like plants of the field
   and like tender grass,
like grass on the housetops,
   blighted before it is grown.

²⁸ I know your rising up and your sitting down,
   your going out and coming in,
   and your raging against me.
²⁹ Because you have raged against me
   and your arrogance has come to my ears,
I will put my hook in your nose
   and my bit in your mouth;
I will turn you back on the way
   by which you came.

This poem is formally a response to Hezekiah from God (v. 21), but substantively it is addressed to the king of Assyria, who has violently threatened Zion. The poem begins in verse 22 with an assertion to Sennacherib that Jerusalem detests him. This statement functions as an opening denunciation of the king as an overture for what follows; it also asserts that Jerusalem has not been cowed or intimidated by the harsh rhetoric of the empire. This characterization of Jerusalem's attitude toward Assyria suggests some considerable buoyancy, no doubt enhanced by confidence in Yahweh who is stronger than Sennacherib, though appeal to the Yahweh connection is not here explicit.

   The two rhetorical questions state the harsh indictment of Sennacherib. The verbs "mock" and "revile" (v. 23) reach back to the statement of Hezekiah (v. 4) and the oracle of Isaiah (v. 6). One might expect that after verse 21 the subject of Sennacherib's belittling would be Judah and Jerusalem. But the stakes are now much higher. Sennacherib has been more daring, for the subject of the belittling has been none other than *The Holy One of Israel*. Indeed, the Assyrian king has dismissed Yahweh by comparing Yahweh to the no-gods of other peoples. Yahweh is mocked by not being recognized as the incomparable *living God*. It is Sennacherib's arrogance and pride that have prevented him from knowing what he should have known about Yahweh.

   The long statement of verses 24–25, placed in the mouth of Sennacherib, gives content to the charge of mockery. The verses are dominated by first-person pronouns, as though Sennacherib were the dominant player in the geopolitical process. The rich assertion of "I, I, I" is a staggering acting out whereby Sennacherib does not say "Thou" to Yahweh and does not recognize that it is Yahweh and not himself who is the initiator in the public process. The "I" of the Assyrian king has acted completely without restraint, without noticing the purposes of Yahweh, without regard for the well-being of the environment, without limit to the reckless use of natural resources. This lack of restraint, characteristic of unbridled superpowers, is expressed as military adventurism, as the destruction of trees, as the manipulation of water in an arid climate, until the Assyrian king claims to dominate even the Nile, the ultimate source of life. Sennacherib is the cipher for every shameless military power that imagines it can operate without restraint on the abuse of the environment and on the brutal exploitation of the population. Indeed, the mention of the Nile may be a hint that Assyria has now taken over the representative role of pharaoh as the quintessence of anti-Yahwism as a spiritual force. The poem is arranged for Sennacherib's self-indictment.

The question of verse 26, perhaps parallel to the questions of verse 23, breaks up the pattern of boasting in verses 24–25. The right answer to the question of verse 23 is "The Holy One of Israel." In parallel fashion, the question of verse 26 leads to the entry of Yahweh into the rhetoric. Now Sennacherib is confronted with an alternative "I," the self-assertion of Yahweh who easily and categorically trumps the "I" of Assyrian arrogance. If Sennacherib can do the deeds of verses 24–25, consider what the holy "I" of Yahweh can do! The divine self-assertion of verses 26–29 is dominated, in the first instance, by the two powerful verbs of verse 26: "I determined"; "I planned." The verbs are stronger than the NRSV suggests. The career of Sennacherib was not only planned and thought, it was effected long ago by this acting, decisive, creating God. It was Yahweh who caused Sennacherib to destroy cities. It was Yahweh who caused conquered inhabitants to be reduced to dismay, making them vulnerable and shriveled. All Assyrian success is authored by Yahweh. All the things Sennacherib brags about are the work of Yahweh. The governing question of verse 26 is in fact a scolding: Have you not heard yet? Sennacherib should have heard. Everybody except Sennacherib already has heard and knows!

The statement of Yahweh in verses 28–29 runs beyond the intended mandate of verses 26–27. Yahweh is the one from whom no secret can be hid (v. 28). Yahweh knows all about Sennacherib, all his ventures, all his plans, all his success, all his outrageous boasting. Indeed, Yahweh knows all about Sennacherib's restless defiance of Yahweh. The strong term "rage" is used twice. Yahweh knows about Sennacherib's self-importance, autonomy, and pride. Yahweh knows that Sennacherib has run well beyond his mandate. The violation is not that he has abused Judah (see 10:6–7), but that he has imagined himself beyond the governance of Yahweh (see 10:15).

The indictment is the indictment Yahweh characteristically asserts against unrestrained superpowers. And so follows the sentence, dominated by yet two more first-person verbs: "I will put"; "I will turn" (v. 29). Yahweh will bring Sennacherib under control; Yahweh will "break" Sennacherib the way a wild horse must be broken. Yahweh calls off the Assyrian incursion into Jerusalem and causes Sennacherib to return home. This later verdict echoes verse 7 and anticipates verses 36–38. The intended mandate of Sennacherib given by Yahweh is in verses 26–27. The violation of that mandate, however, leads to the severe curbing of Assyrian maneuvers. The rule of Yahweh will eliminate the Assyrian threat to Jerusalem. The poem is set up to show the will of Yahweh and the will of Assyria in conflict. According to the claim of this text, it is no contest. Yahweh ends up as subject of all the decisive verbs.

A Product of Yahweh's Zeal
(37:30–32)

> 37:30 **"And this shall be the sign for you: This year eat what grows of itself, and in the second year what springs from that; then in the third year sow, reap, plant vineyards, and eat their fruit.** 31 **The surviving remnant of the house of Judah shall again take root downward, and bear fruit upward;** 32 **for from Jerusalem a remnant shall go out, and from Mount Zion a band of survivors. The zeal of the LORD of hosts will do this.**

This report of a sign seems to parallel the sign offered to Ahaz in 7:14–17. The sign itself is not very clear. It seems to suggest that because of devastation, agriculture will cease in the first year after the devastation, and in the second year only volunteer crops will produce food. Only in the third year will serious farm produce resume. Thus the sign, not unlike the sign to Ahaz, sets a time frame on the devastation, asserting a limit to the destruction Assyria may do.

Two other matters in the paragraph may be noted. First, in verses 31 and 32 the announcement twice uses the term "remnant" and twice the term "survivor." This double usage is faithful to the expectation of the Isaiah tradition that after devastation through foreign invasion—first by Assyria, then by Babylon—surviving Judaism will be only a fragment of the original community. We have seen that such a notion can be a threat—*only a remnant.* Here the same assertion is a promise—*there will be a surviving community.*

The second observation concerns the final phrasing concerning "the zeal of the Lord." The phrase is taken directly from 9:7. In the long run it is Yahweh's passion—for David as in 9:7, for Judah, for Jerusalem—that will guarantee this surviving community. Although the phrase seems an addition, it is congruent with the entire prophetic poem. Sennacherib imagined he would stride the world as he pleased. What he did not count on was Yahweh's resilient resolve and passion that every time will outflank the superpower. This zeal is the ground for Judaism's well-being in time to come.

For My Own Sake (37:33–35)

> 37:33 **"Therefore thus says the LORD concerning the king of Assyria: He shall not come into this city, shoot an arrow there, come before it with a shield, or cast up a siege ramp against it. 34 By the way that he came, by the same he shall return; he shall not come into this city, says the LORD. 35 For I will defend this city to save it, for my own sake and for the sake of my servant David."**

The oracle reiterates the assurances concerning Jerusalem given in verses 6–7, 29. Sennacherib was aimed precisely toward Jerusalem. His own annals attest that Jerusalem is the prize he has yet to take. Hezekiah, moreover, recognized the exposed place of Jerusalem's jeopardy. From the perspectives of both Sennacherib and Hezekiah, the military fate of Jerusalem needs only to be played out. However, there is yet the purpose of Yahweh who *does and forms.* And there is prophetic utterance of that purpose that disrupts both the resolve of Sennacherib and the fear of Hezekiah. The inevitable course of history is to watch the destruction of the city. Only now, "the inevitable" is defeated. The intervention of the superpower is not inevitable because there is a more elemental resolve at work. Sennacherib will not succeed. He cannot win. He will go home without victory.

Sennacherib will not succeed because Yahweh will protect the city and deliver it. The prophetic tradition testifies to a purpose other than the evident one. It is a purpose lodged in God's holiness and is available only in prophetic utterance. A "prophetic view" of history does not rest the future upon the achievements of zealous human persons. Rather, there is a purpose not contained within our common historical explanations. In the end, a trust in "biblical authority," in this context, consists in affirmation of this seemingly outrageous claim.

The ground for this resolve is Yahweh's zeal (see v. 32). Yahweh will protect Jerusalem "for my sake" (v. 35). It is as though Yahweh has a vested interest in the well-being of the city as Yahweh's own natural habitat. This claim represents the core truth of Zion theology. But as always, the claim of Zion is linked to the claim of David (see Psalm 78:68–72). It is for David's sake, for the sake of the dynasty. God's ancient commitment to the dynasty operates (see 2 Sam. 7:1–17; Psalm 89:3–37). This utterance is the extreme use in Isaiah of David theology. This uncompromising resolve is the antidote to hostile imperial strategy. It is a strange mismatch, but this tradition does not flinch in its claim, even against the formidable imperial presence.

An Angelic Deliverance (37:36–38)

37:36 **Then the angel of the LORD set out and struck down one hundred eighty-five thousand in the camp of the Assyrians; when morning dawned, they were all dead bodies.** [37] **Then King Sennacherib of Assyria left, went home, and lived at Nineveh.** [38] **As he was worshiping in the house of his god Nisroch, his sons Adrammelech and Sharezer killed him with the sword, and they escaped into the land of Ararat. His son Esar-haddon succeeded him.**

These verses purport to be historical documentation, and indeed they do correspond, to some degree, with Assyrian records. In this context, however, they are intended as more than history, serving to confirm prophetic utterance. In verses 6–7, 29, 33–35, the prophetic assurance concerns the well-being of the city. And now it is so! It is accomplished by "the angel of Yahweh," which means that historical agency is hidden and inscrutable, but freighted with holy power. That is, the tradition scarcely knows how to say what must be said.

The oddity is that this inscrutability effects the real world of power. The king went home, short of success, perhaps to quell a rebellion. The king of Nineveh, like the king of Jerusalem, is a pious person, as are all kings. He also worships, not unlike Hezekiah. However, unlike Hezekiah, he receives no prophetic assurance. What he receives instead is murder from within his own family. The throne passes to his son Esar-haddon, perhaps a party to the bloody coup. But the affairs of Assyrian politics are no concern of our tradition.

What counts is that Zion is delivered. The king in Jerusalem is safe. The city is rescued. The prophet is vindicated. The miraculous deliverance of the city in 701—done by Yahweh's angel—is the pivot point in the tradition of Isaiah and surely a decisive reference point in Judah's self-understanding. Judah is able to imagine that it has received a "safe conduct" in the midst of the vagaries of imperial power. The moment of deliverance is surely one to savor, vindicating Isaiah's urging of faith. The moment of well-being reaches back into the oldest liturgical claims of Jerusalem in order to assert: "God is our refuge and strength,/a very present help in trouble./Therefore we will not fear" (Psalm 46:1–2a).

It is plausible to imagine, as well, that this staggering time of affirmation that exhibits Yahweh as the governor of imperial processes now becomes the source and engine of subsequent false confidence. It was the Jerusalem leadership, surely with the deliverance of 701 directly available, who can say: "'Peace, peace,' when there is no peace" (Jer. 6:14; 8:11; Ezek. 13:10). It was more than likely this same miracle that beguiled Hananiah a century later into a false judgment (see Jer. 28:3–4).

The miracle is a source of powerful assurance in Judah. It was as well a source of costly self-deception. Statements against that self-deception came only later. For now, the tradition invites only wonder, amazement, and gratitude. The Isaiah tradition offers a peculiar view of history. This time it worked visibly. Faith is indeed the victory that has overcome the world.

FAITHFUL KING, FAITHFUL GOD
38:1–22

This chapter is preoccupied with the sickness of King Hezekiah, who, we have seen, is presented as a model of piety and fidelity to Yahweh. The text consists of a transaction between king and prophet concerning the illness (vv. 1–8), a song of thanksgiving offered to Yahweh by the recovered king (vv. 9–20), and finally two enigmatic verses that in fact offer no conclusion (vv. 21–22). The primary affirmation of the text is that there is *an inscrutable healing* wrought by the power of Yahweh through the good offer of the prophet.

The text as we have it does not read easily. When it is compared with the parallel account of 2 Kings 20, one gains the impression that some elements of the text may here be disordered. Thus it is asserted in verse 9, after the "sign" of verses 7–8, that the king is healed. Indeed, the poem of verses 9–20 (which does not occur in the parallel narrative of 2 Kings 20) is a song of thanksgiving (see v. 19) that characteristically is uttered only after healing. And yet in verse 21 the prophet now undertakes what may have been a conventional medical practice "that he may recover," suggesting that recovery for the king is still anticipated. Verse 22, moreover, has the king ask for a sign, though the sign of healing is already given in verse 7.

In any case, the main narrative line of the chapter is not difficult to trace. It concerns the dramatic movement *from sickness to healing* by way of prophetic intervention, which evokes a response of gratitude on the part of the king. This same sequence is the standard plot line of "narratives of miracle" in the ministry of Elijah and Elisha and is the pattern of lament Psalms and songs of complaint in the Psalter. That in itself would be enough to see that Hezekiah, the good king, prospers and has his life extended because of the special attentiveness of Yahweh. Seitz goes further, on the basis of verse 6, to suggest that the healing of Hezekiah is a foreshadowing of the *healing of Jerusalem*. It is the "sick city" (cf. 1:6) that becomes the healed city by prophetic intervention. Either way, this narrative reflects the accents of Davidic theology that presents the well-being of the king as pivotal for the faith of Hezekiah, the consequence of the faithfulness of Yahweh. In the end, the king can affirm as does faithful Israel, "The Lord will save me" (v. 20). The response (v. 20) is inescapably doxology sung in the temple:

> The LORD will save me,
>> and we will sing to stringed instruments
> all the days of our lives,
>> at the house of the LORD.

A Sign to the Faithful, Sick King (38:1–8)

This narrative unit consists of a prophetic verdict (v. 1), a royal petition (vv. 2–3) and a divine oracle (vv. 4–6), followed by a prophetic sign of assurance (vv. 7–8).

38:1 **In those days Hezekiah became sick and was at the point of death. The prophet Isaiah son of Amoz came to him, and said to him, "Thus says the LORD: Set your house in order, for you shall die; you shall not recover."** **2 Then Hezekiah turned his face to the wall, and prayed to the LORD: 3 "Remember now, O LORD, I implore you, how I have walked before you in faithfulness with a whole heart, and have done what is good in your sight." And Hezekiah wept bitterly.**

⁴ Then the word of the LORD came to Isaiah: ⁵ "Go and say to Hezekiah, Thus says the LORD, the God of your ancestor David: I have heard your prayer, I have seen your tears; I will add fifteen years to your life. ⁶ I will deliver you and this city out of the hand of the king of Assyria, and defend this city.

The narrative introduction creates the scene of crisis: The king is sick to death. The prophet Isaiah, who has ready access to the royal presence, confirms that the king is terminally ill (v. 1). There is no hint that the illness and impending death are punishment. The situation is simply a given necessary to the narrative, though the prophetic oracle confirms that Yahweh is lord of life and of death.

The verdict of the prospect of death evokes a prayer of lament on the lips of the king (vv. 2–3). We are not told what it means that the king "turned his face to the wall." Most likely the act bespeaks discouragement, sadness, and defeat. In any case, the king does what any faithful Israelite would do; he submits his need to Yahweh in petitioning prayer. We have already observed "the good king" as a man of prayer (37:4, 15–20). The king is deeply embedded in the petitionary cadences of Israel and knows how to pray. He prays a prayer of petition. Oddly, however, the prayer is truncated in its articulation. There is not even a petition for healing. All that is uttered is a statement of Hezekiah's fidelity that functions as a motivation. That is, Hezekiah's piety provides for Yahweh a ground and reason for answering with healing. Hezekiah identifies himself as *faithful*, with a "whole heart," one who does good. In the textual parallel of 2 Kings 18:5, the positive verdict on the piety of the kings is even more fully voiced:

> He trusted in the LORD the God of Israel; so that there was no one like him among all the kings of Judah after him, or among those who were before him. For he held fast to the LORD; he did not depart from following him but kept the commandments that the LORD commanded Moses (2 Kings 18:5–6).

It is clear that the prayer operates on the assumption that such virtue may expect positive response from Yahweh, even if it is not a strict quid-pro-quo transaction.

And indeed, the response of Yahweh suggests that the prayer and tears of dependence have moved God to a fresh decision. Thus Isaiah speaks a second time, to nullify the verdict of verse 1 (vv. 4–6). It is made explicit that *the prayer of the king* has changed *the inclination of Yahweh*. Prayer is not simply a subjective act of emotional posturing and submissiveness. It impinges upon God. The divine assurance takes place through four verbs: I have heard, I have seen, I will add, I will deliver. The sequence of verbs is a determined resolve on Yahweh's part, not unlike the series of verbs in Exodus 2:24–25 and 3:7.

Two important matters may be noted. First, the promise "to add" is a remarkable one, indicating that the "times" of the king are "in God's hand" (see Psalm 31:15). God's generosity in response to piety adds to Hezekiah's life. (See the same pattern in 1 Kings 21:27–29 concerning Ahab.) Second, the last verb "deliver" pushes the promise beyond the personal fate of the king to "this city." The phrase extends this narrative about royal illness and recovery to the destiny of Jerusalem, echoing the promise of 37:35 and linking this chapter to chapters 36—37. The prayer of Hezekiah evokes God's new acts for king and for city. The promise of Yahweh is not doubted. What is at issue is the prayer that can evoke and mobilize Yahweh's good generosity. That generosity is always there; it only needs to be triggered, as it can be by a pious king.

38:7 "This is the sign to you from the LORD, that the LORD will do this thing that he has promised: ⁸ See, I will make the shadow cast by the declining sun on the dial of Ahaz turn back ten steps." So the sun turned back on the dial the ten steps by which it had declined.

The oracle of assurance to Hezekiah and to "this city" would seem to be complete in verse 6. Verse 7 appears to stand alone, almost as an addition. The pious Hezekiah did not need a sign in order to trust Yahweh and did not ask for one. In chapter 7, we have seen that King Ahaz disputatiously negotiated about a sign from Yahweh. There is none of that disputatiousness here. The sign is simply an extra gift of Yahweh to the king whom Yahweh highly regards and whom Yahweh is eager to reassure.

A sign is a freighted happening that is taken by the faithful as an underscoring assurance. In this case the sign does not closely match the assurance of verses 5–6, except that both sign and oracle concern time. The oracle adds fifteen years to the life of the king; the sign adds time to daylight before the sun sets. The "natural act" is taken as a signal that Yahweh can indeed disrupt the normal flow of time in order to fulfill a quite specific promise. That is, in behalf of the king, Yahweh makes "time stand still." There is no point in "explaining" this odd event. We deal here with the creator of heaven and earth, the governor of all the seasons, who guarantees the regularities of life (cf. Gen. 8:22), but who may disrupt those regularities on specific occasions. The most dramatic such "disruption," perhaps echoed here, is the miracle of "the sun stood still" (Josh. 10:12–14), in order to allow the armies of Israel time to win a victory. Healing is in any case a miracle that outruns scientific explanation. Here the miracle of healing is connected to the immediate hands-on governance of Yahweh. The sign, bespeaking God's powerful sovereignty, attests to the reliability of the oracle just uttered.

Thanks to the Faithful God
(38:9–20)

The poem of thanksgiving on the lips of the king was probably inserted here after having existed as an independent poem. It is not present in the parallel account of 2 Kings 20; the capacity of the editorial process to insert such poems into narrative is evident, moreover, in 1 Samuel 2:1–10 and Jonah 2:2–9. In this case, the poem fits nicely, for thanksgiving is apparently on the lips of the king after the oracle of assurance (vv. 5–6) and the accompanying sign (v. 7).

38:9 **A writing of King Hezekiah of Judah, after he had been sick and had recovered from his sickness:**
10 **I said: In the noontide of my days**
I must depart;
I am consigned to the gates of Sheol
for the rest of my years.
11 **I said, I shall not see the LORD**
in the land of the living;
I shall look upon mortals no more
among the inhabitants of the world.
12 **My dwelling is plucked up and removed from me**
like a shepherd's tent;
like a weaver I have rolled up my life;
he cuts me off from the loom;
from day to night you bring me to an end;
13 **I cry for help until morning;**
like a lion he breaks all my bones;
from day to night you bring me to an end.

14 **Like a swallow or a crane I clamor,**
I moan like a dove.
My eyes are weary with looking upward.
O Lord, I am oppressed; be my security!
15 **But what can I say? For he has spoken to me,**

> and he himself has done it.
> All my sleep has fled
> because of the bitterness of my soul.

The introduction makes it appear that the prayer of the king is a formal production (v. 9). The verse may reflect the practice of "writing letters to the gods." The prayer is a song of thanksgiving, characteristically offered after a positive intervention by God, in this case healing, though a poem like Jonah 2, offered as a confident prospect, may be placed in the narrative before the rescue.

It is usual in a song of thanksgiving to review the past trouble in order that present well-being may be more fully celebrated as a contrast. Thus the speaker not only describes the past misery but may also report on past prayers of petition offered to God in order to move God to act. In these verses, the king as the speaker remembers what he thought and what he said in the midst of his acute trouble. It is clear that the king had abandoned hope and had arrived at resignation, acknowledging that death would come, that he would "depart and be removed" (vv. 10–12a).

The most striking rhetorical feature of this complaint is the fivefold use of simile employed to voice richly and densely what the sense of impending death is like (vv. 12–14). Thus his life is *like* a shepherd's tent, fragile and easily dispatched; his life is *like* woven material cut off from the loom. God is *like* a lion who crushes; the king is *like* a crying bird, *like* a moaning dove. His life with God is not any of these; it is *like* these in that it is vexed, troubled, under threat, and in jeopardy.

The speaker dares to make a plea: "Bail me out!" (v. 14). The image is juridical. The king asks God to pay what it would cost to free him of the bondage of death. The prayer, however, is fleeting, for in verse 15, Hezekiah admits defeat. Yahweh has done it. There is no recourse. All is lost.

38:16 **O Lord, by these things people live,**
> **and in all these is the life of my spirit.**
> **Oh, restore me to health and make me live!**
> [17] **Surely it was for my welfare**
> **that I had great bitterness;**
> **but you have held back my life**
> **from the pit of destruction,**
> **for you have cast all my sins behind your back.**
> [18] **For Sheol cannot thank you,**
> **death cannot praise you;**
> **those who go down to the Pit cannot hope**

for your faithfulness.
¹⁹ The living, the living, they thank you,
    as I do this day;
fathers make known to children
    your faithfulness.

²⁰ The LORD will save me
    and we will sing to stringed instruments
all the days of our lives,
    at the house of the LORD.

Having conceded the destructive enmity of the lion-God, the speaker nonetheless must appeal to that same God for succor. The movement from verses 10–15 to verses 16–20 is characteristic of these songs of thanksgiving. It may be that the complaint is strategy, to prepare for the petition that follows. But theologically, the prayer recognizes that the one who causes the jeopardy is the only one who can deliver from the threat. Kaiser understands the problematic well:

> As in the case of Job, he is smitten by God himself, and can only appeal to God against God (cf. Job 9:13ff. and 19:6ff.). The poet is well aware that this is the real difficulty for the petitioner, if he is to turn to God in his distress. What can he say to him who himself has caused his suffering, and is not just anyone, but is Yahweh himself? (*Isaiah 13–39*, 406)

Verse 16 is a twofold petition: "restore . . . make me live." Even in resignation, the speaker does not doubt that God can override the threat of death. Even though the speaker has concluded that he will not be "in the land of the living" (v. 11), nonetheless he dares to pray for life.

Verses 17–19 move tersely through a series of moods. First, in verse 17, it is acknowledged that the suffering was in the service of well-being, for in fact God has not given his life over to death and has indeed pardoned his sin. That is, the speaker affirms that what God has done is not God's "alien work" (see 28:21) but is a show of God's good intention. Second, verse 18 voices what is a studied motivation for God, suggesting that God has fended off death, because the dead do not thank or praise or hope or witness to God's faithfulness. The motivation is characteristic of this kind of prayer and seeks to find something in the rescue that benefits God as well as the sufferer. Verse 18 seems to provide the grounds on which God has kept the king from death.

In verse 17, what interests us most is that the motivation suggests that God wants people to hope in God's faithfulness. The use of the term "faithfulness" in verses 18 and 19 is, I suggest, the pivot point of the passage. The healing results from God's faithfulness that endures into and through deathliness. It cannot be unimportant that Yahweh's faithfulness here moves beyond the king's faithfulness (same word; v. 3) that could not save. Yahweh's reliability is more fundamental, more elemental, more decisive. The linkage of *Hezekiah's faithfulness* to *the faithfulness of God* is not unlike *human righteousness* juxtaposed to *God's righteousness*, which Luther noticed in Psalm 143:1–2. The rescue of the king is rooted in the very character of God. The king has no other appeal and needs none.

Finally, the doxological conclusion is drawn in verse 18, as it characteristically is in a song of thanksgiving. The king who was sick to death now is among the living. God had "held back my life" for "the land of the living." It is the *gift of life* now affirmed and guaranteed that becomes the supreme gift of God and the ground for gratitude. The living—those not given over to death—give thanks. The thanks is to give voice to Yahweh's fidelity, which is the powerful alternative to death. There can be no ultimate claim made by death, and it is this that faithful Israel teaches its young. Notice, the poem has turned away from the king and his illness. The king no longer interests us. The real subject is Yahweh and Yahweh's fidelity.

Verse 20 seems to summarize the entire poem: *God saves/we sing*. What else could Israel do with such a miracle but to sing in pre-rational exuberance! No calculation about miracles, no explanation—only glad ceding of life over to the Lord of life!

Odd Healing, Odd Question (38:21–22)

> 38:21 **Now Isaiah had said, "Let them take a lump of figs, and apply it to the boil, so that he may recover."** [22] **Hezekiah also had said, "What is the sign that I shall go up to the house of the LORD?"**

These two verses seem odd in their placement, perhaps being mislocated in the editorial process. Verse 21 shows the prophet engaging in what must have been routine, hands-on remedial work. This is strange in that we have already learned in verse 9 that the king is healed. The question of Hezekiah in verse 22 is a wonderment about a sign, but the decisive sign has been given in verse 7. Moreover, the question is not answered. The two verses are completely enigmatic. We note only that the king's wonderment concerns the temple. As a pious king, he is one for whom the temple is a delight (see 37:1, 14). We can imagine Hezekiah saying:

> Surely goodness and mercy shall follow me
>   all the days of my life,
> and I shall dwell in the house of the LORD
>   my whole life long.
>
> (Psalm 23:6)

The whole of the chapter is odd and unclear. What is clear is that the king in his piety must fully entrust life to the faithful God from whom comes healing and a chance for life. As for the king, so for the prophet. Jerusalem has been a city sick to death (1:6). And now healing! The tradition of Israel moves to gratitude, to thanks for the gift of life it could hardly expect. The gift of God outruns the expectation of Israel that at times borders on resignation. The prophet has urged that Judah must have faith and must trust. That faith is visible in the piety of a good king. But Yahweh's faithfulness, Judah's true hope, is well beyond even the piety of the good king. Life in "the house of the Lord" is a match and meeting of faithful king and faithful God. The future depends upon that match.

AN ANTICIPATED ENDING
39:1–8

This concluding narrative of "First Isaiah" is likely rooted in a historical event. Scholars suggest that in perhaps 703 (that is, before the miraculous deliverance of the city in 701), Hezekiah was engaged in "coalition diplomacy." As a party to such policy, Babylon may have been a restless subordinate of Assyria and ready to cooperate with Hezekiah in resistance to Babylon. Such a diplomatic-military mission might indeed be conducted as reported here, with a friendly welcome and a joint review of resources and plans.

The narrative is introduced by reference to the healing of chapter 38, reported here as known in the international community. The reference is perhaps an editorial device for linking that "internal" narrative to this "external" one. The narrative of chapter 39 is divided into two parts, royal hosting of allies (vv. 1–4) and prophetic intrusion (vv. 5–8). Thus the narrative is credible as historical documentation.

It is generally agreed, however, that whatever the historical foundation of the narrative may be, the text now functions in the structure of the book of Isaiah to conclude the long account of "First Isaiah" and the Assyrian threat. Thus the chapter serves to admit *Babylon* into the horizon of the book (see 13:1–14:23; 21:1–10), a coming superpower that will dominate Judah's life and that will evoke the coming chapters of Isaiah. The chapter now functions not as an eighth-century account but as a prelude to the sixth century, the destruction of Jerusalem, and the termination of the Davidic dynasty. The illness and recovery of Hezekiah, however, may be read symbolically to refer to the time of *exile* of Judah and to its long-term *expectation of homecoming*. Thus, what appears to be a straightforward royal narrative is likely more complex and complicated in its present canonical function.

A Welcome to Babylon (39:1–2)

39:1 **At that time King Merodach-baladan son of Baladan of Babylon sent envoys with letters and a present to Hezekiah, for he heard that he had been sick and had recovered.** 2 **Hezekiah welcomed them; he showed them his treasure house, the silver, the gold, the spices, the precious oil, his whole armory, all that was found in his storehouses. There was nothing in his house or in all his realm that Hezekiah did not show them.**

Although the Babylonian king may be more precisely identified, it is necessary only to recognize that he is a Babylonian and thus a long-term antecedent to Nebuchadrezzar, who will finally bring disaster on Jerusalem and its ruling dynasty (see 2 Kings 24:10–17). The introduction of this royal character introduces at the same time an ominous note into the narrative that runs well beyond eighth-century documentation. Judah must now get used to Babylonians who will move in and take over. The reader is put on notice that we must know more about Babylon than the innocent and celebrative Hezekiah can yet recognize.

The representatives of Babylon come to Jerusalem bringing "a present" (= tribute). This need not mean that Hezekiah is the stronger party to the relationship, but only that it is good diplomatic form to come with a gift in hand. Hezekiah shows them everything. He reveals to them the revenues and resources of his treasure house, the exotic goods of his commercial enterprise, all his storehouse as well as his armory. He reviews with them the extent and limit of every facet of royal splendor. The Babylonians are able to assess completely how much of an effective ally (or adversary) Jerusalem may be. The narrative underscores the point: Everything was made available!

It is not easy to determine either Hezekiah's motivation or how the narrative intends us to assess the king. The review of resources may have been a routine act of policy making. However, if we remember that in every international relationship the pattern of alliance and opposition changes often and quickly, we may judge that he committed a serious breach of security and discretion by disclosing too much to an ally not yet proven to be reliable.

Beyond what may be a decision that is foolish for a pragmatic practice of policy, we may also wonder about the theological intention of the narrative. It is clear that Hezekiah is pleased about his resources and eager to exhibit them. No theological judgment is explicit, but one may conclude that he is excessively proud, excessively dependent upon his resources, and is indeed boasting of his wealth and effectiveness, flexing his muscle, much like his exhibitionist predecessor Solomon (cf. 1 Kings 10:1–13).

If we are willing to go beyond *pragmatic foolishness* to an implicit *theological verdict*, it may be inferred that Hezekiah has in fact turned from Yahweh to more concrete and familiar forms of security. If that either/or is implied, then we may anticipate the savage contrast made by Jeremiah:

> Do not let the wise boast in their wisdom, do not let the mighty boast in their might, do not let the wealthy boast in their wealth; but let those who boast boast in this, that they understand and know me, that I am the LORD; I act with steadfast love, justice, and righteousness in the earth, for in these things I delight, says the LORD (Jer. 9:23–24).

One may detect here cadences of the regular polemic against a self-sufficient monarchy, too impressed with its own achievements, slowly but decisively turned away from Yahweh. Such a reading may be against the grain of the otherwise pious Hezekiah. Such seduction, however, is slow, sneaky, and relentless, and does not give in, even in the face of reputations for piety.

A Prophetic Intrusion (39:3–8)

39:3 **Then the prophet Isaiah came to King Hezekiah and said to him, "What did these men say? From where did they come to you?" Hezekiah answered, "They have come to me from a far country, from Babylon." ⁴ He said, "What have they seen in your house?" Hezekiah answered, "They have seen all that is in my house; there is nothing in my storehouses that I did not show them."**
⁵ **Then Isaiah said to Hezekiah, "Hear the word of the LORD of hosts:** ⁶ **Days are coming when all that is in your house, and that which your ancestors have stored up until this day, shall be carried to Babylon; nothing shall be left, says the LORD. ⁷ Some of your own sons who are born to you shall be**

taken away; they shall be eunuchs in the palace of the king of Babylon."
[8] Then Hezekiah said to Isaiah, "The word of the LORD that you have spoken
is good." For he thought, "There will be peace and security in my days."

Be that as it may, the prophet enters. The appearance of Isaiah reminds us
that we are not here treated to royal documentation. Rather, the king's activity seems to be only the occasion for the prophetic word. The text ex-
ists for the sake of prophetic utterance that characteristically reshapes and
redefines royal reality.

In verses 3–4, the prophet's stance is that of a fact-finding mission. He
conducts an inquiry concerning the king's behavior. Hezekiah is forth-
coming, nondefensive, and seemingly innocent. His response in verse 4 is
dominated by comments on his "house": "my house, storehouses." Although the term "house" clearly refers to the royal buildings, the use of
the term inevitably refers, in royal context, to the dynasty, the promises of
Yahweh to David's family, and the commitment of Yahweh to that house
(2 Sam. 7:11–16). The exchange of verses 3–4 by itself makes no interpretive comment or judgment. The question and the answer appear to be a
straightforward offer of information.

The second speech of the prophet, however, moves from information
to a characteristic prophetic speech of judgment (vv. 5–7). The introductory formula is anticipatory of a long-term future: "The days are
coming." It is important to notice that the oracle contains no indictment.
It is not asserted that Hezekiah's activity in verses 1–4 is the cause for the
consequence now to be asserted. Therefore the reader must judge to
what extent the following threat is consequence (which would indict
Hezekiah) and to what extent it is only an announcement of impending
reality (which would leave Hezekiah's action without condemnation).
My own judgment is that the former is the case: Hezekiah is indicted and
evokes the speech of judgment. Readers may come to an alternative
conclusion.

In any case, the divine oracle is harsh (vv. 6–7). The prophetic verdict
is that the royal house—goods and people—will be deported to Babylon.
Thus the present ally of verse 1 is identified as the coming adversary. The
Babylonians will seize everything of value. The royal heirs, moreover, will
be taken away to become lesser court functionaries in the Babylonian royal
entourage (see Jer. 22:28–30). The promise has run out. The possibility of
the Davidic monarchy is terminated.

The response of Hezekiah, like the verdict of Isaiah, is open to more
than one reading (v. 8). One reading, the one toward which I am drawn,

is that the king's response to the prophetic oracle is a cynical, self-satisfied response. The verdict of Yahweh is acceptable, because it will come *after me*. There will be "peace in our time," as though the king does not care about subsequent trouble or judgment as long as he is not involved in it.

An alternative reading is that Hezekiah is an obedient, pious king who docilely accepts the harsh verdict of Yahweh, because he is prepared to accept whatever Yahweh gives as decree. In this reading, the final statement is that Hezekiah's fidelity has evoked Yahweh's fidelity, and so secured well-being for his own time and place. Hezekiah obediently affirmed that trouble does not come "on his watch," and for what comes after, he yields gladly and trustingly to God's intention. This affirmation, which seems to me against the grain of the text, evokes Calvin's comment:

> [W]hile he wished well to those who should live after him, yet it would have been undutiful to disregard that token of forbearance which God gave by delaying his vengeance; for he might have been led by it to hope that this mercy would in some degree, be extended to posterity. . . . We ought to labor most for our own age, and to pay chief regard to it. The future ought not to be overlooked; but what is present and immediate has stronger claims on our seriousness. . . . When he [Hezekiah] is informed that the promise is ratified, he gives thanks to God, and bears more patiently the calamity which was to come, though he felt it to be grievous and distressing (*Isaiah* III, 193–94).

We ought not, in any case, puzzle too long over the intended nuance concerning the prophet and the king. More important is the function of this brief chapter in the book of Isaiah. Whatever may have been the historical detail, the chapter now serves (a) to put the Babylonian threat front and center, and (b) to give strong voice to the coming deportation that entails the termination of political Jerusalem. This chapter then is a pivot that *looks back* to vindicate the sustained, ominous warning of the prophet, and *looks forward* to the struggle in and through exile to Judaism.

The verdict of chapter 39 reflects a deep break in the life of Judah, a historical break that is matched by a literary break in the text. Thus we may imagine a deep break in the book after chapter 39 and before chapter 40. The literary pause reflects a deep historical break wherein Jews were deported and forced to live in a strange land. The *literary break* bespeaks a costly *historical discontinuity* that is, in the end, a *theological datum*. The break witnesses to Yahweh's relinquishment of old faith arrangements with king, temple, city, and people, and the resolve of Yahweh to do a new thing—the emancipation of exiles and the formation of Judaism. The break toward which chapter 39 looks is decisive both for Judah's identity and for the shape of the book of Isaiah. That break is also a witness to the strangeness of Yahweh, who is at work in the break for newness, a newness now given speech in chapter 40 and following.